AF316651

# From Kingdom Come To
# The Fringes of Outer Space

# From Kingdom Come To The Fringes of Outer Space

## A Father's Memoir

Edited by Harold Speer Jr.

# Harold Speer Sr.

ISBN Paperback: 979-8-218-40344-7
ISBN Hardcover: 979-8-218-39887-3
ISBN eBook: 979-8-218-39888-0

Book Cover and Interior Design:
Creative Publishing Book Design

Printed in the United States of America

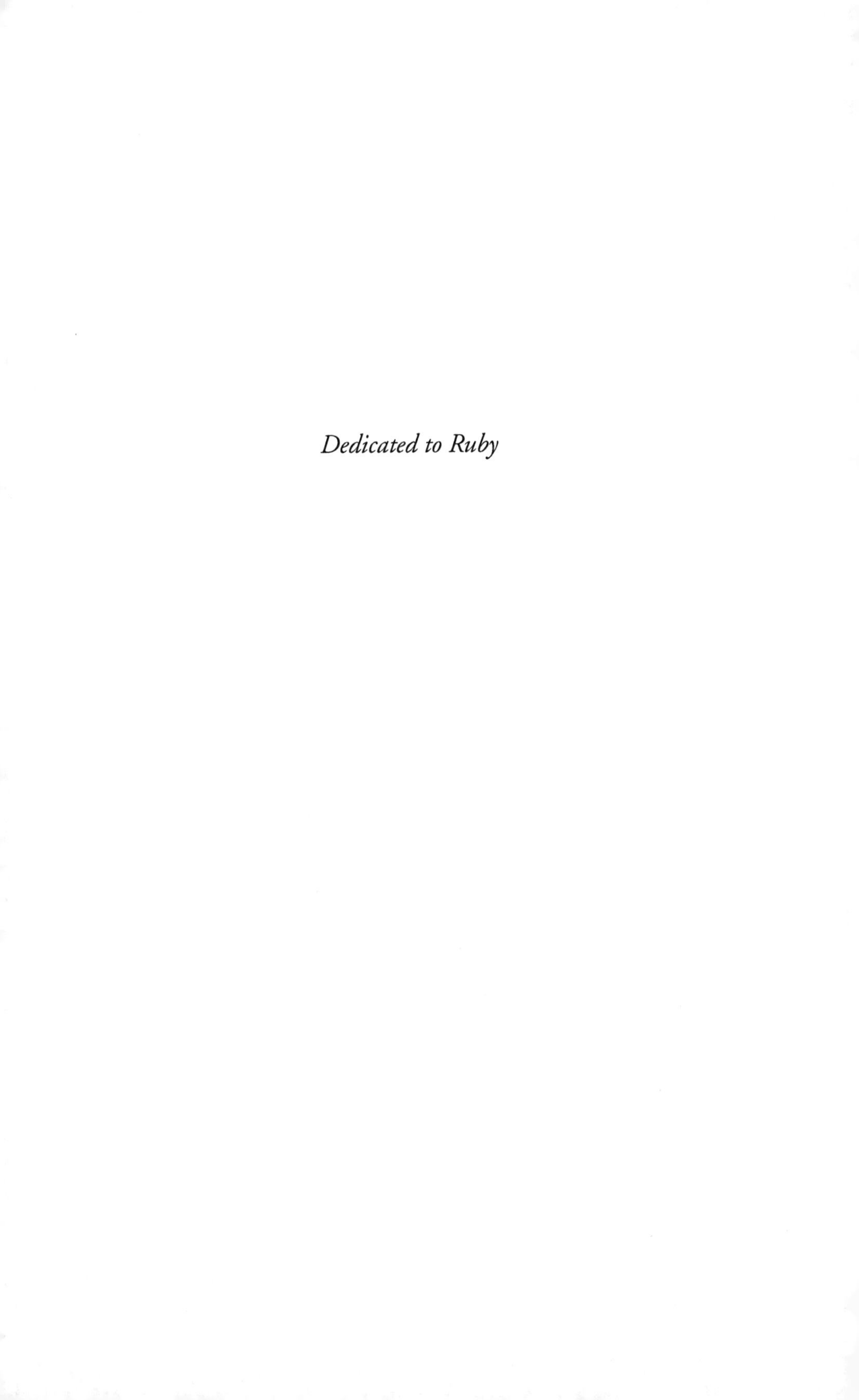

*Dedicated to Ruby*

# Acknowledgments

Many thanks to the following people who assisted in the editing and publication of my memoir: my son Harold Speer Jr., editor, and his wife Grace, who never failed to provide insightful feedback; my grand-daughter Zoe Speer, who helped create the book's covers and assisted greatly with editing; Sarah Beth Menck who assisted with editing; my grandson, Harold Speer, III and his wife Ausra, who helped with publication; my grand-daughter, Shannon Bingham; and my sister, Lois Baird, and her children, who provided several old photographs.

# Preface

My father was always a hero in my eyes. He was one of those lucky individuals who achieved his far-fetched dream beyond his wildest imagination. If the goal in life is to have fun, then my father accomplished that goal in spades. He couldn't have succeeded without the instrumental support of his wife, but I have never met anyone more determined or more optimistic than my father. His optimism was contagious, and he loved to help others "reach their full potential." Whenever he was asked how he was doing, he always responded, "I'm sitting on top of the world." He spent many hours writing and typing his recollections of his vivid childhood and flying experiences. He lived a full life in every sense of the word, and he died one month short of his 92nd birthday in 2017. I feel truly fortunate to be able to finally bring his cherished opus to publication.

# Table of Contents

# List of Photographs

# CHAPTER 1

# Dead Stick Landing

It was a dark overcast night in December 1958. I was a thirty-three year old Air Force Captain cruising along in an F-86H Sabre jet heading east over El Paso, Texas at 45,000 feet. Earlier that day, I had picked up the overhauled F-86H from the refurbishing factory in Ontario, California, and was enroute to the delivery destination of Andrews Air Force Base in Washington, D.C. I had checked the weather report before departing Ontario and the weather was good in Arizona, but an overcast sky was moving into the Texas panhandle. The overcast was expected to arrive in Dallas late that night, causing me to change my first stop from Phoenix to Hensley Naval Air Station in Dallas. The Dallas airport was reporting visual flight rules up until midnight.

I ran into the weather around Big Springs, Texas. The top of the overcast was 38,000 feet, which was 7,000 feet below my current altitude of 45,000 feet. I didn't know at what altitude the bottom of the overcast ended. Thus, I didn't know at what altitude I would break out of the overcast during my descent. Dallas was still reporting clear weather, and it appeared that I was going to beat the overcast to Dallas. It was about 8:30 p.m. and the stars were shining brightly. The top of the cloud coverage looked dark and foreboding with the moon casting an eerie reflection on the murk. I had passed Sweetwater, Texas and was about ten minutes west of Abilene when I felt the engine quiver just for an instant. The RPM (revolutions per minute) gauge fluctuated about one-half of a percent, then immediately returned to the original setting. As a precautionary measure, I reduced power and calculated that I was about eighty miles west of Abilene. The engine seemed to be running normally. Having experience with overhauled automobile engines, I was meticulous in keeping an eye on my engine instruments.

I tuned in to the Abilene radio beacon because I had a position report due there anyway. I was on course, at altitude, and at cruising speed, when all of the sudden, the unthinkable happened! It felt as though I had been hit by a rocket, possibly one that the Army had accidentally discharged from their missile range at White Sands Proving Ground, just north of El Paso. The explosion rocked the aircraft, and I could hear metal breaking and parts clanging together. The aircraft began to vibrate violently. I experienced explosive decompression as the air left the cockpit too quickly and caused it to fill with condensation. The rubber inflated canopy seals went flat, and the canopy was rattling on the rail like it might come off. I made sure to lower my head because I didn't want the canopy to come off, catch my helmet, and take my head with it!

My instruments showed that I was losing my RPM, my tailpipe temperature, and other associated instruments. I could tell the engine had blown up and flamed out. I had lost some compressor blades, which were causing the engine to be out of balance. As the engine lost those 10,000 revolutions per minute, the out of balance jet turbine spool was causing the severe vibrations. The instrument panel gauges and my canopy were frosting over due to the -60° Fahrenheit outside air rushing inside the cockpit that had just been a comfortable 72° F moments before. I figured the back of my seat must be full of compressor blades from the exploded engine.

My heart was racing, but I knew that I would have to stay calm to survive this emergency. I took stock of my predicament. I was gliding at 45,000 feet at 8:30 at night over a 38,000 foot overcast with the possibility of the battery going dead in eight minutes, at which time the controls would freeze. I had seven minutes to make my decision and follow through.

I was flying with my knees bracing the control stick, while I pulled out one of the letdown books from under the bottom of my parachute. I hurriedly flipped through the pages looking for Abilene, when I realized that I had the eastern instead of the western letdown book. Quickly, I reached behind me and pulled out the correct book from under the other side of the parachute. I flipped through the book until I found what I needed. There was a military base called Dyess Air Force Base just eight miles west of Abilene on a heading of 270 degrees from the Abilene radio beacon.

I realized that I would have just enough time to give a routine position report to Abilene radio before I drifted down 7,000 feet and entered the murky overcast. I gave the position report in an extra calm voice. I knew that if I didn't get that position report copied correctly before I declared an emergency, I would not get the chance again. Once an emergency was declared, well-meaning ground control personnel and other aircraft would unintentionally jam the frequencies asking for information.

After I transmitted the position report, I gave the emergency remarks. I told the Abilene radio, "Alert all aircraft flying on Green Five Airway, within fifty miles of Abilene, to move away from the center of the airway. I'm attempting a flame out (no engine), dead stick (limited ability to maneuver the controls), instrument penetration (through the overcast) landing."

I prayed that I'd break clear of the bottoms of the cloud in time to glide to a successful landing at Dyess Air Force Base. I informed the airfield radio operator that I had to turn off my command radio to conserve battery power now that my generator was no longer being powered by the engine. I shut off the command radio and all nonessential instruments. I began to monitor the bird-dog needle in the navigational radio to note station passage over the Abilene radio beacon. I kept having to wipe the frost off my flight instruments to read them because the moisture inside the instruments was fogging the lenses.

I noted that the elevation of Dyess was 2,275 feet. This meant that I would have to break clear of the overcast at 7,000 feet to have the minimum safe altitude to complete a dead-stick landing. Otherwise, I'd have to eject at 5,000 feet, since that would give me the required 3,000 feet to accomplish a night ejection.

Anxiously, I waited for the navigational bird-dog needle to swing on the Abilene radio beacon to tell me that I was in position to begin my instrument approach. I got that swing of the needle over Abilene at 18,000 feet. I noted that I was gliding down at 230 knots per hour, and my rate of descent was around 1,000 feet per minute. Following the instrument approach guidelines, I would arrive over the beacon at the low cone at 8,000 feet, and then arrive over the field at 6,000 feet. Given that the field elevation was 2, 275 feet, I would have 3,725 feet to make my night flame out approach.

The Air Force did not recommend these types of approaches because of the many calculations that had to be made, and the difficulty of judging distances at night. I had the added problem of being in the clouds. I completed my penetration turn, came inbound, and crossed the low cone at 8,000 feet. My freezing cold canopy fogged up when it hit the warm air at lower altitude. I rushed to wipe the canopy off with my sleeve and I spotted a small hole in the clouds. It looked like I might be gliding out of the clouds in another 1,000 feet and finally be in the clear. I made sure to closely monitor my instruments for any changes.

I broke out in the clear at 6,000 feet over the air base. If it hadn't been dark, I couldn't have seen the runway lights through the foggy canopy. Remembering how slow the gear comes down with a windmilling engine (jet engine turbine fans turning without power and only by virtue of the incoming air as the plane glided down), I knew that I would risk being blown out of the sky if I attempted to perform an air start in the presence of fuel lines that had been cut during the explosion. Time was of the essence, so I decided to take the risk. I had to attempt an air start to get my hydraulic pressure up to drop my gear and to get a little heat to the windscreen to decrease the fog to complete the landing.

I hit the air bottle and got 12% revolutions of the clanging engine turbine fans. I hit the spark and thrust the throttle outboard to get the fuel to vaporize and blow into the combustion chamber. Unbelievably, I got an air start without blowing the engine. The engine ran up to 58%, then I got another explosion and the engine flamed out again! I dropped the gear while I still had some RPM, and the landing wheels came down and locked. The inside heat didn't warm the canopy as much as the warm Texas air did. I thought that I might have to blow the canopy to see, but looking into 160 knots of wind would have made my eyes water so badly that I wouldn't have been able to see anything anyway. So, I shelved that thought.

I knew I was going to make the runway, but I worried that if I turned on the landing lights, they would pull so many amps that I might get a big light for a moment, and then everything else would go dead from the lack of battery juice. I remembered that I could drop the drop tanks if I found myself coming in short to increase my gliding distance. I rolled out on final with my gear and flaps down. I could see the runway lights, and I was going to touch down just between them.

When I couldn't see if I was short, I lifted the flaps. I touched down a little hard on one wheel, but I recovered on the bounce and made a nice two-wheel touchdown on the next contact. When the nosewheel dropped onto the runway surface, I began braking with much relief.

I slowed down and began looking for a turn off finger to the taxi strip. About halfway down the runway, a large vehicle passed by me on the left side of the runway going in the opposite direction. I switched on my radio and asked the tower what was on the active runway. The tower replied that I had met the fire truck, which was heading for the end of the runway on which I had landed. The tower operator explained, "The fire truck was dispatched to the end of the runway. We thought you had crashed! We didn't see your landing lights."

I realized that I had been incredibly lucky again — I had landed in the middle of the runway, and therefore missed colliding with the fire truck. I switched on my taxi lights, turned off on the last taxi way, and stopped. I requested that the tower operator have base operations dispatch a tug with a tow bar to my aircraft to pull me into the parking apron. The tower operator replied that this was a bomber base, and it didn't have a tow bar for a fighter jet. I then told the tower operator that they'd have to send the tug out with a rope to do the job.

I turned off my taxi lights and left my navigation lights on. I didn't want the tug operator to run into me after I had gotten this far along without a mishap. I saw the tug coming with its lights on. I turned on my taxi lights as he pulled around and stopped in front of my nose wheel. He got off the tug and tied the rope to my nose wheel strap while I told him that I would hold just enough pressure on the brakes to keep the rope taut. He pulled me up to base operations and stopped. I got out of my Sabre after he put chocks under the wheels and a ladder up to the cockpit.

I wrote up the condition of the aircraft on Form One. I stated that the aircraft "had a tendency to explode while running." Perhaps an understatement.

I got my clothes off the back of the pilot chair followed by my boots and shaving kit out of the gun bays. I walked into base operations and was greeted and congratulated by the airdrome officer of the day. He asked me what my intentions were. I told him, "I want to catch a flight back to California tonight." He recommended that I stay for the night while he called a SAC (Strategic Air Command) general officer to give me a commendation for the job I had just done. I told him, "I'm in a hurry and I don't need a commendation."

I requested a staff car to take me over to the commercial airport since there was nothing moving west out of Dyess that night. The officer told me that he would drive me over to the commercial airport himself. I loaded my bags into the staff car, and we started driving to Abilene.

The airdrome officer was fascinated at the way I had handled this incident. He wanted to know "Why didn't you eject? Why try to make the more dangerous dead stick landing at night? Especially one requiring a weather penetration!" He reminded me that the standard operating procedure plainly stated that a pilot should not attempt a dead stick landing approach at night. I asked him, "Have you ever considered the possible malfunctions during ejections at high altitudes?" I told him that a long list of items must happen correctly to have a successful bail out.

In the first place, the canopy must jettison, otherwise you will have to eject through the canopy. You must have your arms in the armrest and your feet in the stirrups. You must brace your head against the headrest. Once you blast out of the cockpit, the seat will be rotating, and you must separate from the seat without getting hit. Sometimes the wind will dig behind you and blossom the chute while you are still in the seat. This would make the shroud lines wrap around the seat, making you a prisoner in the seat. If you do not get clear of the seat, you must rely on your freefall mechanism to deploy the chute at the proper altitude. You do not want the chute to open at altitude, because of the -60° Fahrenheit temperature and the opening shock of the chute could jerk off your shoes, gloves, oxygen mask, and helmet. You would be traveling at high speeds, and you would have to fall some distance to slow down to a maximum speed of 120 feet per second before you could consider opening your chute. The little bottle of emergency oxygen that is attached to your parachute lasts only ten minutes. Thus, in those ten minutes you would need to freefall about five miles to get to air that you could breathe without oxygen. You would be freefalling at about seventy m.p.h. or one mile per minute.

So, from 40,000 feet, it would take a freefall of around five minutes just to reach the lower atmosphere where you didn't need oxygen. If your parachute accidentally deployed at altitude, you could come close to freezing to death, or dying from lack of oxygen before you descended to the warmer breathable air at lower altitudes. While you were falling through the weather, your aircraft could circle and strike you, or an airliner could plow into you in the soup and butcher you with those four bladed propellers. Even if you descended properly, you could hit wires or land in a lake or on a highway at night and suffer unknown consequences, especially if a strong wind were blowing when you landed. You could be dragged along the desert cactus and get all skinned up. Besides, I said, "I would lose my civvies, my cowboy boots, and my shaving kit with the aircraft. I'd rather take my chances with an emergency landing."

By this time, we were approaching the Abilene civilian airport. We pulled into the terminal, and I informed the airdrome officer that, "I have a Christmas dance to make in Grundy anyway." The airdrome officer stopped the car and got out to help me carry my luggage into the terminal. He departed without a word. He had the expression of someone who could not believe what he had heard and seen.

I asked the ticket agent if I could get a flight to California, so I could pick up another jet to deliver to an eastern destination close to Grundy. She told me that there was nothing going west that night. I then asked her if there were any flights going east. She looked surprised. She told me that I could catch an eleven o'clock flight to Dallas. I told her that I would take that flight. She said, "I thought that you wanted to go west." I told her that I could find something going west out of Dallas. I boarded a Trans Texas flight, and we soared off to Dallas. We arrived in Dallas at the Amon Carter field in time to connect with an American Airlines flight going to Los Angeles where I would pick up another F-86H for delivery the following day. I boarded the American Airlines flight and relaxed in my chair.

My mind was still racing, and I began to contemplate just how lucky I had been in my Air Force career as a pilot. This emergency landing wasn't my first stroke of luck, and it wouldn't be my last. It had all started with a boyhood dream in the Appalachian foothills of Eastern Kentucky.

# CHAPTER 2

# The Beginning and the Family

The name "Cumberland" has always evoked the same kind of excitement for me as does an approaching birthday. Both are markers for my life's journey that encompasses five careers and travel in forty countries. "Kingdom Come" is a name that early settlers gave to a spot on Pine Mountain in Eastern Kentucky near the small mountain hamlet and mining town of Cumberland. The Mighty Pine Mountain range stretches from Pineville, Kentucky to Elkhorn City, Kentucky, flowing northeasterly along the Kentucky and Virginia border by way of Harlan, Cumberland, Whitesburg, and Jenkins, Kentucky.

The Pine Mountain has maintained its beauty largely because it is an outcropping unsuitable for mining coal seams and too rugged for timbering. The oak and evergreen pines cling to the rocky ridges. Moss and pine needles cloak the top of the ridge like a magic carpet. Sparkling mountain springs are plentiful, ferns grow green, and the

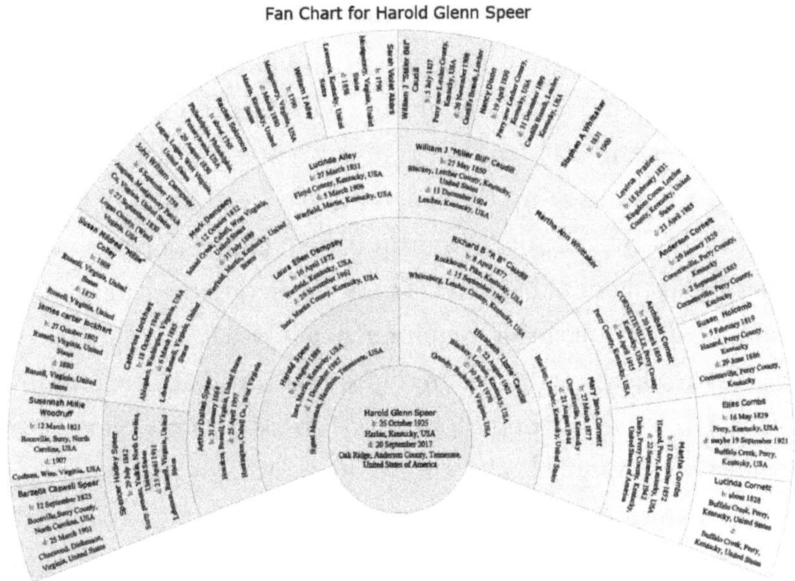



mountain laurels lattice the slopes of the mountain, catching the rainfall momentarily before it drips into the rich soil. The quail, squirrel, rattlesnake, and hare share the big pine with the hawk and the four seasons. The headwaters of the Cumberland River begin just above the sleepy town of Cumberland, as a clear brook in a beautiful mountain top meadow. The river winds and twines ever so gradually down the mountain, through and beyond Cumberland on their westerly course. The natural beauty surrounding this area explains why this little "Switzerland of the Bible Belt" comes as close as one dares to heaven. It also explains why the state park atop of Pine Mountain is called "Kingdom Come State Park."

The Appalachian Mountains proved to be good hunting ground for the Cherokee Indians high in the Smokies, as well as a land rich in mineral deposits for my forefathers who arrived from the British Isles and Western Europe. My great grandfather, Spencer Hadley Speer, journeyed out of the Yadkin Valley of North Carolina through the Damascus pass into Virginia and settled in Lebanon, Virginia, near the Holston River. All Spencer Hadley brought to Virginia was the horse he used in his courier duty with General Robert E. Lee's forces and a mini ball in the calf of his leg. He met and married Mary Catherine Lockhart[1] in Lebanon, Virginia. In addition to farming, he learned to practice dentistry through an apprenticeship with his father-in-law, James Lockhart[2]. The State of Virginia had no dental school or dental licensing requirements at that time. Spencer and Catherine ushered eight children into this world at Lebanon, four boys and four girls. All of the four boys, Patrick, Thomas, Samuel, and Arthur Dallas Speer, also became dentists through apprenticeships.

Dr. Arthur Dallas Speer, my grandfather, was a short and stocky man with dark brown hair and a freckled face, told me many stories about his early life in Virginia, West Virginia, and Kentucky. He was the town champion wrestler. On one occasion he locked legs with a challenger as the town folks gathered around to watch the action.

---

1 Catherine's father, James Lockhart, was a dentist, and his grandfather, William James Lockhart, fought in the American Revolutionary War for which he received a 100 acre land grant. A couple of Speer relatives, William, and his brother Henry, also fought in the Revolutionary War. Almost every generation of the Speer family had at least one member who fought in some war. Spencer Hadley Speer's great-grandfather, Aaron Speer, fought the Indians in Indiana during the War of 1812. Spencer Hadley Speer and his brother James, also a dentist, fought in the American Civil War. Harold's great-uncle Arthur Speer fought in World War I and was institutionalized for the remainder of his life because of his exposure to mustard gas during the war. Harold Glenn Speer and his brother Keith fought in World War II, and Harold served during the Korean War. Harold G. Speer, Jr. and his wife, Grace E. Speer, served in the U.S. Army Reserves during Desert Storm.

2 There have been twelve practicing dentists among the Speer family in Eastern Kentucky, Southwestern Virginia, and Tennessee. *See,* Speer, Jr., Dr. Harold Glenn, "Five Generations of Dentists in Virginia, Kentucky, and Tennessee," *Tennessee Dental Journal,* Fall 2022; 99(1): pp. 14-18.

When the dust settled, Arthur had a broken leg, but he had thrown the challenger. Arthur, along with two of his "go-getter" brothers, Thomas and Samuel, would drive a herd of sheep from Lebanon to the Washington, D.C. market and return with supplies of all kinds to supplement their income.

Arthur Dallas rode horseback, carrying his little black bag of dental instruments into Buchanan County on Knox Creek at Hurley, Virginia to follow the new coal mines that were opening in that area. When those mines slowed down, he moved again and became the first dentist ever to enter Pike County, Kentucky. He would also ride from Pikeville, Kentucky to Williamson and Logan, West Virginia staying with families, such as the Lawsons, Goffs, Williamsons, and Scotts while delivering dental services. His last move took him to Martin County in Warfield, Kentucky on the Tug Fork of the Big Sandy River where his office was set up in a store in Warfield owned by Lewis Mark Dempsey. From this association, he met and later married Laura "Little Ma" Ellen Dempsey, a schoolteacher, and the daughter of his landlord. The Dempseys were a prominent family in both Kentucky and West Virginia with land holdings that included nineteen natural gas wells and the rich, but undeveloped, Alma Coal Seam deposits.[3]

Arthur Dallas and Little Ma had four children. Three boys, Russell, Arthur, and Harold were born in Warfield. Irene, their

---

3 The Dempsey Family controlled around 4,000 acres around Warfield, Kentucky in Martin County. This acreage included a 1,600 acre tract on Wolfe Creek and a 2,400 acre tract in the lower end of Warfield, as well as another 150 acres over on the West Virginia side of the Tug River just above Kermit, West Virginia. The Dempsey family relatives also included the famous heavyweight boxer, Jack Dempsey, whose family originated from the mining town of Logan, West Virginia, but moved for a period to Colorado after being converted to Mormonism, but later returned to West Virginia during Jack's boyhood.

only girl, was born after they moved from Warfield to Inez. Arthur Dallas bought the entire hollow at the upper end of Inez, called the "Kingfisher." He set up his dental practice on the second floor of a different Dempsey store in Inez.

My paternal grandparents lived very graciously in Martin County. In addition to Arthur Dallas's dental practice, they continued to trade cattle at the stock market in Paintsville, Kentucky. They farmed the Kingfisher, tended the bottoms,[4] and managed the bee hives. In a rock cellar under the little yellow house on the upper side of their property, they kept delicious wine that they made using their own grapes they had harvested from the farm. The barn up the hollow housed the horses, cattle, and hay for the winter. The corn crib was well supplied, and the hogs were put on a wood floor to eat corn at fattening time to bring them to over 400 pounds each.

My father, Dr. Harold Speer, was the third child of Arthur Dallas and Little Ma. He was one of the first two graduates of Martin County High School in Inez. He learned to play the piano and became a talented musician.[5] Harold was also an excellent swimmer, even though the creek at Inez was small. He mastered the currents and swirl pools of the Tug River, which drowned many an unprepared swimmer. My father attended the University of Louisville School of Dentistry for three years before graduating from the Cincinnati College of Dentistry in 1922 at the age of twenty-three.

Dad wanted to set up his dental practice in the populated coal camps, but Martin County did not have a big coal industry, so he rode a horse over to Letcher County where several coal mines were in

---

4 Fenced, plowed, planted, harvested, and mowed the fields, while managing the livestock in or around those fields.

5 In his later years, Harold's grandchildren used to love to hear him play the piano and sing one of his favorite songs – "Crazy" by Patsy Cline.

operation at the top of the mountain seams around Blackey, Kentucky. In addition to working in Blackey three days a week, dad also had several temporary locations which he worked a couple of days a week.

My maternal grandparents, R. B., and Jane (Cornett) Caudill, met in Hazard, Kentucky while training to be teachers. They got married and settled in Blackey, Kentucky, where they bought and operated the big general merchandise and feed store located next to the railroad siding just below the Blackey Depot. They sold everything from candy to feed, pianos, and even coffins upstairs. The feed store was lucrative, but the depression was a blow to the bank account of my grandparents, and they never trusted banks after that.

My father befriended the Caudills, who had four children about his age: Lottie, Dennis, Elizabeth, and Hubert. Elizabeth, a strong individual who always seemed to "be in charge" of her surroundings, was the postal clerk in the feed store, and Dr. Harold did not take long in deciding to marry her. They were married on July 24, 1924.

**CHAPTER 3**

# Early Childhood

The mines around Blackey were not running every day and Dr. Harold got word that more permanent mines were in Harlan County, Kentucky. Mom and dad, packed up their life, said goodbye to the Caudill family, and followed the work to Cumberland where the miners from the big deep mines at Lynch and Benham provided numerous patients for dad and his colleague, Dr. Little Whittaker. Unlike the Pine Mountain, the Little and Big Black Mountains on both sides of the Pine Mountain were mined extensively.

Four children were born to Elizabeth and Harold between 1925 and 1929. I was the first born, and then in rapid succession came Keith Dempsey, Lois Irene, and Mildred. We lived in a boarding house that Mother ran behind Creeche's Grocery Store. Dad's dental office sat on top of the Florence Dress Shop.

Life went along smoothly for us in the beginning. I remember playing with my brother and sisters in our red and white sunsuits, inside the picket fence behind the boarding house. My mother's sister, Aunt Lottie Caudill, came over to help Mom and "Aunt" Ellie Loggins manage the boarding house and us children.

Our first experience of tragedy came when my youngest sister, Mildred, stood too close to an open grate fire and caught her dress on fire. Before Aunt Lottie could wrap her in a bed sheet, Mildred's back was severely burned. Mildred was taken to the Valley View Hospital at Benham, Kentucky and was attended to by Drs. Mullen and Schosser. The whole family, including my grandparents, came down to see her, so I knew how serious the situation was. At first, Little Mildred's condition seemed to have stabilized — she sat up in bed and passed a silver half dollar from each one of us to the other as a sign of recognition. Unfortunately, an infection developed, causing the burn to become fatal on March 18, 1931. Penicillin wasn't used on patients until almost ten years later in February 1941.

On a rainy day, Mother let my brother and I go with dad up the hill behind Cumberland to dig Mildred's grave. I was only about six years old, so we were too little to help much except for moving rocks. Dad dug the grave just outside the fenced area before the cemetery expanded. I could tell this was a terrible ordeal for mom and dad — my previously bright and happy mother was suddenly quiet and at a loss for words, while my dad threw himself into his work. Grandfather R. B. Caudill placed a little blue ceramic lamb on Mildred's tombstone, which he told me would watch over her. As far as I know the lamb is still there, and I hope it is. The hospital bills and funeral expenses were devastating to my father's savings.

A lot of things seemed to happen to our family around this time. I was too young to understand that with a depression in progress and with the unions trying to get started in Harlan County, a lot of people were put out of work. Of course, this had a bad effect on my dad's dental practice. I can remember the wrecker hauling away our new Chevrolet and when I asked Mom why, she told me that we couldn't pay for it right then.

Dad got sick with the flu and had to go stay with his parents in Inez. Mother took us to stay with our Caudill grandparents in Blackey. I got to know a lot of relatives on the Kentucky River very quickly. It seems like we were kin to everyone. We met our cousins, Andrew, and Taylor Dixon,[1] who looked out for us. We played in our grandfather's big feed store and ran along the river road down to Elk Creek. We rode the boat and fished for bass and catfish behind the old barn next to the Caudill Cemetery.

One afternoon, I was over at the feed store and heard my Uncle Hubert start up his Model-A Ford. He and my brother Keith headed down the dirt road toward Leatherwood. I tried to run across the swinging bridge in time to catch them, but they did not see or hear me. I kept running long after the car was out of sight, all the way past Elk Creek. My side was hurting, so I would walk some then run some as I cried.

I met a man on a horse just below the mine cable car below Elk Creek. He had curly hair, a big smile, and a peg leg. He stopped his horse and asked, "Where are you going?" I told him, "I'm going to catch that car." He leaned over, extended his big hand, and said, "Grab my arm." He swung me up behind him on the horse and told me that the car would return shortly and that he would take me back to Blackey so I wouldn't have to walk. I didn't realize that he was Mace Whitaker, who was also a relative.[2] My curiosity got the best of me, and I couldn't help but ask how his leg got cut off. He

---

1 Harold Glenn Speer's maternal great-great grandmother was Nancy Dixon, who married "Stiller Bill" Caudill.

2 Harold Glenn Speer's maternal great-grandmother was Martha Ann Whitaker, who married "Miller Bill" Caudill.

told me it was a logging accident. Then he told me that the peg leg had saved his life once! When the brakes failed on a dinky train that was hauling logs, Mace jumped off and stuck that peg leg in some loose dirt to stabilize himself while the train went on to wreck. You can see that it didn't take him long to make me forget the auto trip I missed. This kind of familial treatment surrounded me during my time in Blackey. Mace Whitaker let me off his horse in front of the R. B. Caudill place where I noticed a black Whippet Coupe parked in front of the house. I heard guitar music and singing. Someone told me that the red letters on the door of that coupe spelled "Red Foley."[3] My grandfather's place was a common stopover for visitors of all types in the area.

On Sundays after church, people would come to eat dinner at the R.B. Caudill place. I remember three tables would be placed end to end with cane bottom chairs lining each side. As a seat became empty, one of us children would squeeze in the empty chair. The chicken and dumplings were my favorite, and there was always plenty for everyone. Desserts of strawberries, Irish cobbler, cake, or pie always finished off the meal. If the kids weren't at the table eating, they could be found playing with little toy cars at the back of the house along the rock wall until the guests left.

Around 1932, my father had a house built near his parents in Inez across Rock Castle Creek on the first flat on the hill. We arrived in Inez in a truck loaded with furniture which we parked down at

---

3 Clyde Julian "Red" Foley was a country music star born in 1910 into a musical family from Blue Lick, Kentucky. He played the French harp, piano, banjo, trombone, harmonica, and guitar. Besides country music, his genres included gospel, rockabilly, boogie, and rhythm and blues. He eventually sold 25 million records and was inducted into the Country Music Hall of Fame. *See, Colin Larkin*, ed. (1993). *The Guinness Who's Who of Country Music* (First ed.). Guinness Publishing. pp. 140/2. ISBN 0-85112-726-6.

the corn crib near the creek. We helped carry the pots and pans up the path to the house while the heavy furniture was handled by the movers. The house was about 300 feet above the dirt road which ran along the creek.

Grandfather Arthur Dallas brought over a jersey cow and some chickens. We had Dommer Necks, Rhode Island Reds and White Leghorns. The jersey heifer grazed in the big pasture by the house while the chickens scattered all around. This pasture was our new playground from which we could see across the creek to the main part of town. We found three big sycamore trees which had grape vines in them. It was not long before we were swinging out over the flat on these vines. Fortunately for me, the vines did not break on the out swing but gave way gradually while inbound to the tree roots. We immediately abandoned this activity.

# Early School Days

Although the public school was just across the creek from our place, we started school in Inez at the Presbyterian Church school because Arthur Dallas was the superintendent. Our grandfather was quite influential in church activities and was instrumental in bringing gentleman and scholar Dr. Courtney into the Inez Presbyterian Church to preach on Sundays and teach school through the week. The preacher - teacher lived in the brick manse below the red brick church. My father had been traveling to Betsy Lane and Beaver Creek in Floyd County, Kentucky practicing dentistry around the new mines in that area. He realized that he needed a car, so two car salesmen each brought a car to the Kingfisher. This prompted a family gathering there. Both salesmen and cars were in the driveway; one a gray Buick and the other a gray 1929 Model A Ford.[1] Uncle Russell told dad to get the Buick,

---

1 Henry Ford famously stated that the customer "can have any color you want as long as it's black." This policy on Model A Fords, however, ended in 1925. After that time, four colors were offered – Black, Bonnie Gray, Andalusite Blue, and Balsam Green. *See, The Expanded and Annotated My Life and Work: Henry Ford's Universal Code for World-Class Success.* (2013) by Henry Ford.

*Harold, brother Keith, friend Jimmy,*
*and sister Lois in Garrett, Kentucky, circa 1933*

but dad decided on the Ford because some of the roads required big wheels to negotiate. We only saw dad on weekends after that because he traveled to the coal camps with his dental satchel and foot pedal drill in his new car.

Before long Dr. Courtney had married his new assistant and taken her back to Pennsylvania to be with family. Once Dr. Courtney left the church, we kids joined the public school. The Inez public school was a busy place because the classes were so large. It was obvious that we weren't going to get the attention that prevailed in the previous Presbyterian Church School. Basketball was the predominant sport in the Inez public school. The team played on a dirt court beside the school because they had no gymnasium. Baseball was a favorite adult pastime, and we went to see Pickle Beans Slone pitch for the Inez Baseball Team on Sundays — he was a professional as far as we were concerned.

The biggest event to occur in Inez while we lived there was the Mills trial. John Henry Mills choked his mother to death with a chain around her neck in a religious rite. She was supposed to come back alive in three days. Unfortunately, she did not revive. The spectators at the trial almost caved in the second story of the courthouse. John Henry got loose during the trial and ran down the street before being caught.

For entertainment, our family enjoyed brief visits to our cousins Clyde and Earl Cassady,[2] who lived on Main Street in Inez. We loved to listen to Cousin Clyde play classical music on his grand piano. After Clyde was finished, dad would play "Ragtime" and popular tunes like "Casey Jones."

Dad was still working away during the week and only coming home on weekends. He made the right payroll connection at the Big Elkhorn Mines in Garrett, Kentucky in Floyd County where he opened an office. The mining officials allowed him to "cut through the office" for services rendered to miners. This guaranteed payment to the dentist by payroll deductions from the miners. So, dad decided to move the family to Garrett. The moving truck came to Inez, and we all helped load our belongings. I was about ten years old then in 1935. My brother Keith and I got to ride in the big ton and a half Ford truck bed for the trip to Garrett. After a long slow trip, the truck finally turned down the road between the Freddie Williams Hotel and the old barn just below Garrett Hollow. Dad had rented a tan company style house in Garrett, which sat on stilts with the front porch facing the railroad. Dad had his dental office in the front room. The patients would wait on the porch in cane bottom chairs until their turn came at the dental chair.

Bill Sexton, an Inland Natural Gas maintenance man for Beaver Creek, lived just below our house. Bill and his wife, Aunt Martha, had seven boys. We spent so much time with the Sextons that Bill and Martha became "Uncle Bill" and "Aunt Martha" to us.

---

2 Clyde and Earl Cassady were Little Ma Dempsey's nephews, sons of Little Ma's sister Mary Dempsey Cassady.

The railroad ran up Beaver Creek right through the middle of Garrett, which was a "Company Town," that is, the coal company owned all the businesses and the 500 coal camp houses rented by the miners. Old Doc Dempsey and his son Chester lived in an odd brick home with seven fireplaces across the creek below town in West Garrett. He was from Elkhorn City, so he must have been some relation to my paternal Grandmother Laura Dempsey. Dr. Dempsey was a good friend of my dad.

Aunt Lottie Caudill had been in Louisville, Kentucky staying with her cousin, Gladys Buckhold, getting her beautician training. In 1935, she came to Garrett and put a beauty shop in our house while she built up clientele. In the meantime, my mother was learning the hair styling business by helping Aunt Lottie. The ladies paid in Big Elkhorn script, which the company gave the miners for wages instead of money. The script could be exchanged for money, but you only got seventy-five cents per dollar. The script had to be spent at one of the company enterprises, and the company store prices were considerably higher than regular stores.

Dad gave Mom about $7.00 to $10.00 per week for us to live on. This must have been a tight budget. We supplemented our diet by picking poke salad greens by the railroad, a traditional Appalachian food. Although pokeweed is poisonous, it could be eaten if cooked by boiling two or more times with the water drained and replaced each time.

Preacher George Patrick and his wife, Ange, moved into the house next door. My mother and Ange made friends quickly, since they both had a young family to raise and very meager funds. We got along with the three Patrick children, George Jr., Patrick, and a younger sister named Mary. Preacher George was a watch repairman during the week and a circuit riding preacher on the weekends. Preacher George bought himself an old green Buick convertible for $20.00. He couldn't wait to drive that car to a "preaching." He didn't get far when one of the tires blew out — the tire, rim and all came off, which cost as much as the whole automobile to fix! He sold the car because the "upkeep" was too much.

My father came home one weekend and parked his Model-A Ford on the little dirt road between our house and the railroad. Someone had shown my brother and I how to change gears by using the clutch. When we saw the car empty and the key in the ignition, we drove that Ford back and forth. It had only gone about fifty feet when the fan belt came off or broke. We didn't realize anything was wrong, so we kept driving until the engine was red hot. Someone mentioned the heat problem, so we quit driving the car. My father never noticed a problem with the engine when he left on Sunday evening. That sold me on the Ford engine for life.

Around late August of 1935, I started school over at the mouth of Rock Fork. Lawrence Bailey, who lived down the road in West Garrett, went to school at Rock Fork with me. He could play the guitar, sing, and was good at reciting poetry. He asked me to go home with him for dinner and I agreed. At West Garrett he bought a plug of Brown Mule chewing tobacco and he gave me a chew. I was sick by the time we got back to school from swallowing too much tobacco juice. I had never learned to chew tobacco and keep it in a lump. After class began, I began to crave water and drank the bucket dry. I stacked my books up on my desk and laid my head on them. Then it happened, I tossed the entire contents of my stomach out all over my books and desk. Man, I was sick but tremendously relieved. The teacher let me go home early. I never told her what made me sick.

Mom saw me coming down the railroad tracks early from school. She came out to meet me and I told her what happened. She told me to stay away from Lawrence Bailey. Lawrence remained my friend, but I did stay away from chewing.

When the creek went down, my friends and I would go swimming below the bridge which crossed Beaver Creek to the schoolhouse at the mouth of Rock Fork. I didn't know how to swim, but quickly realized the value of such skill. Patrick Jr. enticed me into neck deep water. He told me to take a big breath, spring off the bottom and start dog paddling. He then pushed me into water over my head. I learned to swim immediately to get back to shore.

Saturday was the big action day in town. The miners would get drunk on the "Pickle Lo" row side of town, then cross the tracks on the way back through the commissary complex to Garrett Hollow and home. The company deputies would pick up a portion of the drunk miners as they passed through the incorporated complex. The fights would start, and it would take several deputies to get some of those miners to the jail house behind the meat market. The miners gambled a lot on the creek banks and fights would start over poker. Most of the miners traded guns and swapped knives. Therefore, many shootings took place at the taverns, in town, and up Garrett Hollow. We knew that someone had been shot whenever we heard a gunshot.

We would run up the railroad to the company doctor's office to see who would be brought there. The Doctor's office was a little yellow company building not much larger than a corn crib. It was located just above the drugstore. The wounded men would be carried to this building and laid on the porch until the doctor arrived. This was where we would find out who was shot and who shot him. I'd hear other miners ask the man, "Who killed you?" Usually there was no reply. Eleven men were killed during the three years we lived in Garrett.

There was plenty of action in the mountains, the miners supplemented their cash income by hunting aggressively for squirrels, quail, and rabbits. Sometimes the mines only worked two or three days a week, so the miners *had* to hunt to eat. Once, as we were wading in the creek down Garrett Hollow near the jail, we heard a rifle ring out.

Someone shot a big black dog that belonged to one of the children in our gang. The dog had been wading with us. We looked for the assailant to no avail. That dog was picked out as a target right among us kids. I admit the dog was a little on the mean side. Maybe he had bitten someone. Our attention was soon diverted to the open space in front of the commissary where several deputies were in the process of overpowering a drunk miner. Epp Laugherty, the deputy, got tired of man-handling this miner and asked for assistance from the crowd. The crowd responded, otherwise he would have been forced to knock the miner out.

My brother Keith had found out a way that we could see parts of a movie at the company theater for free. Someone had drilled several one half inch holes in the front wall of the theater and here we took turns watching the movie. This led to us going to see our first movie in Garrett – Hop Along Cassidy's "Last Round Up."

George Patrick's friend, Hershel Griffith, who lived two miles up Stone Coal Hollow, had a girl's bicycle that he wanted to sell. George Jr. rode that bicycle down to show to us and taught us all how to ride. He approached my mother and asked her to buy the bicycle for us. They negotiated a deal for six dollars – two dollars down, then a dollar a week until it was paid off.

We began to really cover ground on that bicycle. I went up to the company store and let the miner's children ride it for a nickel a ride. One boy ran off with the bike, but soon returned pushing the bike and looking for the company doctor. He had met a car on the road and the dust blinded him so badly that he crashed into a road sign and cut his chest.

I used to ride that bike up Garrett Hollow where there were about 500 company duplexes. The folks had a lot of dogs up that hollow, which meant there were a lot of pups around. I was offered seven pups in one day. I accepted all the offers and took them home to raise. My mother made a big fuss but eventually, after some pleading, let me keep the dogs.

A fine man by the name of Frank Davis had a dry-cleaning plant at Weyland, Kentucky and he came to pick up dry cleaning in Garrett. My Aunt Lottie Caudill was one of his stops. It wasn't long before Frank and Lottie were married. Uncle Frank was a gregarious man[3] with a stocky build and a receding hairline, and Aunt Lottie was a resourceful, no-nonsense woman. She had been raised during the depression and always feared another depression. For this reason, she always stocked multiple "canned" mason jars filled with vegetables obtained from the big garden behind their house that she and Frank meticulously and laboriously worked. Frequently, Frank could be seen smoking his pipe while walking behind the tiller along the long rows of the garden on the hillside behind the Davis house. The grandchildren were also often enlisted to help hoe the garden or help Aunt Lottie string the green beans. Frank and Lottie had no children and were like second parents to Harold and his siblings[4].

I always went barefoot with the other children in the summer, and I only wore shoes during the winter. One winter I outgrew my shoes and went to school barefoot because we couldn't afford another pair. I would walk the railroad cross ties on the way to school because

---

3 Uncle Frank always smoked a pipe and in between puffs would mutter, "Mmm … Yeah … Mmm." Years later, he moved to Knoxville, Tennessee and worked at a service station/fire department below his house where he gladly let the grandchildren play on the Fire Engine parked in the garage of the service station. He also was very proud of his green and white 1950's era Oldsmobile that had a push button start; a feature that disappeared until reintroduced in the early 2000's.

4 They both were always quick to help, and on one cold snowy night in 1968, Frank drove his truck 30 miles north of Knoxville to tow Harold's broken down VW Beetle into Knoxville for repairs. Uncle Frank and Aunt Lottie magnanimously loaned Harold the money for his car repairs on that occasion.

that was the last place the snow lay and the first place it melted. Dad came home one weekend and brought me and my brother each a sheepskin lined leather jacket and some shoes. I figured I had it made, and I welcomed the cold and snow.

CHAPTER 5

# Farm Experience

**M**y maternal grandfather and grandmother Caudill came to Garrett to take me to Blackey in Letcher County for a vacation. My trips to the Kentucky River had always been most enlightening and rewarding, and this trip did not prove to be different. I always received the royal treatment. This trip was to be especially influential in building my practical education relating to work skills and the ramifications of property ownership.

My grandmother, Jane, was one of eight children born to Arch Cornett and his Combs wife in Daisy, Kentucky on Big Leatherwood. Arch was a timber cruiser for many years for the Ritter Lumber Company in Daisy. He acquired the Cornett Plantation which encompassed Depot Branch and both sides of Big Leatherwood Creek about three miles above Daisy. The farm took in over 1,000 acres of bottomland, woodland, and hills.

My great grandfather Cornett had been dead for some time, and during the depression his children had not paid any taxes on the

Arch Cornett property. The farm came up for sale for the $6,000 outstanding taxes. My grandparents raised the money and paid the taxes, thereby getting a lien on the property. The heirs were to reimburse my grandparents, but failed to do so. Consequently, the farm was placed in the name of R.B. and Jane Caudill.

I arrived in Blackey just at the moment that my grandparents were establishing possession of the Arch Cornett place. They had gathered a large crew of men to get the Daisy farm in working order. Without knowing it, I was moving right into the workforce along with Preacher Haze and his son, Mace Whitaker, Taylor and Andrew Dixon, Frank Davis, and anyone else my grandfather could lay his hands on.

I stayed in Cornettsville with my grandparents in one of the houses that was included in the Arch Cornett holdings. Grandfather Caudill decided to have a lot plowed next to the house in Cornettsville. After rigging up the horse and plow and plowing a few rows himself, he called me to get into the harness behind the plow. That plow was tricky to keep in new ground, it would hit a rock and I would get thrown down the sloped field when the plow came out of the ground. By the time the lot was half completed, I had begun to control the plow and the horse

My next work experience came when my grandfather gave me a four-pound lard bucket to try my luck at milking a cow. He told me to go to the barn and milk the cow by myself. Not sure what to do, I grabbed some hay and a couple of ears of corn with me to the stall, hoping to distract the cow. While the cow was eating, I got my stool, and washed my hands and the utter, hoping to get her used to the idea of being milked. I finally began milking and when I had the bucket full, I started to get up to take the milk to show my grandparents. Right then, the cow spooked when I stood up causing her to knock the bucket of milk over. Unfortunately, I had to be satisfied with only telling my grandfather about my success, since I no longer had the proof.

Plowing more new ground above Depot Branch was the next project. Grandfather Caudill took me there to the barn below R.B. Whitaker's cabin[1] and took me straight to the big mule's stall. The big mule, "Big Head," was giving Grandfather a hard time getting the plow harness on. "Big Head" hated the work rig so he would fight you on it in the stall, but he was fine once you got him out of the stall into the field — that being said, he sure did make you work for his services. The rest of the crew had already taken the horse up the hollow and were plowing on one side of Depot branch. Grandfather hooked the big mule to the plow and began on the other side of the branch. I fell in behind the planter throwing rocks on the rock pile to make the hoeing easier later. At noon we all assembled at a cool spring at the head of the branch to eat lunch: a pone of cornbread with an eight-pound lard bucket full of milk.

Grandfather usually had some difficulty keeping "Big Head" plowing just before the 5:00 p.m. quitting time. The mule would constantly try to break down the hill with the plow and head for the barn thinking he could get out of work. Grandfather would grab the mule around the neck and put his thumb in the mule's eye to gain control. That was about the only way to turn around an animal weighing 1,200 pounds and standing fourteen hands high.

The work crew would follow the horse and mule out of the hollow in the evening while the cows were headed for the barn. The path from the pasture ran along the creek above a cliff. It was dangerous terrain, and it wouldn't be hard to slip off the path and fall fifteen feet into the river below. On one occasion a cow fell over the cliff

---

1 R.B. Whitaker was a brother of my Great-Grandmother Martha Whitaker. Martha married William J. "Miller Bill" Caudill.

onto a flat river rock below in the shallows. The cow broke her leg, so grandfather quickly killed it and butchered it right there on the spot. The meat was divided among the work crew and the neighbors.

Late in the evening after supper, I would often go swimming with my cousin Aster Whitaker in the swimming hole in the mouth of the branch while grandfather read his Bible by the pine knot light. He was always preparing for the next Sunday's church service.

My Caudill grandparents were active in the Baptist Church. The Baptist services included foot washings. Grandfather used to wiggle his big toe at me when he noticed that I was watching that part of the service. I always enjoyed the chanting messages because they were easy to follow. The membership always sang between the changing of preachers at each service and the voices were spontaneous and rich in harmony and tone. This fellowship carried throughout the work week. The Frog Creek Baptist Church only met once a month, so my grandparents visited Carr Creek or some other Baptist Church on the other Sundays.

It became a tradition for all of us to meet the passenger train when it came into Blackey on Sunday afternoons to pick up passengers, relatives, or the mail. There was a long train and a short train, which we designated a "long dog" or a "short dog" depending on the number of cars. One of my first big thrills came when I accompanied Grandfather Caudill on the train to Hazard for a business trip. I had never ridden a train before, so naturally, I looked forward to the trip with great expectation. I was not disappointed once we boarded the train.

I felt especially important when we took our seats, and I still could not believe it until the train pulled out of Blackey. I was impressed with the cleanliness of the train and the professionalism of the conductor. The whistle blew and I was looking out the window across the Kentucky River through the trees watching the well-wishers waving good-bye to us.

I never knew exactly what the business in Hazard was, but I wanted to be in on the transaction anyway. As we walked through the town I gazed in the windows and realized that I had never seen so many gold watches before. As we would pass a storefront, Grandfather would say, "Let's go in here and see if our money will spend."

Before I knew it, the corn was ready to hoe on the Arch Cornett place. Grandfather took me on the one-eyed horse to the upper field. He gave me a hoe and told me to cut the weeds in front of Taylor Dixon. I didn't realize how fast someone had to move to stay ahead of the crew. After a couple of rows, I asked Grandfather how long I was going to be cutting weeds and moving rocks around the tender corn stalks. He told me, "You'll be on every stalk in the field until it's hoed." I got busy because some of those rows required half a day to hoe on one side of the branch alone. By noon, I had plenty of appetite and didn't care as much about my finicky eating habits.

One day Taylor Dixon and I were hoeing one of those long rows of corn. At about 2:00 p.m., we had just stood up for a short break and we both heard some distant engine roaring. We were trying to identify or place the noise. It got louder and seemed to be coming up Leatherwood fast. It couldn't have been a train because it was going too fast. Besides, there was only a dinky railroad track there. For a moment I thought that the passenger train had split a switch down on the Kentucky River and was coming up Leatherwood Creek.

Then like a flash, I caught them with my eyes. There were two yellow P-40 Army Air Force fighter planes majestically buzzing about eye level right up the middle of Big Leatherwood Creek. The planes were in a loose echelon (diagonal) formation. Although the planes were only in our sight for a couple of minutes, they made a life-long impression. I realized then that the mule, the dinky railroad, the automobile, and the passenger train were no comparison to the airborne locomotion. I decided then and there that I could handle a cockpit job. I knew I would apply for a job as a pilot when I was old enough. Eventually, Taylor Dixon nudged me, and I began hoeing corn in that new ground again. Summer was about over, and I had to go back to Garrett to get ready for school.

# CHAPTER 6

# Transitioning from Kentucky to Virginia

When I got to Garrett, I discovered that my father not only had an office in Pikeville, Kentucky, but he had established part time offices in Big Rock and Harman, Virginia as well. Around 1938, mother told us that a Mr. James Belcher was constructing a house in Harman, Virginia for us to move into in the near future. A big mine called the H.E. Harman mine had just opened in Bull Creek. There were 1,100 miners working there who needed dental attention, and father was lucky to get in on the ground floor.

In the meantime, the big news in Garrett was that the miners had tied heavy cables around the jail house and attached the other end to the coal shifter. The jail was all busted up from when the shifter pulled the coal cars out of town. We never figured out why the miners wanted to bust up the jail.

The very night we returned to Garrett a black ambulance came down the road by our house and stopped at Bill and Martha Sexton's.

I saw someone lying down in the ambulance with a white sheet covering all of him except for his head and arms. Someone else got into the ambulance and it headed back out to the main road again. Next morning, we got the story: Deputy Sheriff Lafferty had shot Kermit Sexton in the arm over on Pickle Lo Row. The ambulance was taking Kermit to the hospital, but sadly he bled to death enroute. We knew that Sheriff Lafferty was in for some difficulty in getting out of this situation. The Sextons were outraged and full of vengeance, but "Uncle" Bill made sure they stayed within the law, so they wouldn't get themselves into trouble.

When dad went to work, mom would help Aunt Lottie give perms in Aunt Lottie's beauty shop. One night, we were walking from Aunt Lottie's house to our house with our dog "Bill" when directly in front of Frank Daniel's house, we met some other folks who had a big dog. Well, our dog lit into this part-bulldog, and it wasn't long before the bulldog had a death choke hold on our dog. We yelled at our mother to do something. Mom laid down on the bulldog and opened its jaws with her bare hands. This proved to be a great error because Bill went right back to work on the bulldog. Mom couldn't keep the dogs apart. "Uncle" Bill Sexton heard the commotion and ran out to help. It was very dark, and he couldn't see very well so he pulled out his pistol and shot our dog. The fight stopped immediately, and we asked him why he did that. He exclaimed, "I thought the dogs were attacking your mother!" He didn't know which dog was which. In all this melee, mother had been bitten several times without realizing it. We went into our house where mother cleaned and dressed her wounds. She told us that she had taken a very foolish chance of being seriously injured by trying to break up a dog fight with her bare hands.

The next big event was the arrival of a carnival in Garrett. A little Calliope (an organ on wheels) came down the railroad beside the tracks one day. This little truck had an organ in the bed with pipes of every size hanging upright like three-inch stove pipes. The organ was playing, and all the kids surrounded the Calliope when it stopped. The driver told us a carnival was coming to town — the bottom just across the railroad tracks from our house would be the location. He told us that we would receive free tickets for rides if we helped set up the tents and things. Well, he got the fullest cooperation. We raced each other to try to get more tickets. We carried water, pulled tents, drove stakes, and did whatever other chore that was assigned to us.

Dad came home just before the carnival was ready to open. Dad and mom decided that we should be out of town while that carnival was in progress. Aunt Lottie had bought a 1935 Chrysler with a rumble seat from Dr. Isom. Mom and Aunt Lottie took us children to Blackey for a short vacation. We were always well received in Blackey by the adults and many cousins while Dad went back to his Pikeville office.

When we got back to Garrett, I had hoped the carnival would still be there, but we saw the bottom was empty except for a few pieces of heavy equipment that were covered with tarpaulin awaiting shipment. We pieced together what happened to the carnival from the neighbors. Everything had gone well at the carnival until someone cheated Lacy Triplett and some others in a poker game. Shortly thereafter, twelve sticks of dynamite blew the Calliope into a thousand pieces along the railroad tracks. Someone must have thrown dynamite from the road above our house because a few sticks of it were lying on our roof top. We surmised that the hole in front of our house resulted from dynamite which hit short. The sticks of dynamite must have broken apart when they hit the roof of our house. We also found several sticks of dynamite when we were cutting the grass with a reap hook, and more sticks of dynamite were found around a water tank at Freddie Williams' Hotel. The dampness around the tank had put the fuse out and thankfully saved the water tank.

The children told us that the local people set off the dynamite to flush the crowd off the carnival ground. Then there was a shoot-out where two or three people were wounded. Someone commandeered the carnival owner's touring car along with a five gallon can full of nickels. The carnival folded their tents the next day and pulled out of Garrett in great haste.

In light of the carnival incident, dad decided that it was time to move the family full-time to Harmon, Virginia. He traded the 1929 A-Model Ford for a 1935 Plymouth Coupe, which had a "mother-in-law" or rumble seat. He had his dental equipment loaded on a truck and we left Elkhorn City heading up the Levisa River. I was twelve years old and excited about the move. The mountains got higher, and the valley got narrow — the dirt road created a lot of dust as we traveled along. About a mile or two above Elkhorn City, the road became a ledge running about 300 feet above the Levisa River for about three miles. Dad put the Plymouth in low gear to motor through the narrows. There were shallow ruts in the road, and it was obvious that a car could not afford to get out of the ruts because the ledge was just inches from the lower rut. Frankly, I was ready to hop out of the rumble seat just in case the car hopped out of the ruts and plunged over the edge. I saw blue smoke curling up through the pines over Potters Flats and I realized that a cabin was tucked away in those pines. I thought this isolation was something rare and resembled a resort type existence. About two-thirds of the way through the narrows we passed a wide place in the road where we saw a grave monument beside the road. The inscription on the grave marker read: "Here lies a Confederate soldier known but to God. Struck down by an assassin's bullet while returning home after the War Between the States." We stopped to ponder this, and I was emotionally moved by the inscription. The remoteness and slow pace of the setting enhanced my appreciation of all things.

We crossed the border between Kentucky and Virginia just before the road turned up a left hand fork of a creek running into the Levisa River where there was a novelty and coke stand which sold fireworks and kept snakes as a draw. The road turned right for the ascent of the mountain leading up to the flat of the mountain called the "grassy flats." We climbed up the winding road through the oak trees, maple trees, and pines until the road narrowed beside a cascading mountain stream filled with all sizes of boulders interlaced with mountain laurel. The water spray cooled the hollow. It was not only refreshing, but it cooled the engine of the car, which had been pulling hard in low gear for a long period of time. I thought that I got a whiff of a mash odor in that laurel breeze too.

We finally popped up on the flat of the mountain at Judge Mullins' store in Breaks, Virginia. This creek valley was a wide meadow filled with rich green grass. Grassy Creek narrowed to a small brook meandering through the meadow. Across from the meadow was the Breaks Canyon, which ran along the border separating the state of Kentucky from the state of Virginia. It was 1,600 feet deep in places and was called "the Grand Canyon of the South." After refreshing ourselves at Judge Mullin's store, we motored up the grass valley to the foot of Bull Mountain, our last steep climb. We finally reached the top of Bull Mountain at the Yates' farm and apple orchard. We stopped and looked down into the valley floor below. It was not only steep, but narrow and rugged as well. I realized then the difference between a valley and a hollow right there — the hollow was so narrow that the mountain sides touched the stream. The automobile was geared down before starting down the other side of the mountain. Each curve was a switch back elbow turn. Finally, we began to see evidence of a coal camp near the bottom of the mountain.

We saw the machine shop on the hill side where the mining motors and buggies were repaired and serviced. All kinds of copper wire, roof bolts, motorized equipment, and tools were stored in this shop and the shop yards. The mining dolly's motor arc flashed[1] ever so often as the motor ran on the tramway while being powered electrically by the overhead copper cable via the roller dolly pole connector. The welding torches flashed inside the shop as the repairs continued. We saw the company official homes just across the creek from the coal tipple and railroad siding. The company store and the bath house were the two largest buildings straddling the creek.

We came down the creek below the coal tipple to the familiar grounds of the little white grade school. Our brand-new six room house was located at the lower end of the Harman school lot just above James Belcher's conveniently located general store. The living room was in the front center of the house and served as a reception room for dad's dental office located in the left front room. There were two bedrooms and a kitchen in the back of the house next to the school lot. The outhouse sat beside the school outhouse.

Dad was glad to move his temporary office out of the back of the Belcher Pool Room. On one occasion a cue ball jumped the table and struck a patient on the head. The curtain which separated the dental office from the Pool Room wasn't heavy enough to stop the ball. Dad's new location was ideal because of its proximity to the drift mouth (an opening on the slope of a hill for an underground mine) and the Post Office.

The entire community wasted no time in patronizing the services offered by dad and mom, and we immediately befriended

---

1 An arc flash is a phenomenon where a flashover of electric current leaves its intended path and travels through the air from one conductor to another. *See,* KM Kowalski-Trakofler, EA Barrett, CW Urban, GT Homce. *Arc Flash Awareness: Information and Discussion Topics for Electrical Workers,* Archived 2017-08-29 at the Wayback Machine. DHHS (NIOSH) Publication No. 2007-116D.

the local children who played in the school yard.[2] We noticed right from the start that the law and order observed by this Virginia community was much more than was the case on Beaver Creek in Floyd County, Kentucky. Perhaps the influence of the old Virginia justice system extended throughout the reaches of the Old Dominion. Mines were a relatively new industry to that portion of Virginia, and the company only constructed homes for the top officials. So instead of a company owned town, the miners by and large owned their own homes. Most of these miners were native to this area and had a relatively stable family existence. Before the mining industry came into Buchanan County, the timber industry was the big capital industry.

We children wasted no time exploring the area with our bicycles. We would race each other up and down Bull Creek — we even became bike experts and started doing tricks on our bikes. We'd ride our bikes backwards, jump over items, and blaze off the road to bike trails in the woods and over slate dumps. We explored all the hollows which emptied into Bull Creek, including Deel Fork, Star Branch, Belcher Hollow Branch, Stiltner's Creek, and Convict Hollow.

The miners lived up these hollows. The roads had slate on them to cover the mud holes. However, as you traveled further up the hollow, you would eventually hit just a creek bed type road. The water was clean near the heads of the hollows. You could smell the rich dirt and fresh undergrowth and hear the cricket and June bug sounds amidst the stillness.

Most of the farmers in the Bull Creek area were old homesteaders. They had two storied farmhouses with their log barns built on the

---

2 Some primary family names included Belcher, Elswick, Looney, Ratliff, and Stiltner, but there were other families who came into Buchanan County with the mines themselves.

only bottom or flat land where rail fences outlined the perimeter of their holdings.

The coal shifter or steam engine train would churn up Bull Creek daily – pushing those empty coal cars up to the tipple and beyond. The smoke coming out of the shifter's stack was thick and black. We soon discovered that if we got one of those cinders in our eyes while riding our bikes, we would be immobilized for a few minutes. We learned to squint our eyes when we rode by a shifter that was chugging hard and puffing black smoke. The grade was steep, and the shifter would spin its wheels many times while shifting the empties and hooking up to the loaded cars. The shifter would run over the lead warning caps, and they went off like big firecrackers. When the train left, we gathered the lead remains to use for fishhook sinkers when fishing in the Levisa River.

Our next big social event was a Colley Reunion in Breaks Park. During music breaks, the politicians spoke, and the children slipped off to pick blueberries out of the laurel thickets. I often get nostalgic when I remember the serenity of that pine studded, mossy, rock out-cropping with the laurel growing out of the cracks of the rock formations. As we got further back from the brow of the cliff, the dirt became deeper and richer — the undergrowth became difficult to penetrate and the danger of rattlesnakes kept us from venturing under the laurel. Those big diamondback rattlers blended in with the roots of the laurel along those moss patched rock layers just above the ground. It wasn't uncommon to see rattlesnakes with heads as big as a miner's palm.

# CHAPTER 7

# Our First Vacation (Virginia Beach)

Our next big excitement came when Wiley Beglet came to visit us. Wiley was an automobile salesman and an old friend of dad and mom from Whitesburg, Kentucky. The way Wiley and my parents reminisced; you would never have guessed that a car sale would be an incidental part of this visit. Wiley knew that mother wanted a four-door car, but dad didn't want to trade. He was satisfied with the two-door car. However, my mother knew our family was getting too large to ride the rumble seat on the vacation she had planned for us. Finally, dad agreed to the terms, but he only had about $400 plus his car. He had to borrow another $135 to make the deal. Wiley was well paid for his visit, and we had a 1937 Plymouth four door car.

Dad and mom worked hard for about another month, saving up for the vacation. They soon had the money that they figured they needed for our trip. We loaded up in the Plymouth and dad tied a small mattress on the roof of the car — he didn't want to rent any more rooms than were absolutely required. I don't remember where we slept along the way, but I do remember arriving at Virginia Beach. The water had a salty odor as we waded out in the surf to swim. We soon noticed jellyfish everywhere, and we returned to the beach as fast as we could. Dad couldn't get us back into the water.

Dad hired a couple of row boats to take us out a little to fish. I wasn't all that carried away with saltwater fishing, but we dropped the lines into the water and let them sink to the bottom. Then we lifted the lines until the bait was just off the bottom. We caught several fish, but I'm sure we lost as many as we pulled into the boat. We didn't keep the line taunt until the fish were in the boat and the fish would throw the hook the minute the line went slack.

Dad decided to drive over to York, Virginia and rent a forty-foot boat. He took me and my brother Keith. Even though we thought that was a big extravagance, we climbed aboard anyway. The captain took the boat out into the Chesapeake Bay and dropped anchor. We had good luck and caught plenty of fish.

Dad's big moment came near the end of the day when he hooked a big fish. We all came over to dad's side and watched him pull in the fish. When the fish got up to the boat, the captain told dad that the fish was a sand shark. Man, this really excited us. The captain offered to cut the shark loose, but dad insisted on hauling the shark on board. The shark was about thirty or forty inches long. Dad was really proud — he put the shark in an ice cooler, so he could have it mounted.

We finished with the beach – sunburns and all. Dad and mom loaded us up for the trip to Monticello, the home of Thomas Jefferson, which was near Charlottesville, Virginia. We drove onto the grounds at Monticello, which had the atmosphere of a school of learning. When we saw the circular building called the rotunda, I thought that Jefferson must have entertained congress right there in his living room. I could see why the University of Virginia was located here.

Next, we journeyed to the Mt. Vernon Plantation near Arlington, Virginia. George Washington had built a villa on the Potomac River with the land to match the mansion. My impression of Washington and Jefferson was that anyone who would build such beautiful homes had to have noble political ideologies. We drove over to Washington, D. C. where the Capital and government buildings were massive and elaborate. The cherry blossoms gave warmth to all that granite built around the Potomac River. We went up inside the Washington Monument and looked over the city. We visited the Lincoln Memorial that night. The next day we headed back down the Shenandoah Valley toward our home in Harman, Virginia. Dad and mom were satisfied to have provided us with a little tradition.

# CHAPTER 8

# Outside Activities

**M**y dad had several patients named Bingham who were great fishermen and hunters. They showed dad their fishing equipment, pistols, and hunting rifles. Many of these men hunted and fished in faraway places on their vacation. I became educated in hunting and fishing equipment just by listening.

Before the 1938 school year was about to begin, I received an exciting invitation to a possum hunt up Belcher Hollow with Frank Clevenger and his brothers. We followed the dogs into the mountain, chasing a rabbit into a hollow tree. Frank twisted a branch into the fur of the rabbit trying to pull it out, but it wouldn't budge. We built a fire with leaves and tried to smoke him out, and he still wouldn't come out! Then Frank said he would borrow a ferret for the next hunt. The ferret is a domestic weasel, which I had seen in Garrett, Kentucky. Miners used them when they were meat hunting. We treed a possum or two, and then found our way home in the night by carbide lamp.

When the snow came, we rode our bikes on the slippery roads and spun the rear wheels on the ice patches. We learned how to handle these icy patches on wheels. We used to create these icy patches by pouring water on the gentle slope behind the schoolhouse near the pump house, and letting it freeze overnight. All the kids sat along the stretch of ice while one person performed his bike slide — if the rider fell, everyone piled on him.

Spring brought an end to school programs. All the school children had a part in the May Pole dance. The children sang and danced around the May Pole in costumes, and a May Pole King and Queen were selected. After the program, the school children auctioned off their box suppers. Naturally, the parents bid on their own children's supper because the parents had prepared the supper. Everyone had a good time, and the school raised some money for whatever was needed.

When the summer began to get hot, we rode our bikes down Bulls Creek looking for minnows. When we had enough minnows, we rode to the mouth of Bull Creek to fish in the Levisa River. If the fish didn't bite, we just went swimming.

We met more children as we spent more time away from home. The Elswicks down below Belcher Hollow owned a restaurant and beer garden called the Blue Moon. On the hill behind the Blue Moon, the Elswicks owned some rental property. A family by the name of Powers built an inexpensive home there. They built a frame of two by four lumber on a wooden platform floor, boarded up the sides about six feet, then placed a tent over the top of the wooden rafters for a roof. Mr. Powers had been a coal miner from over in Wise County. He had changed his occupation to mending shoes. The Powers family had two children, an eleven-year-old girl named Lugene, and a nine year old boy named Gary. These children melded into our little society without a ripple.

One day, Mr. Powers came up to my father's dental office and wanted to have his teeth extracted and dentures made. However, he told my father that his finances were meager. In lieu of this information, Dad agreed to attend to Mr. Power's dental needs in return for the regular delivery of a number of quarts of buttermilk over a certain period of time—happy to make a trade for his services during the hard times of the Great Depression. Mr. Power's son Gary, who we played with as kids, later gained international notoriety when he was shot down while piloting a U-2 spy plane over the Soviet Union in 1960 when Dwight Eisenhower was President.

The population of Bull Creek had increased to a point where the little creek began to fill up with refuge, and only hard rains would clean the creek out. Many of the miners began killing rats with .410 gauge shotguns and .22 rifles. I wanted a .22 rifle like many of the other boys my age. My bicycle was pretty beaten up from all my racing and stunt activity. A boy from Belcher Fork offered to trade me a .22 rifle for my bicycle, and after gaining my parents' permission, I took him up on his offer. I felt like I could make my way through the world as a hunter alone. I became a pretty decent shot. That peep sight wasn't highly effective late in the evening, an open sight was better when the sun went down.

I went hunting a couple of times on the hill behind our house. That mountain was certainly rugged — the steepness and the briars made hunting a real chore. No wonder the local people didn't hunt that hill with guns and dogs. I planned to hunt where the terrain was more traversable in the future.

My dad continued to barter for his dental services. Later, someone traded a couple of pigs to my father for their dental work and Grandfather and Grandmother Caudill had to come over to help butcher the hogs. Naturally, they planned to take some meat back to the Kentucky River. I was allowed to go back to Blackey with them for a short visit — I took the necessities, my rust-colored checkered jacket, and my rifle. I wanted to hunt that backcountry, and I did just that.

When I got to Blackey, I went up the hollow behind Grandaddy Caudill's house. I climbed up the moss-covered rock ridge where pine trees scattered along the ridge. I was looking for yellowhammer birds. Moving slowly, I walked up to a little pine tree about the size of myself and I heard something chirping and scratching just beyond that tree.

I froze in my tracks. I was finally able to make out a covey of quail busily scratching around the moss, feeding on insects and seeds. I slowly raised my gun to my shoulder and aimed at the covey. I didn't want to shoot them on the ground because I might accidentally hit a sick bird. So, I made a noise to flush out the covey. As the covey fluttered to lift off, I trained my rifle on a rising wad of feathers that appeared to be a bird and fired. My first quail fell back on the ground. Feeling good, since I was a meat hunter for sure, I took the quail down the mountain to grandmother, who plucked the bird and prepared it for my supper dish. I was practically a king at King Arthur's Round Table that evening. I returned to Harman like someone who just returned from a Safari — a hunter of sorts.

# CHAPTER 9

# High School Days (Grundy, Virginia)

I graduated from Harman Elementary School and was scheduled to attend Grundy High School. The yellow school bus ran from Harman to Grundy every morning and brought us back in the evening. Grundy was a beautiful little landlocked mountain hamlet. The cool, clear waters of Slate Creek and the Levisa River parted the forest, and mountains were steep on all sides of Grundy. Evergreens dominated the rock cliffs — I can still smell the pine needles. The courthouse was literally a pillar of granite. The main street paralleled the Levisa River, while Walnut Street ran along Slate Creek. Walnut Street intersected Main Street by the courthouse. When you stood on the courthouse steps, you were in the center of human activity in Buchanan County.

My father decided to put a dental office in Grundy. He rented an office from Truly Goff. The Goff building was located directly across from the Morgan theater on Main Street. Slate Creek and the Levisa River joined just behind the Morgan theater.

It was five miles from Harman to the mouth of Bull Creek, and six miles further up the Levisa River to Grundy. The Virginia convicts were in the process of building a new road from the mouth of Bull Creek to Grundy. That old road to Grundy was rough. Part of the new road was open, but only when it was dry and dusty. When it rained the new road would stall a tank – motorists drug off mufflers with regularity in those muddy ruts. Oil pan plugs were scrapped off and tires were busted.

Mom and dad always gave me fifteen cents for lunch. We ate at all the different restaurants and drug stores in town until we found the best buy. Harve Roberts had the best hot dogs with the best chili in town. Two hot dogs and a coke would satisfy an appetite for as long as you can expect in a growing boy.

I had enrolled in the four basic academic subjects for freshman in Virginia public High School. These subjects were English, Mathematics, History and General Science. Mrs. Trimble taught English, Mr. Roller — History, Mr. Blevins — Mathematics, and Miss Wolfe — General Science. My homeroom teacher was Mrs. Trimble.

The four major sports were available to the student body. Those students who lived out in the county were unable to take part in the after-school athletics, because of the problem of getting home after the bus left. Therefore, basketball and football were recruited from students who lived within walking distance of Grundy High School. Since I lived in the county and had to take the bus home, I didn't get to participate in basketball and football at that time. I maintained bicycle racing as my extra-curricular activity after the school bus delivered us to our homes in the county. We pursued this activity with the same fervor that we would have pursued the major sports.

I was, however, able to join the High School band because we could practice during school hours at our study hall periods. We could attend the weekly Friday night football game to play in the band because our parents could take us that one evening a week during football season to the High School to catch the school band bus. Our parents followed the school buses to the games and back to the High School grounds after the games. Our parents picked us up there and took us home.

It was the fall of 1940, when we moved to Grundy. My Grandfather and Grandmother Caudill had helped my parents buy a nice lot on Walnut Street 2,000 yards up Slate Creek from Grundy High School. Grandfather Caudill had Mace Whitaker and his work crew dismantle a house next to the big feed store in Blackey, then haul the material to Grundy and reconstruct the house on the new lot.

*Liza Lee Place - Grundy, Virginia*

Dad maintained his office at Harman, but he switched his days. He spent the first three days of the week at Harman and the last three days at Grundy. Mother moved one-half of her beauty shop beside dad's office in the Trula Goff building. We children were pleased about moving to Grundy because we could ride our bicycles or walk to town and to school. We liked our neighborhood because of the beautiful view. There was a big rock in the creek right behind our house which sat on its edge. This rock literally turned the creek water, making a natural swimming pool about four feet deep. There were plenty of fish in Slate Creek too — the State of Virginia released trout periodically in Slate Creek above our place.

Not long after, we took a trip to Princeton, West Virginia., In our new silver four-door Oldsmobile. I don't remember what we attended, but I do remember us stopping on the way by Doran, Virginia and watching a Ford Tri-Motor plane hauling passengers out of the Doran Airport near Richlands, Virginia. On our return trip, we stopped just outside of Princeton at a little air strip where a pilot was barnstorming and hauling passengers around the town for $1.50 per person. My parents let my sister Lois and my brother Keith take a flight. I didn't want to just take a flight. I wanted to learn to fly. I figured there would be a time in my life when I would learn to fly. I was surprised how simple flying appeared to me.

When school began that fall, the band was becoming a big thing. The County School Superintendent, Percy V. Dennis, Sr., had hired Miss White from Radford College, who was going to go places and do things with the Grundy band. Miss White had us all buy $125.00 uniforms, which was a big thing at the time. We practiced and learned to march. I played the trumpet, Keith played the drums, and Lois played the clarinet. When the band started to look and sound fairly good, Miss White began to organize a trip to Richmond, Virginia to a big statewide band festival.

My mother and Mrs. Laura Harman chartered a railroad Pullman car in Bluefield, Virginia, to carry us to Williamsburg, Virginia. We drove to Bluefield in the '39 Oldsmobile and then we loaded onto the Pullman car. We got out of the car in Williamsburg and took a chartered bus to Richmond, Virginia. That was the biggest event we had ever attended as participants. It was beautiful! That night we stayed in the homes of local bank members, who showed us exceptional hospitality. The next day, we did the long trip back to Bluefield in reverse. Our parents met us at the railroad depot, and we began to relay our experiences to the family on the seventy-two mile trip back to Grundy.

*Grundy High School Band – 1942.*
*(Harold is 3rd from left on the front row and his brother Keith is*
*on the drums. Harold's sister Lois missed that picture day.)*

Squirrel season had opened — I got my rifle with its scope sights and headed up the piney point right in front of our house. It was early and the fog was lifting as I quietly moved my feet from one moss covered rock to another. I had gotten almost a thousand feet up the point, when suddenly a squirrel dropped a hickory nut in the leaves and went leaping from tree to tree down the opposite side of the point. The squirrel made a beeline for the pines along the creek, then he disappeared. I knew that I had spooked every squirrel on the hill, so I came back down the hill and decided to catch him the next morning. Well, the next morning I went through the same experience, the squirrel was outsmarting me. I came home again and on the third morning, I slipped about halfway up the hill. I threw a pinecone up the hill where the squirrel was cutting hickory nuts, then I made a fast trip down the hill to the big pine tree next to the creek where the squirrel had always disappeared. I crouched low behind a moss-covered rock with my rifle trained on the likely limb of the tree. Sure enough, the squirrel came bouncing down the hill and jumped on this limb. He sat just long enough for me to squeeze a shot off, and the squirrel dropped dead at the foot of the tree. I had mastered squirrel hunting.

I turned sixteen years old in October of 1941 and got my driver's license. After football games, the school bus would take us to the High School and several of us band members would get together at my house for a jam session. We later started getting together after a game at the Hi Hat in Little Prater or the Blue Bonnet restaurant in Clay Pool Hill, where we would play while the other students danced with the permission of the restaurant owners. In a short time, we were invited to perform at student dances. We got so good that the restaurant owners began to pay us $10.00 each Friday night. The Buchanan County Country Club even engaged us on a regular basis.

My carefree high school days were rudely interrupted one day in December of my senior year. My brother and I were accompanying my father on a business trip to Inez, Kentucky. On our way back to Harman, we listened to the radio. It was December 7, 1941, and the newscaster announced that the Japanese had attacked Pearl Harbor. My father said, "We'll surely be at war by tomorrow."

The next day President Franklin Delano Roosevelt, in an eloquent and emotional speech, asked congress to declare a state of war between the United States and the Japanese Empire. We were officially at war, and the recruiting began immediately. The war bond drives featured the Hollywood stars at the big whistle spots. The draft board went into operation. Mr. Lewis B. Hershey, Manpower Chief for Buchanan County, started calling the boys up for physical examinations at the local draft board.

The pace of the war related industry and the pulse of the nation quickened. Defense contracts were numerous and local boys went to work in new defense plants and ships building in Baltimore, Norfolk, Radford, Bristol, and Oak Ridge. Everyone seemed eager to serve their country in whatever capacity they could. We started following the conduct of the war in the newspaper every day. There was a lot of flag waving and hoopla on all occasions — everyone wanted a part in the action. We were soon fighting the German, Japanese, and the Italians. The axis powers had a lot of victories before the Americans and the allies got rolling.

In 1943, I took aeronautical mathematics under Principal John Meade. I was seventeen and it looked like I might have an opportunity to serve in one of the armed services before the war ended. I figured I would need that mathematics if I got a chance to fly. I remember our aeronautical class had a model plane building project. I took balsam wood and carved out the likeness of a P-51 North American Mustang fighter plane. I thought it was a rather good job. Next, I carved out a sharp likeness of a P-38 Lockheed Lightning fighter plane. I figured that I wouldn't be able to get into the war in time to fly the Lockheed Lightning anyway. That model is still in the showcase at Grundy High School as far as I know.

*Harold Glenn Speer – age 17*

# College Admission and Enlistment

Father wanted me to go to dental school at the University of Louisville. After I graduated from High School in May 1943, he took me to Louisville and introduced me to one of his former classmates by the name of J. T. O'Rourke. Dr. O'Rourke was the Dean of the University of Louisville Dental College. He told my father to fill out an application when the time came for the next school year, and he would make sure that my application got due consideration.

My grandfather Caudill arranged for me to enroll in Murray State Teachers College at Murray, Kentucky that summer. Dr. Caudill was the president of Murray State Teachers College at that time. Father and Mother drove me to the campus and introduced me to Mr. Caudill, who cordially welcomed me. I was quartered in a private dwelling just across the street from the college president's house where my roommate was Mike Caudill. I was given a part time job cleaning the president's home and I enrolled in General Chemistry and Trigonometry for the summer session. I got an A in chemistry and a B in trigonometry for both terms of summer school.

I enjoyed Murray State, but I was ready to catch the Greyhound for the trip back to Grundy when the summer quarter ended. I came back to Grundy proudly wearing a Murray State T-shirt and I went back to work for Gene Matney at the Esso Service Station in Grundy.

When the fall semester started, I decided not to go back to Murray State, because it was too far to come home on the weekends. Instead, Father and Mother let me enroll in Eastern State Teachers College at Richmond, Kentucky that fall. They drove me to Richmond and the beautiful campus of Eastern State Teachers College. There was an Army WAC (Women's Army Corp) detachment taking training there. The student union building had all kinds of action— There was a pool table among other recreational devices in the student center lounge in the basement of the student union building. I made several good friends in the student center, including Johnny Pace[1] and Chad Howard.[2]

---

1 "I went home with Johnny one weekend. Johnny's family owned a grocery store and Johnny had the key. The first night we stayed at his home, Johnny and I went down to the store to make a late phone call to some girls. We went inside and began to use the phone when we heard a commotion at the door. When we came to the front door, the people went away. The next day we heard that the police had arrested a couple of transients who had broken into several places the previous night. The robbers told the police that they had started to rob the Pace store, but someone else had beaten them to it. The robbers had mistaken Johnny and me for burglars."

2 "Chad, a bit of a daredevil, one day borrowed his father's 1941 Packard and we took a couple of girls to Cumberland Falls State Park. Chad was following an A Model Ford. The Ford just would not lay over so we could pass. Finally, on a straight stretch, Chad floor-boarded the gas pedal on the Packard. We started around the Ford and, just before we got to the Ford, its left rear tire blew off, taking the left rear fender with it. Chad did a great job dodging the fender and missing the Ford as he passed in all the dust stirred up while the Ford swerved off the hardtop. Chad didn't bother to tell Mr. Howard how close we had come to crashing his Packard."

A lot of the freshmen at Eastern were planning to enter the service when they became eighteen. I wanted to do that myself, but I knew my father wanted me to go to Dental School. On the other hand, I wanted part of the war action before it was over. I stayed eight weeks at Eastern.

My eighteenth birthday arrived on October 25, 1943, and I decided to go back to Grundy and enlist or volunteer in the service. A U. S. Army Air Force recruiter came on campus and gave us an aviation aptitude test. I took the test and passed with flying colors. I got an appointment at Godman Field, Fort Knox for a personal interview with a board of U. S. Army Officers. When I came back to Grundy at the end of the term, I told my parents of my plans and actions. Naturally, they were disappointed about my dental career, but enthused with my ideas of a flying career.

I had to catch a bus to Louisville, Kentucky to keep my appointment at Godman Field. I arrived in Louisville four hours early so I would be sure to find the airfield and the office where the board met. I got a local bus to the airfield. After asking several people regarding the meeting place of the cadet board, I discovered that I was at Bowman Field in Louisville, instead of Godman Field at Fort Knox. I grabbed a bus for Fort Knox and finally found the examination board. I was wearing a new blue tweed suit with a soft blue shirt and a blue tie to match. I looked my best with my black shoes shined. I met the board and passed easily. I returned to Grundy to initiate the entry procedure that the board had given me.

I stopped by the local Grundy draft board number 19 and asked to be drafted in the next allotment. The board gave me papers indicating that I would be leaving in a couple of weeks and instructed me to give my aviation cadet records to my induction center when I arrived at the location.

**CHAPTER 11**

# Enter U.S. Army Air Corps – World War II

In December of 1943, I was called to active duty and reported to the Buchanan County draft board. I loaded up with other draftees into two buses headed for Abingdon, Virginia. Mr. McGuire's son was put in charge of the first bus, and I was put in charge of the draftees on the second bus. We were interviewed individually when we arrived in Abingdon. I gave my aviation cadet folder to the interviewer, but he just continued to ask me questions while filling out a vital statistics form. The Doctor examined me briefly and then told me that I had been assigned to the U. S. Army. For a moment I was thankful that I wasn't assigned to the Navy or the Marines or even the Seabees.[1]

---

1 **United States Naval Construction Battalions**, better known as the Navy **Seabees**, form the U.S. Naval Construction Force (NCF). The Seabee nickname is a *heterograph* of the initial letters "CB" from the words "Construction Battalion." Chapter VI: The Seabees. *Building the Navy's Bases in World War II: History of the*

REGISTRATION CARD (Men born on or after July 1, 1924, and on or before December 31, 1924)
(Also for the registration of men as they reach the 18th anniversary of the date of their birth on or after January 1, 1943.)

SERIAL NUMBER: W 367–
1. NAME (Print): Harold Glenn Speer
ORDER NUMBER: 17688–A

2. PLACE OF RESIDENCE (Print): Grundy, Buchanan Co, Va
[THE PLACE OF RESIDENCE GIVEN ON LINE 2 ABOVE WILL DETERMINE LOCAL BOARD JURISDICTION; LINE 2 OF REGISTRATION CERTIFICATE WILL BE IDENTICAL]

3. MAILING ADDRESS: 440 Oak St Richmond Va

4. TELEPHONE: 136 Grundy Va
5. AGE IN YEARS: 18 — DATE OF BIRTH: Oct 25, 1925
6. PLACE OF BIRTH: Cumberland Ky

7. NAME AND ADDRESS OF PERSON WHO WILL ALWAYS KNOW YOUR ADDRESS: Dr. Harold Speer Grundy Va

8. EMPLOYER'S NAME AND ADDRESS: student

9. PLACE OF EMPLOYMENT OR BUSINESS: Eastern Ky S. N. Y. J. C.

I AFFIRM THAT I HAVE VERIFIED ABOVE ANSWERS AND THAT THEY ARE TRUE. Harold G Speer

D.S.S. Form 1 (Rev. 11-16-42)        (OVER)        (Registrant's signature)

*Harold's Selective Service Registration Card – 1943*

We boarded a troop train that night bound for Ft. George G. Meade, Maryland. We filed off the train and lined up for our haircuts and our shots. We were issued our dog tags and a uniform along with two pairs of shoes, which I thought rather generous. We were quartered in nice clean barracks. The next morning, we dressed in U. S. Army uniforms and marched to another troop train headed for Greensboro, North Carolina. We arrived in Greensboro that evening and filed off the train to those waiting olive green U. S. Army buses,

*BuDocks and the CEC 1940–1946.* Vol. I. Washington, DC: U.S.GPO. 1947. Retrieved 18 October 2017 – via HyperWar.

Naval Construction Battalions were conceived of as replacements for civilian construction companies in combat zones after the attack on *Pearl Harbor*. At the time civilian contractors had roughly 70,000 men working U.S.N. contracts overseas. International law made it illegal for civilian workers to resist an attack. Doing so would classify them as *guerrillas* and could lead to *summary execution.* Seabee History: Formation of the Seabees and World War II. NHHC. 2017.

which hauled us to the beautiful Greensboro basic training center. Those tall southern white pine trees were standing everywhere in the sandy, loamy ground. The barracks mess hall and parade grounds were laid out like a college campus or a military prep school. The parade ground was in the center of the arena and the auditorium doubled as an indoor classroom and a recreation center.

I was assigned to the Aviation Cadet Pilot Class of 1943. I didn't see any airplanes or a landing strip — I figured we would get the groundwork out of the way first. We began taking basic training and wwere restricted to the base on the weekends. However, one of the local women's colleges sent their choir over to the auditorium to present a singing program for us to enjoy. We were certainly impressed by the tranquility and beauty of the group, as well as the harmonious tone of their voices. We immediately looked forward to getting off base restriction to pursue social activities on the weekends.

Mom and dad paid me a much-appreciated visit the next weekend. They were surprised that I was enjoying myself. They returned to Grundy reassured that I was making the most of my opportunity.

We took some final aptitude tests just before completion of basic training. As soon as we graduated, the base commander told us that only a few college-trained men would be selected to attend flight school because the demand for pilots had decreased dramatically. This was quite a jolt to me, and I realized that I would have a little harder route to the cockpit now. The commander said that we would be assigned to other essential technical fields as dictated. I immediately thought of parachute school, however, I was selected for radar scope operator's school at Savannah, Georgia.

I boarded a troop train again, headed for Savannah. I found Hunter Field very suitable. The radar academic course was superb. I was impressed with a squad of marines who attended the same course. These marines impressed everyone with the way they excelled at marching everywhere they went in a squad. They were all business. I'll never forget those green uniformed marines. The radar training was thorough, and I found the course a pleasant experience. When I completed the academic portion of the radar course, I was sent to Drew Field, Tampa, Florida, and out in the back country to operate a radar scope in a training status. We would be vectoring B-17 and B-24 bombers along certain routes within our range. Then, we would direct P-39 and P-51 fighters toward the B-17 and B-24 for practice intercept missions.

This was interesting work, but it seemed to leave me on the ground. I needed to get in the air some way. There was a lot of publicity about Major Clark Gable attending the Panama City aerial gunnery course. I applied for aerial gunnery school and was accepted. I boarded an Army tractor-trailer type bus with other selected troops for the trip to Panama City. We got off the bus at Lyndall Field just outside Panama City, Florida.

I fell in love with this place. There was an air of drama about any flying operation that I didn't feel with any other operation. We were given full choke shotguns and taught how to use them by shooting clay pigeons, also known as skeet. When we became proficient at shooting skeet from a standing position, we were allowed to shoot from a machine gun mounted shotgun turret. Next, we were put on flatbed trucks which would drive through a series of skeet houses. As the truck passed a skeet house, a skeet was thrown up by a spring-loaded skeet thrower. The skeet came up from all angles and we had to fire them all while on a moving platform. This practice was plenty of fun and there was never a dull moment.

Next, we learned to field strip a fifty-caliber machine gun. Then we climbed into a Martin top turret or a Sperry ball turret where we learned to rotate the turret by sitting on a bicycle seat and turning the handlebars to turn the turret to the left or right. We elevated or lowered the twin fifty caliber machine guns by rotating the handlebars upward or downward. There was a projector screen over the blackboard at which our guns were pointed, and an electric spot on the screen indicated where we were aiming the guns. A film showing a P-39 in a pursuit attack on our bombers would pass across the screen from one position to another. We would track the fighter image and squeeze the trigger when we had the spot on the fighter. An electrical device sounded when we were on target and scoring hits on the fighter. We enjoyed operating in the air-conditioned training rooms —You not only learned the skill, but you beat the heat.

Next, we practiced shooting the twin fifty caliber machine guns from a real turret with live ammunition. A jeep ran around a circular track out in front of the line of turrets. When the jeep went behind a sand bank at the back of the circle, a ten-foot square rug target showed above the sand dune. We fired away at the target while it traveled behind the sandbank. We really got the feel of the turret and the machine guns in action versus the simulation we had been doing previously. The vibration and the chatter of the machine guns gave us a sense of reality which was an essential element in our training.

Our next class involved a trip to the parachute loft, where we learned to pack a parachute and to get in and out of the parachute harness. Finally, we learned the proper way to bail out of the aircraft and how to land in the chute and collapse the chute.

Next, we learned how to release a rubber raft from an aircraft, how to board the raft from an aircraft partially submerged in a pond of water, how to use the oxygen mask at high altitude, and all about the emergency operations of equipment in subzero temperatures. Finally, we were hauled to Apalachicola, Florida for actual flight training on a B-17 Flying Fortress. The big moment had arrived; we were going to leave the ground!

I made three good friends in my class – Francis C. Mears from Scottsdale, Pennsylvania, and Jack and Mike Epperson, twins from

Haleyville, Alabama. Our first flight consisted of tracking a real P-39 making passes on our B-17. There was no ammunition in the P-39 fighters and they took only a few seconds to commence and break off their attack. That was fun!

Finally, we got a run over the gulf with "hot" guns. Our targets were floats at different points in the water. The B-17 banked left then right so the Martin top turret could get a chance to shoot into the water. Our last flight was one in which we would demonstrate our ability to field strip a fifty-caliber machine gun in high altitude flight with gloves on, which required considerable finesse.

Mother and father came to Panama City for my graduation and I introduced them to my friends. We visited the beautiful white, sandy beach in Panama City, and later went out for dinner. Again, my parents were amazed at how well I enjoyed the training. They were more impressed with my promotion to Corporal than I was.

*B-24 aircrew training — Panama City, Florida - 1944*
*Harold Speer in the center of the first row in the picture on the left.*
*Training buddies included the Epperson twins (Mack and Jack), Francis*
*C. Mears, and Art Aro. Harold with cigar in picture on the right.*

After graduating from aerial gunnery school, we boarded a troop train again to Mitchell Field on Long Island, New York. I was assigned to a B-24 training crew that was shipped by troop train to Chatham Field in Savannah, Georgia. Our crew consisted of a pilot, copilot, nose gunner, tail gunner, Sperry ball gunner, flight engineer, radio operator, waist gunner, navigator, and bombardier. There were twenty B-24 crews in training at the same time at Chatham Field. The aircraft were flown 24 hours per day as long as they were "in commission" (safe to fly) and the crews were scheduled in three eight-hour shifts or flying periods. The B-24 pilots and crews received every conceivable training mission, day or night, including practice executing the many different aerial battle formations. When the weather got too low for pilot training at Chatham, the pilots flew to Batista Field, 37 miles southwest of Havana, Cuba to complete their practice bombing and high altitude precision instrument procedures -- the crews were left at Chatham to continue military training for about a month.

When we completed combat crew training, we were allowed to go into Savannah on the weekends. We headed for the USO (United Service Organization) centers, where coffee and donuts were always available, and a dance was always on the agenda. The local girls showed up for the dances in abundant numbers. We had to get back to the base by midnight, which was always a scramble.

When the pilots returned from Puerto Rico, we were ready to fly to Mitchell Field, Long Island to get our overwater equipment. We loaded up in the B-24 and blasted off for Mitchell Field in December of 1943 and landed just before dark. The wind was cold, and the snow blasted across the icy runways and taxi ramps. We chalked and tied down the B-24 and buttoned up the aircraft, then made a dash for the waiting U. S. Army bus that took us to our quarters. We were extremely glad to get inside those warm barracks.

The next day, we began a two-week training program, which included an altitude pressure chamber course. We got our overseas immunization shots, our winter uniforms, and our winter flying suits. Our aircraft was given its final overseas inspection, and then we waited until the weather was favorable enough to start our overseas flight.

The crew got a weekend pass and we headed for the railroad stations and a trip to Hempstead N. Y. where we visited one of the crew member's home in Brooklyn, N.Y. Afterwards, we went our separate ways to explore the "Big Apple." We learned quickly that the U.S.O. Centers were the place to go because people our age were there, and we could afford the refreshments. The evening was ever too short! We grabbed the train bound for Mitchell Field to be back on the base before midnight.

Finally, the weather report became favorable for our first flight to Europe. We loaded up the Consolidated Liberator B-24 and took off toward Bangor, Maine. We were cruising about ten thousand feet over the snow-covered New England countryside. It was late on a winter day and very cold inside the plane. The scattered farmhouses we passed had their porch lights turned on, and as I looked down, I wondered what those people were talking about around those cozy fireplaces while our crew was moving on in the real danger.

Suddenly, out of nowhere, a Republic Thunderbolt P-47 fighter plane made a couple of practice gunnery passes at our B-24. He came out of the remaining sun in the sky from our left side. The fighter pilot began his simulated attack on our bomber three thousand feet parallel and about one thousand feet above our altitude. To reach this position, he flew the same heading that we flew. However, the fighter pilot flew about 100 miles per hour faster than our bomber.

Once the fighter pilot got to that imaginary point called "the perch," he began a slightly descending curve until the nose of his fighter pointed right at the middle of our bomber. Then the fighter pilot reversed his bank and began a left hand turn to keep the nose and the gun camera in the middle of our bomber. As the fighter pilot closed the distance between the fighter plane and our bomber, he drifted to the rear of our bomber. He was flying faster than we were, but he was flying a curve, therefore, our bomber began to move ahead of the fighter plane. Once the fighter pilot arrived directly behind our bomber in a trailing position, he turned sharply to the right and began a climb up to another attack position on our left side into the sun.

The fighter pilot completed the second pass at our bomber, then flew his plane up to join us in flight formation. We waved at each other. The fighter pilot rocked his wings and rolled left until his plane was upside down. He then pulled the Thunderbolt through a split-S maneuver, which took his plane about four thousand feet below our bomber where he leveled out going in the opposite direction from our bomber. The Thunderbolt had white contrails coming off each wingtip like white smoke as the pilot pulled the Thunderbolt through the dive in that cold air. That was an especially beautiful sight for me. I felt like I had gained enough knowledge of fighter tactics right then to be able to fly a fighter if the chance came by later.

We landed after dark at Bangor, Maine, touching down on the icy runway. Our pilot taxied our bomber to the parking apron, where the crew chief blocked the wheel with chock blocks and tied the wings and tail of the aircraft to the tie down in the concrete.

Dow Field was the name of our base. The town of Bangor was within walking distance of about twelve miles. The North Country was beautiful even covered with a couple of feet of snow. The airfield was well organized, and the personnel were efficient and satisfied with the location and their relations with the townsfolk. I was impressed with the quality of life.

Since everything was secret about troop movements in those days, the transient troops were not allowed to go into Bangor on weekend passes. However, shortly after we arrived, this policy was modified, and we went into town with the first transient troops that Saturday. I walked the length and the breadth of this town, getting acquainted with the physical aspects of the township. I was amazed to find out how the people I met were as friendly as the folks back home. I was under the mistaken impression that "Yankees" didn't have time to be friendly folks.

In time, I found the USO entertainment facility. The red brick two story building had a library downstairs. The upstairs had a recreation area, where coffee and donuts were available. I noticed that a dance was scheduled right there that evening. Naturally, I planned to attend.

When I returned to the USO, the place was rather crowded with our age group. I mingled with the crowd around the edge of the dance floor until I spotted a girl with whom I wanted to dance. She was apparently delighted with my approach. We spent the evening together, and I forgot about the war for one evening. I had to get back to the base by midnight, so I caught the last bus back. The girl told me that she could come to the base USO reception and dance Sunday afternoon. We made arrangements to be together for that occasion. Her parents escorted her to the occasion. I was impressed by her parents too.

The weather began to look good between Dow Field and Goose Bay, Labrador. Our crew was restricted to our quarters for the earliest possible movement. The sky was clear, but the north winds stayed rather brisk in the Canadian wilderness along the coast. When the wind report became favorable, we loaded up in our B-24 for take-off. We roared off the runway and headed north for Goose Bay, Labrador. I studied the terrain from the plexiglass waist gunner's position. After we crossed the mouth of the blue St. Lawrence River, the countryside was a snow barren wilderness. The evergreen white pines were about all that stuck up out of the white desert of snow.

We had previously been told that every 100 miles on our overland route, there were shelters with caches of food and other provisions stored for our benefit just in case we had to bail out. This was some comfort; however, airmen have a great deal of confidence in their flying machines. We didn't figure we would get to use those shelters.

When we arrived at Goose Bay, the winds were so high that we had to circle a couple of hours before the winds subsided enough for us to land on that icy runway with eight feet of snowbanks on each side. When the wind shifted and lined up with the runway heading, our pilots motored in for a real smooth landing with no problems.

Eight feet of snow covered everything at Goose Bay and the buildings were underground. Boarded up walkways connected the buildings to protect the troops from the wind, rain, and snow. I can't remember how long we spent at Goose Bay but, the weather forecast finally became favorable enough for the flight from Goose Bay over the Atlantic to Bluie West One on the southernmost air strip on the continent of Greenland.

Our crew loaded all our belongings back on the B-24, including many items we had purchased from the Post Exchange. My Post Exchange items included a box of three musketeers. Our engineer had the engines pre-heated with a ground heater unit with twelve-inch heating pipes running into the engines. We found everything frozen in the aircraft with a glazed ice covering. It took a while for all the instruments to warm up before they were readable or usable. You couldn't touch anything metal without gloves, otherwise your fingers would instantly stick to the metal. You would lose your flesh when you tried to turn anything loose. We got a healthy respect for the sub-zero temperatures right away.

We blasted off the runway and headed out across the cold choppy Atlantic on our way to Greenland. I looked at the ocean from the window, and the waves looked at least sixty feet high. The white caps sprayed in the air from one wave to the next. I realized that a ditch in the ocean would be quite a challenge should the occasion arise. About halfway across our route, an ocean station "Bravo" ship with communication equipment stood by in the event of problems. There were some SA 16 "Flying Duck Butt" twin engine boat aircraft stationed at Goose Bay, as well as at Bluie West One, Greenland, which could come to our rescue in the event of an emergency. I learned years later that those flying boats cannot land safely or take off in swells that are six feet high.

We arrived at the mouth of the fjord at Bluie West One. The light brown lava walls of this canyon were 300 to 500 feet high. We entered the boxed canyon-looking inlet at an altitude below the walls and flew directly over the radio station located on a little rock in the mouth of the fjord. We flew about ten or twelve miles up the inlet before we spotted the single landing strip on the right side of the gorge just four feet above the water on our approach end. The runway ran up a steep hill before one could turn an aircraft off the runway onto the parking ramp. This base looked like the canyon wall had been blasted off into a gravel pile next to the water at the base of the cliff. It was barren and only the gray coarse gravel rock protruded out of the wind-swept base camp.

The familiar Army barracks and gymnasium with the gray colored perma-siding dotted the bank before the runway and above the ice-frozen inlet. We approached the end of the runway making sure we didn't land short because that four-foot lip would jerk our landing gear off easily. We didn't want to land on thin ice either. We also had to be careful not to land too far down the runway, because a go around would be hazardous with the far end of the runway ending so near the canyon wall.

We touched down and slowed down before turning off the runway on the slanted ramp. The ice-covered ramp made taxiing hazardous.

The pilot had to use the engines more than the brakes to taxi into the tie down locations. We deplaned with only our flying suits, mess kits and overnight bags. The wind made walking on ice a real chore. The bus, which picked us up, took us to the barracks and drove like a block of ice. I bet the grease was frozen in everything but the motor.

The maintenance crew at Bluie West One didn't impress me for looks, but their efficient operation made the grade. Their uniforms were a little on the untidy side. We went to the NCO club after we got squared away. We found out that life on the rock was frugal. I expected Greenland to have more inhabitants. The only folks around that camp were Inuit natives, who lived across the fjord from the base and were hired to do odd jobs.

Instead of group exercise, we went individually to the gymnasium to work out in sweat suits. The gymnasium was loaded with training equipment that we shared with the Inuit inhabitants as well. You could play basketball or work out on parallel bars, punching bags, medicine balls, etc.

I asked some of the permanent party troops what they did in their spare time, and they told me that, outside of the radio, books and hobbies, the only entertainment was the USO troops that came by Greenland on their way to and from Europe. They told me the Inuit village was off limits to the troops.

Once the weather cleared, we loaded up the B-24 for our trip to Meeks field at Keflavik, Iceland. Before we taxied out on the runway, we discovered someone had taken our Post Exchange goodies out of the B-24. The runway didn't lend itself to an abortive take-off – we would surely have slid into the fjord if we ever tried to stop. Thankfully, our crew didn't have any trouble lifting off the runway. When we reached the radio station that stood on the flat one-half acre of lava rock sticking up about twenty feet out of the fjord, we turned left and climbed to our cruise level on course to Meeks Field near Keflavik, Iceland.

About half-way to Iceland, we passed over the ocean station "Charlie" rescue ship. As we approached the southern tip of Iceland, we noticed that this island was covered with brown and purple lava rocks about the size of wash tubs. The snow didn't lie well on these rocks because the wind blew the snow off and melted it. When we were approaching Keflavik, the snow began to fall, and the terrain looked like smooth, covered topsoil under the snow.

We spotted Meeks Field as we were descending in a left-hand circle. We could see another air strip over at the capital city of Reykjavik. I saw Bell Air Cobra P-39 fighters taking off and landing on that strip in the distance. The fighters looked about the size of lightning bugs from my vantage point. I made another mental note to remember where I would land if I flew a fighter across the ocean later.

After we secured the aircraft, we were housed in Nissen huts[2] provided by the British. After we settled in our quarters, we went to the mess hall to eat. After supper, we visited the Post Exchange, where we met some attractive Icelandic girls, before going to the NCO club. I was looking forward to visiting the capital city of Reykjavik. When I inquired how to get into the city from the base, I was told that transients were not allowed in Reykjavik. I learned that the political situation was touchy with Iceland. I don't think the Icelandic establishment wanted Americans taking over their city during the war and then leaving it when peace came. Then again, the U.S. Army may not have wanted us in town for security reasons. Anyway, I was disappointed about missing the opportunity to get to know the Icelanders better even though I realized that the war was the top priority, not tourism. Someone told me that the city really was beautiful.

---

2 The Nissen huts were shaped like a barrel split down the middle. The metal frame of the Nissen hut was covered with galvanized corduroy tin. This was a very efficient structure, especially in high winds.

# CHAPTER 12

# England – B-24 ("Wandering Wanda")

**W**e had been enroute from the states for about two months. Of course, the dead of winter was not the best time to cross the Atlantic by aircraft at the time. Finally, the fog of England let up and the weatherman gave us the "go" signal. We headed east toward England and passed over the last rescue ship, the ocean station "Delta," about half-way to our destination. We spotted the green countryside of Ireland as we approached the British Isles. I felt like I had much the same view as the famous aviator Charles Lindbergh had during his first Atlantic crossing. We then arrived over "Bonnie Old" England, where the countryside looked so green and orderly. We landed at Vaccey, Wales where the British gave us a quick "glad to see you Yank" and loaded us on a lorry.[1] We were hauled to the USAF airfield at Stone,

---

1 British term for bus.

England near the town of Bangor. We were housed in Nissen huts again, and the blankets on the bunks were blue-gray, heavy woven wool, or as we liked to call them, "horse blankets."

It was February 24, 1944. We stayed at Stone Field for about thirty days. I pulled KP (kitchen patrol) for thirty days. One morning the Sergeant woke me to go to KP and I fell back to sleep. For that little tardiness, I pulled cabbage stalks every night at a nearby garden for a week. I managed to get up on first notice after that with ease.

Finally, we loaded on a troop train and headed for our combat unit. We got off the train at Norwich, England. We boarded a Lorry and journeyed to Ipswich, then to Attleborough, and lastly out to Old Buckenham Airfield. We were assigned to the 8th Air Force (under the command of Major General Jimmy Doolittle), the 453rd bomb group (H) under the command of Colonel Ramsay D. Potts (and later under Colonel Edward F. Hubbard) in the Norfolk/Suffolk region of eastern England. Our squadron was the 732nd briefly, then the 735th squadron. Major Donald Heaton was the commander of the 732nd Squadron. The 453rd bomb group operations officer was the famous Hollywood actor, Major Jimmy Stewart. I was assigned to the B-24 H named "Wandering Wanda."[2]

The aircrew of "Wandering Wanda" was alerted for several missions that were scratched because of bad weather. Then on April 4, 1945, it was clear as a bell and we were given a mission to bomb the German Messerschmidt (ME) 262 Jet airfield at Wesendorf, Germany. We

---

2 In one of those strange coincidences only to be found out at a later date, the mother-in-law of Harold's future son, Stephanie (Jackson) Hall, was stationed around the same time (October 1944) in nearby East Anglia around Kettering, working as a Red Cross Aide and serving the American and Allied soldiers from the ClubMobile called the "Maine." She later married an American P-47 fighter pilot, Leroy Hall, from Hillsboro, North Carolina, who saw action in Italy.

scrambled to "Wandering Wanda," fired her up, and manned the guns. We taxied out with a full bomb load and took off when our turn came. We joined the one thousand plane formation and headed for the continent. There wasn't a cloud in the sky. We left the White Cliffs of Dover and were approaching the French coastal city of Le Havre. This was our diversion route before heading for Germany. Our pilot started a turn back toward England and we asked what happened. He said we were scratched because the effort was not considered a "mass effort." I took this to mean that the commander didn't want any new crews going to Germany on such a clear day. He must have felt that fighter attack and flak would make dense traffic more hazardous. We returned to Old Buckenham where we were debriefed and given a shot of scotch as a reward for our efforts. When we got back to the barracks, I discovered that I had been promoted to Buck Sergeant. I had been a Corporal since I graduated from gunnery school.

We were allowed to go into town that night. We soon found a dance hall crowded with a wedding celebration, and we were invited to join the celebration. I discovered that the British Isles had one big advantage over America. That is, Britain had more girls per square yard than anywhere I had been, and they were receptive to company. For a moment I again forgot about the war.

When I got back to the barracks that night, I leaped into the top bunk and had just gotten to sleep when someone shook my leg and told me to go outside the barracks and get into the air raid ditches. The air raid sirens were blasting the base. I intended to get up, but it was dark. I figured that JU-88 called "Bed-check Charlie" couldn't find our base, much less hit my barracks on his harassment mission. So, I stayed in my bunk. However, the base commander came through shortly thereafter checking on new crew members. He roused me outside in my long johns. I jumped into the ditch, which had about a foot of water in it. I got plenty muddy.

Just a short time later "Bed Check Charlie," a Junkers JU-88 light twin engine bomber, came right over our quarters at a low altitude. Fortunately for us, the English fog concealed our location. "Bed Check Charlie" continued over to the next air strip and dropped two bombs on a mess hall where someone had left on a kitchen light. I later heard that about sixteen men were killed in that one incident. From then on, we rolled out of the barracks every time that air raid signal sounded at night. On most all the other air raid alerts, we came out at night and watched the orange contrails of the high-flying German V-Bombs on their way to London.

My last mission of aerial warfare over Europe occurred on the foggy morning of April 10, 1945, on Mission # 258. I was a waist gunner on the four engine B-24 "Wandering Wanda." 2nd Lieutenant Joseph C. Somers was pilot in command and Warrant Officer Henry M. Barker (from Knoxville, Tennessee) was co-pilot. That morning all crew members attended the mission briefing in the Quonset hut. Our mission was to bomb the jet fighter experimental station over Rechlin, Germany about fifty miles north of Berlin. In the event the weather prevented identification of our primary target, we would proceed to our secondary target which was the railroad yards located south of Berlin at Wittenberge.

The weather was a 500 foot ceiling and three miles visibility at take-off time. The weather was "broken to overcast" at the primary target and "broken" over the secondary target. We were instructed to depart "Old Buckenham" to the northeast and to form up in formation while climbing to an altitude of eighteen thousand feet. We would fly northeast across the North Sea to a point between Hamburg and Kiel, Germany before turning southeast toward our primary target.

Once over Germany, we could expect flak and enemy fighter aircraft enroute to the target and concentrate flak on the bomb run. We departed the briefing building and rode jeeps out to our awaiting heavy bomber loaded with sixteen 500 pound, penetrating bombs plus full fuel tanks and yards of fifty caliber bullets. We preflighted the aircraft, donned our flak suits, and the pilot cranked up the four big engines.

The operation officer in the tower fired two green flares. We roared down the runway and lifted off into the wild blue yonder. We formed up as we climbed through the overcast and leveled off on course like an assembly line operation. We arrived over Germany and turned the corner at Kiel-Hamburg, then turned southeast toward our initial point.

We were flying in the high right squadron behind the lead squadron. Lt. Love and command pilot Major Clingan were piloting the lead B-24 and leading the 735th Squadron.[3] When we began our bomb run, the flak batteries opened up and saturated the area with exploding purple brownish, flower-looking puffs of flak. The lead squadron was able to drop their bombs on the primary target, however, the high right and low left squadrons were not able to drop their bombs because the hole in the overcast closed up before the bombardier could fix his bombsight on the target. After the lead squadron's "bombs away," the flak stopped. It was eerily peaceful, but also a time to beware of the ever present threat of attack by enemy fighters.

Our three squadrons continued on course to our secondary target, the rail yards at Wittenberge. We were approaching our bomb run when the flak batteries let loose with a barrage of withering flak that was deadly more accurate than the flak we had experienced over our primary target. We had lots of cloud coverage over the primary target, but we only had scattered to broken cloud coverage over Wittenberge.

---

3 *See,* Staff Sergeant William Voight's description in *Last Mission – Lasting Memories* – pg. M-43, in the "Memories" Section … "The Liberator Men of Old Buck." *See also,* William E. Brown, Jr. Diary entry – April 10, 1945, for notation of this event and a copy of the "After Action Report."

The B-24 piloted by 2nd Lt. William H. Powell, Jr. (from Nash-ville, Tennessee) received a direct hit. His B-24 then struck our right wing tip as it plunged earthward out of control and on fire. Our tail gunner reported seeing two parachutes open, but he said the chutes were on fire. The B-24 exploded below us and broke in half just behind the wing.[4]

We opened our bomb bay doors on the bomb run. Suddenly, *WHAM!* The jolt sounded like lightning striking our aircraft. The flak knocked out our number three engine. Our aircraft immediately began falling back in the formation even though our pilot adjusted the power setting on the three remaining engines. We dropped our bombs on target anyway.

We turned west on course for Old Buckenham. We were now a "straggler" because the other aircraft had left us behind. Bomber planes were safer while in a large formation. Stragglers who had fallen out of the formation were preferred targets for enemy fighter aircraft. It wasn't long before the inevitable happened! The tail gunner called, "Bogey closing in at six o'clock high." I said, "It's probably an American P-51 pilot." The co-pilot put his Navy field glasses on the plane. He said, "If that is a P-51 pilot, then he is flying a German FW-190." Lt. Somers and Warrant Officer Barker pushed our B-24 nose low and made a rapid descent into the fourteen thousand foot solid overcast, which fortunately protected us from detection by the enemy fighter planes. We had too much precious cargo to risk being sprayed with machine guns and cannon fire after we had completed our mission. We needed to get home and get another load of "goodies" for the Germans.

---

4 *See, The Mighty Eighth Roll of Honor*, pg. 443 – Serial Number 251089, 10 Apr 45, 453rd BG, Missing Air Crew Report 13897, Pilot, 2nd Lt. William H. Powell, Jr., KIA (killed in action), hometown of Nashville, Tennessee.

*Wandering Wanda Aircrew – With permission, Copyright B-24 Best Web:* http://www.b24bestweb.com/.

<u>*Standing (L-R):*</u>
*Cpl. Harold Speer of VA (Waist Gunner), Cpl. Mack Epperson of AL (Waist gunner), Unknown (Flew once), 2nd Lt. Morton W. Gleisher of NY (Navigator), Henry M. Barker of TN (Co-Pilot), 2nd Lt. Joseph C. Somers of NC (Pilot).*

<u>*Kneeling (L-R):*</u>
*Sgt. Earl Hill of NJ (Tail gunner), Sgt. Norman J. Bressette of VT (Flight Engineer), Sgt. Hiram B. Eldon of MA (Radio Operator), and Cpl. Anthony J. Alfano of NJ (Nose gunner).*

We made it back to Old Buckenham, landed, completed our debriefing, and collected our two shots of scotch before settling in our bunks for a good night's sleep before our next mission. In the meantime, our ground crew would repair the B-24 "Wandering Wanda," refuel, and refill our bomb bays with more high explosives.

# Some Statistics

Statistically speaking: The life of an aircrew member in World War II was a precarious existence. According to "Real Clear History," the United States "suffered 52,173 aircrew combat losses in WWII. Another 25,844 died in accidents. More than half of these died in the continental United States. The U.S. lost 65,164 planes during WWII, but only 22,948 in combat."

According to the National Museum of the Mighty Eighth Air Force in Pooler, Georgia, "The cost of ridding the Nazi scourge was staggering. The Mighty Eighth airmen suffered the most casualties of any command in World War II – 26,000 men were killed in action; another 28,000 became prisoners of war. Their valor was unparalleled. As the teenagers and young men of the Eighth battled the enemy at 25,000 feet, such bravery earned them 17 Medals of Honor, 220 Distinguished Flying Crosses, and more than 420,000 Air Medals."

The fate of aircrewmen for America's allies during World War II was similarly precarious. According to the Imperial War Museum in Duxford, England, "51% of aircrew were killed on operations, 12% were killed or wounded in non-operational accidents, and 13% became prisoners of war or evaders. Only 24% survived the war unscathed."

**CHAPTER 13**

# On the Continent (Hell Drivers 36<sup>th</sup> TX-OK Infantry)

**J**ust a few days later I went on a local flight with a veteran crew to check out as an assistant flight engineer. When we got upstairs, the old crew chief asked me to change an inverter. When I told him how I was going to do it, he said, "Never mind, you have just passed the test." When we landed, someone told me that our crew was being split up because the war was just about over. He told me that I was being assigned to the infantry.

I couldn't believe what I was hearing until I checked the bulletin board. Sure enough, I was scheduled to catch a troop train for Tidworth Barracks near Southampton, England to get a six-week hot infantry refresher course. That night my crew was to fly supplies to the Remagen Bridge Head Infantry, who were trapped across the Rhine River. I was assigned to guard the aircraft and supplies that night. Consequently, I did not get to go on the mission the next day.

The rest of the crew went on the mission and dropped the supplies. However, flak shot out their brake lines and the crew landed "Wandering Wanda" at Bentwaters Airfield near Woodbridge for emergency repairs. When the crew finally got back, we were briefed on a mission to the ball-bearing plant at Swineford, Germany. Before the mission came off, I was sent to Tidworth Barracks. I asked why I was being sent to the infantry and the rest of the crew were being sent elsewhere. They told me, perhaps for my satisfaction, that I was a draftee and had no choice.

When I got to Tidworth Barracks, I found the camp a beautiful place ideal for a Boy Scout jamboree. I had finally arrived at a permanent military training camp which was going to prepare us for live fire in six weeks. We trained like Rangers. We went day and night methodically mastering each phase of ground combat. I volunteered to fire every weapon at our command and was put in charge of a squad of trainees.

On occasion, the drill instructor would have us fall out and dig fox holes. He would say that we were going to be run over by some tanks. We dug the fox holes three or four times without being approached by any tanks. After digging the holes, we were just told to fill them up again and fall in. This routine became a ritual. I figured this was designed to break up any monotony. Consequently, we stopped digging such deep fox holes. When the drill instructor caught us digging short, he marched us to a nearby gulley and ordered us to dig fox holes. We obliged half-heartedly. When we were about half-way through digging, we heard tanks coming out of the gulley. Once we saw those three giant tanks coming out of the gulley, we quickened the pace of our digging. Sure enough, the tanks ran right over our fox holes, turning back and forth. We were covered with dirt, but unharmed. We dug deep every time after that episode.

We had some soldiers who didn't want to go to combat. They were in the stockade. Each squad leader was assigned a couple of these soldiers to run through the qualifying combat infantry course along with the regular squad. I had to watch these people carefully. They would seize any opportunity to go over the hill or take your weapon. For these reasons, we did not take these guarded soldiers on night missions, and I kept them at arm's-length at all times. Consequently, I got good cooperation from them. They qualified right along with the rest of the men.

An opportunity to train for officer candidate school came through our camp, and I applied. My commanding officer assigned an evaluation officer to observe my performance and submit a report.

One day we had a visitor to our camp. Tommy Farr,[1] the great boxer, showed up and refereed several boxing matches between volunteers at the camp. After Tommy left, a General spoke to us and wanted us to volunteer to go into combat with only four of the six weeks course completed. Before the end of the day, May 8, 1945 (VE Day), we learned that the war was over in Europe. We continued our training, but the officer candidate school quota was dropped.

Upon graduation at Tidworth Barracks, we were given a three-day pass to London. After we returned from our London pass, we were loaded on a troop train for Southampton. We arrived at Southampton and were loaded on a troop ship named "The Exchequer." We sailed out of the port of Southampton on a beautiful day – the sky was blue, and the Channel was smooth as velvet. The wind was calm, and the sun was shining. I felt more like a tourist than a soldier headed for

---

1 Thomas George Farr was a Welsh boxer, who became the British and Empire heavyweight champion on March 15, 1937. He is considered one of the "greatest British heavyweight fighters ever." He was inducted into the Welsh Sports Hall of Fame in 1997.

foreign soil. I remember the trip across the Channel so well because half-way across, the radio announced the death of President Franklin Delano Roosevelt, who had died earlier on April 12, 1945. The news struck me like he was a member of our family. I couldn't hold back some private tears.

We docked at Le Havre, France where the commanding officer ordered us to fix bayonets before we marched off the dock. We marched past several hedgerows that still had "knocked-out" tanks sticking out of the rows. I found out that some Frenchmen were bitter at the Americans for having leveled Le Havre with bombs. There were some French communists who were hostile too. Occupation troops were in for some challenging experiences.

We marched to Camp Phillip Morris, which was just outside Le Havre. The American troops were either enroute to the United States or to Germany. We processed at Camp Phillip Morris for shipment to the various replacement centers throughout the European Theatre of operation (ETO). My group was put on a troop train bound for Worms, Germany just west of the Rhine River. I never saw so many blown up railroad tracks in my life. Because of blown out bridges, we traveled back and forth to reach our destination. The "forty and eight"[2] cattle cars in which we rode were neither comfortable nor heated. By the time we had finally arrived at Worms, we were worn out from the train ride, but our spirits brightened upon getting off the train.

The town of Worms was in the Rhineland area called Westphalia. The camp was in a blue green wheat field, and the compound was enclosed with barbed wire. The place was a tent city where we were

---

2 These cars received their names because they could carry 40 men or eight horses, as was clearly painted on each boxcar. During World War II, the infamously uncomfortable "forty and eight" boxcars still transported supplies and troops to the front, but they also returned to Germany with new cargoes. *The American Legion.*

quartered in field tents, and Military Police patrolled the camp. Inside the camp, we shot crap and played cards, while waiting to be picked up by units stationed in Germany through a requisition program. A policy of non-fraternization with the conquered enemy was in effect. The Army still had a mission to capture many of the German troops that were hiding in the Alps, as well as, in other places. These troops were dangerous —they could kill, and would, as we later discovered.

About three days later, a two-and-a-half ton GMC truck pulled up to the gate. The markings on the bumper indicated that the truck belonged to the 36th Texas, Oklahoma Infantry Division Quartermaster Company. The Sergeant had a requisition with my name on it. He had me hop on the bed of the truck along with my barracks bag and eight or ten other troops. I was impressed with the professional attitude of these two drivers, who drove the "Jimmy" two-and-a-half-ton GMC truck and hauled us to Germany. They were soldiers who had conquered the enemy. They were as friendly as cousins, but you sensed that they didn't have any trouble handling their job. These soldiers were well fed, and their uniforms were cleaned and pressed. The truck was clean, well painted, and marked. The mechanical condition of the vehicle was in top shape too. I was glad to join an organization like the 36th infantry Division. We were part of General Wade Haislip's 7th Army.

We crossed the Rhine and went through the bergs and hamlets until we arrived at the beautiful blue Danube River at Ulm, Germany. This was like a dream coming true to me. I never thought that I would see the beautiful blue Danube, much less be stationed on its banks. The truck pulled up to the bridge across the Danube, then turned left in front of a cigar factory which fronted the banks of the river. We dismounted with our barracks bags in hand and were taken to the First Sergeant's office and signed into the company. Then we were quartered in the lower end of the factory. We were individually called to the Sergeant's office for a brief interview. When my interview came, the Sergeant asked me what I wanted to do, and I told him that I wanted to drive a jeep. He assigned me to the Supply Officer's jeep. My first trip came just a few minutes later. We were dispatched to Gunsberg, Germany, between Ulm and Munich. We got on the Autobahn or "superhighway" just below Ulm and headed for Gunsberg.

The autobahn was beautiful on the green rolling terrain with the evergreen pines lining the edge of the highway through the forest portion of the journey. The highway was straight enough to use as an aircraft runway. That thought had just raced through my mind when I saw these marguerites hacked out in the forest along the superhighway. In each park, there sat a bright new Messerschmitt 262 German Jet Fighter. The Germans had used this stretch of the auto-bahn as a take-off and landing strip for a squadron of Messerschmitt ME-262's. I realized that the Germans had been ahead of the allies in the fighter business. I recalled our last briefing in England had given some indication of the new jet fighter and its superior performance. We thought that the Germans only had a few prototypes roaring around the sky. I remember our B-24 crew talking about a German jet meeting a formation of American B-24's head on. Although our pilot called out that the jet was at the twelve o'clock high approach position, because he noted the black smoke trailing the jet, our nose gunner never saw the jet. Thus, the gunner's chance of shooting down one of the first jets slipped right by him. He said he wasn't looking for something so fast and small, and without a propeller.

We finished our business in Gunsberg and returned to Ulm. When I went to eat that evening, I discovered that we had a kitchen, a beer hall, and a private swimming pool all right there in the rear of the factory in a private courtyard. I thought these 36th division folks showed a lot of resourcefulness.

When the Captain noticed that I was a Buck Sergeant, he had me taken off jeep driver duty and put me on guard duty. This guard duty was a special assignment. I had a squad of men, and we had a roadblock set up on the bridge which crossed the Danube just next to our quarters. We searched everyone who came across that bridge for weapons. The 36th Infantry Division was searching for weapons in each town in their jurisdiction.

I was sent to Goppingen just south of Ulm where I was put in charge of a squad of men to systematically search a particular section of town. I assigned two men to search each house on each side of the cobblestone streets. We completed our details in about a week. We didn't find any weapons. About the only difficulty we had was a troop of arrogant Austrian actors who "claimed" that the military government had excluded them from search. They even had an order posted on the door that stated military personnel were prohibited. I had never seen such an order and I was suspicious of its authenticity. As commander of my squad, I was obligated to search them to verify their truthfulness. A policy of non-fraternization was still in force. We followed orders and did not socialize.

Upon completion of my special patrol search mission, I found the 36th Company going out to a local parade field. A U.S.O. troupe which included Jack Benny and Helen Hayes was scheduled to put on a performance for us. In the meantime, the 36th QM had planned a Texas Oklahoma rodeo for the entertainment of the U.S.O. troupe as a surprise. We enjoyed the Jack Benny jokes and the singing of Helen Hayes. After the U.S.O. finished their act, the rodeo got underway. I don't know where those horses and cattle were requisitioned, but the cowboys had their hands full roping and riding those German animals. Everyone had a grand time, including the U.S.O. troupe, just watching that production.

This part of Bavaria was incredibly beautiful with green rolling hills. The weather was ideal, and the fraternization policy was about to be changed. The troops sensed the drift. There was a beach directly across from our quarters. The German youngsters would go swimming there every day. It wasn't long until one of our troops discovered that the Germans had thrown their weapons in the Danube from the bridge near our quarters before the Americans arrived. Suddenly everyone was going swimming and recovering all kinds of pistols as souvenirs. We were not allowed on the south side of the river, but who could tell the difference between a German and an American in a bathing suit?

One of our troops found a heavy wire cable and took the cable up to a clump of trees just downstream from our quarters. He fastened the cable to a sturdy tree about twenty feet above the ground. Next, he swam across the Danube dragging the cable across the river with him. He attached this cable to a tree on the south side of the river about four feet above the ground. He took another cable and put it twenty feet up a tree on the south side of the river. He swam back across the river and tied this second cable to a tree about four feet above the ground on our side of the river. This enterprising soldier then rounded up a pulley wheel and a fork hook. He bolted the forks onto the pulley wheel after placing the pulley wheel on top of the cable. He had a one-man overhead monorail, better known as a zip-line.

He held his hands to the fork hook and swung out over the Danube River. His weight caused the pulley wheel to carry him down the cable and across the Danube. He would touch the far bank with his feet and stop the pulley before he ran into the tree. He would return to the north side of the Danube by the same method. Eventually, two or three more pulleys appeared. The German girls caught on and began to come to the beach in numbers on Sunday afternoon.

I climbed up the tree with a pulley in my hand. When I got up to the cable, I put the pulley on the cable. I attached the forked hook to the pulley wheel by putting the long bolt through the forks and through the pulley wheel. I swung out over the river. I got about two thirds of the way across the river and the nut on the bolt came off and the bolt came partially out of the pulley wheel. This position of the pulley wheel caused the wheel to bind on the cable. I was about twenty feet above the water. I tried to release the pulley hook, but each time I tried to release my hands, the cable simply went up and down as I jostled my weight. I was stuck. My hands began to hurt from my weight just dangling there. Finally, I discovered that I could cause the pulley to move toward the south bank by swinging my weight to the south. I made the distance in about six or eight swings. I went swimming with the rest of the troops. On my return, I made sure I had a pulley with a bolt and nut securely attached.

There was a little park on the north side of the Danube. I went out to the park one day and was sitting on the bench when a young German girl came by and sat down on my side of the bench. Apparently, she didn't know about non-fraternization. I just sat there wondering what would happen. About that time, I heard Captain Madox say to me, "Soldier, you know the policy of non-fraternization is still in force?" I got up and headed back to our quarters. Captain Madox patrolled that park to make sure that non-fraternization was enforced.

Captain Madox planned for me to take charge of a squad of truck drivers and their two-and-one-half ton GMC trucks. My platoon leader sent me with a driver on a couple of orientation trips. We were dispatched to Stuttgart to get a truck load of Coca-Cola. The countryside around Stuttgart was beautiful. Our next trip was to Heilbronn to get a load of coal — this trip was as much fun as the first trip. Around this time, the 36th QM Company also had to relocate some Polish displaced persons.

Captain Maddox told us at Reveille why we had searched Goppingen sometime earlier — we were moving our company into an empty factory (Fabrik) the next day. Goppingen was the town which manufactured those little toy trains which were sold worldwide. We were happy to move to Goppingen, but I hated to leave Ulm because the beer bar and swimming pool set up was hard to come by. The beer in Germany really had a head (foam at top of beer) on it when you drank it from cold steins.

We got settled in the factory on the south end of Goppingen in one day. The 36th QM Company moved in short order, and I was put in charge of a squad of truck drivers. I was dispatched with my first convoy of eight trucks up into the mountains. The supply officer had made arrangements with a woodsman (Forster) to furnish the 36th Division with firewood for the winter. As I rode up the forest trail, I was impressed with the way the Germans kept their forests manicured. I could tell the forest had been cut and replanted for years. The trees were similar in size and were growing in rows with the trees being equally spaced. The woodsman had the wood piled by the cords. He checked each cord off on his record sheet as we loaded the trucks. We hauled enough wood for the Division to burn all winter.

A requisition came into the company for a squad of drivers to go to Marseille, France by train to drive some new dump trucks back to Germany, and our squad was selected. We were hauled to the French border in trucks, and we then boarded the French passenger train. We rode passenger cars this time with slat bench seats. As we rode down the valley in southern France the country was beautiful and green. Even though the sun was bright, the wind was bitter cold. We passed convoy after convoy of destroyed German trucks beside the roads. Our Air Force must have caught an entire German Army on the road headed back to the Rhineland. We arrived in Marseille early in the morning. A bus took us from the train station to the dirt storage field where the new dump trucks were parked. Each dump truck had an army jeep loaded in the dump bed to haul back to Germany.

We ate K rations[3] while we were drawing our dump trucks. We built a fire by putting a little gas in a C ration can. We lit the gas and warmed our hands and our K rations on that little blaze. I noticed the azure blue Mediterranean Sea in the distance from our truck marshaling yard. This was a breathtaking, beautiful sea. I promised myself that I would spend some leisure time on that beach when I was on my own time one day.

*Harold on the right in Marseille, France as Truck Driver with 36 Texas, Oklahoma Infantry Division Quartermaster Company – 1945*

---

3 K ration consisted of three separately boxed meal units: breakfast, dinner, and supper. It was intended for issue to mobile units of short duration. K-rations were lighter than C rations (prepared, canned food), and three meals a day netted only 2,830 calories. A-ration consisted of fresh food and B-ration consisted of packaged, unprepared food.

We lined up our dump trucks in a convoy, and the convoy commander led the procession. Some of the dump trucks didn't have the windshield up. It wasn't long before the drivers of those trucks pulled over to the side of the road and began to uncase the windshield and set it upright so the soft canvas roof could be attached. Fortunately for me, my truck had the windshield and roof already properly in place. We roared up the gradually rising terrain of the Rhine Valley. In addition to beautiful green grassland, we saw some large vineyards. We stopped from time to time to see that the convoy didn't stretch out too long. We also wanted to make sure that we didn't lose anyone for mechanical difficulties. A French girl brought me a flask of wine at one of those roadside stops. I gave her a box of K rations in return. I didn't speak French and she didn't speak English, but the transaction went off without voice communication — language was not a barrier.

Our twenty-four dump truck convoy rolled into Dijon. The cold wind began carrying traces of snow. The road forked somewhere north of Dijon. The left fork of the road went to Paris and the right fork went to Reims, France. We barreled through the junction taking the right fork. However, four of our trucks took the left form by mistake and went to Paris. I don't know whether this was a planned mistake or not. At any rate, we rolled on toward the Reims without really knowing where the four trucks went. Each truck was pulling a small metal trailer full of "Jerry" cans (five-gallon containers) full of gas.

We ran into snow and ice near Reims. We came to a town or city with a moat built around the outskirts. The moat was thirty feet deep and about one hundred feet across. The highway crossed the moat by a stone bridge which had been off set about one hundred feet from a straight course through the city. The bridge was covered with a layer of blue ice. One of the trucks in front of me made the first turn to the right but went over the side of the bridge as the driver tried to make the left turn onto the bridge. Luckily, the driver jumped out of the dump truck before it toppled over the side of the bridge. The driver slid along the ice and didn't get hurt. The dump truck landed upside down with the jeep and trailer in the dry moat. Our truck convoy had a big wrecker following us which took the wrecked truck to the nearest U.S. Army depot.

The convoy commander called all drivers together for a word of additional caution. He counted heads and discovered four truck drivers missing. He said those truck drivers would be court-martialed when they arrived at Frankfurt, Germany. The convoy commander moved out in front again and we drove through Saarbrucken. We crossed the Rhine River and finally reached the big Frankfurt truck depot on the outskirts of Frankfurt on the Main River. We turned our trucks into the motor pool. A 36th QM truck was waiting for us. We loaded up in the bed under the canvas top and relaxed as our driver drove us back to Goppingen.

Captain Maddox informed me that I hadn't had a leave since I had been overseas. He asked me if I wanted an R and R (Rest and Recuperation) leave to visit England for a week. I didn't realize that a person got leave in Europe. I told him that I would like to take that R and R leave for England. I got my uniform and "Ike"[4] jacket cleaned and pressed and took a small flight bag with my shaving kit and clean undies in it. I also took my camera and plenty of film.

---

4 "The Eisenhower or "Ike" jacket, officially known as the Jacket, Field, Wool, Olive Drab, is a type of waist-length jacket developed for the U.S. Army during the later stages of World War II ... it featured a pleated back, adjustable waist band, fly-front buttons, bellows chest pockets, slash side pockets, and shoulder straps." Shelby Stanton (1991). *U.S. Army Uniforms of WWII.* Stackpole Books. ISBN 0-8117-2595-2.

A 36th QM truck driver hauled me to Frankfurt where I joined a group of vacationers. There were some U.S. Army nurses and WACS (Women's Army Corps Service) on vacation with us. We all got on a vacation bus for a tour of Old Heidelberg. We visited the castle on the mountain overlooking the Neckar River and took pictures of each other around the castle. We were astounded at the giant wine keg in the wine cellar that was fifteen feet in diameter! We sampled a little and he told us about the German University students who did a lot of beer drinking and singing. The most interesting detail that we learned involved the men students, who loved to fence with swords. They liked to have a scar on their face, which identified them with the educated class. They fenced in the streets on occasion too. Those Germans loved to play soldiers and they enjoyed the drama of combat competition.

We returned to Frankfurt by bus and loaded on a C-47 twin engine passenger plane. The weather was perfect. We took turns taking pictures of the German countryside from the cockpit of the C-47. The English Channel was a familiar sight, and the White Cliffs of Dover rose abruptly about one hundred feet above the English Channel. The English countryside was so beautiful and green even in winter. London is a big city even when flying over it. We landed at Heathrow Airport in London. After we cleared customs, we were taken by bus to Wimbledon House. One of the English Royal families had temporarily made this mansion available for vacationing Americans. The grounds reminded me of our Old Kentucky Home in Bardstown, Kentucky.

I wanted to see the famous English University of Oxford. So, I got on a train and rode to Stratford-upon-Avon where I got off and strolled through the giant Oxford University campus all day. The grounds and gray stone buildings looked the part of a university. I didn't really see a lot of students. I did notice the English were quite proper and serious about everything. I didn't see the English lounge around carrying books like Americans do at their universities.

When I was satisfied with my visit to Oxford, I boarded the evening train bound for London. Our vacation group met back at Wimbledon House and boarded the bus bound for Heathrow Airport where our C-47 was waiting for us. We loaded up on the aircraft and strapped ourselves in the seats. The C-47 lumbered off like a big bird into the blue sky. We studied the English Channel and looked for the famous beach of Dunkirk. I saw a lot of sunken ships and wrecked boats along the French Coast. We landed at Frankfurt where a 36th QM jeep was waiting for me. The jeep driver had brought the supply officer down to Frankfurt on business. The Supply Officer knew I was scheduled to be at Frankfurt airport at that time, so he had the jeep driver pick me up. We motored back to Goppingen.

When we arrived in Goppingen, I found out that the 36th QM company was "pickling" (cocooning) their vehicles getting ready to rotate back to the states as a unit. I had not acquired enough overseas points to be eligible to return to the States with the 36th Division. Therefore, I got orders to report to the 3rd QM Company in the 3rd Marne Division near Castle, Germany in the little town of Zeigenhain.

Several other troops were sent with me in a truck to the 3rd Marne Division Headquarters at Bad Kissinger. Bad Kissinger was a little resort town with hotels built around hot artesian wells. Folks vacationed there to drink mineral water and take hot baths. The white buildings of the town were beautifully designed. There were weeping willows located throughout the grounds with pedestrian paths lined with flower gardens connecting the buildings. Many of these walkways were covered with an arched roof. The 3rd Marne Headquarters was in the most beautiful building of all. It was on a slight rise overlooking the complex. The horseshoe driveway passed by the Headquarters front door where the American flag, along with the 3rd Marne Division color flag, were gently waving in the breeze.

A 3rd QM jeep picked me up along with my barracks bag at Headquarters. We rode down the cobblestone streets to Ziegenhain, which was a typical provincial German village with a small stream running through the town. There were two streets in town, and they came to a junction in the middle of town near the little bridge that crossed the brook meandering through town. The 3rd QM Company occupied several private homes in this little berg. I was quartered upstairs in the home which was temporarily serving as the supply building. The mess hall had been a restaurant. The 3rd QM Company had German maids and German cooks. Those German Frauleins cooked very well. That was some of the best food that I had ever eaten. That night, the entire company went to the local beer hall to drink steins of beer and dance with the Frauleins to the music of the little German band.

I was assigned to a truck squad the next day. I was dispatched along with the rest of my squad to Bad Eisenach. One of the 3rd Marne Infantry Companies had to pull back out of the Russian zone of Germany as the Russian and Americans adjusted the borders. A twelve-inch snow fell on our convoy enroute to Eisenach, and the heavy snow had caused a big tree to fall across the little mountain road. One of the truck drivers hit his brakes too heavily and slid and crashed into the butt end of that tree. Our convoy stopped briefly to render any assistance possible. Someone supplied a blanket to cover up the driver who had been killed by the tree when it crashed through his windshield before his truck had stopped. We drove on to Eisenach, where we loaded up an Infantry Company and hauled them to their newly designated patrol site at Ziegenhain.

The next day, we were dispatched to Furstenfeldbruck, located in the heart of Bavaria, to shuttle German prisoners of war to various permanent prisons throughout the American sector. As we drove to southern Bavaria the countryside quickly became flatter and more rolling. We drove out to the big German training base near the military airport and stopped in front of the longest barrack I had ever seen. These white three-story stucco barracks were at least a mile long. The Americans had every German "Nazi" soldier in Bavaria housed in these barracks. The guards loaded our trucks with P.O.W.'s, and then climbed on board last. We pulled out of Furstenfeldbruck and headed for the special prison complex in Marburg with our load of high-ranking German officers. The barracks were first class brick structures. These ranking officers must have been scheduled for war crimes trials which would happen in due time. After we unloaded our passengers, we drove back to Ziegenhain.

Thanksgiving 1945 rolled around, and the 3rd Marne Division had just discovered forty thousand cases of the best French champagne that the Germans had taken from the French. The Seventh Army was about to take the champagne from the 3rd Division, so the commander of the 3rd Division had the champagne issued to his troops. I got four bottles. The mess sergeant scheduled us for a big dinner with a band scheduled to make special music for the occasion. The mess sergeant even had fruit baskets made up for the troops.

On Thanksgiving Day, we had a visitor from 3rd Marne Headquarters, Sergeant Audie Murphy, who came to have dinner with us. He had been stationed at Headquarters pending his return to the States. I didn't recognize Audie when I met him informally outside the mess hall. Someone told me, "That was Audie Murphy." I asked what he did, and someone volunteered that he had kept three German Tiger tanks from over-running a 3rd Marne Infantry Company by using a bazooka. That Thanksgiving dinner was so good that the troops were in extremely high spirits after dinner.

The 3rd QM Company had a couple of British counterparts visiting us to study our method of operation for a couple of weeks. Luckily for me, I was dispatched to drive these troops back to Hamburg by myself. I loaded ten or fifteen cans of gas on my GMC "Jimmy" truck and drove to Hamburg with the help of the British who had to give me directions. I drove almost to the north seashore before I came to the British unit. In the British zone, there were warning signs reminding us to be armed while passing through that unpopulated area. We were instructed not to pick up anyone either. There had been some murders and hijacking of trucks and equipment along this route. The British couldn't take pistols home as souvenirs, like the Americans could, so before I left, my British passengers gave me a total of nine pistols as souvenirs.

# CHAPTER 14

# U.S. Army Ski Team (Bavaria)

There had been a policy in the 3rd QM to let drivers use their trucks on the weekends. I planned to visit the parts of Germany that I had not seen on the weekends that I had left, but we got a new first Sergeant. The troops said he went by the name of "Court Martial Shaffer." He was born in Germany but grew up in America. He had about twenty years in the U.S. Army. I asked the Sergeant if I could go to Nuremberg for the weekend in my truck. He informed me that the weekend trips were over. He told me to start thinking about furthering my education. I responded by filling out an application for an Army School. He told me to learn a trade, but I had the idea of going to Oxford to an intelligence school or something similar.

In just a few days, a quota came to the 3rd QM Company for two soldiers to attend a welding school in France. Sergeant Shaffer called me in, and I told him that I would pass up this opportunity, but I would take the next school quota that came down from headquarters. There had been a lot of talk about training the infantry troops to snow ski. This would keep the troops occupied and prepared for winter fighting if the occasion ever arose.

A few days later, a quota came in for several troops to attend a two week ski school at Fulda, Germany. I was properly notified, and I promptly accepted. Three of us were selected from the Company. We took one of our trucks and picked up the rest of the troops at Bad Kissingen. We drove to the little resort hamlet of Fulda. I had never seen such luxury in a rural setting. We were quartered in a resort hotel called SkyTop Manor. The rooms had light colored wooden double bunk beds. The bedspreads were red and white square cloth. The dining room resembled a ballroom. The ski pro shop was next door in the basement of the hotel which housed the ski school staff.

The townspeople all gathered at the little beer hall each night to dance and drink beer to the music of the German band. We even had American USO girls who served us donuts and coffee during our breaks on the ski slopes. We were served a seven-course breakfast, as well as a seven course supper. I can still remember those big peaches that started breakfast. We had our classwork in the morning, then we went to the ski shop to prepare our skis for the afternoon slope work.

We were anxious to get up on the slopes. The "Jimmy" hauled us steadily up the winding road to the training slope. When we got to the bottom of the training slope, we put on our skis and followed our German instructor with the eagerness and enthusiasm of ten-year-olds. We put all our energy into our training and advanced rapidly in our lessons. We were tired when quitting time came, but we still managed to go to the beer hall for entertainment after supper.

I was particularly impressed with the methods utilized by the ski school staff in teaching us the basic rules of skiing. Every day we would scrape the wax off our skis and rewax the skis according to the weather conditions for the next day. In cold, hard, and dry snow conditions, we waxed our skis with paraffin. In warm, soft, and wet snow conditions, we waxed our skis with a soft sticky wax. We carried different types of ski wax with us along with our first aid pouches. We used snow goggles to keep from going snow blind, and we dressed in ski parkas and pants over insulated underwear. The parkas and pants had string ties at the arm and leg openings like a sweat suit, so we could control our temperature by loosening or tightening our strings.

Skiing was just like any other sport once the basics were learned. Our proficiency and speed had a direct relationship to our physical condition. On one occasion, the USO girls had two ten foot tables set up at the bottom of the slope. There was a ten-gallon aluminum container full of coffee sitting on each table. Donuts were piled high on the tables too. Those donuts were big and soft and coated with a real sweet crust. The USO girls rang a little dinner bell when the refreshments were ready. We all skied down the hill to take a coffee break.

I was feeling rather confident in my skills and decided to show off for the USO girls. As I skied down the hill, I planned to come to a quick stop by turning my skis sideways and spraying the girls with a bit of snow for some fun. However, the snow had been packed down from all the passersby and had turned to ice. When I tried to turn, I hit the ice, and my skis flew out from under me. I slid into the table and knocked the coffee and donuts off. I not only felt bad for spilling the coffee, but I felt a little foolish. I decided I would have to keep practicing before I started showing off.

The ski staff had a practical test for us at the end of our beginner's ski course. The test consisted of a slalom race downhill with flags wide enough apart for beginners. We lined up in a single file to run the course and I observed many of my friends trying to ski too fast. They would either fall or miss one of the flag gates. My strategy was first not to fall, and second not to miss any flag gates. Once I accomplished these objectives, I would then concentrate on speed. I made it down the course in thirty-eight seconds without falling or missing a flag gate.

When everyone had finished the race, the officials assembled us for a little graduation exercise. We were declared "basic ski troops" at the exercise. Before we were dismissed, the senior military representative called out the names of those soldiers who had been selected out of this graduating class to attend the advanced ski course at Obers Dorf, Germany on the Austrian border. I was surprised to hear my name called, but I was all for this extended vacation!

The next day, we loaded up on an olive-colored Army bus, and the driver drove south to southern Bavaria. The roads were covered with snow and ice, and the further south we went the more snow we encountered. It was dark by the time that we started up the Southern Alps toward Obers Dorf. The road was so narrow that the bus driver had to back up a couple of times to make the hairpin switchback curves. On one of those curves, we broke a fan belt. Fortunately, a jeep was following us. We got the jeep driver to go to the motor pool at Obers Dorf and bring us back a belt, which took about an hour. We finally arrived high in the Alpine village of Obers Dorf, a chalet village in a very exclusive setting. We ate at the dining hall, which was more like a ballroom in the big hotel. We were quartered in a second hotel.

The next morning, when we fell out for reveille, we could see how high up we were in the Alps. The T-bar ski lift went to the top of the mountains, above which was just blue sky. The Austrian-German border ran along the top of that mountain range. We headed over to the cafeteria where we discovered a group of Army nurses had arrived to take the advanced training. We anticipated a social every night in the ballroom.

The Seventh Army competitive ski team was practicing at this location. I realized that we had arrived at one of the best ski slopes in Europe. We had an instructor for each of seven levels of ski instruction, and we advanced from each level until we reached the top level or wherever we felt comfortable. I advanced myself as fast as I could to get exposed to all the fundamentals of skiing. A German woman instructed the top class, which had only six skiers. I was told these skiers were formerly members of a Yale Ski team.

We began to ski in teams rather than as individuals. We were taught ski safety procedures and how to ski in deep snow. We would keep one ski about six or eight inches ahead of the other ski so we could step over any obstacles when we needed. We also skied with our skis about six or eight inches apart so we could hold our balance when gliding over obstacles. We never skied alone or during periods of restricted visibility.

After a couple days of skiing as a team, the instructor let us ski for a day by ourselves. I immediately rode the T-bar up the mountain as far as it would go and then climbed to the top of the mountain with a couple of other skiers. We walked around the stone marker which separates Germany and Austria. Then we came down the mountain through the deep snow and the trees to where the top of the ski run began. The run was narrow and very steep at first, but it became wider when we made it to the first slope. We enjoyed increasing our speed as we made it all the way down the slopes.

I finally promoted myself to the top class. The German Fraulein instructor knew her business and taught us well. The ski staff at Obers Dorf was building us up for an eight kilometer (about five miles) cross-country endurance race to be held at Mittenwald. The course ran through the forest and across the meadows and gullies in the foothills of the Alps. A trail breaker preceded us that morning, leaving a trail we could follow through the course.

I had my wax, first aid kit, and emergency rations on my pistol belt. I had placed the paraffin on my skis for speed. I figured the weather would be cold and crisp in that mountain pass. I started very well; however, the temperature suddenly went up, and a little blizzard came. The flakes were so big, I could hardly make out the trail blazers' tracks. The heavy wind was blowing the snow here and there in swirling motions.

I knew that I would have to stop, clean off my skis, and put on soft sticky wax. I delayed this procedure, however, because I was having difficulty following the course. The snow was covering the trail quickly. The heavy snowfall and swirling wind coming up through the mountain pass made it hard for me to keep my orientation. I didn't know, but the race had been called off. The snow began falling wet, then it froze to the bottom of my skis as I slid over the slushy snow. The snow caked about three inches of snow on my skis, which made my ski feel like a heavy snowshoe. I stopped and tried to scrape off the wax and snow. I rubbed on the sticky wax, but it came right off again. I surmised that the ski must be dry to hold a wax coating. I could have taken my skis off and walked in just as fast. I was glad just to complete that cross-country race! The ski staff was happy that I finished the race under the circumstances without getting lost.

We boarded the bus and returned to Obers Dorf. The next day, I went deep snow skiing with the top team on our last day of skiing. I came out of the mountain through the woods and saw a little road. I was confident that I could jump off the bank, land sideways on the road, and stop before I got to the edge of the road. I leaped and hit like I planned, but the road was icy, and my skis flew out from under me. All my weight landed on my right knee. It was so dumb in retrospect! At any rate, the snowmobile came up and hauled me back to the doctor's office. Fortunately for me, I only had a bad bruise. I graduated as an "intermediate skier" with the rest of my class.

# CHAPTER 15

# Jeep Driver (UN Relief Organization Mission)

We loaded the bus and drove back to our units. When I was dropped off at Ziegenhain, the First Sergeant had a new assignment for me. The Supply officer wanted me to drive a jeep for him. I accepted the new assignment with great expectations. My first assignment was to lead a squad of trucks from Ziegenhain to Antwerp, Belgium to pick up a shipment of scotch whiskey. Ice and snow covered the roads. As we drove through the mountain roads of Luxemburg, one truck slid off the road and flipped over a couple of times. The truck went off the road and the driver was badly shaken up after having jumped out. The officer in charge had one of the trucks take this man back to Germany to the hospital for a check-up and observation.

As we continued toward the lowlands of Brussels, the weather got warmer and the snow melted off the wet roads. The fields were still partially covered by the snow. We drove through Brussels and arrived at the shipping docks in Antwerp that evening. The dock troops loaded our trucks full of whiskey. The officer in charge got in the jeep with me and gave me the go ahead to move out with the convoy.

The officer had a bottle of scotch, and he started drinking as I drove. He then ordered me to let him drive. I was very reluctant to relinquish the wheel but did so under mild protest. The officer did all right until we reached the mountains. He was going too fast and would not take my advice to slow down. Then it happened! He slid off the road into a deep ditch on the upper side of the road. Fortunately for us, the jeep didn't turn over, but it was at a dangerous angle. I had the first truck pull up to the edge of the road next to the ditch and then I hooked the winch on the front bumper of the truck to the rear bumper of the jeep. I went down to the jeep to back it up the bank with the help of the winch. The officer would not relinquish the jeep. He insisted on backing the jeep out himself. I was near the end of my patience with this officer. Thankfully, the winch did its job.

When the jeep got back on the road, the officer failed to let off the accelerator and the jeep went past the front end of the truck. Fortunately, the winch was still attached to the jeep bumper. This prevented the jeep from going off the cliff on the lower side of the road. It became obvious to everyone that this officer was in no condition to drive. I simply told him, "I am driving my jeep back to the unit. You can either ride with me or in one of the trucks." He realized the wisdom of that move even though he was a little drunk. He agreed with my plan, and we drove on back to Ziegenhain that night without a hitch.

My next assignment was to drive the supply officer and two United Nations Relief Organization officials to Herford, Germany. These troops got on board the jeep with their duffel bags, and we left Ziegenhain early in the morning. The UNRA troops had a couple of bottles of Benedictine with them. The officer and the

UNRA troops proceeded to get highly inebriated. I stopped to get them some coffee and a bite to eat. They caused the Innkeeper so much trouble that he called the British Military Police. The police took the two UNRA troops to the stockade. I followed the British Military Police to the stockade. I pleaded with them to let me take these troops on to their destination.

The British wisely agreed to let the men go after a four-hour rest in the cooler. I stayed with the British Military Police while the UNRA troops slept it off. When the BMP were satisfied that the UNRA troops could behave themselves, they released them. I drove on to Herford, where we went into the British Headquarters. The hospitable British insisted that I have dinner with them in their Officers club. They put one of the UNRA jackets on me to stay within their tradition of segregation of the ranks. I had an enjoyable meal and then we retired to the bar. Scotch was rationed in the British sector. However, on this occasion the British opened the bar. The officer insisted that I have a few drinks with them, but I declined. I knew that I had to stay sober because the supply officer certainly would not. After we exchanged all the jokes we could think of, I told the supply officer that we had better hit the road and he reluctantly agreed. Later that night, we had a flat. I fixed the flat and drove into Ziegenhain early the next morning. I took the supply officer to his quarters and turned the jeep into the motor pool. I checked in with the dispatcher and he told me to get four hours of sleep and report back.

When I reported back to the dispatcher, I asked to see the First Sergeant. I decided to do something besides just driving. He asked me what I had in mind, and I told him that I would like to become a maintenance mechanic. He agreed that I would make a good one and he assigned me to the motor pool. The motor pool was a quiet place, but the mechanic job was different. I was learning a trade that I could use no matter where I eventually worked.

# CHAPTER 16

# Going Home (37th Anti-Aircraft Company)

One day, the First Sergeant came by the motor pool while I was under a truck replacing a bogie drive shaft connector. The First Sergeant tapped me on the bottom of my shoe with his shoe. He told me to get back to my quarters and pack my duds. I had acquired enough points to rotate back to the States.

I packed my barracks bag and loaded on a truck headed for Darmstadt, Germany. I was attached to the 37th Anti-Aircraft Company which was rotating to the States as a unit. The truck made several stops to pick up rotating troops on the way to Darmstadt. We were a happy group when we arrived at Darmstadt. The 37th AA gave us a welcome like we had pulled a tour with them. We stayed in Darmstadt for a couple of nights and then we loaded on a truck bound for Le Havre, France. We really enjoyed the ride out of Germany through that portion of France.

It was the first day of April 1946. The bright sun bathed the lush green countryside. We were leaving the continent like finishing a good book. We arrived in Le Havre and were dropped off at Camp Phillip Morris tent city. Some of these camps handled inbound troops, while other camps handled outgoing troops. We stayed overnight at Camp Phillip Morris. The next morning, we marched down to the waterfront dock and walked up the ramp of the liberty ship called the "Sea Porpoise." We were taking an ocean cruise back to the States.

I took my barracks bag below and found my hammock. We got out mess kits and went to dinner. The step ladder down to the galley was a lot of fun. We stood up to eat at those tall tables and then we went back to our quarters. We were called up on deck to fall in formation where the crew gave us instructions to follow while we crossed the Atlantic Ocean on board the ship.

We waved good-bye to France as we pulled out of the harbor and moved smoothly out onto the high seas. When we hit that rolling ocean, some of the troops got seasick. I managed to keep from getting sick, but I felt a little woozy at times. I just got in the hammock when the ship started going up and down and rolling a little at the same time. I had an Army manual about electricity, which I managed to read through as we crossed the Atlantic. The trip across the Atlantic was a loss of time as far as I was concerned. I could see why folks would rather fly than ride a ship. As the Sea Porpoise approached New York, we passed the Statue of Liberty. We docked at New York Harbor and were transferred to Fort Dix, New Jersey to process for honorable discharge from the Army.

The last thing the Army did for me was to offer the opportunity to sign on with the reserve corps. I passed up this opportunity because I had my own career plans. I was given an honorable discharge on April 12, 1946. I rode the bus to the train station and got a ticket on the train for Roanoke, Virginia. I had to change trains in Washington, D. C., but I finally arrived in Roanoke, Virginia early the next morning.

I window shopped in the men's stores until I found a suit I wanted. I waited in front of the store for about an hour until it opened. I went into the store and bought a complete set of clothes and accessories. I donned these civilian clothes and caught the bus home. My bus schedule took me to Bluefield, West Virginia where I was supposed to change buses to get to Clay Pool Hill near Richlands. However, I went to sleep on the bus and when I woke up, I didn't recognize the road. I asked the driver if we had come to Bluefield yet, and he said we had stopped in Bluefield before continuing toward Charleston, West Virginia. I explained that I had been asleep, and he said he would flag the bus coming the other way from Charleston, so that I could get back to Bluefield. The mountain road was wet, and the night was foggy. The bus driver had to go slow. When we met the Charleston bus, it was easy to get him to stop. I got my barracks bag and got off the north bound bus and loaded on the southbound bus.

We rolled into Bluefield in the wee hours of the morning and I caught the early morning bus bound for Clay Pool Hill near Richlands, Virginia. As the bus motored through those limestone-based, bluegrass pastures in Tazewell County, I remembered the day that I had left this area to fight a war in Europe. I felt like I was returning home from a big vacation.

I hadn't told my folks that I was back in the States because I didn't want them to fret about the journey. The bus driver shifted his gears to make the long climb up the rising slope leading to the lone restaurant on top of Clay Pool Hill, which also served as the bus station. When the bus stopped behind the two gas pumps in front of the restaurant, I stepped off onto the fresh gravel and walked into the restaurant some ten feet away. I went inside and ordered a cup of coffee. I asked the waitress when I could expect the Black and White bus from Grundy. The waitress popped her bubble gum and told me it could be from ten to fifteen minutes or one to two hours depending on the road, weather conditions, and breakdowns. Fortunately, "Old Faithful" (converted school bus) topped the hill coming from Richlands as we were talking. The bus pulled up to the gas pumps and the driver told the attendant to fill her up. The driver helped a couple of passengers off with their suitcases and paper box luggage. He then came inside and picked up some auto parts which had been ordered for some garage on the route.

I left the restaurant with my barracks bag on my shoulder and loaded onto the bus. The driver drove out of the station and shifted gears to start down the long hill which led to Pounding Mill and Richlands. We drove by the old "Fruit of the Loom" water mill at Pounding Mill and continued on parallel to the railroad tracks and the river into Richlands. We stopped in front of the restaurant in Richlands to drop off a package.

The driver reboarded and drove up the narrow winding creek that led to Shorts Gap and the Buchanan County line. When we crossed over Shorts Gap, I knew I was home, because I could walk to Grundy from Shorts Gap. We drove down the Levisa River stopping at each little post office looking for passengers. We picked up a couple and let off a couple of coal miners' family members.

Finally, we drove by Garden Creek High School, and I began to look for someone I knew personally. We drove through Vansant and then through Roosevelt Row on the upper edge of Grundy. We passed the hospital curve and rolled across the little rise in the road in the upper end of downtown Grundy on Main Street. The bus turned right at the courthouse on Walnut Street and drove one block before turning left to the little bus shack facing Main Street. I got my bag and walked off the bus. I got a cab, which always waited for bus passengers, to run me up Slate Creek to the Liza Lee Place. The cab driver only charged me a quarter.

I entered the front door, sat my barracks bag down, and went into the kitchen. There was dad eating at the table in the breakfast nook overlooking Slate Creek. I said, "Hello Dad!" It took him a few moments to realize I was home. He called mom, who was outside gathering some clothes off the line. She came in and we had a little reunion. They both wanted to know why I didn't write. I told them that I was pretty busy and, since the war was over, I didn't think that they had anything to worry about. I suddenly realized how much they looked forward to hearing from me on a weekly basis.

My brother, Keith, had gotten out of the Navy and entered Virginia Polytechnical Institute in Blacksburg, Virginia. My sister, Lois, had enrolled in Berea College in Berea, Kentucky.

We made plans to visit every member of the family on the weekends. After I finished catching up with all the family, I went looking for a job until school started at Centre College in Danville, Kentucky in June 1946. People didn't want to hire anyone for a couple of months, so I joined the "52-20 club." I drew a twenty dollar check at Richlands every week for being unemployed. There was one distinct possibility for work. I could have bought a surplus Army 2 & ½ ton GMC truck and started hauling coal. The little independent coal mines, which hauled coal to the tipples in tandem dump trucks, were in their infancy. My parents dismissed the possibility of me entering the coal trucking business as "out of the question." I was going to complete college.

Those two months went by all too quickly. I met a lot of my friends who had also gotten out of the service. They were either going to college, getting into the coal business in some capacity, or following their parent's profession.

# CHAPTER 17

# Centre College (Chemistry, Biology, Humanities, Football)

I had always wanted to go to Centre College, a small Presbyterian college located in Danville, Kentucky in the center of the bluegrass state, because my mother's brother, Uncle Denys Caudill, had gone there. He had great success both in academics and sports. He played first string center on the Centre College Praying Colonel football team in the late twenties when Centre beat Harvard at Harvard 6-0, breaking Harvard's thirty-three game winning streak in 1929. Uncle Denys was nicknamed "Jumbo" by his friends at college because of his achievements on the football field.[1] Father and mother drove

---

1 Several other Caudills also attended Centre in the nineteen twenties. Uncle Denys's cousin, Dr. Fred Caudill, graduated from Centre around the same time that Denys graduated. Dr. Fred Caudill served on the medical staff at the State level in Frankfort, Kentucky in controlling venereal disease throughout the state.

me to Danville in our new black 1947 four door Land Cruiser Studebaker. We drove onto the old Centre campus and stopped by the administration building that had impressive large white columns. I went inside and registered, while Dr. Heffelfinger came out to the car and met my parents. He helped me carry my trunk into Wiseman Hall Dormitory. After I was secure in the dormitory, my parents drove back to Virginia. Centre was a striking campus with an impressive staff. The college had twenty-six doctors out of a faculty of thirty instructors. Some very notable persons had gotten their undergraduate education at Centre, like United States Supreme Court Chief Justice Carl Vinson.

I was impressed by the cafeteria, because we sat at round tables and were served by maids. The furniture, which looked like maple, was beautiful, and the red tile floors in the cafeteria were spotless. The food was excellent.

I met Dr. Wilbur E. Cook, who was the head of the Department of Biology and had taught my Uncle Denys. He was like an uncle to me throughout my college career. I was a health enthusiast because my father had always placed heavy emphasis on our physical condition. I saw the football players working out in shorts and tennis shoes on the practice field. I joined the fun, and they invited me to come out for football that fall. I told them that I would. So, we worked out together every day after evening classes.

Centre had played teams such as Army up until 1941, when the faculty had elected to discontinue big football in favor of playing teams that recruited players only from their student body, like Centre did. This proved to be a break for me that fall. I went out for football and made the team as a tackle and guard on the red shirt squad. We lost every game that year while I sat on the sideline and watched. The coach never gave up and was bent on building a winning team. He didn't do that by giving up – he just kept adjusting.

The Sigma Chi fraternity put the rush on me, and I joined that fall too. I was honored because the "Sigs" were noted for their academic standing. The second year, the coach sent me a postcard inviting me to early spring practice. I didn't realize that this was an opportunity to make the traveling squad. I didn't bother to go because I was too busy having fun with my friends in Grundy during the break. My laboratory course kept me tied up four afternoons a week, so I had to be satisfied with playing on the red shirt squad. I was in good shape my third year, but I got mouse-trapped by Art Schriber, and injured my right knee again. However, I continued to play and finally got to play as a tackle in the homecoming game against Carson Newman. I dropped the ball carrier on my first play by shooting the gap where a guard had pulled. The coach left me in a full quarter. The next game was with Tusculum in Greeneville, Tennessee. I did all right in that game, but again injured my knee. It would get out of place at times, and I couldn't run full speed for a while.

I graduated from Centre in August of 1949 and my entire family came to the ceremony. By that time, my brother had graduated from East Tennessee State at Johnson City, Tennessee, and my sister had graduated from Berea College in Berea, Kentucky.

**CHAPTER 18**

# High School Teacher-Coach and Marriage

After my graduation, we drove back to Grundy to the Liza Lee place. On the way home, we discussed my future. I decided to get a summer job in the mining industry until I could get into dental school. I discovered that several local people were in the same situation as me. One day, we all met at the local drug store in the morning to discuss our past, present, and future. One of the group was a college graduate named Frank Pierce, whose father was the Grundy Methodist Church minister. We decided to look for a job together. We wanted to get a job outside of a mine around the tipple, on the slate dump, or in the sand house. He and I figured that these types of jobs lent themselves to temporary labor, but of course, we would gladly accept any available semi-skilled positions in an apprenticeship category. We hoped for a job "picking bone" (chipping slate off lumps of coal with a prospector's pickaxe) in the tipple coal separator conveyor system.

119

The tipple was very noisy and the "bug dust" (coal dust) was always heavy in the air. This job was very hazardous because the chips flying from the coal and slate could injure the workers. We also thought we might get a job filling the ruts in the roads leading to and from the mining property. A truck had to constantly haul "red dog" (burnt slate) along those roads to keep the ruts filled.

We began making the rounds to the different mines in the county asking for employment. We would drive up to the tipple and go into the mining shop or sand house looking for the outside foreman. We felt that the outside was the only place temporary employment was available. The inside positions were reserved for the career miners. We got two answers everywhere we went. One was a plain "no help wanted," and the second answer was "we only need experienced men." In the meantime, we enjoyed chasing girls at the new tent skating rink at Royal City and Hungry Mother's Park at Marion, Virginia.

One day Frank's father found a job which was open at the county agent's office. The county agent needed someone to measure all the tobacco allotments in the county. Frank accepted the position, and he offered me half the money to help him. We covered the county in about two weeks. We really had a ball. Frank had to redo the paperwork a couple of times, but we completed the job.

I decided to apply for a teaching position just in case I didn't get into dental school. Father and mother took me over to the Superintendent's office to fill out an application. The Superintendent indicated that he might have an opening over at Hurley High School.

At about this time, I was due for my six month dental checkup. I went up to my father's office to make an appointment. The receptionist, Ruby Cox, was a cute little blue-gray eyed blond barely over five feet tall. As she made an appointment for me, I asked her a few questions and found out that she had just graduated from Grundy

High School. In fact, my sister Lois had taught her English and had gotten her this summer job.

I left the office, but I couldn't get the receptionist out of my mind. She was several years younger than me and hadn't gone to college. She might not have even been interested in me. At any rate, I went back to the dental office when my appointment came around. I had to wait in the waiting room for a few minutes, where we had another brief conversation. I was surprised at her efficiency and learning for such a tender age. She was father's chairside assistant during the cleaning procedure, but father had a different experienced assistant for major surgery.

*Ruby Cox – age 17*

After my teeth were cleaned, I waited in the waiting room until she got off from work. I asked her if I could take her home and she agreed. She lived in Deel, Virginia, about three miles above Grundy. She got her coat, and we went to my father's car. I drove her up to her home in Deel, where she introduced me to her parents, Mr. Cecil, and Mrs. Lottie Cox. Her father was a coal miner who worked outside now building coal tipples at drift mouths and on railroad sidings. Her mother ran a beauty shop in Big Prater just below Deel.

I enjoyed meeting her family, they seemed of a gentle nature. I drove back to Grundy thinking what a rare occasion this had been for me. I felt like I wanted to pursue this relationship in the future.

In the meantime, I applied for Dental School at the University of Louisville where my father had attended. My brother, Keith, had just returned from the Navy. He applied to the University of Virginia Dental School. In due time, we were notified that our applications were late, and we would have to apply the next year. My brother and I applied for school teaching positions. I applied with the Buchanan County School Board in Grundy, and my brother applied near Johnson City, Tennessee.

I was accepted as a Chemistry and Math teacher at Hurley High School in Hurley, Virginia. I also got the job of coaching the Hurley High major sports teams. Hurley was sixteen miles from Grundy, so I needed a car before school started. I went over to Harold Smith's Ford dealership in Grundy, where I met Ralph Watkins, the main salesman, in the office. I introduced myself and told him to order me a 1949 black two door Ford V-8 coupe with white sidewalls, radio, and heater. He said that he would put in the order. I talked to my mother, who said she would make the down payment for me, but I would make the monthly payments.

About a week before school started, I went over to the Ford place to see if my car had arrived. To my dismay, Ralph had not ordered my car. Apparently, he did not know that I meant business. I selected a black two door sedan in the basement with a V-8 engine and a straight shift. This car didn't have a heater, but I figured that I could get a heater later if I found that necessary. Mother paid Harold Smith $600 down. Harold gave me eighteen months to pay the rest at eighty-eight dollars per month. I got my insurance with State Farm Insurance from Bob Hale at Royal City. I hand-washed that black Ford that day. The next day, I discovered that I could haul

Gladys Horn to Blackey, Virginia in my car on my way to Hurley. She taught school at Blackey Elementary, and that was a break for both of us. She would pay part of my gas bill.

I went inside and there were several teachers in the auditorium talking with the Principal, D.A. Justus, and his wife. I was recognized immediately and introduced to the entire staff. I felt like I was back in the old Presbyterian group. We were given our clean-up assignments. I was supposed to get the school grounds ready for recreation. I was surprised to find that Hurley had no football team. Right away, I planned to organize one. Mr. Justus was delighted and told me that although the high school enrollment might support a team, the school had never really had a teacher who had played football before I came along. He told me to lay out a football field on the playground.

I got a couple of posts put into the ground on the edge of the field. I had a bar put across the top of those locust posts. I made them so that the children could do pull ups. I marked the boundaries of the football field with lime. Next, we moved the rocks off the surface of the football field. Some of the prospective football players came in early to voluntarily lend a hand. By the time school started, we had set up a recreation program.

On the weekends, I took Ruby to visit my relatives. We drove all over southwestern Virginia, as well as eastern Kentucky. My folks thought the world of this wonderful person. One day I told my mother that I had decided to marry Ruby. Mother was pleased, but my father had some misgivings about Ruby's lack of a college education.

One day I took Ruby for a picnic in Breaks Park. After we ate, we strolled over to Lover's Leap and looked at the beautiful gorge and the forest beyond. I felt that this was the time to make my proposal. She only asked that I get the permission of her parents as well. We watched the sun set in the west and got back into the '49 Ford. We drove through the grassy flats and over Bull Mountain. I drove on to Deel, where we went into the Cox's home. Mr. and Mrs. Cox were expecting us. I talked to Mr. Cox for a couple of minutes. He noted that his daughter was short on formal education, and he suggested a later date. He finally agreed to go along, if I agreed that Ruby could go to Radford State Teachers College after our marriage. That seemed more than reasonable to us. Mr. Cox insisted that he pay for his daughter's college.

We set October the first, 1949, as the wedding date. I gave Ruby an engagement ring and we planned to be married in the Sinking Springs Presbyterian Church in Abingdon, Virginia. We were going to Gatlinburg for our honeymoon. In the meantime, I had this football team to get together.

I recruited the best students that I could find. I had about every available ball player in the school sign up. We did not have any uniforms. I taught the players the Frank Leahy[1] type of football. We had to play touch ball until I could borrow some uniforms from the Grundy High School football club. We were ready for a game, but still needed uniforms. I got the full cooperation of my former coach and the county Superintendent in getting the football uniforms and the bus to transport the players over to Grundy to play Grundy's "B" team. In fact, I was allowed to collect the fifty cents gate fees to help purchase our own football uniforms later.

The game was sensational! What our Hurley boys lacked in experience, they more than made up in enthusiasm on the field. The

---

1 Francis William Leahy was an American football player and coach at Notre Dame in the 1940's and 1950's. His winning percentage of .864 is the second best in NCAA Division I football, trailing only that of fellow Notre Dame coach Knute Rockne. Leahy's Notre Dame coached teams won four national championships in 1943, 1946, 1947 and 1949. *See,* College Football Hall of Fame profile for Frank Leahy.

game was a runaway for Grundy. Although Grundy had a score of twenty-six, our offense grabbed a kick-off near the end of the game and Harold Ling ran that pigskin all the way up the field for our first touchdown. We didn't make the extra point, but as far as the Hurley team was concerned, that six points was the only score of the game. Hurley was in the football business for good. The parents and teachers knew that Hurley was in for some big excitement in the football arena soon.

October 1, 1949, finally arrived. I had picked up my first paycheck of $190. I drove up to Deel, where Ruby was expecting me. She came out of the house with a little light blue suit and a matching set of high-heeled pumps and matching blue handbag. We drove off from Deel into our own world. It seemed so natural between us, which certainly wasn't the problem that we had heard other people having. We drove directly to Abingdon, Virginia, where we were married in the manse with the Minister's wife and family witnessing the ceremony. We left Abingdon and drove toward Gatlinburg, Tennessee.

We decided to spend the night in Morristown, Tennessee at the King Myer Hotel. We met my family the next day in Gatlinburg. Our entire group went up to the Great Smokies National Park and had a big picnic together. The only thing different about this gathering from usual was the fact that the family had enrolled an additional member, Ruby. Might I say, the watermelon was mighty sweet, and life was feeling that way too.

On our way back to Grundy, we discussed the problem of Ruby going to Radford. She would have to go up there by herself and I would drive up to see her on the weekends. Teaching was an extremely rewarding profession in every way except for remuneration. After I paid my car payment, gas bill, and jewelry bill, I didn't have any money left. I could see that I would have to make some other arrangements. I had a major in Chemistry, so I decided to apply for a position as a chemist in the Radford Arsenal in Virginia. That way, I could be near Ruby, and there was a good financial future in chemistry. My teaching paycheck made it abundantly clear to me that I needed a better paying job no matter how much I loved teaching and coaching. I applied for the job as a chemist at Radford and was accepted. I went to the Superintendent to get a release, and he let me know that he couldn't release me until the year was completed. So, unfortunately, I couldn't accept the position at Radford and went on teaching and coaching at Hurley. Ruby and I would have to make it work for a few more months.

# CHAPTER 19

# Korean War – Basic Pilot Training (Waco, Texas)

Shortly after I completed my first year as a teacher at Hurley High, the Korean War started on June 25, 1950. One day, I read in the paper that the Air Force needed jet pilots. I had always wanted to be a pilot and I had missed my first chance through no fault of my own. Although I had already been assigned a position as a teacher and assistant football coach at Garden Creek for that fall, I went to the local recruiting sergeant who gave me the necessary papers to fill out to enlist in the aviation cadet program. I got an order to report for a physical examination, but my tonsils had swollen up and blocked my eustachian tubes. I wrote to the Air Force asking for a later date for my physical due to my condition to give myself some time to get better.

I drove to Knoxville and stayed with my Aunt Lottie and Uncle Frank Davis until I could get an appointment to get my tonsils removed at Fort Sanders Hospital. I remember going to Fort Sanders Hospital well since it was my first hospital experience. Dr. Eugene Haun was my surgeon. When I woke up, my precious Ruby was there, and since I was feeling okay, I started to get out of bed. I quickly learned that one is a little wobbly after surgery.

Ruby and I came back to Grundy, and I went to teach at Garden High School right on schedule. I also began assisting with coaching the football team. One day I got another physical reporting date from U.S.A.F. headquarters —I was scheduled to take my physical at Langley Field, Virginia. When I arrived at Langley, the eye examination "dark room" had light rays coming through the cracks between the boards of the walls. I pointed this out to a Colonel who happened to come by. He thanked me and had the technician cover up the cracks. I didn't want anything to interfere with my passing this physical. Once the cracks were covered, I went on with my eye test. After I finished all the tests, I was interviewed by the doctor. He surprised me when he said that I had failed my physical! I asked him on which particular phase, and he told me that I had some hearing loss which was unacceptable. I told him about my recent operation and explained that this could be a temporary situation and asked to take the hearing test over again. I held my breath and listened to those tone levels as best I could. When I came out of the audiometer test, I went back to the reviewing doctor. He said that I passed the second time. I didn't have to take the review board, because I had passed it at Ft. Knox earlier. However, I insisted on taking the board again. I was afraid that the two sets of reports would not get together.

I drove back to Grundy with deep satisfaction and great expectations about my future. In the meantime, I continued to teach and coach at Garden Creek. One day in October 1950, I got a telegram from USAF headquarters ordering me to report for the aviation cadet class of 1951 at James Connelly Air Force base in Waco, Texas. I took the telegram to the courthouse and showed it to the Buchanan County School Superintendent, who said that, under those circumstances, he would release me from my teaching contract.

My wife drove me to the train station in Abingdon, Virginia. She planned on going to Radford to continue her classes while I completed my first year of pilot training. I kissed her goodbye and got on board a car full of young Army troops going west also. I hung up my coat and placed my handbag containing my orders in the car. I sat down with the men, and we started swapping stories right away. I quickly forgot civilian life, it felt like I had just been on a long furlough.

When we got to Dallas, I caught a bus to Waco where I presented my orders at the gate to the Air Base. The Air Police directed me to the correct barracks, which was full of incoming student pilots. We got to meet everyone in the barracks before the processing began.

We were assigned to four flights, and we had a tight schedule. In the morning, we did our exercises and intramural sports, and in the afternoons, we attended ground school, which included studying the earth's surface, map reading, and navigation. We also studied flight characteristics, aircraft engines, weather, federal air regulations, flight instruments, and the medical aspects of flying.

Our physical training encompassed a series of exercises in the swimming pool wherein we practiced swimming certain strokes, floating, and treading water. To become qualified in water survival, we had to pass a practical swim test, which included removing our flying suits in the water and fashioning them into a life preserver by tying the legs and sleeves and blowing air into them.

Finally, after passing our ground school and practical swim test, we were marched down the flight line and assigned flying instructors. Those rows of yellow AT-6 aircraft looked mighty good. This was our big day! I had waited a long time for this moment, and I was mentally up for this occasion. My instructor was a combat veteran who had flown P-51 Mustangs in the ETO (European Theater of Operations) and had five confirmed kills to his credit. He was a Captain who didn't talk much, and he just told me when to meet him at the aircraft.

The next morning, I excitedly met the captain at our assigned plane. After carefully reviewing pre-flight inspections, he told me to get up on the wing and put my parachute in the back seat. He then buckled my parachute correctly and fastened my seat belt and shoulder harness properly. Before buckling in himself, he gave me one last piece of advice, "Remember that in the event of a bailout situation, you climb out of the cockpit and dive out and downward toward the surface of the wing, and let the slipstream do the rest." This procedure was necessary to avoid hitting the horizontal stabilizer or the tail of the aircraft in the case of a bailout.

The captain then flipped on the battery and master switches in his front cockpit. The lights came alive in my cockpit at the same time. The captain hollered for the ground crew to clear the propeller area, then he pressed the starter switch. The propeller started turning on the eight 150 horsepower Pratt and Whitney radial engine. I saw the red mixture lever go full forward. Then the throttle lever moved forward about one quarter of an inch. The engine caught once, and then belched a big puff of rich blue smoke out of the exhaust stack on the left side of the engine. The throttle again wiggled forward about an inch and the engine coughed once again but started for good. The turning propeller blades swirled dense blue smoke over our canopy. That rich gasoline odor caused me to gasp for breath. I learned then to always take a big breath of air before the engine belched.

The captain switched on the radio switches, and I could hear the tower controller issuing taxi and take-off instructions. We taxied out to the runway and the captain pushed the throttle slowly and steadily to the firewall. The aircraft started moving forward down the runway. When the aircraft reached lift-off speed, the captain put back pressure on the stick and, suddenly, I felt a temporary heavy feeling in my stomach as the wheels of the aircraft left the runway and the aircraft became airborne. It was exhilarating!

The captain proceeded to perform numerous flying maneuvers while explaining the workings of the controls and instruments. After a time, he asked, "Do you want to follow my pressures on the controls?" I quickly responded, "Yes." He made a few maneuvers, then he told me to take over full control. The aircraft was flying straight and level when I took control of the stick and rudder pedals. I noticed that the aircraft flew itself – all I had to do was put the pressures where I wanted them and operate the trim wheels to take the pressure off the controls. I told the captain that this was a "lead-pipe cinch."

The captain completed his orientation flight and returned to the base. He lined the aircraft up with the runway, pulled out the carburetor heat control, and slowed the aircraft to about 100 miles per hour. The aircraft was descending at 500 feet per minute. He started his round out about ten feet above the runway surface. He then started using back pressure on the stick to attain the landing attitude by holding the nose up about ten degrees above the horizon so the main gear and the tail wheel would touch down at the same time. The airspeed dissipated and the aircraft set down on the runway surface with a little screeching noise when the wheels touched the surface. The captain opened the cockpit canopy as we turned off the active runway onto the taxi finger. The sudden intake of air was refreshing. We taxied back down the main taxi strip and turned into our parking position. For the first time, I knew that I was going to be a pilot!

Somehow those white barracks looked more important to me than any fancy hotel that I had ever seen. As I walked into the barracks, the other cadets who hadn't flown yet asked me how the flight went. I told them that it was like "duck soup."[1]

The next day, I went flying again with the captain. This time he let me get in the front cockpit. We repeated the previous lesson and added a series of power on and power off stalls. We also went through a series of spins. I learned that altitude is a real factor in all maneuvers, just as much as speed. Before I knew it, I was doing barrel rolls, loops, low rolls, Immelmanns, lazy eights, cloverleafs, and Split S's.

The time to solo was rapidly approaching. All the cadets put money in a pot to give to the first person to solo with the least number of hours. For some reason some of the cadets wanted private bets with me. I obliged them because I felt that I would solo at the earliest permissible moment. The regulations required twenty hours of dual time before one could solo. Sure enough, I soloed first. The other cadets not only paid off in cash, but they threw me into the showers and sprayed me down in full uniform.

Christmas was coming up fast. Some of the instructors were taking the AT-6's on cross country flights with the blessings of the flying school. The trick was to get a ride with an instructor who was going near your home for Christmas. I lucked out and found an instructor who was from Harlan, Kentucky. I asked him to let me go with him, but he said someone else had already asked him. I talked to the other cadet, who lived up North, and he agreed to let me go to Bristol, Tennessee with this instructor because Bristol didn't help him that much on his trip home. He went commercially.

---

1 "Duck soup" means extremely simple, easily accomplished. This American colloquialism dates from about 1910 and is no longer known. It gained currency after it became the title of one of the Marx Brothers' zaniest motion pictures (1933). *See,* The Free Dictionary by Farlex.

We took off from James Connally Air Force base that afternoon. I had called home and my mother had arranged for a friend of mine, None Nicewander, Jr., to drive my '49 Ford to Tri- City Airport that evening and wait for us to arrive. Unbelievably, we got to Tri-City and found the runway socked in by bad weather. We instead went on to Charlotte, North Carolina and landed. We had to stay overnight in Charlotte. I called the Tri-City Airport and told None to go back to Grundy, and that I would get a bus home the next day.

We flew back to Tri-City Airport the next morning and landed without problems in clear weather. Tri-City sure was a beautiful airport. I thought that any airport close to home was a beautiful sight because the country had always been beautiful anyway. I took my barracks bag with me to the bus station. When I got off the bus in Grundy, I was wearing my flying suit and carrying my parachute. I walked down the street greeting my friends. I told them that I had flown from Texas to Tri-City Airport. My paraphernalia convinced those doubting my endeavor that I was truly in pilot training and now traveling by air courtesy of "Uncle Sam." I walked to the Liza Lee Place and went in to see my family, who had a million questions. I convinced them that flying was the only way to travel and I assured my folks that I was headed for a great career in the Air Force. I had a wonderful Christmas with Ruby and my family!

After Christmas, the instructor flew me back to Waco without a hitch. When we landed at James Connally, I was a lot wiser, and my morale was over 100%. I was ready for the rest of my training. We flew the remaining missions like seasoned pilots even though we were cadets.

# CHAPTER 20

# U.S.A.F. Jet Fighter Pilot School (Williams AFB, Arizona)

**W**hen we finished the first phase of our air cadet course, we all went to the bulletin board to see where we were scheduled to attend advanced flight school and what type of aircraft we would be flying. I found my name right away and was pleased to see that I had been one of the "select few" who were scheduled to attend jet fighter school at Williams Air Force base, near Chandler, Arizona. Some of the cadets were scheduled to attend the multi-engine school at Enid, Oklahoma, while other cadets were scheduled to attend the piston driven P–51 Mustang four bladed propeller fighter bomber school at Craig Field in Selma, Alabama.

I caught the bus to the cadet training quarters at Williams Air Force Base. I was assigned to my barracks, where I met several other cadets who had already reported. We exchanged formalities and introduced ourselves. Everyone had come a long way and made some definite commitments to arrive at this point in our training.

We all decided to walk down to the flight line and look over our training aircraft. We approached the flight line and were amazed to see so many aircraft. There were those yellow AT-6's, but many more silver Shooting Star F-80 single-engine jet fighters. There were also some propeller-driven, silver T-28 North American tricycle landing gear training planes, which were bigger and more powerful that the AT-6's.

We came back to the barracks jabbering about the aircraft we'd seen. I felt like I had hit the jackpot. The other cadets said the payroll for one month at the Williams Air Force Base was $1 million. I doubted that any other school that I had attended had any such inventory of material and instruction staff. This was like getting to Hollywood, only this was not just for the picture—it was for real!

The next morning, we all mustered into formation after we were flushed out of the barracks clean shaven and in full uniform with shoes shined. The training officer marched us over to the auditorium where we were processed and given our assignments and schedules. We were marched to the various places where we would be attending training, and we were introduced to our instructors. The training went by rapidly, afterwards we marched to the flight line, drew our flying gear, and were introduced to our flight instructors.

Our training started for real the next day. We marched to the flight line and reported to our instructors at the operation building and were greeted with a pleasant surprise. We were training with some Norwegian and French cadets. I was assigned to Captain O'Brien along with three French cadets. Capt. O'Brien was a pipe-smoking XV-25 pilot who was methodical and by the numbers. He did not instill the confidence in me that my Captain in Waco had, nevertheless, I was glad to have any instructor.

Our first flights were orientation rides on the AT-6 so that the instructor could evaluate our previous training and give us a physical orientation of the flow of aerial traffic in the surrounding military and commercial airfields. Williams Air Force Base was a terribly busy place and looked like a beehive during the weekdays. Those AT-6's and AT-28's were moving only half the speed of those F-80 Shooting Stars. You might say that Williams AFB was the "Wall Street" of aviation in that portion of the United States.

Our subsequent training started with the two-seater T-28, which handled better than the AT-6. We really enjoyed our "buddy" rides with one of our classmates. We tried all maneuvers with comments from our classmates. I discovered that you can only reach 400 knots per hour when flying the T-28 straight down. The propeller reaches its maximum revolutions per minute and then becomes a brake. I also discovered that if you pull negative G forces for any length of time, the oil will spill over the left side of your engine cowling and leave a telltale slick that you would have to explain when you landed. I quickly completed my fifty or sixty hours in the T-28.

Next, I completed twelve hours of ground school in the mobile training unit on the F-80 Shooting Star. I was then taken to the alert hangar where a real live Shooting Star was bolted intact to three concrete pillars just out back of the hangar. I simulated all aspects of a flight from the start-up and taxiing procedures to the take-off, in-flight maneuvers, and a landing. Starting the engine in an F-80 Shooting Star in those early models required some delicate manipulations. The pilot had to use both feet and both hands, as well as his ears and sense of smell. After plugging in the APU (auxiliary power unit), the pilot would switch on the master and starter switch until the turbine began to indicate a steady rise in RPM. When the RPM reached ten to twelve per cent, the pilot switched on the ignition switch to get spark in the two combustion chambers before any jet fuel arrived there. Next, the pilot opened the throttle wide open to get all the fuel pressure that he could muster with that low RPM. Once the two combustion chambers ignited with a rumbling sound, the pilot had to reduce the throttle to about idle to keep the engine from over-speeding, and the aircraft from jumping the chocks on the ramp. The other twelve combustion chambers or cams were ignited from the little connecting crossover tubes between the combustion cams.

After we completed our simulated practical emergency operation test, we were sent over to the base hospital for our altitude chamber indoctrination, where we experienced decompression at a simulated 35,000 feet. When we finished with our altitude chamber exercises, we were marched over to the base hospital again, where we were gathered around a 75 foot tall shaft with a metal chair attached. The chair had a roller which would allow it to move up and down the shaft. When the instructor asked for a volunteer to demonstrate the ejection seat, I immediately raised my hand because I wanted to know how it felt to have two 75 mm cannon shells blast me and the seat up in the air – just in case I might later find it necessary to bail out of a jet fighter. As I got into the chair and strapped down, the instructor told me to put my feet into the stirrups, keep my arms in the armrest, keep my chin tucked in, and hold my head back against the headrest.

After I was solidly in the ejection seat, the instructor said that I was to squeeze the trigger on the right raised armrest to simulate the ejection of the canopy, and then to squeeze the trigger on the left raised armrest to discharge the cannon shells. When I squeezed the left arm rest trigger, I discovered that this was no simulation! The chair and I shot up the pole 49 feet and stopped. My eyeballs felt heavy and the smoke from those two cannon shells was putrid. I had just experienced 16 "G" forces. The instructor cranked the chair with me in it down the pole by a sprocket wheel arrangement. Once I got back down to earth, I started to get out of the chair, but the instructor indicated that I should remain in the chair for a second trip, because the base photographer had arrived and wanted to get some action shots. They loaded the cannons again and I was blasted off two more times before the photographer got the shots he wanted. Frankly, I had been kicked in the bottom enough for the day. I was an "expert" on the ejection seat operation before I left the seat.

I was soon given an orientation ride in the two seated T-33 by Captain Nishaan. The aircraft climbed like it couldn't wait to get to altitude. We climbed right on up to twenty thousand feet before we leveled off. That baby could really tram – we were going about 600 mph with no strain at all. The captain demonstrated the maneuvers and then let me practice them. The jet flew itself more so than any aircraft that I had flown. We headed back to the base after about an hour of flight. When I came onto the initial approach, I overshot. Captain Nishaon explained to me that we were traveling twice as fast as a propeller aircraft and the side and back pressure required to bank and yank the jet was about twice that of any conventional aircraft. I brought the aircraft around for another pass at the field. I banked, applied back pressure, and rolled out on the centerline. The aircraft was mine from then on.

I flew several more flights with Captain Nishaan. On one flight the captain let me take command of the entire flight and perform all the aerobatic maneuvers. When I finished, the captain told me to "take her to the barn." I entered the traffic pattern and touched down like I had flown the aircraft for years. I was taxiing to my parking space when the base Colonel came by in a jeep and stopped near our parking space. I eased the jet around the corner so as not to perturb the Colonel – that was a mistake! The jet lost its momentum and the nose wheel cocked. I had to blast the throttle to get the jet going again and uncock the nose wheel. I didn't realize the force of that jet blast on the ground, and I almost blasted the Colonel out of his Jeep.

When I stopped and chopped the throttle, I noticed the Colonel standing by the boarding ladder that the crew chief had put on the aircraft railing so we could climb down. The Colonel's face was red, and his eyes were bloodshot. I knew he was upset but I didn't know why. He waved for me to get down out of that aircraft. I unstrapped and climbed down the ladder. I didn't take off my helmet or my oxygen mask because I didn't think I wanted to hear what he had to say, and I certainly didn't want to be recognized. He was blowing his top and finally reached over and unsnapped my oxygen mask and took off my helmet. By this time, he was through with me and began telling the captain a thing or two about taxiing a jet aircraft. After the Colonel left, the captain had a few choice words for me. However, he started laughing about the ridiculous situation which I had presented to the Colonel by staying under cover behind my oxygen mask until he had his say. The captain told me he wasn't going to be embarrassed again that day with me. He assigned me to a single seated F-80 Shooting Star and told me to blast off by myself.

My instructor had just told me to go solo the single seated Shooting Star! I wasted no time filling out the special visual flight plan format at the operation desk and I caught the shuttle buggy to the single seated Shooting Star ramp area. I hopped off the shuttle buggy when I spotted the big blue tail F-80 with my tail number on it. As I was walking out along the row of aircraft to get to my Shooting Star, the base public relations officer and a group of French Air Force public relations officers stopped me. The public relations officer wanted the French Officers to be able to interview a jet pilot cadet on the ramp in action. These folks had moving cameras and writers with them, and I agreed to give them what they wanted. I told him what a fabulous opportunity this jet flying provided for a young man. I let them take several still shots of me and the blue tail Shooting Star that I was about to fly. They filmed the walk around inspection with me as I explained the what and why of my efforts. I climbed up the step ladder to the cockpit and put my blue helmet on the canopy rail on the far side. I checked the Form One, climbed into the seat, and strapped on my seatbelt and shoulder harness. The filming photographer was up on the ladder shooting the camera down into the cockpit. I explained to him the delicate starting procedure of the F-80 and told him that if I got the sequences out of order, it could cause the engine to catch on fire or explode. Upon hearing this explanation, the photographer climbed back down the ladder to the ground to make his movie.

I fired the old powder can up and signaled the crew chief to pull the chocks from under the wheels. He disconnected the APU generator that supplied the electric power while on the ground and then pulled the chocks. I waved goodbye to my public relations friends and called to get taxi information. The tower gave the taxi information and an active runway. I jazzed the throttle to get the initial forward momentum and then chopped the throttle to idle until I made the turn. I was on my way to my first solo Shooting Star flight! As I turned down the taxi strip, which was parallel to the active runway, I could see my French friends still getting some footage. They were going to use this film in recruiting French cadets in France for the cadet program in the United States.

As I taxied toward the run-up area, I thought of how those public relation officials failed to realize that this was my first solo flight in a jet fighter. Well maybe they couldn't tell the difference. I went through the pre-takeoff checklist and stopped short of the runway. I had noted my start up time on my flight progress card, which was strapped on my left leg with a pencil stored on the holder to record the statistics. I got clearance to take the active runway and closed the canopy and locked it in place. I taxied onto the active runway, lined my nose up on the centerline, and pushed the throttle full forward to the far wall.

The Shooting Star lunged forward. As I approached takeoff speed, I came back gently on the stick, and was off the runway and climbing. I lifted the landing gear handle and heard the wheels lock into place.

I was climbing at about 3,500 feet per minute, and I figured that I would climb to 20,000 feet in about seven minutes and burn about sixty gallons of fuel. That would leave me roughly 250 gallons of fuel to complete my flight. I went through all the aerobatic maneuvers that I knew, including loops, chandelle and barrel rolls, and slow aileron rolls. Soon it was time for me to return to the base. I saw the airport and turned on initial approach about three miles out while cruising at 275 mph. When I passed the runway, I chopped the throttle, actuated the speed brake, and began my turns. I lowered my flaps and gear before my round-out and held the aircraft about six inches above the runway at a speed of 105 mph until the main gear brushed the pavement, producing two little puffs of blue smoke. I continued holding the back pressure on the stick until the nose wheel dropped to the runway. I had just made my first solo landing in a jet engine airplane!

I taxied off the runway to the parking area, unstrapped myself, and climbed down the ladder to the ground. To my surprise, the public relations crew was there to film my shutdown and closing of the flight plan. They had filmed my takeoff and landing, which required some persistence to say the least. I explained to them that my flight had been full of the ordinary aerobatic maneuvers that one only experienced in a jet program such as this one. Although I appeared calm, I was excited about the opportunity and experiences that I was currently enjoying and relayed this good feeling to the director of the public relations operation to be used as he saw fit.

With boundless confidence and exhilaration, I continued to fly additional solo training missions in the F-80 during my time at Williams Air Force base. Always experimenting and testing the limits of the airplane, on one mission, I attempted to break the sound barrier by diving straight down, but the F-80 wasn't designed with thin enough wings to push through the barrier. On another mission, I looked up and saw an XC-99 at about nine o'clock. I couldn't believe it! That aircraft was so big that it blotted out the sun. I climbed up on what is called a perch. I was flying parallel to the XC-99 and about a mile out and a mile above it. When I got just a little in front of the XC-99 I turned in toward it and reversed my turn to keep the XC-99 in my imaginary gun sights. I kept this pattern until I was very close. I broke away by reversing my turn and going behind the XC-99. Just as I reversed my turn to climb back up on the perch on the other side of the XC-99, I ran into the prop wash of the six propellers of the XC-99 and got some severe jolts. I could easily see why one should be strapped to the seat of the jet and why you needed a football helmet to wear inside the cockpit. I came out of the propeller wash with no damage and pulled up on the perch for another pass. I made the pass and broke off above the propeller wash that time.

During one morning briefing, the captain indicated that we would lead a group fly-by over the field at a designated time. As we were taxiing out to the active runway, a very embarrassing thing occurred. The full, right 230 gallon centerline drop tank rolled off the end of the wing. The other drop tank was so heavy not being counterbalanced that it caused the wing to almost touch the ground. The fuel running over the taxiway from the ruptured tank was causing an additional fire hazard. The big drop tank lay on the taxi strip like an overripe tomato just spewing jet fuel. Captain Nishan yelled at me, "Did you punch the jettison button on the stick?" I replied, "No Sir!" Then he realized it must've been a malfunction because when you punch the drop tank switch on the stick, the left tank drops first. The right tank would only drop on the actuation of the second punch. We taxied a safe distance from the jet fuel and shut down after calling for a maintenance crew. The captain was quick to see that the maintenance crew got the correct information on the accident down on paper before he signed anything. We went back to the operation shack on a jeep and waited for the drop tank to be installed on the aircraft.

Finally, the ground crew called us and told us that the aircraft was ready to go again. The maintenance crew assured us that the conditions that had caused the malfunction had been corrected. We found the aircraft ready to go with the right tank replaced and serviced. We climbed aboard and fired up again. We still had time to make the fly-by formation. We taxied out to the runway and waited for permission to take the runway for takeoff. The tower finally gave us clearance to take the runway for takeoff. When we took off, we waited until we had 500 feet before turning left on our crosswind leg.

As we were turning, both fuel centerline drop tanks flew off the aircraft and burst open as they hit the open Arizona desert. Fortunately, nothing was under us out in that spot in the desert. We realized that maintenance had some real rewiring to do when we got back. In the meantime, we joined up with the fly-by formation. Since we had no tip tanks, they decided to let us lead the fly-by. That way the folks on the ground would not notice the drop tanks missing on the lead aircraft so much as they might if we were a wingman without drop tanks while all the other wingmen had drop tanks. Consequently, I led the entire gaggle of twenty-five aircraft on a fly-by inspection over the main active runway at Williams Air Force Base for the base commander to review.

After the fly-by, we pulled up and broke away from the formation. We entered the traffic pattern shortly thereafter, landed, and taxied over to the maintenance hangar where the maintenance officer was waiting to investigate the malfunction, along with a panel of officers representing the base commander. The drop tanks cost money and an investigation had to determine the cause of the malfunction and recommend corrective action to headquarters, which would disseminate the information throughout the Air Force for compliance. We gave our statement to the investigators and were allowed to go on our way.

On one weekend flight to Riverside, California, I was able to attend an evening dance at the Orange County Ball Auditorium. It only cost about fifty cents to go inside, and I met the nicest crowd of Mormons. The female guitar player had a particularly good voice, and I asked my friend, "Who is she?" He replied, "She is Bonnie Lou with Buster Moore."[1] Well, I certainly enjoyed the evening dance.

The next day we were scheduled for a low level spread formation flight. We taxied out like four ducks in a row and were waiting at the end of the runway for take-off clearance, when we heard some pilot's communication over the radio that his wingman's aircraft looked like it was on fire. Three cadets immediately shut down their aircraft in the air. However, only one of them should have. The other two cadets unnecessarily shut their aircraft down before verifying their own instruments. So, there were three aircraft in the air making a flame out pattern to Williams airstrip. The tower closed the runway to normal traffic to give the three emergencies priority use of the field. Any aircraft that were too low on fuel, were advised to land at Luke Air Force Base or the municipal airfield as their fuel status dictated. During the next few minutes, the tower and the involved

---

1 Bonnie Lou and Buster Moore gained fame as a touring variety show act playing country, bluegrass, and gospel music with careers spanning from the late 1940's to the mid 1990's. Buster got his start at WROL radio in Knoxville, Tennessee. *See,* Biography of Bonnie Lou and Buster, Archives of Appalachia, East Tennessee State University.

pilots began to realize that only one aircraft had a real emergency. The other two pilots accomplished an air start and continued with their mission and the aircraft with the probable engine fire landed safely at "Willie."

On our next mission, we got to experience flying at full speed close to the ground. We dove down and leveled off at 500 feet above the terrain. We discovered that the desert looked very rugged at 500 feet above the terrain. It was quite different from the smooth looking desert floor that we were used to seeing from high altitudes. We completed our mission and headed back to the base. After landing and as we were taxiing back to the other end of the runway, we noticed another jet aircraft in the pattern. We held short of the active runway until the aircraft aloft could complete his pattern and land. As the aircraft in the pattern turned base, his nose was too high. I figured that if he didn't lower his nose and add some power quickly, that he might stall out. While I was thinking about this possibility, he stalled out. The jet hit hard just short of the runway and the dust swirled all over the aircraft as he slid toward the overrun. Fortunately, there was no fire and the rescue squad got to him in short order. He had broken his back and couldn't get out of the aircraft by himself. After this incident was cleared up, we taxied across the runway and parked in our usual parking spaces in the jet section of the ramp.

We caught the shuttle buggy back to the operations shack for the captain's critique. He told us that we had the makings of fine fighter pilots, and that we could next start thinking about turning the aircraft into a platform on which to use a machine gun and from which to drop bombs. I knew that we were getting close to graduating by the way the instructor was talking. I wanted to get in some formation aerobatics, but that was for a special few. I asked the captain when I could get some formation aerobatics and he told me that he would get me a familiarization ride with the Thunderbirds the first time they performed at Williams. I thought to myself that maybe they would perform at our graduation exercises. I didn't know what influence the captain had on the Thunderbirds, but I was going to hold him to his promise.

The next few days included training in night flying, after which the captain told me that I had completed my cadet training. Graduation exercises were coming up that weekend and our next assignments would be posted on the barracks bulletin board. When we received the graduation schedule of the event, I noticed that the Thunderbirds were scheduled to perform, so I asked the captain about his promise. He told me that I could ride with them in a T-33 the day before graduation when they went out to do the routine practice session. I went back to the barracks thinking about how I was going to observe their methods and retain the information. I decided to take a pad and a pencil to record the speeds and the G forces involved throughout the maneuvers. We had to get ready for the banquet and the dance at the graduation. I would have liked my wife and family to come, but I knew this was too far for them to come for one evening.

When I reported to the operations shack the next day, the captain told me that I was to report to the Thunderbird leader when they came down to the flight line that evening at about five o'clock. I couldn't wait! I went down on the flight line to see if the aerobatic team had arrived on the base and saw the aircraft parked in the privileged area in front of base operation. I knew that I was about to experience what few pilots at my stage of the game had ever had the opportunity to experience. I met the aerobatic team at the aircraft on schedule with my personal equipment. The team introduced themselves and the leader told me to climb aboard. I rode in the back seat on this flight.

We roared off in formation and the leader cleared the area by making a few sweeps of the base at 400 miles per hour. Then he came over the active runway at about 200 feet and pulled the nose up to do a loop. I noticed that we had 400 miles per hour in the beginning. We registered four G's in the initial pull up. As we went over the top of the loop, we still had 200 miles per hour. This gave the wingmen plenty of control to maintain their position. The G forces were only two G forces on top of the loop. The airspeed and the G forces increased coming down the backside of the loop up to 4G forces again and the airspeed built back up to 400 miles per hour. We did barrel rolls, slow rolls, Immelmanns, and finally the bomb burst.

In the bomb burst, all aircraft lined up with the leader until they were all going straight up like the beginning of a loop, but at the top of the straight up portion of flight, all aircraft took off on individual loops so they each occupied one of four quadrants. All aircraft met and crossed paths at the same time and at exceedingly small differences of altitude at the bottom of the loop at about 400 miles per hour. It was quite a spectacle for the folks on the ground.

We came on in and landed. I thanked the Thunderbirds after I got out of the aircraft at base operations. I also thanked the captain for getting me the ride. I grabbed the shuttle buggy to get back to the barracks to tell the other cadets about this crowing experience. The other cadets were extremely attentive, and I felt sure that I satisfied their curiosity to a sufficient degree.

The big parade came on Saturday. We marched and passed in review before we stood by to hear the guest speaker impart words of praise and words of wisdom to our graduating class. After the speaker stepped down, we marched in line up on the stage to receive our commission and our silver wings. After everyone had graduated, we took our places in the audience to watch the Thunderbirds put on another jolly good show.

When the activities were over, we headed to the barracks to see what our assignments were on the bulletin board. I was going to Luke

Air Force Base, Arizona to fly the F-84 fighter bomber. I could've gone to Nellis Air Force Base, but they were only flying the F-80s. I didn't know that the Nellie Air Force Base, Nevada group had an air superiority mission and were flying the C version of the F-80s. Otherwise, I would have requested Nellis and most likely have gotten the assignment. At any rate, I would have a fighter bomber mission and maybe get an air superiority assignment later. I needed to get into an outfit with an air superiority mission to get my opportunity to become a jet fighter "Ace" by shooting down enemy aircraft. You do not get much recognition for bombing and strafing enemy troops, although the job is just as essential.

We attended the gala affair at the base Line Grill. The famous cartoonist, who had followed our class of 1951 G by running a cartoon version during our training in the syndicated column, was one of the honored guests. In the informal ceremonies that preceded the dinner and dance, the instructor pilots voted on the best all-around cadet for 1951 G. To my amazement, astonishment, and delight, I was the winner! I surely was blessed with this outfit.

# CHAPTER 21

# Commissioned Officer and Pilot (Documentary Movie)

The next day was October 27, 1951, two days after I had turned 26 years old. We reported to the squadron headquarters in the barracks area. The public relations officer was there. He asked for volunteers to stay three or four weeks longer at Williams Air Force Base, Arizona to participate in a documentary movie for the benefit of Norway. I was surprised when only five Americans and one Norwegian volunteered. Naturally, I was one of the Americans. I had not previously had a chance to participate in a movie of any kind.

The rest of the new Officers and pilots were dismissed. We stayed with the Public Affairs officer and went down to the public relations office. The Public Affairs officer explained our role in the documentary. We would be the principal characters in the cadet class.

We would wear the cadet uniforms throughout the film. We would be followed through every phase of the aviation cadet program from ground school through the flying phases and our weekend or leisure hours. We would not have to learn any lines since the movie would be a monologue dubbed in Norwegian. The next cadet training class would be used as the background shots. This sounded good to me.

The next day, we met the photo and film crew at the Public Affairs office. The Public Affairs officer told us that our first scene would be our welcome to Williams Air Force Base, Arizona. About three or four convertibles drove up to the Public Affairs office loaded with local models from Phoenix. The first scene had the models meeting us at the Phoenix municipal airport, where the band played the two national anthems. Then we loaded into the convertibles with the models and headed to the base.

When we arrived at Williams Air Force Base, there was much pageantry and fanfare which the camera caught rather well. The training group commander and the base commander were on hand to greet us, as well as the base band. We were given a few words of praise and welcome in the base auditorium by the dignitaries. Then we were released to visit the various recreational activities in and around Phoenix. The models accompanied us in the convertibles as we looked over the country clubs and golf courses.

Our next scene was a reception on the top of the Adams Hotel by the city fathers. We played games in the swimming pool with the girls until it was time for table tennis. We dressed for the buffet which followed and danced to the music provided by the Base combo.

The next day, we were filmed attending classes and participating in class discussions or select demonstrations. Each of us was filmed as a leader in those particular events. We were filmed in every phase of the ground school and associated activities. That weekend, we were invited to a Dude Ranch west of Phoenix to make a trail ride and have a chuckwagon supper while we listened to the songs of the west played by the best western music stars. The camera crew was "living it up" right along with us.

The next week, we were filmed in the actual flying activities. The film crew would film us going to and from the aircraft and would get in the back seat of the T-33 to film the actual in-flight shots. The film crew wrapped up the movie with a moving graduation scene. We were sad to see the filming end, but we were anxious to get home on our leaves before reporting to our next duty stations. The Public Affairs officer released us to take our leaves. We said goodbye to the models and the movie crew and packed our bags.

As I went down to base operation to see about catching a military transport going east towards Virginia, I thought about the number of Norwegian recruits who would be prompted to join the program when they saw that documentary. I thought I'd go to Norway sometime myself and visit some of the bases and see if any of the cadets or officers would recognize me. My luck was still running high in base operations. I caught a C-47 on a flight from Williams Air Force Base to Chattanooga's Lovell Field that evening. I climbed aboard, took a seat, and began to run over in my mind what had happened to me in the past few months. Before I knew it, the C-47 was in the traffic pattern for Lovell Field in Chattanooga. I must have fallen asleep for most of the night flight. I disembarked and went to a phone in the terminal and called my sister who lived in Rossville, Georgia. She and her husband came down to the airport to get me.

**CHAPTER 22**

# F-84 Fighter Bomber School (Luke AFB, Phoenix)

Next morning, I boarded a bus bound for Knoxville, Tennessee and Bristol, Virginia. I got off the bus in Bristol and caught the bus for Clay Pool Hill just outside of Richlands, Virginia. At Claypool Hill, I caught the black and white bus for Grundy, Virginia. I got into Grundy about 5:00 PM and got off the bus in downtown Grundy. I visited with my friends and acquaintances as I walked through town up Slate Creek to the Liza Lee place. I walked through the big yard and went into the house without being noticed. My father was in the kitchen again. Mother was putting supper on the table. I said, "Hello folks." They were obviously as overjoyed as I was. After a few moments of reunion, I sat down at the table to eat supper. My folks began to tell me what had been going on in Grundy during the past six months. My wife had gone to live with her folks in Abingdon, Virginia to attend a beautician school at Virginia Vocational School there.

152

After supper, I cranked up my 1949 Ford, which had been sitting by the carport since I had been in cadet training. I backed out of the long driveway and headed towards Richlands. When I got to Richlands, I turned down Highway 119 towards Abingdon. This road ran through the rolling bluegrass plantation country of Virginia where several big mansions sat on hilltops amongst clumps of big oak trees overlooking the pasture lands and the grazing white-faced Herefords. I drove by the Stuart mansion and the Pratt mansion.

I knew that Lebanon was just past the Elk Garden School. I slowed to a crawl while driving through Lebanon. I always glanced into Jessie's Drug store to see if the town was still alive. I would always wonder, when I looked at those big white pillars on the courthouse steps, how my great grandfather must've hung around there during court time. I would look over the beautiful campus at the high school right there in Lebanon where my grandfather attended the Academy. It was always a pleasure for me to visit that little hamlet even though I was just passing through.

I increased my speed as I left the city limits on my way to Abingdon. I rolled down the pike by the Hansonville Junction. I crossed the gap on Holston Mountain and slacked off the power as I rolled down the long hill and crossed the crystal-clear Holston River. I applied power again as I climbed the other side of the valley slope. I rolled down the long straight stretch into Abingdon and turned right out of Abingdon towards Bristol on the Lee Highway Route 11. After three or four miles out of Abingdon, I slowed to a crawl before I found the little clay road which turned right off the main road to the little farmhouse where my wife was staying with her parents. I traveled only a few hundred yards before I turned into the yard at the little farmhouse. My headlights notified the folks that they had visitors. I stopped the car and opened the door. As I stepped out of the car the friendly bulldog named Jack welcomed me home.

The porch light came on and my wife appeared at the edge of the porch. When she determined that her husband was in the yard, she said, "Come in out of the night." I walked up to the steps and shook hands with my father-in-law, who escorted me into the living room. My wife had gone back into the house to comb her hair and pretty up a bit.

After we exchanged a few pleasantries, my in-laws went back to bed. My wife came into the living room with my six month old daughter Rebecca Lynn. This was the first time that I had seen my daughter. She was so cute with her curly red hair and pleasant disposition. She was just a little butterball. She obviously had had the best of tender loving care from everyone near her. Rebecca looked at me as I held her. Finally, she smiled and pushed her little hand over my mouth as if to say welcome to my world. After the initial excitement, Rebecca fell into another deep slumber, because it was after her bedtime. I spent some time telling my wife briefly about my training. She told me about her beauty school class, and we turned in for the night.

*Doc and Mrs. Speer, Lois and Calvin Baird, Ruby,*
*Becky, and Harold beside '49 Ford and in front of*
*Liza Lee place in Grundy, Virginia – 1952*

My leave was up too quickly as usual and I left Grundy in my '49 Ford on my way to Luke AFB in Glendale, Arizona. I made a stop in Knoxville to visit my Aunt Lottie and Uncle Frank Davis, a stop in Nashville to visit Andrew Jackson's home – the Hermitage, and then I continued traveling west through Memphis, Little Rock, Dallas, El Paso, and Las Cruces to Phoenix. I drove through Phoenix and headed west for another 12 miles to Luke Air Force base. I drove up to my new quarters and checked in with the Officer in Charge of Quarters, who gave me my room assignment. I moved into my room and cleaned up to go to supper at the officers club. When I arrived at the officers club, I ran into my 51-G classmates who had gone to advanced P-51 Mustang fighter school at Craig field in Alabama. They had arrived at Luke to attend the gunnery camp for conventional fighter aircraft. I also ran into some of my 51-G classmates who had come over from the jet fighter school at Williams Air Force Base. They were all about five weeks ahead of me because of my TDY (Temporary Duty) on the documentary movie.

The next morning, I reported to my operation shack and drew my flying gear and helmet. I was sent over to the mobile training center to attend the F-84 ground school. After completing the ground school, I was sent over to the hospital to undergo another physical examination. The Air Force required that pilots get a physical once a year. After my physical, I was given a front seat orientation ride in a T-33, after which the instructor was satisfied that I was ready for the F-84. He scheduled two F-84's for us the next morning.

The Hogs performed sluggishly in comparison to the Shooting Stars. The Hogs had a big spool in the engine which gave more thrust but took longer to reach the desired RPM's. The hogs were also heavier than the Shooting Stars. Notwithstanding these disadvantages, the Hog was a more advanced fighter than the Shooting Star. The instructor took me to the transition area where we performed a series of aerobatic maneuvers and a practice flameout pattern. We then returned to the airport where we landed without incident. After shutdown, I followed the instructor into the debriefing room where he went over the fight with me. He was satisfied that I could handle the aircraft.

Next day, we were scheduled to fly to Las Vegas, land at Nellis Air Force Base, and return after dark. This would give us time to go into town and see the sites before we returned to Luke. Those instructors had that program figured down to a science. We blasted off in a four-ship formation. I was scheduled to fly in the number four position because I was the strongest wingman. We climbed out over Wickenburg and leveled off over Prescott before turning on course to Kingman. Prescott looked refreshing because of the mountains and the forest growth of pine trees. There seemed to be enough rainfall in the mountains to support green pastures. By the time we approached Kingman, we were over desert country. We passed over Kingman and turned toward Las Vegas. The leader had us fly in spread formation so we could observe the countryside.

When we had the Hoover Dam in sight near Boulder, Nevada, the leader rocked his wing signaling us to join up in close formation before we commenced our penetration at Nellis Air Force Base. We joined up and the leader made a jet penetration on the low frequency radio beacon at Las Vegas. After the leader broke over the end of the active runway, we followed consecutively with the appropriate spacing. We all landed and taxied to the transient parking ramp where we shut down and chocked the aircraft.

We caught the shuttle buggy and rode over to the base operation where we got transportation to the BOQ so that we could take a shower and put on our civilian clothes to catch the blue bus for downtown Las Vegas. Downtown Las Vegas looked like a penny arcade for side-walking cowboys. We soon tired of the sidewalks and grabbed a city bus for the famous and lovely strip. The hotels and motels of the strip were evenly spaced and, due to irrigation, the landscape between these castles were green extensions of the golf courses that stretched out into the desert behind the casinos. The first casino was the Riviera on our left. I went into the pink castle, but I didn't care for the floor show because it wasn't well lit and there was a table charge. I left the Riviera and walked into the Flamingo, a really nice place with a superb floor show. There was a good place for the visitors to sit and watch the gaming tables. I felt more welcome at the Flamingo, and I caught their floor show before moving on down to the Desert Inn, which had a flagstone rock face and a marble tile floor. The floor shows at the Desert Inn were also to my taste.

I caught the blue bus back to Nellis in time to meet my flight at base operation. We saddled up our iron horses and blasted off for Luke in close formation at night. The moon was shining, and the stars were bright. While running through some occasional clouds, we heard the radio communications of another flight returning to Luke from Las Vegas that was having some trouble. We penetrated Luke and landed in a normal manner. After we got to the operation debriefing room and finished our critique, we heard that one of the flights to Las Vegas had run into trouble and lost one student pilot and his F-84.

We went back to the barracks, changed clothes, and went down to the Officers club to try to get the details. We learned that the flight had hit some clouds unexpectedly in loose formation. Those F-84's saw extensive use for aerobatics and gunnery training. All those gyrations were not good for the instruments in any type of aircraft, much less jet fighters. The Maintenance Crew were terribly busy at these training bases just keeping the training aircraft in commission for VFR (visual flight rules) on the gunnery range, much less, maintaining instruments for night use on these training aircraft. The instrument training was accomplished in the T-33 aircraft. This flight had a number four man who was flying an aircraft with some flight instruments in poor condition. As we gathered the details, he was trying to fly instruments through the clouds until he could visually see the lead aircraft. He got spatially disoriented while trying to interpret his fight instruments. He called his leader once and said that he thought he was upside down, losing attitude, and gaining speed at a high rate. The instructor advised him to bail out if he could not control the aircraft. Unfortunately, the aircraft was observed exploding on top of Chloride Mountain before the pilot could eject.

Another pilot on the same flight got so separated from the flight that he got lost and had to make an emergency landing at a small dirt airport at Kingman, Arizona. He didn't know where he landed until he got out of the aircraft and asked someone where he was. Miraculously, he was able to stop the aircraft on the overrun in the desert without damaging the aircraft, except for blown tires and bent wheel fairings. The leader of that fateful flight and the number three wingman returned to Luke and landed where they were investigated by the usual aircraft accident board. I'm sure the instructor was transferred out, if not grounded permanently. Training bases have the most accidents because they fly the most hazardous missions with the most inexperienced pilots.

For my next flight, I came out of the operation shack and walked down the ramp towards my aircraft. I heard one of those P 51's having engine trouble on the base leg, and I noticed that the engine was backfiring and puffing smoke. The pilot landed long, got a bad bounce, and pushed in the throttle to get the aircraft to settle down. His next touchdown was in a hazardous crab, and something fell off the cowling. The pilot poured the throttle to the aircraft again. He got the aircraft off the runway and initiated a go around. The engine was running rough as he climbed out to turn left on the cross-wind leg and it worsened on the downwind leg. When the pilot turned base, the engine quit and began belching fire and smoke, greatly restricting his visibility. He had to turn on final approach short of the runway and land in the sand with his gear up. The crash crew headed out to the aircraft across the taxiways and were able to get the pilot out of the cockpit, but he was severely burned. He had a broken back from the hard landing for which the ambulance took him to the Base hospital. This was one of Colonel Martin's pilots from Craig Air Force Base, Alabama. I went to the hospital with several of the other pilots to see how he was getting along. A lot of my classmates were there also. His wife was there along with some of the other pilots' wives. He was conscious and I talked to him briefly. He was bandaged up, taking glucose intravenously, and in shock. We sat around the waiting room talking about old times and trying to comfort his wife. I thought he would recover, but I knew his future flying status would be a problem. We finally left at the doctor's recommendation. When we got over to the club, we talked about how the accident happened. While we were in the club, word came that the pilot had expired.

On my next flight, my leader leveled off at twenty thousand feet and had me fall in trail. He began trying to shake me off his tail, performing every maneuver in the book. I would get a quick glance at my engine and flight instruments every now and then. I noticed that we were hitting twenty thousand feet in the top of our loops and were dissipating three or four thousand feet in our maneuvers. I got a quick glance at my fuel gauge and gave the leader a fuel report. I noticed a surge of warmth come over my body and I checked my oxygen gauge. I had only fifty pounds showing on the gauge. I knew that this required a ground crew to purge the oxygen system when we got on the ground to keep the tanks from developing sweating inside. I notified my instructor of my oxygen supply and he said that we would head back to the base after this maneuver. I was on my back and at the top of a loop in trail position. Suddenly the aircraft lost its thrust. I notified my leader that I had just flamed out. I pulled the nose of the aircraft through the horizon and rolled right side up in a slight dive to get the desired airspeed for an air start. I set the attitude to hold about 200 knots. I located the air base and turned toward the runway as I attempted an air start. Nothing happened! I checked my circuit breakers – they were all in place. I tried another air start, but nothing happened. I told my instructor that I was going to glide to the base, set up a high key point, and attempt a landing without the engine. He acknowledged and notified the tower of the situation.

I arrived over Luke Air Force Base and hit my key point about five thousand feet above the runway. I started my left-hand descending circle toward the runway. I threw my gear down, but they came down slowly without the aid of the hydraulic pressure produced by an engine in operation. I made my circle a little wider to allow time for the gear to lock. I saw that I would need flaps to make the runway. When I lowered my flaps, it used all of the remaining hydraulic pressure the plane had stored in the system. My flaps came down, but my nose gear still didn't lock. I was too close to the ground to put my head into the cockpit and start cranking the manual system with a hand pump. I thought that I could set the aircraft on the runway and the weight of the aircraft would cause the nose wheel to lock since the nose wheel stuck out forward like a table leg. I touched the main gear, but when the nose wheel touched, it collapsed. I was going down the runway on two main gears and the nose of the aircraft itself. The sparks were flying!

When the aircraft came to a complete stop the nose was smoking. The firetruck came out very quickly and squirted foam all over the nose. I climbed over the edge of the cockpit and a fireman let me slide down on his shoulders to the ground. The Air Police came up and took my parachute. The ambulance took me over to the flight surgeon for a routine examination after an accident. When I got back to the flight line my buddies had heard that I "went in." They didn't know that I had survived, so these friendly colleagues had made up their own flying equipment shortages by dividing up mine! I got it all back but my flying jacket for which I signed a statement of charges. I'd been using a brown leather jacket that I had bought in Phoenix that would pass as a regulation flight jacket anyway. I still had my soft white scarf which I purchased with the civilian jacket. My operations officer told me to go to the barracks and wait until I was called to the accident investigation board. I figured I was "grounded."

The next day I was called up before the accident investigation board. I didn't know that this board was a joint accident investigation board and a flying evaluation board all rolled up in one. I reported to the board in a formal session, and I sat down with my counsel. The board members asked me to go over the incident as it happened. I relayed the incident as I could remember it and the board excused me. When the board came out of session, I was permanently grounded due to flying deficiency. I was disappointed to say the least.

**CHAPTER 23**

# Armament School (Denver, Colorado)

The next day the commanding officer told me that I was being transferred to the military aircraft transport command in Kelly AFB, Texas. I got my orders that evening. I ate supper at the club and packed my duffel bag in my car. I was leaving the base that night. I bade my friends goodbye and proceeded to my '49 Ford. I drove out the base gate, then started down the road to Glendale. I drove straight through to El Paso and on to San Antonio. I arrived at Kelly Air Force Base the next evening and checked into the BOQ. I cleaned up and went over to the officers' mess. I got a good impression of the MATS (Military Air Transport Service) command at the club. Those pilots fly the big ones all around the world and have the best quarters with a golf course at the base.

The club had a big happy hour and the WACS (Women's Army Corps) were swarming. I joined in the gala affair. Next day, I reported to my commanding officer who was a lieutenant colonel who had just returned from Saudi Arabia. He told me that I would be the group training officer who saw that the troops got all the training on time and on record. This job wasn't as exciting as flying and paid about $150 per month less, but I could live with it for the time being.

I went about my business during the day and made the rounds at the officer clubs at night. I still wanted to fly, and I couldn't understand why the Air Force had been so harsh on me. I continued to attend the Link trainer course which was readily available at Kelly Air Force Base. I wrote letters to my friends at Luke asking how I could attempt to get another hearing on the accident. No one was familiar with those procedures.

One day, I was gassing up my '49 Ford at a service station next to Kelly field. I was talking to a couple of "light" colonels who were from the command inspector general's office. I told them what had happened to me, and they told me to report to their office the next morning. I reported the next morning, and the officers asked me if I had gone through my group inspector. I told them that I didn't know the group had a representative with the inspector general's office. They contacted the group representative, who took down my story and told me that they would check it out.

In the meantime, my commanding officer had submitted my name for an armament officer maintenance course to be conducted at Lowry Air Force Base in Denver, Colorado. I was dispatched to Denver around the middle of July 1952. As I drove out of Kelly field in my '49 Ford, I decided to make a detour to Chickasaw, Oklahoma to visit my Great-Aunt Crittie Caudill Andrews who owned a restaurant there. I rolled out of San Antonio and headed for Austin, Waco, Dallas, and Oklahoma City. I hadn't seen Aunt Crittie since 1937. That Ford ran like a top and I drove all night as usual. I rolled into Chickasaw about 8 o'clock in the morning and knocked on Aunt Crittie's door. She came out and was pleasantly surprised to see me. She took me over to the restaurant and we had a big breakfast. I told her the family news and then listened to her news. I had a deadline to get to Denver, so I reluctantly had to leave after our pleasant visit at breakfast.

I rode that '49 Ford hard to Dodge city and headed west towards Denver. Not far out of town, I came to a sign that said Highway 50 and Highway 50 N. Since Denver was north, I took the 50 North Rd. Early the next morning, I stopped in Big Bend, Kansas to rest a bit and get a haircut. I went to the barbershop and while I was waiting, I asked how far it was to Denver. They told me that it was a little over 400 miles. I told him that I was only 300 miles from Denver last night when I left Dodge City. That is when I discovered that I had backtracked.

I quickly left the barbershop without getting a haircut and headed out on Highway 96 towards Eads, Kansas. I was barreling along on that straight highway at about eighty mph trying to make up for lost time when the left front tire blew out. I had my hands full trying to keep that car on the road. Fortunately, nothing was coming from the other direction, and I managed to slow the car down and pull over to the side of the road.

There wasn't anybody around and I hadn't seen a house for miles. All I had seen was a couple of red necked pheasants, which I had flushed when I came up upon them. My tire was ruined along with my wheel. I put on the spare tire and placed the ruined wheel with hanging strands of rubber in the trunk.

I cranked up and headed towards Denver again. I passed through Eads and rolled on to Kit Carson highway. I rolled into Lyman and picked up Highway 70 W. for Denver. As I began to approach Denver, the flat prairie became covered with lush blue green grass. The snow-capped Rocky Mountains gave Denver a backdrop like a painting. The mountain breeze penetrated the prairie for some distance. That was really a stimulating experience! I hadn't expected Colorado to be so beautiful.

I finally rolled into the clean suburbs of Denver, where the lawns and shrubbery were nicely manicured. The streets were square, and the main drag was wide. The many small blue spruce trees reminded me of Christmas trees. I drove down Colfax Avenue until I came to the sign pointing to Lowry Air Force Base. Just after I passed the big Fitz Simmons Veterans Hospital and the Stapleton airport, I turned left at Quebec Street then made another left off Quebec into Lowry Air Force Base, which looked like a college campus. I drove to the BOQ and checked in with the CQ. I went over to the training squadron and signed in to report for class the next morning at 6:00 am. Afterwards, I went over to the club to eat dinner.

The club was so plush that I thought it must have previously been someone's private residence. I asked someone how this happened. They told me that General Eisenhower came by there on occasion. After I ate, I ran into some other officers who had reported earlier that day to go to the same school that I was attending, and I introduced myself. One officer was Gerald Dotson James from Texas – he resembled Roy Rogers, and I told him so good naturedly. He rather enjoyed the likeness. He lived in Kingsville, Texas down near Corpus Christi. Another officer was Lieutenant Collis, who was a real farm boy from Tennessee. He was the "salt of the earth" type. We all three became fast friends. We made plans to enjoy ourselves while in Denver for those three months.

We hopped in my '49 Ford and toured the city, taking in the night spots. We really didn't care for the bar type entertainment, so we drove out to the airport and began investigating the surrounding recreational areas. We decided to take in the resorts in the high country on the weekends.

Next morning, that bright sun woke me up, shining through the window. I got up and looked out at that beautiful blue sky.

It reminded me of the ski area in Bavaria, except that the Rocky Mountains had prairies in the distance. Denver was a first-class city with a high standard of living where people enjoyed a good economy and good health. The streets were clean and wide. I knew that we were going to enjoy our tour in Denver.

I shaved, jumped into the shower, and shined my shoes before putting on a clean uniform and heading over to the clubhouse for breakfast. My friends were already eating. I ordered ham, eggs and coffee and joined them. After breakfast, we headed for the barracks, where the classes were held. Our instructor outlined our course and gave us an option to attend either an early class from 6:00 AM to 12:00 noon or a later class from 12 noon to 6:00 PM. We chose the early class, which allowed the possibility of spending a lot of time in the afternoon in the mountains. In fact, I decided to tour the entire state of Colorado while I was there.

The altitude affected the performance of my '49 Ford. I thought that my engine was losing compression, so I decided to buy a new Ford. I had seen a new 1952 ivory Ford convertible in the showroom of the downtown Ford dealership. I usually shopped at three places when I traded automobiles to make sure that I would get the proper allowance for my vehicle. The other two Ford dealers didn't have what I wanted, but I did learn that I could expect about an $850 allowance for my '49 Ford. I drove back to the downtown Ford dealership where the ivory Ford convertible was located. When I went inside the salesman asked me if I wanted to drive the convertible. I told him, "I don't want to drive it — I want to buy it." I asked him to allow me $900 on my '49 Ford. We traded in short order. I was financed through CIT which handled Ford purchase contracts.

Next order of business was a trip to the sporting goods store. I wanted to go trout fishing every day that I could while I was in the vicinity of those high-country trout streams. I also wanted to clear my

*Harold in his ivory colored 1952 Ford Convertible*

thoughts and contemplate getting back on flying status or preparing myself for any other outcome should the inspectors general fail in their review to get me reinstated to flying status without restrictions.

I found a sporting goods store loaded with fishing gear. I wanted a sports fishing outfit, so I asked the management to introduce me to a salesman who was an avid trout fisherman. I figured that he could help me get the proper gear and steer me in the right direction as to the places to go fishing. I greeted the salesman and told him to give me an outfit that he himself would like to have. He picked me out a Shakespeare automatic reel and a Hunter seven and one-half foot rod with 70 feet of tapered line. He also selected a dip and creel, hip boots, and an assortment of wet and dry flies. I asked the salesman where the best trout fishing locations were situated, and he told me to go to the head of the South Platte River just below the Denver city Reservoir near the little resort restaurant of Deckers.

I paid the salesman $60 for my outfit and thanked him. I couldn't wait to get back to the base and show my friends my new automobile and my trout fishing gear. I found my friends at the barracks writing letters and studying. They came out and looked at my convertible and examined my trout fishing outfit. I asked them to go to the mountains with me, but they didn't seem to share my enthusiasm for going to the mountains so quickly. I figured they might want to wait until payday to buy their equipment, so I took them for a ride through Denver with the convertible top laid down. I dropped them off at the base and told them that I would reconnoiter the mountain areas by myself until they were ready to make the journey.

I headed down Highway 87 south towards Colorado Springs. This highway ran on the prairie parallel to the Rocky Mountains. I passed Castle Rock and beautiful Palmer Lake and rolled into Colorado Springs. The prairie was still green around Colorado Springs, but I began to see signs of reduced rainfall. Colorado Springs was a clean little resort town with a small college there. The most prominent landmark was the Broadmoor Hotel on the south side of town overlooking the prairie and located in sight of Pikes Peak. I planned to spend a vacation there one day.

I turned west on Highway 24 out of Colorado Springs and drove past the Garden of the Gods as I started up the mountain. The higher I got the dustier the country became because of the lack of moisture. The soil became a red, pink clay like ash, which was common to the far west. The grass was located along the streams, but the high country was covered with pine trees. I passed some nice-looking house ranches along the way. I finally started down toward the South Platte River and arrived at the little resort of Deckers. I parked my new '52 Ford convertible along the camp site near the stream and donned my fishing garb. I started going upstream casting about 50 feet of line back-and-forth on the water on the far side. By going upstream, I avoided scaring the fish with muddy water churned up by my boots. I fished about a mile upstream, noting the likely fishing holes.

I started back down the stream walking on the bank where my shadow would not fall onto the stream. I cast my line on the lower end of the fishing holes near the rapids where the fish tended to lay waiting for food to float their way. I could see that I would arrive at the restaurant about the time for supper. Unbelievably, I found the best fishing hole right out in front of the resort. I caught about six trout right there. I turned all of them loose except for the two that I wanted to eat.

I noticed that I had attracted a group of fishing fans when I walked into the restaurant parking lot. They had been watching me catch those fish. Apparently, no one else had tried that spot with any success. The restaurant had a policy of either frying two trout for two dollars or fixing two of their trout for two dollars for supper. That way everyone was happy. The personnel in the restaurant were glad to have us tourists and we were glad that the restaurant was open for business.

I had dinner and played the jukebox a time or two. Then I headed back to Denver for the night. I found my friends in the barracks studying and eating snacks. I told him that I had found a nice spot to fish, but they still weren't actively interested. I went to bed contemplating fishing all around those mountains, and I slept well.

The next day after school, I hit the trail again. This time I went up to Estes Park where I fished in the lake. However, I preferred to wade the stream, rather than fish from the bank around a pond or fish out of a boat. The stream was too deep to wade in the park where I wanted to fish, so I drove over to Granby and Fraser on the western slope of the continental divide. Those aspen trees were a beautiful sight with the fall colors waving at me like tensile dressing. The weather was quite cool in the Fraser area because of the extra high altitude. After fishing for a while, I decided that Decker should be my headquarters.

The next day I headed for the North Platte River right after school. By this time, my friends had begun to get interested in what I was doing every day. When I came back from fishing on that particular day, the boys told me that they wanted to go with me that weekend. I told him that we could either get a tourist cabin, sleep in our sleeping bags in the roadside park above Decker's, or just drive back to Denver every night. It was only about 50 miles from Denver.

They got their fishing outfits, and we took off in my '52 Ford convertible that Friday. I took a shortcut to Deckers by cutting off at Castle Rock and taking the back roads through the forest to Deckers. The boys loved the backcountry. When we finally reached Deckers, my two friends were ready to go fishing. They finally saw what a playground I had discovered.

We arrived at Decker's around two o'clock in the afternoon. My friends wanted to go into the restaurant and have a beer before they undertook the rigors of a fishing expedition. We parked the Ford convertible in the parking lot in front of Decker's restaurant and walked up the steps of the porch. We sat down at one of the small tables and cranked up the jukebox. The college-age waitresses wore red and white checkered aprons that matched the tablecloths.

My friends and I ordered three Coors beers. After finishing those beers, we ordered another round of beers and three sandwiches. When we finished eating, we headed for our fishing gear in the car and then started wading up the stream. We didn't go to the Reservoir because we weren't getting any bites – we were making too much noise talking. Finally, my friends wanted to go swimming in the big hole about one half mile above Deckers. I saw that they were in a playful mood, and it was too hot to fish anyway. We went into the water, but it was too cold to enjoy swimming. We decided to go back to the restaurant and change into some dry clothes. After changing into our dry clothes, we got a bite to eat and headed back to Denver.

My friends were bitten by the fishing bug. I told them on the way to Denver that we could catch some fish if we were quiet and fished when the fish were biting. They agreed we could do some serious fishing the very next weekend. I hit the books with my friends that week because the instructors began to give us some tests. The following weekend we headed for Decker's resort again. This time I took the boys down the Colorado Springs route so that they could see the beauty of that route.

We ran into some local people who owned nearby ranches on that trip. They invited us to fish in their private fishing holes. We went with an insurance salesman to his ranch where we fished in his private trout farm. I didn't care much for that type of fishing because the trout didn't have a chance. We then fished in some smaller streams on the ranch. We even startled a big buck deer along one of the paths through the underbrush. The path went around a steep bank, and it was covered with underbrush. I met the big buck in the tunnel. For a moment I didn't know whether he was going to charge me or backtrack. He whirled around and took his doe to the backcountry. Frankly, I was a little bit apprehensive at that moment. We left the ranch after we discovered that it was a better place to hunt than to fish. We returned to Decker's resort to eat, and then drove back to the barracks that night.

The next day, we hit the trout trail again. We ate breakfast at the restaurant – my friends liked to have a Coors before going fishing. We fished all day. In the middle of the day, we laid down on some big rocks in the middle of the stream and took a snooze. We woke up after that little rest and went back to trout fishing. That evening we ate at the resort and enjoyed the company of the table help and the jukebox music. We returned to Denver late that night.

We rested Sunday until about twelve o'clock, then we hit the trout trail again. We were regular tourists at Deckers. Those people thought we were residents after a while.

The next weekend, we went to Leadville, Colorado for a change. We loved that tourist town. Those old saloons were cranked up with live entertainment in our age group and the player pianos continued to play during the live entertainment rest breaks. After we satisfied our curiosity by making the rounds, we headed back to Denver.

Our armament officer course had become quite challenging. We were not only identifying the different types and kinds of explosives from the different color codes, but we began to explode them in target application. We had begun to disarm duds too.

I decided that my wife should enjoy this wonderland. Our baby daughter was about eighteen months old and able to travel by then. I wired my wife to fly out to Denver. I met Ruby and little Rebecca as they got off a commercial fight at Stapleton field in Denver. The flight had originated in Tri-Cities Airport in Bristol, Tennessee. Gerald James had been instrumental in helping us acquire a cottage in Aurora with a little piece of land for only $75 per month.

I drove my little family out to the cottage like in the movies. It was a dream come true for us. I immediately planned to take my wife around to all the sites of significance in the area. The next weekend we went to Estes Park and Aspen. The following weekend we made the Colorado Springs and Deckers run. The next weekend we visited the University of Colorado at Boulder. My wife would take me to work and drop me off when she wanted to use the car to shop.

One day I got orders from my parent base of Kelly Air Force Base, Texas, which said that I was returned to full flying status as of August 17, 1952. I could hardly believe my eyes! Although I had not given up, I didn't expect such efficiency from the inspector general's office. I had a month more of school to finish before I was scheduled to return to my home base of Kelly Field.

I knew that the authorities at Kelly would want me to go to my overseas assignment in Saudi Arabia as an armament officer. I realized that I had to get reassigned to a primary cockpit position to consolidate my flying training. In fact, I found a regulation that stated that a pilot graduating from a flying school must be assigned to a cockpit position for one year at least after graduating. Eight months had passed since I had graduated from flying school. I had to get assigned immediately to a flying unit to regain my currency, maintain my flight proficiency, and get my flying pay.

I completed the armament officer course and drove my family back to Grundy, Virginia on my leave. I left them in Grundy until I could get things straightened out. My wife decided to go to Knoxville and stay with my Aunt Lottie Davis and go to Knoxville Business School while I was working out my assignments. The Saudi Arabian government would not allow me to take my dependents to their country.

# CHAPTER 24

# Tripoli, North Africa (Mediterranean Circuit)

**I** drove back to Kelly Field, Texas and reported to my squadron commander. I explained my predicament. He said that it would be a big inconvenience to accommodate my case, but he managed to assign me to Brooks Air Force Base air evacuation unit in San Antonio to fly as a secondary duty until I could work out other details. Those air evacuation pilots and flight nurses were the greatest! We went all over the United States hauling wounded Korean War veterans, as well as other service personnel who needed airlift transportation to and from the various services, Veterans hospitals, and convalescent centers throughout the United States. We flew mostly twin engine Convair 440's and the four engine Douglas C-54 aircraft.

I was piling up enough flying hours to get back my flying pay and get back into the swing of flying. I had just a short time to get everything up to date before I departed for overseas. I wanted to get assigned to a jet fighter squadron before I went overseas, but I just didn't have enough time. It would take so long to put in an application and process it that I would be in Saudi Arabia before command could react to my application anyway. So, I figured that I would just have to proceed as time permitted on getting reassigned to a jet fighter squadron overseas.

On my appointed day to ship out overseas, I boarded a MATS C- 54 flight from Kelly Air Force Base, Texas to Wheelus Airport in Tripoli, Libya. We first flew to Dover Air Force Base, Delaware, where we got our overseas briefing and overseas survival gear. We next flew to Gander AFB in Newfoundland, then proceeded to Goose Bay, Labrador, Bluie West One, Greenland, and then landed at Keflavik, Iceland, where we spent the night in the BOQ. The Comedian Jerry Colonna[1] was on our bus to the officers club. We noticed that the Scandinavians were very reserved and typically had fair skin, blonde hair, and blue eyes.

The next morning, we continued to Prestwick, Scotland. The ocean traffic was picking up and we soon saw the green countryside of the British Isles. We landed at Prestwick and had some time to shop in the terminal. I was pleasantly surprised at the high-quality merchandise that was available in the terminal shop. The material was expensive but worth every penny in quality. I bought a Scottish tam or two. Those British Isles had more beautiful women than any place I'd been outside of America. We ate in the local restaurant and went out to board the aircraft. We climbed out over England and on course for Frankfurt, Germany. We weren't long crossing the

---

1 Jerry Colonna was an American musician, actor, comedian, singer, songwriter, and trombonist who played the zaniest of Bob Hope's sidekicks in Hope's popular radio shows and films of the 1940s and 1950s. He also voiced the March Hare in Walt Disney's 1951 animated feature film *Alice in Wonderland.*

North Sea. We flew over the Netherlands and observed the beauty of the lowlands. Finally, we arrived in Frankfurt, Germany at the Rhein-Main air base[2]. We checked into the BOQ and headed back to the club to eat by way of the post exchange. We ate and enjoyed the entertainment at the club until the club closed at twelve o'clock when we turned in for the night to our barracks.

The next morning, we ate breakfast at the club and then loaded up the aircraft for our leg to Rome, Italy. We had to climb up to fourteen thousand feet to cross the Alps. As we gained altitude, I could see that the countryside was much like the green countryside in England and France. A blue haze covered the land just north of the Alps. We climbed over the snow-capped Alps through the Bremen overpass and could see the sheep and cattle herds grazing on the green pastures below. We crossed into northern Italy and let down to about six thousand feet while flying down the "boot." I could see some grape vineyards below. The pilot pointed out the Leaning Tower of Pisa and we soon saw Rome on the famous Seven Hills. We flew past Rome and landed in Naples. In the traffic pattern, we noticed the tree lined road surrounding the airport. The pilot said that the Romans had planted those trees so the Roman soldiers could walk and march in the shade. We deplaned and went into the terminal building, which quickly acquainted us with the condition of the economy of Italy. The building was made of low-grade concrete blocks and stucco. There were no shops in the terminal and the customs agents were dressed in adequate but unimpressive uniforms. We only stayed in the terminal for about ten minutes before loading back onto the aircraft and heading south over the blue Mediterranean Sea on course for Tripoli, Libya, North Africa.

---

2 The Rhein-Main airport became the main American terminal in Western Germany for the Berlin airlift during the Cold War.

The weather became warmer, but it was still brisk. The sky was blue and there were some scattered clouds below us. We could see the many fishing boats and cargo ships below us. There was a lot of commerce in the Mediterranean Sea, and I realized that our chances of survival in a ditch in this body of water would be much better than a ditch in the North Atlantic. I felt relieved as we crossed over the beautiful island of Sicily. After we flew over Malta, we soon saw the brown hue of the coast of North Africa in the distance. We finally saw the palm trees which lined the boardwalk of the city of Tripoli.

The city of Tripoli was a beautiful resort on the coast. The hotels were white stucco and Spanish looking. Although Tripoli was a modern metropolis by European standards, the surrounding countryside was the sparsely populated Arabian desert. The only roads were little asphalt roads along the coast. The Arab men in the Outlands rode the donkey, lived off dates from the palm trees, and fished along the coast. The Arab women walked behind the donkey.

As we let down into the traffic pattern at the big American base of Wheelus Field, just east of Tripoli, I saw the big civilian airport of Idris just south of Tripoli. We landed on the two-mile-long asphalt runway at Wheelus Field. While we patiently waited for the ground crew to come out of the service shacks, we noted the gentle swaying of the palm trees which covered the base housing area. The foreboding and eternal desert wind impulsively kicked up the sand around the base operations building. The whole pace of living shifted into a lower gear than we had experienced on the continent of Europe. Finally, the ground crew came out to the aircraft, secured the landing gear, and put up the ladder to the passenger door. The crew chief opened the passenger door, and we walked down the gangplank to set foot on the sands of North Africa. The blue bus picked us up and took us over to the BOQ where we checked into our rooms and cleaned up. We were told to report the next morning to base operations.

We headed for the post exchange where we found merchandise of lesser quality than we had seen in Europe. I soon learned that the products available in the German base post exchanges were acquired out of the United States and Europe. However, the products available in the Tripoli post exchange were acquired out of Britain, which had the North African economy tied up from their historic control of the markets in that area.

I walked over to the officers club, which looked like a casino. This perception was confirmed when I walked inside and saw a slot machine room, a ballroom, and a bar and nightclub section. Although I was stationed in an American enclave on the outskirts of the old city of Tripoli, I couldn't wait to visit the city of Tripoli out of sheer curiosity.

After I ate dinner at the club, I went into the bar, and it was humming with activity. The officers, their wives, and their adult offspring were milling about all over the place. The music was blaring like a cabaret in New Orleans. There were officers in white visiting from the Navy and many other allied officers, including a lot of transient American officers at the bar. They were going to and from various bases located in the Middle East. I was at "Grand Central Station" for the Middle East. I fully expected a belly dancer to step through the beads draping the backstage bandstand.

I worked my way up to the bar beside some officers in my age bracket. They were psychological warfare officers who had just been shipped from someplace in Idaho to Tripoli to be disbursed to the various stations throughout the Middle East theater of operations. I engaged their spokesman and gained an amazing bit of insight into the challenges that America faced in the Middle East. Those officers were certainly up on their history, both current and ancient, in the Middle East.

I found out that a bus left the officers club about every thirty minutes and took military personnel into the city of Tripoli. I decided to catch that bus. I was told to travel with someone and to stay out of the old city. I was also told to frequent only the places that the Americans and the British visited. Finally, I was told to eat and drink only at the first-class hotels and casinos and to visit the British officers club downtown called the "Bath Club" if I got the chance.

I got on the bus, which drove along the seashore as it left the gate to the airbase. I could see Arabs and their date farms. The camel was the beast of burden in North Africa, and it carried the workload for the natives. We passed the big Muslim Mosque and entered the city of Tripoli proper. The horse drawn carriages, "Garis," were making their taxi runs for the tourists all along the boardwalk. Private automobiles were noticeably absent – petrol or gasoline was too expensive.

The blue bus let us off in front of the biggest casino in the center of the affluent section of the city. I elected to walk downtown with one of the officers whom I had met in the club. We found what we were looking for in the inner city where the British sports cars and lorries stirred our curiosity. The natives looked like they were only slightly better off than the American Indians on the reservations in the United States. The Italian women were distant and scarce.

We decided to go to the British Bath Club to mix and mingle. We were welcomed at the Bath Club, however, we soon learned that the British officers club was too reserved to suit our disposition. We went outside and caught the blue bus back to Wheelus field. We stopped by the club and had a "nightcap," as the British called it. We left the club when it closed and turned into the barracks.

The next morning, I reported to base operations. The officer of the day told me that I had been pulled out of the pipeline for Saudi Arabia and I was to report to the Wheelus Air Base support group. My orders stated that I was to be assigned to the airbase support group with a primary duty as a passive defense officer, but I was attached to base operations for flying purposes as a secondary duty.

I was pleasantly surprised. Because of the proximity, I had a better chance to swing a transfer to a jet fighter outfit on the continent.

I reported to my new commander, who welcomed me and explained my duties in detail. I didn't mention my plans to my new commander because I figured I had better get settled and caught up on my flying time before I initiated a request for a transfer. I kept in mind the regulation which stated that I should be assigned to a flying unit with a primary duty as a pilot for one year after graduation to consolidate my pilot training. I planned to make sure that I got the full benefit of that regulation. I got permission to go down to base operation and get some flying time until I was caught up on my flying pay. I had a little cold, but I didn't think that would bother me on that old, two engine C-47 that I had seen down at the base operation when I came onto the base on my first day. The base operations officer cut orders assigning me to a western Mediterranean flight on the C-47 which would give me some quick flying time.

I was assigned as a third pilot on a C-47 Mediterranean flight. We loaded up our cargo and passengers, and taxied out to the run-up area to give the old war Relic the engine run up to see if all engine indicators were in the green. Everything checked out okay and we taxied onto the runway. The pilot pushed the throttles to the firewall and the co-pilot held the throttles in place so that they would not creep back from the vibrations. The plane lifted off the runway and climbed to six thousand feet where the pilot leveled off the aircraft, set up the cruising speed, and put the aircraft on autopilot. We chatted about the weather enroute and at our destination. The weather was forecast to stay clear for the entire flight. We headed for Malta on our first leg. We spotted Malta and commenced a gentle, gradual letdown. We arrived over the island and entered the traffic pattern. We landed on the macadam (crushed stone) runway and taxied into the little Nissen hut, which served as a terminal building.

We deplaned and a British officer cleared us through the informal custom routine.

An attractive and well-dressed red-headed woman came out to meet the pilot. There was a little informal, friendly reunion. The red-headed woman was a German nightclub singer who made the rounds to various Mediterranean Resorts and clubs. She was a friendly person and not without influence and connections. In a brief moment of privacy, she lowered her blouse just enough to show us a little of her bosom and several packs of cigarettes she had stuffed in her blouse around her bosom, thereby circumventing customs. This was a little private joke. She was scheduled to fly commercially to Morocco in the next few minutes.

We boarded a British lorry. The first and second pilot got in the front seat with the driver and the rest of us climbed up in the truck bed to ride standing up along the cab rack. We took off toward the town. We had driven about a mile when we came into the city outskirts where the streets were lined with high walls. We met another truck coming from the opposite direction and I thought we were going to hit the oncoming vehicle for a moment. We passed each other on the wrong side! I told the pilot that I wanted to talk. He asked why. I said, "This fellow is driving on the wrong side of the road." The pilot informed me that Malta was a British protectorate and the drivers all drove under British law, which stated that everyone drives on the left-hand side of the highway. I was a little embarrassed, but I soon recovered. We went into a little British restaurant and had a mild and bitter sandwich. We reloaded up in the lorry and drove back to the airport.

We got aboard the aircraft, cranked up the engines, and made a rolling take off. We climbed to about six thousand feet and set course for Algiers. We had to fly just off the coast of Tunisia to pacify the Tunisians. We crossed the sea again and spotted the airfield at Tunis, which we bypassed on our way along the coast to Algiers. We landed on a remote base several miles south of the city of Algiers. We refueled and took off immediately, headed for Oran, Algeria. We flew over the desert, where we could see tank tracks still left over from WWII. We refueled at the remote base of Oran and got our new manifest for Rabot, Morocco. We took off and flew over more desert before arriving at the remote Salé International Airport outside of Rabot, where we refueled and took off for our home base of Tripoli. We arrived in Tripoli that night.

I was building up flying time. However, my base operation normally didn't have much time allotted for the training of new pilots, because most pilots were already checked out in the type aircraft and the mission before they were sent overseas to perform the duties of a pilot in that mission. Therefore, I was not getting the individual attention needed to check out in the C-47 aircraft as an aircraft Commander cleared to carry passengers. I knew this was a dead-end street.

The next day, I applied for a transfer to a jet fighter unit on the continent. In the meantime, I elected to get as much flying time as possible while my application was being processed. I was sent downtown to Tripoli to apply for a passport which would allow me to take those MATS C-54 flights to the Eastern Mediterranean ports. There were only seven college graduates in the whole of Libya. These scholars ran the Libyan government after the Italians and the British recognized the independence of Libya after the war. I found one of those graduates in the passport section. He was pleased to have a customer and was most polite. He told me to leave my application in his basket and come back in three weeks. I did as I was instructed and returned to the base.

I was told to set up a training program for military personnel to learn how to decontaminate equipment, as well as how to avoid radiation. Bomb shelters had already been designated. I had to see that the supplies were inventoried and kept current in those shelters. I worked diligently at my job, although it wasn't very exciting.

I had an annual instrument check flight coming up. I really wasn't up-to-date on instrument flying in the C-47 because I had flown only as a third pilot on that type of aircraft. I was not allowed to fly instruments because there were passengers on board, and I was a trainee. Consequently, I was scheduled to take an instrument flight check in an aircraft in which I was not checked out, and at a time when I was less than current. I took the flight check nonetheless and passed. However, the check pilot noted that I was not cleared to carry passengers. He indicated that I needed more time in that type of aircraft.

I got a local flight the next day to practice some instrument flying. We took the twin engine C-47, cranked her up, and headed for the runway. There were only three of us on board. One other pilot was going to get an instrument check ride after I got in some practice instrument approaches. I was the third pilot for takeoff purposes. After we taxied into position for takeoff, the tower cleared us for takeoff. The pilot in command gave the order to take off and pushed the throttles to the wall. The co-pilot held the throttles to the wall. We broke ground and were about 200 feet in the air when the pilot ordered the gear up. The co-pilot started the gear up procedure. Suddenly, the right engine started running uncontrollably. I knew that those old aircraft were subject to problems, but nothing that we couldn't handle. I happened to look out the windshield and saw the propeller come off the right engine and start rotating like a toy propeller as it hit the runway and bounced over the heads of some Arab workmen, who were digging a ditch along the runway for placement of the wires for the new runway lights. The Arabs never saw the propeller as it cleared their heads by twenty feet or so. They wouldn't have believed it if they had seen it. I could barely believe it myself. Anyway, the co-pilot was still trying to reduce RPM on the right engine. In retrospect, I don't think the pilot or copilot saw the propeller leave the aircraft. At the time, I assumed that all three of us had seen the propeller. The pilot elected to take the aircraft around and land with one engine. This was a poor decision, but the pilot in command had the option. He may have acted in the best way possible, considering his estimate of the situation.

We turned into the now-dead engine and flew over the bay trying to reach the other runway. We almost had it made when, unbelievably, the left engine failed. We glided down and landed on the side of the runway in the sand because we were too low to continue our turn to the runway when the engine quit. Fortunately, only the aircraft was damaged and there was no fire. We all got out in a calm manner. The rescue fire trucks, and ambulance got there on time, but there were no casualties or injuries. We rode back to the base operation with the officer of the day.

My next training flight in the C-47 allowed me a three day a stop in Rome, where I got the opportunity to visit the Coliseum and Saint Peter's Cathedral and climb the steps of Trinita Dei Monti to look at those flat-topped stone pine trees dotting the landscape. The Italian populace appeared more reserved than the British or the French, and too busy to stop and interact with an American soldier, but this could have been the nature of "big city" inhabitants. Occasionally, a street vendor would approach me to try to sell me postcards or something along those lines. I was surprised to see some women with green and purple wigs going to and from the streets – this must have been a fad. I soon discovered that I had to go to the Embassy restaurant or one of the church U.S.O's (United Service Organizations) to meet Americans of my age group.

There were a lot of pedestrians, bicycles, and motorcycles of all descriptions in Rome, but few Italian automobiles, which roared through the city like the Grand Prix was in town. I couldn't get over how those cars blinked their lights at night when they came to an intersection, rather than stopping and looking before they proceeded. They flicked their lights and, if they saw no lights coming, they sped through the intersection without stopping. I don't know whether this was the rule or if this was an innovation. Buses and trucks were plentiful.

The three days went by too fast. We caught the blue bus back to the airport, cleared customs, and boarded the aircraft. The weather was cooperating beautifully as we took off heading south to Tripoli. After we landed at Wheelus Field, we were able to catch a little of the 1953 "New Year" spirit at the club that night.

The next day, I was sent down to the passport office to pick up my passport. I found that my application had not left the basket into which I had deposited it. I was told to come back the next day, and it would be ready. I went back the next day, and the passport was indeed ready. My friend just didn't want his basket to look empty throughout the holidays.

I got my next flight on a four engine C-54, which was making the Eastern Mediterranean "milk run." I got on board as the third pilot at the base of operations. We had a full load of passengers and a full load of fuel. We were scheduled to fly to Cairo, Saudi Arabia, Bahrain in the Persian Gulf, Nicosia, Cypress, Athens, Greece, Naples, and return to Tripoli. We roared down the runway and climbed to ten thousand feet, where we leveled off and turned on the automatic pilot. We studied the scary cold front we were about to enter. The blue-black frontal cloud looked like it might generate heavy turbulence and icing, but we plowed straight ahead. Sometimes those things just looked mean. However, we soon found out that the weather front was the "real McCoy." We got turbulence and icing in its worst form. The deicer boots were having a hard time keeping the one-half inch ice off the leading edge of the wing and the engine icing was causing fluctuating engine temperatures. The propellers were throwing off the icing and it was striking the fuselage like someone was throwing bricks at us. We were having trouble holding the proper airspeed and altitude due to the accumulation of the ice. Then it happened, the number two engine on the left wing failed. The pilot in command feathered the propeller on that engine and let down into warmer air to help melt the ice. We were closer to Benghazi than to Tripoli, so the pilot elected to make an emergency landing at Benghazi. We radioed Tripoli about our intentions and our predicament. Tripoli acknowledged receipt of our transmission. We hit some clouds as we approached Benghazi, but luckily we penetrated them by letting down a couple more thousand feet. We were in the clear at about five thousand feet. We needed all the visibility that we could get because the runway at Benghazi was only five thousand feet long.

We were loaded with passengers and fuel and had to land a little faster than we normally did. We were concerned that the required heavy braking might cause a fire – because there was no firefighting equipment standing by at Benghazi. The Libyan government could not afford to maintain that wartime base as a full-scale operation. The tower was the only facility. The veteran pilot in command made a good landing and we were able to stop without incident. The other aircraft was already enroute before we touched down and we stayed on the plane until it arrived.

When the other aircraft arrived, we exchanged planes and continued our mission to Cairo. As we crossed into Egypt, we saw the thought-provoking pyramids. We landed in Cairo just as dusk was fading into the darkness of night. We deplaned and caught the blue bus to the officers' mess where we ate camel steak - at least the management told us it was a camel steak. The steak was tough.

The officers' mess was a Casino Hotel in downtown Cairo which handled the American traffic for the Air Force. It was a first-class hotel for that part of the world. We finished eating and adjourned to the nightclub bar room where we caught the stage show. A real belly dancer came out and went through her paces – it was better than a movie! We mixed and mingled a little until the bar closed and then turned in for the night in our assigned rooms in the hotel.

The next morning, we got up early, ate steak and eggs, boarded our C-54, and roared off towards Saudi Arabia to the east. We leveled off at ten thousand feet, placed the plane on autopilot, and had coffee while we discussed the prospects of encountering a sandstorm in Saudi Arabia. The pilot in command said that it could be clear and seventy miles visibility one minute, then a desert "Ghibli" or sandstorm would come out of nowhere and sock the place in for several hours. We had an alternate landing site on the British island of Bahrain in the Persian Gulf.

We flew across the largest sand pile that I had ever seen and spotted the airport near Riyadh, the capital of Saudi Arabia. The location looked like a tent city in the desert. We landed, taxied over to the terminal building, and were searched by the Saudi guards. That seemed rather primitive because we were only going to stay a few minutes. The guards were a crude lot and were more curious than suspicious. The kingdom of Saudi Arabia was a primitive society, and the King of Saudi had the population under control.

The local Air Force personnel told me that the king didn't want any alcoholic beverages brought into the country because his cousin had gotten drunk and killed someone. So, the king had decreed that no alcohol would be brought into the country. The king also didn't put much stock in the oil roughnecks who were in his country drilling for oil. He made the law apply to all personnel in his kingdom. Consequently, the oil drillers took up gambling to replace drinking. The local personnel told me that thousands of dollars changed hands in those oil fields every night at the gambling tables.

Women were in short supply in Saudi Arabia. The oil drillers frequently took off to Cairo for entertainment. The Egyptian Casino operators had many women entertainers on their circuit from night-clubs all over Europe and the oil rich drillers paid well for their entertainment. We ate at the officers' mess, but the food was not sumptuous due to the heat and the flies. There was a slight wind blowing all the time and the fine silt sand was in everything. We found ourselves coughing and sneezing a lot because our nostrils were not used to constantly filtering out the desert dust. After we ate, we went back to the aircraft and boarded. The pilot took off for the island of Bahrain about one hundred miles to the east. We flew over the Persian Gulf, which was very blue and clear. That was a welcome sight after seeing all that desert. We landed at the island of Bahrain and found the airport much like the one in Saudi Arabia. The asphalt strip looked like an abandoned drag strip with sand blowing across it in little waves or "dust devils." We taxied over to the terminal building and went through customs again. However, the custom inspections were mostly informal and the people were glad to have visitors.

We also got a pleasant surprise. We were allowed to go into town and take a little tour. We found a row of black Studebaker taxi cabs waiting for us at the rear of the terminal building. We boarded the taxis, but soon found out that the Arabs were dangerous drivers. The road was straight and level, but there were pedestrians, camels, and donkeys walking along both sides of the narrow asphalt highway. Those cab drivers drove through all that congestion like it didn't exist. How those walking Arabs got out of the way was a mystery to me. Perhaps they were used to the "races."

We arrived in the Arabian town and were met by a walking tour guide. He took us to the various sites around the village. The most impressive sight was the Virgin pool – this was a villa where the king kept his next wives-to-be. They all swam in the beautiful virgin swimming pool outside the villa on the grounds. While we were there, some little Arab children came out of the sands calling for "buck sheath" or gifts. The guide said they were begging, so we tossed some coins into the sand, and the kids found the coins easily. They had no trouble looking through the sand.

We went back to the taxi stand and were waiting for the taxi when we saw a big crowd of Arabs dragging a couple of thieves down the street. We were told that the thieves were being dragged to the city square to have the hand which had stolen the object cut off with a sword. A pot of boiling oil served to cauterize the stub arm. We did not see the ceremony, but we were shocked at these methods, which appeared way behind our view of civil liberties. The state didn't seem to have much invested in their population. There was no employment for the masses, and they had to live off the desert and the sea.

An Arab vendor approached me with a little match box containing three light blue pearls about the size of a dime. The pearls were stuck in the cotton bottom. He could not speak much English and I could not speak any Arabic. He started the bidding process by asking me for $30. I said, "No." He then asked for $15. I said, "No." Finally, he got down to $1. I said, "No." He said $0.90. I said, "Yes" and gave him 90 cents. Then I tried to sell them back to him for $0.50. He said, "No." I offered them back for nothing. He said, "No" and ran off. I figured that he had come by these pearls in a nefarious way. The taxis arrived and we raced back to the airport. We went through customs again and went out to board the aircraft.

The pilot in command cranked up the aircraft and took off to the Northwest. We climbed to ten thousand feet and leveled on course for the island of Cypress in the Mediterranean Sea. We had coffee and looked out at the desert as we crossed the country. We finally arrived over the Mediterranean Sea and the coastline became green from the available rainwater. We crossed the strait and found

Cypress looking much like Malta. It was very green and flat. We landed at Nicosia, the capital, but we didn't leave the aircraft. We let off a couple of passengers and took on a couple. We taxied back out to the runway and roared off, headed for the island of Crete. We climbed out to ten thousand feet, had more coffee as we flew over the Mediterranean Sea, and arrived in Crete on schedule.

We made a milk run landing at Crete and took off immediately for Athens, Greece. We climbed to our usual cruising altitude of ten thousand feet. We noticed that there were more fishing boats in the coastal waters of Greece. We finally spotted Athens, where we landed, taxied over to the terminal building, and parked. We walked down the gangplank and walked over to the terminal. I soon realized that Greece had an economy much worse off than Italy. The many wars had depleted Greece of most of its resources. The Greek people were left only with the barren hills and the sea upon which to live. We didn't stay long at the terminal because there wasn't anything for us to do. The terminal reminded me of a warehouse. We left this bleak setting and took off towards Naples.

We flew across the blue Adriatic Sea and the boot of Italy at the instep. We flew over Mount Vesuvius and let down to the landing strip at Naples. We landed and went into the terminal building while the ground crew refueled. There was little activity and no shops at the terminal in Naples, but a few people spoke English and were somewhat receptive to conversation. We soon reboarded the aircraft and flew across the Mediterranean Sea to Tripoli and Wheelus Air Base.

I went to the barracks, cleaned up, and went over to the club to eat. I began to realize how fortunate people were who lived in France, Britain, and the United States. As I sat there at the club eating supper, I thought about how people took these modern conveniences for granted. I was glad that I had a part in defending a civilization so advanced as ours.

I ran into some of the psychological warfare officers at the bar again. I was delighted to see them, because I had a few hundred more questions to ask them about the journey that I had just made. I wanted to know how these areas fit into our defense organization. I wanted to know some of the personalities with whom we would be dealing in a future confrontation. These modern historians filled me in quite well in an informal manner. Then we began to talk about the Muslim religion and how it was interpreted by the local Arabs. I was told that the poor uneducated Arabs were so pious that they would let the eye of a child get infected so that the child would not look like Mohammed. I did not know if the world would last long enough to cultivate all the potential human resources in the Middle East. The controlling nobility was in the minority, and they planned to stay that way. These countries were meccas of revolt and turmoil. World stability could certainly depend on the stability of the Middle East in the future. The oil reserves could stabilize the situation by helping the Middle East arm, educate, and employ their human resources. I hoped their oil would hold out long enough to industrialize their physical resources.

We ushered in the 1953 New Year through a series of parties at the club. Each organization had its own separate party. We must have gone to a week of parties before things began to return to normal about a week into January. I didn't know if I would get my transfer to Europe, so I made plans to live in Tripoli. I sent for my 1952 Ford convertible and went down to Tripoli to hire a local real estate agent named Luigi. I gave Luigi six British pounds to find me a house. I was going to send for my wife and child when I got quarters for them. Tripoli wasn't a good place to rear a family, but it would be an experience that would make my family appreciate the affluent lifestyle which they enjoyed back in the U.S.A.

One day, while I was down in the center of Tripoli, I decided to have some of that black coffee that the natives were always drinking.

The local base policy recommended avoiding the native restaurants. I stopped at a nice-looking restaurant and ordered coffee, which was thick as syrup, black as coal, and served in a little porcelain miniature cup. It was hot, so I had to drink it slowly in small sips, but I enjoyed the coffee.

I walked around the center of town trying to find some natives who could speak a little English. I went to several Arab shops, but I found only two or three shop owners who could speak English. The Italian shopkeepers knew a little English, but they were strictly business and a little distant with Americans. They were more used to the British. One Italian woman shopkeeper made a little conversation with me, because she was recently widowed. Her husband had been dead for about eight months, and she was in mourning for one year. I could see that these natives lived on such a tight economic budget that they were not carefree like the people I encountered in the small towns back in the states. I walked down the boardwalk and saw some Italian women, but they dodged Americans. The Italians thought of the Americans as transients, so I caught the blue bus back to the base. On my ride back, those gas pains hit me. I thought the bus would never get to the base. The coffee or "demitasse" (half-cup) that I had drunk gave me diarrhea. I barely made it to the barracks. I knew that I would not be drinking any more Arab or Italian coffee in Tripoli.

I had noticed that the city was surrounded by a twelve-foot mud-brick wall topped by broken glass. I asked some of the officers at the club about this phenomenon. I was told that when the Italians were in power, they had a patrol that ran all the transient Arabs out of town every night at the eleven o'clock curfew. This wall helped keep the Arabs out. I heard some exaggerated accounts of the skill that the Arabs had developed in theft.

# CHAPTER 25

# 48th Fighter Bomber Wing (Chaumont, France)

The daily routine in Tripoli began to catch up with me. I began to feel how remote that station was after all. Everyone looked forward to any opportunity to travel while stationed at Tripoli. In fact, a trip to Europe was a real luxury. One day I got orders transferring me to a jet fighter wing in Chaumont, France. I couldn't believe my eyes -- I had a reporting day! I went to the club that night because I felt like celebrating. I had a few drinks and noticed a crap game in progress. Although I usually abstained from gambling in general, on this night I felt lucky. I started betting with a dentist who was winning. He won a lot of money. In fact, he broke the game. They had been playing on a pool table and the dentist had a bushel of money in front of him. I only had a small amount. He asked me if I wanted to play with him now that everyone else had gone. I responded, "Yes." He promptly broke me. I think the dice were loaded -- I'll never know, but he couldn't lose.

I went back to the barracks in subdued spirits. I had just been paid and had sent all my bills out, but I had lost the rest of my pay. Fortunately for me, the base had a little supplementary pay for the high price of food in the officer's mess. I was told that I could apply for, and draw, $45 for each month that I had been there. I made an application the next day and was paid that same day. I directed that my automobile be diverted to my French station, and I tried to find Luigi to get my six-pound sterling back or some part of it. I found out that every Italian in Tripoli must have been named Luigi. I never could locate him. I left word with his contact for him to cancel the search for a house.

Around this time, I got a letter from CIT in Denver, Colorado claiming that they had not received my automobile payment. What a time to get such news! I was low on funds, so I wired my Aunt Lottie Davis to send the car payment to CIT in Denver. I told her that I would pay her back in due time. She sent the payment and I applied to the post office to be reimbursed for my lost money order for the car payment that I had sent to CIT. I had the stub receipt. It was then that I learned that the post office does not pay off for sixty days. I guess this gave the government time to trace the money order. I made a patch ham radio-telephone call to Grundy telling my folks about my transfer. Then I loaded my personal belongings up in two barracks bags and caught a C-47 for Frankfurt, Germany. We took off from Tripoli on a beautiful day around the 1st of February 1953. We flew across the Mediterranean over Malta and up the boot to Naples. We made the usual landing at Naples, but we didn't get off the plane. We let off some cargo and then took off for Frankfurt on the Main, Germany. We flew over the boot of Italy, crossed the Alps into Austria, and then on to Germany. We flew down the Rhine River and angled off to the Main River before letting down into the traffic pattern at Rhein-Main Air Base in Frankfurt. We landed and taxied over to the base Operation ramp, where we got off the plane and took the blue bus to the officers' billets. I checked in for the night and was told that I would be taken to the railway station the next morning to complete the last leg of my journey by rail.

I cleaned up and went over to the club, where I met some other flyers who had transportation. I was invited to go into town to the Val Holler, a big dance hall. We drove into Frankfurt proper, parked the car, and walked over to Val Holler. We paid a small cover charge and went inside. The dance floor was like the Palladium in Hollywood. Each table had a telephone in the center of the table and couples were dancing on the floor. The unaccompanied ladies or "ladies in waiting" were sitting at tables. When you decided who you wanted to dance with, you just rang her table. I understood there were some "one-hundred dollar marks" available if you preferred. We danced with a couple of girls and then decided to go back to the base Officers club because that activity could become expensive. Besides, we had to turn in early to get up the next morning to make our schedule.

We drove back to the base and turned in for the night. The next morning, I woke up early as usual. I checked out of my room and went over to the officers club for breakfast. The blue bus took me to the railroad station in Frankfurt where I boarded my train with my two duffel bags. This was the same train that I had ridden to Marseille a few years ago. The train pulled out of the station, rolled down the Main River, and passed through the Black Forest. We rolled up the Rhine Valley to Mannheim. We crossed the Rhine River and rolled through Rhineland, through Kaiserslautern, and on to Saarbrucken, where we passed through customs. The French customs agent routinely checked our orders and asked us if we had anything to declare.

The train rolled out of Saarbrucken into France to Metz. We stopped in Metz briefly, then the train rolled on to Nancy. We stopped at all the railroad terminals, including Toul and Neufchâteau. Finally, the conductor came by me and told me that my next stop would be Chaumont on the Marne River. When the train pulled into Chaumont, I took my two barracks bags and got off the train. I saw some Air Police at the station and asked them where the air base was located. They told me that the blue bus ran about three times a day, but they were going there shortly and would be happy to take me with them. I immediately accepted their offer. I loaded my two bags in the back seat of the Jeep and climbed in. Chaumont was a small, rural village that wasn't particularly prosperous.

We left the city square and drove down the narrow, asphalt "cow path" type road. We wound around the river and crossed the bridge under the highstone railroad bridge that crossed the valley at a high level. We drove up to the other side of the valley floor and came to a junction in the road. We took the left-hand prong, which was a gravel road. That French clay was as messy as the Tennessee mud, but not as red. We pulled up to the perimeter fence at the guard shack by the gate. The guard came out to check my orders. After a short exchange of greetings, the gate guards saluted me and waved me through the gate.

I returned the salute and we drove onto the Chaumont base. I saw that the base was a tent city arrangement. It must have reminded the French of the Expeditionary Forces of World War I. We pulled up to 492nd Bomber Group headquarters and I got out. The Air Police saluted me and went on their way. I checked into the C.Q., who let me sign in and assigned me a tent across the street.

I went over to the tent, stowed my barracks bags, and cleaned up at the common shower in the wash house. I went over to the tent which served as the officers club. I went in and found several officers sitting at the tables and standing at the bar. I decided to introduce myself by buying three bottles of champagne and inviting the officers to join me. I did just that. However, there was no response to my invitation. So, I decided to celebrate by myself, and I proceeded to drink the champagne by myself. Finally, one of the officers came over and joined me. He said, "I just can't see one man drinking all that champagne." He introduced himself as Lieutenant Hulen Burk from Amarillo, Texas. He sat down and began drinking with me. Pretty soon other officers came over and we stayed until the bar closed.

Those flyers thought that they had a rough deal because they were stationed in remote France rather than in Germany. I couldn't understand their attitude because they could have been stationed in Africa. At least they were in a jet fighter unit and on the continent. They could fly or drive to Germany on the weekend. I turned in for the night.

The next morning, I reported to the Group Commander Executive Officer. He told me to report to the flight line of the 492$^{nd}$ fighter bomber Squadron. I walked down the planks which were laid down to the flight line to keep everybody out of the mud and went into the Commander's tent by our Squadron operation tent and reported.

The Commander welcomed me to the squadron with a jaundiced eye. He was skeptical of someone coming out of nowhere to the squadron. This outfit had been called up from Alexandria, Louisiana as a National Guard Wing and the personnel were close-knit. They didn't want anyone that they didn't know. The commander checked my orders and told me to take my Form Five or "flight record" to the squadron operation tent and report to the squadron operations officer. I went over to the squadron operation tent as instructed and reported to Major Gravenstein. He took my Form Five and looked it over briefly. He introduced me to some of the flyers who were in the operation shack waiting for a flight. To my surprise there was Lieutenant Hulen Burk. He told the Commander that he would introduce me around. I met Ali Reynolds' brother, Jim Reynolds, a former classmate of mine from Williams Air Force Base, Arizona. He had already pulled a tour of duty in Korea.

*Fighter Pilot Harold with 492ⁿᵈ Fighter Bomber Squadron – 1953*

The weather was bad, so the commander canceled the rest of the day's flights, and everyone retired to the officers club for dinner. I met the rest of the flyers at the club. Some had their families with them, but they lived in a resort hotel in Neufchâteau or in houses in Chaumont or surrounding villages like Longchamp. After we ate, everyone drifted off either to their tents or off the base to their families. I retired to my tent, where I met the single officers and the officers who had not sent for their families. We talked about the situation. The base had some logistical problems because of the reliance on French ground and rail transportation. They also felt that the French were taking advantage of the Americans. We were not treated as conquerors in France like we had been in Germany. The French were an independent lot. They just didn't realize what we were pumping into their economy at the local level. This was probably true of most rural areas where a military base moved in on them.

I wanted to send for my family right away and I wrote to my wife. She told me that she wanted to finish her business course at Knox Business College before she would consider coming to rural France. I decided to get settled and then send for her later. I went down to the flight line every morning. After the morning briefing, I sat around studying the operating manual on the F-84C Thunderjet, which the 48th Fighter Bomber Wing was flying. I also studied the regulations. I went out on the line and got cockpit time in the aircraft as well. I was ready to get checked out in the F-84C. Three weeks went by, and I was still sitting around. They said the weather was not good enough to fly transition. I personally didn't think that was the reason. I felt like they didn't want to check me out.

One day the weather was nice, and I asked if someone would check me out. I was told that the Squadron operation officer had reviewed my records and said that my first flight resulted in a crash. He suggested that I be sent up to group headquarters to fly the Gooney Bird C-47. I had already been that route. I told him that I was checking out in the F-84. No one said anything. They just let me sit around. They were going to let me beat myself through disgust. I had no intention of leaving that Squadron. I had not expected this attitude, but I was ready to cope with it.

One day, ten Yugoslavian pilots were transferred into the 492nd Fighter Bomber Squadron to check out in the F-84's. We were sending F-84's to former Yugoslavia at the time. These Yugoslavians had to be checked out so that they could go back to former Yugoslavia and check out the rest of the pilots. These Yugoslavians had wrinkled uniforms, which looked like Russian uniforms. They even had a red star on their hats and caps. The weather broke for the best and the squadron started checking out the Yugoslavians.

Our squadron commander Colonel William Norris was moved up to Wing. and our Squadron operation officer Major Gravenstein was moved up to squadron commander. Our senior flight Commander Major Degraffenreid was moved up to operations officer. I was still sitting around reading flight operation manuals. I had a belly full of waiting. I asked the operations officer when he was going to check me out. He told me that the squadron commander had to give priority to the Yugoslavians. In short, they had another reason not to check me out. I went into town that night and entered a French hotel to have some champagne. I went over to a local "Ma Companion" dance hall. I was getting plenty drunk as I made the rounds. I thought I would get drunk and figure out how to break this hold up.

It wasn't long until the French bar refused me another drink. I insisted, and they called the Air Police. Fortunately, the bar didn't call the Gendarmes. Those French police were all business with the Billy clubs. The Air Police arrived by jeep. The two Air Police came into the bar and led me outside. They told me that I would have to be taken back to the base. I told them that I would go back when I was ready. I was giving them static that they didn't deserve. They finally forced me into the back seat of the Jeep. I lunged into the street again. I stood off and raised my fists to resist any more restraint. That is when they waded into me. One grabbed my arms and the other parted my hair with a Billy club. I felt the club bounce off my head. It didn't hurt, but I got the message. I told them that I had that coming, and that I would go with them peacefully. We got into the Jeep again. As we drove out to the base, I found out that one of the Air Police was a Hickman from Knoxville, Tennessee.

The other Air Police was a Williams from Sevierville, Tennessee. We made some arrangements on the way back to the base. They decided to take me to my tent and release me to the custody of my flight leader. This was accomplished without further incident. I turned in for the night, but not before having a few words with a senior officer who was trying to scold me for my actions.

The next morning, I didn't wake up from my stupor with the rest of the officers. No one volunteered to wake me either. When I woke up, I smelled like a brewery. I went over to the washroom to shave and shower. I met the other officers, who had already showered and shaved. I jumped into the shower and turned on some cold water. This brought me out of my doldrums. I washed up, shaved, and put on new clothes. I reported to the squadron operation officer. He asked me what I was celebrating. I told him that I expected to get checked out in the F-84, but it looked like I would have to see the Wing commander to get any action. He told me that the Yugoslavians came first. Belligerently, I asked him if I would get any priority if they sent ten Russian pilots in here. I was treading on dangerous ground.

The squadron operation officer called one of the flight leaders who was rotating back to the states and asked him if he would take on the responsibility of checking me out. He said he would be glad to check me out in the F-84. I was still a little flush from the night before. The captain told me to go out to the aircraft with Lieutenant Burke and get in the cockpit to take a blindfold cockpit test to be given by Lieutenant Burke. I climbed up into the cockpit and took a brief look around. Lieutenant Burke climbed up the ladder and told me to close my eyes. He asked me to touch certain switches and levers as he called them out. I showed him that I knew where everything was located. He told me to fire up the aircraft and follow the captain to the runway.

The crew chief plugged in the APU ground auxiliary power unit. I gave him the signal to start up the auxiliary unit and turn the power into my thunder jet. He flipped on the switch and my cockpit lights lit up like a Christmas tree. I made my ground check. After I received instructions from the flight leader in the lead aircraft, I gave the overhead six circle movement with my hand, indicating that I was starting up the engine. I hit the starter switch. When the RPM reached 12%, I hit the ignition and opened the throttle. The engine burped, indicating that the internal firing chambers had ignited properly, and the RPM was rising. When the RPM reached 30%, the engine stabilized. I signaled for the crew chief to unplug the APU. I didn't want to taxi away and drag the APU unit with me. I switched on the radio and contacted my flight leader. He acknowledged and told me to taxi out behind him to the runway. I gave the jet a little throttle and it lunged forward. I reduced the throttle and put on the left brake to turn the aircraft toward the taxi strip. The prefabricated steel plate surface was frosty. The wheel just slid on the frost. I almost slid off the parking apron. I had to get the crew chief and Lt. Burke to help me turn the aircraft toward the taxi strip manually by pushing on the nose wheel. This was a little embarrassing but insignificant under the circumstances.

We got permission to take the runway in formation and takeoff. The flight leader gave the run up signal. We both ran our engines up to takeoff power. The flight leader gave me the signal to roll. Then he nodded his head as the signal of execution. We rolled down the runway and blasted off like two veterans on a scramble mission. We climbed out to the transition area and leveled off. The captain told me that he would fall in trail, and I could ring out the aircraft and get the feel again. I put the thunder jet through her paces over the Argonne Forest.

We returned to the base, let down in the traffic pattern and entered the initial approach. I was in the lead. The flight leader wanted to follow me in the pattern to see that I let my gear down at the proper time and airspeed, that I set my base leg out far enough, that I put the flaps down at the proper time, and that I kept the proper air speed in all legs in the pattern. He wanted to monitor my final approach and see that I was going to touchdown at the proper speed in the first third of the runway. My approach and traffic pattern were satisfactory to my chase pilot. I touched down and slowed down in time to turn off at the proper taxi finger. We taxied over to the PSP (perforated steel plates) ramp and parked. The crew chief put chocks under the main gear and nose wheel. I filled out the Form One and climbed down the ladder. The flight leader took me over to the squadron operation tent and gave me a critique. He also told the operations officer that if I "completed 200 hours, I would make an excellent fighter pilot." I wasn't sure what he meant, but I assumed it was complementary. The operation officer scheduled us for several transition flights to familiarize me with the area, as well as the take off and letdown procedures in instrument weather.

We flew a couple of round robins and landed in neighboring bases in France and Germany. Finally, the flight leader cleared me to fly as number four in his regular formation. I got acquainted with the Yugoslavians, who checked out at the same time. I had something in common with them since I was a student pilot too. The Yugoslavians were professional soldiers, otherwise, their government would not have spent that kind of time with them. They would go back to former Yugoslavia and train their fighter force in our methods.

The squadron leader decided to give the Yugoslavians a three day pass so that they could visit Paris while they were in France. He called me over and told me that I could go too. I told him that a couple American officers had asked me to go to Strasbourg with them. He said, "Go wherever you want."

We hopped in the jeep station wagon that one of the officers had sent over from the states and we drove to Nancy and then to Strasbourg. The countryside became more beautiful as we got to

Nancy – the Rhine Valley countryside was picturesque. We arrived in Strasbourg in the early evening and drove to the middle of town where the cobblestone square was surrounded by four hotels. A music festival was in progress at the best hotel. We were in civilian clothes and went into the hotel ballroom almost unnoticed. We sat down at one of the little round tables and ordered the best champagne. The waitress brought out Piper Heidsieck, popped a cork, and tested the vintage. She poured us three glasses and set the bottle down into the silver ice container with a towel wrapped around the top to keep it cool. We enjoyed the music for a while, then we turned in for the night at the hotel.

The next day, we drove up to Basel, Switzerland and spent the night in a first-class hotel there. We found Basel to be much like Strasbourg, unmolested by visiting soldiers. We liked the resort-like atmosphere of Basel better than the hustle and bustle that we found in Frankfurt and Paris. We drove back to Chaumont the next day and found the weather had changed for the better.

I reported to the squadron the next morning and things were humming. The USAFE had ordered the wing to depart France and proceed to Furstenfeldbruck air base near Munich, Germany in Bavaria to stage out of Furstenfeldbruck to and from the air-ground gunnery range just north of the airbase.

The wing commander gave a big briefing for a mass formation flight to be accomplished from Chaumont to Furstenfeldbruck the next morning. Then the weatherman gave his briefing. The Wing Commander told us that we would takeoff in close formation and climb out in flights of four aircraft in fingertip formation. We would then join the other two squadrons to form a V formation.

We all made a dash for the operations tent to draw our personal equipment. We proceeded out to the runway and awaited our start time signal. Each squadron had a different tail color on their aircraft. Our 492nd had green tails. The 493rd had yellow tails. The 494th squadron had red tails. Each flight had a different call sign, which would end in the color of the squadron tail. Our flight had the "Gander Green" call sign. The wing commander let his element roll at the appointed time. Ten seconds later the second element commenced to roll. We all got airborne and formed up first in elements and then in the V formation. It went off like clockwork.

We flew to Augsburg then turned toward Munich on our final leg. The Wing commander ordered the squadrons into echelon formation. Then the squadrons ordered their flights into echelons. Finally, the flights ordered their elements into echelon formations. The stage was set. The Wing commander reported over the beacon and simultaneously commenced his penetration. Each flight thereafter reported over the beacon and commenced their penetration. Fortunately, the ceiling was about 3,500 feet as forecast by the weatherman.

We all landed in the allotted time. We checked into our quarters and washed up before going to eat. The commander had a little critique party at the bar for us when we arrived at the club. He complimented us on our formation expertise. He told us to be bright eyed and bushy tailed for the combat ready training which would start promptly at eight o'clock in the morning.

We all dashed down to the post exchange. Furstenfeldbruck had the best merchandise in the ETO. We shopped for items and then decided to grab the train to Munich. I hadn't been there in ten years. I rode the blue bus to town and walked to the railway station. I got my ticket and boarded the fast freight for Munich. I got off the passenger train at Munich and walked through town. I wound up at the Hofbrau House where I joined the masses with a cold stein of beer. I drank to the music of the Bavarian band. I had to leave when the last train left for Furstenfeldbruck. If it had not been for the conductor, I would've missed Furstenfeldbruck and gone to another station. I had fallen asleep, and the conductor woke me up at Furstenfeldbruck. Those Germans were efficient. I stopped by the club and turned in for the night.

The next morning, we were awakened early by the commander. We shaved, showered, and had an early breakfast. Then we caught the blue bus to the alert side of the base where we reported to our new operation room in the alert hangar. We noted our schedule to be on the gunnery range and drew our aircraft assignments and takeoff times. We watched the ground crews load the 50 caliber guns with painted ammunition. We had to be airborne in two minutes or write a letter explaining what the delay was. The MATS crews (Military Air Transport Service) and the SAC crews (Strategic Air Command) would never understand that efficiency.

We finally took off in a flight of four. We located the range and contacted the range safety officer in the tower, who gave us instructions. We would be strafing the 10' x 20' targets on the ground from a traffic pattern of two thousand feet for practice. We would break off the run when we were one thousand feet from the target to avoid ricochets and "target fixation" or "flying into the ground." We flew a rectangular pattern and had good spacing because we did not want to open fire until the aircraft ahead had turned on the crosswind leg and was out of our line of fire. Everything went according to plan. We expended our ammo, formed up on the climb out, and leveled out for a straight flight back the first day. We landed that first day, taxied over to the alert hangar, and shut down the aircraft while the crew reloaded our guns for another sortie. We made three fights or "sorties" per day until we all finished that phase of training.

The next phase of training was high angle strafing. We had to pull out at the proper time and altitude using smooth pull-out pressure on the stick. An abrupt pull out could cause a high-speed stall, wash out the aircraft, and be fatal to the pilot. We had a party every night as we met at the club to compare scores. There was plenty of bragging and a few grudge bets.

Our next phase was dive bombing. We used little black five-pound bombs filled with black powder that exploded on contact with the ground. We completed this phase of training without incident and moved on to the next phase of training, which was skip bombing. We would fly about 200 feet above the ground and release the three-foot blue boy bomb and make it hit the target on the first bounce. It was important to release the bomb at the right moment. If you released it early, the bomb would miss the target. A late release would make the bomb jump over the target. If you flew too low, the bomb could bounce back up and strike the aircraft. The black powder charge exploding against the fuselage would damage the aircraft. In fact, it could cause a multitude of problems such as a gear door jamming or a shattered windscreen. If that bomb got sucked into the intake, you could have engine failure. So, it paid to follow the rules. Finally, we started strafing and shooting for record or "qualifying." The weather was a factor. We could get better scores when the wind was calm. We all qualified before we used up our allotted hours. We had a big celebration at the Hofbrau House on completion of our training program at Furstenfeldbruck.

We kissed the Münich kinder (little children) goodbye and saddled up for the big flight back to Chaumont. We had another successful group gaggle on our way back to Chaumont. When we landed at Chaumont, the commander told us that we should get ready for the air-to-air gunnery and high-altitude bombing encampment to be held in Tripoli the next week. We went to the club and discussed the future gunnery camp. We turned in for the night when the club closed.

The next morning, we reported to the flight line operation tent. The briefing on the flight to North Africa began at the squadron level. Then the group commander gave his briefing, followed by the final briefing by the wing commander. We learned that we would fly south of France and across the Mediterranean to Rome on our first leg. We would land and refuel at Rome's Cappuccino Airport before taking off on our second leg over the Mediterranean by Malta to Tripoli.

The air rescue service would orbit their twin-engine flying boats (SA-L6) between Nice and Rome near the island of Corsica. The second flying boat would orbit between Rome and Tripoli near the island of Malta. We waited for the weather to clear. Shortly before we got the word to scramble, I learned that I was one of the new pilots who would have to ride the C-119 that carried the ground crew and support equipment to Tripoli. I resented this because I didn't know that we always had a few aircraft in the hangar for routine maintenance and a few pilots had to ride the "Dollar 19" across the Mediterranean to gunnery camp.

Finally, the weatherman gave us the "all clear" signal. I watched the wing line up on the runway for the blast off. It was quite a sight as I watched the wing roar off without me. While I was looking in the direction in which the jets had taken off, I saw those five C-119's come flying in from Toul-Rosières. They entered the rectangular landing pattern, which was customary for conventional or "reciprocating" aircraft. They landed, and we watched the ground crew load up their equipment. Then we climbed aboard the fourth aircraft and sat there on the ramp waiting for the instrument flight clearance for an hour. The C-119's, heavily loaded with fuel and payload, finally taxied into position for takeoff in turn. The Dollar 19 accelerated slowly and lumbered off into the blue sky. We got into our position with the C-119's already aloft and climbed to ten thousand feet. We flew down to Nice, then turned out over the sea and headed for Rome. We spotted the SA-L6 as we passed by Corsica. We bored on until we made visual contact with the airport at Rome where we entered the traffic pattern and landed for refueling.

We waited in the terminal until the pilot sent the crew chief after us. We loaded up and bored across the Mediterranean where we spotted the second "Duck Butt" or Sa-L6 just off the island of Malta. We continued to fly over the sea until we reached the coast of North Africa at Tripoli where we entered the traffic pattern for Wheelus Field and landed. We taxied over to tent city, where we would make camp for our combat readiness training.

After the pilots shut down the aircraft, we deplaned and went to our assigned tents. The blue bus took us over to the airbase group side of the field where we received a warm welcome from the local base commander in the auditorium. After a briefing on the facilities and what to expect from the airbase support group, we got on the blue bus and went back over to the south side of the field to clean up for supper. I already knew the routine at Tripoli. The base looked better to me as a gunnery camp than it had looked as a permanent station. We hopped on the blue bus and rode back to the club side of the field for dinner and social engagement. Afterwards, we caught the last blue bus back over to the gunnery camp and turned into our respective tents for the night.

The next morning, the operation officer got us up early. We dressed for the flight and had breakfast in the field kitchen, which had been set up in the mess tent by the ground crew. After we ate out of our mess kit, we went through the wash line and dipped the mess kit into the containers of hot water. We put our mess kits and utensils on a tent pole to dry while we were gone. We went to the squadron scheduling board and got our aircraft assignments. We proceeded to our aircraft and saddled up for our flight over the Mediterranean to fire air-to-air gunnery. We went off in a flight of four and rendezvoused with the jet pulling the target over the Mediterranean at twenty thousand feet. The target was a 10 x 20 foot rag which looked like iced glass but was a nylon cloth mesh.

It was connected to the tow aircraft by a one-thousand-foot cable. The tow aircraft would tow up range and parallel to the coast for ten minutes or so and then turn around and tow down range for ten minutes or so. We would climb up between the tow target and the coast to about five thousand feet above and two miles out from the tow aircraft. We would fly parallel to the tow aircraft until we were abreast of it. We would be flying about 100 miles an hour faster than the tow plane when we reached the "perch" or the point in the pattern where we turned into the tow aircraft. We would be coming downhill when approaching the rags.

When we got about one thousand feet from the rag, we would be in the "cone of fire." Our aircraft would be flying about 450 mph, and we would be tracking the rag in the gun sights while the aircraft was pulling about 4G forces. We had just a few seconds to fire before we reversed our turn and broke up to the far side of the tow aircraft. We would climb up and over the tow aircraft until we commenced our second pass.

The trick was to get the correct spacing between our aircraft in the pattern so no one would put "hot" guns on the aircraft in front of him. We had to break off the firing pass while we were still pulling G's so we would not shoot up the tailpipe of the tow aircraft. We would be coming downhill, and the tow aircraft was about 200 feet above the rag because of the weight of the cable and the drag of the rag. An iron bar was attached to the rag from which a twenty-pound lead weight was attached to keep the rag in the upright position.

Theoretically, we would not hit the target ship while firing on the rag. However, timing was critical, and we had to be in the "firing cone." If our sites and aircraft were steady, our bullets would find their mark. We had to fire out to sea to make sure that we didn't hit anyone on the coast. We flew toward Benghazi where there wasn't any air traffic to interfere with our air-to-air gunnery.

After we completed our firing passes, we would form up in fingertip formation and return to the home base at Wheelus Field. The traffic back at Wheelus was quite dense. There were seventy-five takeoffs and landings per hour during the peak traffic hours of the day. Our spacing to get into the landing pattern was a challenge, to say the least. Although we were required to leave the aerial gunnery range with adequate reserve fuel, we also had to expand all our ammo. This left some judgment up to the flight leader. We were usually pushed for fuel when we arrived over the base. We could call "low fuel" and get a priority, but then we would be "on the carpet" for not leaving the range early enough. Therefore, we all played "shut mouth."

We returned from the range, entered the pattern, and landed. We deplaned and waited for the target aircraft to fly over the field and drop the rag. The ground crew would pick up the rag and bring it to the camp. We would hang the target on two posts and begin counting the holes in it. Each of us used ammo with different colors. We could count our scores by noting the numbers of, say, red or green holes in the target. Thirty percent was considered an expert in air-to-air gunnery. It took concentration to score expert. Everyone was in on the count. We had several practice missions before we began firing for record. However, everyone counted all their practice missions. Pilots who had been flying for fifteen years had the same challenge as a brand new pilot when it came to hitting the rag. We had to get the rhythm to really rack up a score.

I had to miss the air-to-air training in Arizona due to my accident, so I was on my own to learn the ropes by observation, conversation, and briefings. I caught on fast … perhaps too fast. I was qualifying in the practice missions and got a little cocky during the night sessions at the bar. I began to forecast what percentage I would shoot the next day. The old pilots who were not having my luck were badgering me about my predictions. They were waiting for me to fall on my face.

To my surprise, I was accomplishing my predictions. I was the first to qualify after we started to shoot for record.

Then it happened. I was on a mission to complete my sorties on the range. I was in the cone when the sun hit that certain angle that you will rarely hit unless you are flying at the right time of day. The sun glare momentarily blotted out the target rag while I was on the firing pass. I should've broken off and made another pass. However, I made the age-old mistake of staying in the cone waiting until I could discern the rag again. When I did see the rag, I was about to inhale it. I broke left but my left drop tank caught the cable. The cable broke, but not before my wingtip light had been broken out and the twenty-pound weight had put a big dent in my left tip tank. The flight leader radioed back to the base camp that there had been a mid-air collision between a fighter aircraft and the target. Usually, the damage was quite heavy, and the aerodynamics of the aircraft was changed. Sometimes, the gear doors would be damaged. There were a number of things to watch out for after a collision. If that twenty-pound weight hit your windscreen, it would be like getting hit with a cannon shell. I took the usual precautions and tested the flight characteristics by going through the stall series. I had the chase aircraft fly around me and report the damage. I made an easy approach and landed without incident. I taxied over to the gallery ramp and shut down. The Wing commander and his staff met me as I climbed down the ladder that the crew chief had put up for me. Colonel Peterson told me to go on about my business and he would handle the subsequent investigation and recommendations.

The squadron operations officer told me to take the day off. He suggested that I visit Tripoli. I caught the blue bus to the main base side of the field. I then caught the blue bus to the Bath Club in Tripoli. I got off the bus and strolled along the boardwalk under the gentle swaying of the palm trees which stretched the length of the boardwalk along the beach. I was reminiscing.

I could visualize what must be going on back at the investigation. One party would want to transfer me out because I had a spot on my record. The other faction would include the mature Colonel Chesley L. Peterson, who had flown with the Eagles squadron in the Battle of Britain. Colonel Peterson would take the incident in perspective and consider the incident as a natural hazard of an aggressive young fighter pilot under the circumstances. Most officials would have transferred their mistakes out, but the mature experience of Colonel Peterson prevailed.

I wondered why a beautiful beach like Tripoli had no bathers on it during the week. I had forgotten how poor the natives were, and the Italians and British lived too austere lives to enjoy the luxury of the beach during the week. I didn't see any tourists. Tripoli was a beautiful place, but it was remote. About the only tourists traveling through were there on business. As I walked toward the center of town by the big "allegedly" mob-connected casino, I noticed an Arab pulling a load of rusty metal pots toward the marketplace on a two wheeled wagon behind a donkey. I wondered where he got those rusty pots. I walked into the marketplace and saw a big commotion. Everyone was gathering around the Arab with the rusty pots. Then, just as abruptly, the crowds scattered like a covey of quail. The Gendarmes escorted the Arab out of the city. The Arab had found a bunch of land mines, which he had dug up and brought to the marketplace to sell. How he was not blown up, I do not know. This incident aptly demonstrated the plight and the education of the Arabs in Libya.

I stopped by a local police station, which served as a precinct center for that part of Tripoli. The Arab "beat pounders" were missing. The Italian squad leader who was on duty summoned the British Corporal in charge. There was no foolishness. I was to state my business. I told the Corporal that I was just passing through and I wanted to chat a bit. The Corporal was courteous enough and answered my questions, but he volunteered no other conversation. I caught the gist, thanked him, and left. I began to realize that we had limited social circles in that part of the world. I stopped by the British Bath Club for a drink, but there was only one customer besides me. I looked over the place, ordered a drink, and decided that the place was too dead for me. I went back out on the street and caught the next bus to my base. I moseyed over to the officers club, went inside, and found it deserted.

I went to the snack bar and got a sandwich and a powdered milkshake. I realized that one must be employed during the weekdays to have any companionship around a military base. It was no place for loafers. I took a stroll to the post exchange, thinking it would be a good time for me to inventory the stock. I lost myself in the PX for a couple of hours. I had one other place to go – the base library. I stopped by the library and browsed for a while, but I decided that I would not have time to read anything, so I went back to the officers club and waited for the fighter pilots to come over after work. Finally, they arrived. We all gathered at the bar to hear about the day's activities. I knew that I would finally hear about my case's disposition when all the other stories were told. Finally, Colonel Peterson came by and told me to report for duty as usual the next morning.

Well, I was "back in the saddle" again. I really appreciated his confidence. I left the club that night with everyone else when the Air Police escorted us out. The permanent party had left much earlier. The temporary duty personnel were making the club money, and we didn't want the club to close, but regulations prevailed, along with the Air Police. As I rode the blue bus back over to the south side of the base to the gunnery camp, I thought of how fortunate Americans were to live such exciting lives like mine. Those Arabs worked twenty-four hours a day just to eke out an existence. It was easy to understand how suspicious and jealous those people were towards Westerners and Americans in particular. I turned in for the night with a lot of satisfaction that I didn't discourage easily.

The next morning, I was in the "wild blue yonder" on the aerial gunnery range as usual. Higher headquarters did not find out about the incident even though they always had spies who wanted to garner some points from the higher ups. It so happened that we had a cover up for the banged-up tip tanks. One of the other pilots had taxied into another aircraft after a night flight and banged up his right tip tank. That made two tanks that had to be disposed of without the knowledge of the higher headquarters. Colonel Peterson devised a plan to get rid of those two ruined tip tanks legally. One of our esteemed flight leaders took off for another night flight. After being aloft for about one hour, he called the tower and reported that the tip tanks were not feeding and that he would have to jettison them into the sea before a night landing. The tower acknowledged and logged the incident. Then our flight leader hit the pickle button and the two tip tanks went twirling down into the Mediterranean Sea. The flight leader came in and landed without further incident.

We started shooting for record and I was having tremendous results. I was the first to qualify. Our nightly sessions at the bar began to involve high emotions and a little betting. I was forecasting my scores, and the old pilots resented this confidence. I remember telling a fellow pilot that I would shoot about 40% on my next mission. Sure enough, I shot 43%. I kept raising my forecast and then going up and shooting that score or more until the operation officer took my aircraft away. Aircraft are like everything else. If you have a new aircraft, it will fly truer. If your crew chief is proficient, you will have guns that are well harmonized, and the mounts will not be loose. The electric gun sight will stand up under the G forces. I took the different aircraft that the operations officer assigned me and checked it out on the ground. It checked OK. However, when I got on the range, the aircraft's guns were loose on the mounts. I could tell they were loose by the noise the machine guns were making when they were firing. When I pulled about four and one-half G forces on the aircraft, the gun site reflection disappeared off the windscreen. I flew out my mission, but I didn't fire out. After I landed, I told the operation officer what a "dog" I had been given. He told me that I should be able to fire as well in any aircraft. I told him that he should try that aircraft on the next mission. He bet me a half case of beer that he could shoot 30%. I told him that I would give him a case of beer if he could shoot 20%. He blasted off with the intent of showing me up. I knew what he was going to run into. When the target ship dropped the rag, we counted the holes. The operations officer had only nineteen holes in the rag out of 180 shots (10.5%). He promptly invalidated both previous missions because of the discrepancy. I won a big decision, but the operations officer never forgot the humiliation he suffered from the incident.

The operations officer had to fly back to Chaumont to arrange a home plate reception for our squadron and to get some parts which were needed to repair some of the aircraft that would be returning. Since I had already qualified as a "combat ready pilot" during the Tripoli gunnery exercises, the operations officer selected me to join him on the flight back to Chaumont as his wingman. We saddled up a couple of F-84's and taxied down to the runway. I noticed in the run up check that my aircraft had an electrical short in the instrument panel. The indicator lights would light up when they were not supposed to. I told the operations officer about the situation, and he said, "Don't worry, that is the reason we are taking the aircraft back to Chaumont." I didn't appreciate the fact that he let me fly that "pinball machine" across the pond.

We blasted off and climbed out over the Mediterranean. We leveled off at thirty-five thousand feet on course for Marseille, France. I thought we should've headed for Rome, but I was eager to get familiar with another airbase. We flew over Sardinia and bored on to southern France. We arrived in Marseille just before dark and I was somewhat anxious because there was always a possibility of an electrical fire in an aircraft within an electrical short.

We landed at Marseille where the French military refueled us. We blasted off again up the Rhône valley for Chaumont. We went to altitude because of the darkness, arrived over the radio bacon at Chaumont, and made a night penetration.

The next morning, Captain Jones rounded up the spare parts for the squadron and placed them in the baggage pod attached to the underside of my aircraft. Captain Jones was flying the pinball machine as we blasted off for Chaumont. My aircraft flew a little sluggishly with the pod hanging under its belly, causing us to lose a little air speed and use more fuel. The weather was beautiful as we flew down the Rhône valley again. We let down at Marseilles and landed to refuel. I got another good look at the blue Mediterranean beach in the letdown. I wanted to spend some leisure time there someday.

We blasted off for Tripoli, but we had spent a lot of time in Marseilles waiting for fuel. We were going to arrive in Tripoli at night. As we roared across the Mediterranean we asked the weatherman about the weather in Rome. We were over Cagliari, Sardinia at the time, and the weatherman came back on the command radio in proud broken English saying, "The weather in Rome, she is afine." The Italians did not like to give bad news to visitors. This report told us only that the weather in Rome was fine for those people who were walking. We continued to North Africa.

Darkness caught us about fifty miles out to sea. We radioed Tripoli for landing instructions. The tower came back on the command radio station stating that a sudden Ghibli or sandstorm had just passed through Tripoli and had knocked out the airstrip landing lights. We were advised to land at the civilian airstrip on the south side of Tripoli at Idris field. Captain Jones did not want to divert and land at Idris, so he told Tripoli that we would orbit a while until the ground crew could get the lights back on. In the alternative, we could land at Wheelus Field without lights when the sand blew out to sea and the ground visibility improved to three miles.

I notified Captain Jones that I only had 400 pounds of fuel. About that time, the ground crew got the runway lights on at Wheelus field using the emergency system. We scooted down to traffic pattern altitude and landed. The Arabs wanted us Americans contained at Wheelus Field. They wanted their civilian air terminal unmolested by military traffic that was not their own. We taxied over to tent city, parked our birds, and buttoned them up for the night.

I told Captain Jones that I was ready to jettison that pod to get some extra range. He told me that he had wired it so that it would not accidentally come off, and I couldn't have jettisoned them if I had hit the pickle button anyway. He said he could not afford to lose those spare parts by accident. We didn't mention this fact for fear of local criticism by the Monday morning quarterbacks and the possibility of higher headquarters obtaining this information. One had to contain every operation that was not specifically covered by the guidelines. This caution was probably true in any business, as well as in one's personal affairs.

We retired to the club to hear about the sandstorm from the squadron. When we arrived at the club, we found everyone inside having a going away party for us. I couldn't tell if they were glad that we were leaving Tripoli or were truly appreciative. At any rate, we made the most of the occasion.

The next day, we saddled up the squadron and blasted off to Rome along with the rest of the wing's other two squadrons. The weather was beautiful as usual, and we passed by Malta again. Malta had a warm spot in our heart because it was British, and it could serve as an emergency landing strip. Also, the air rescue squadron had a detachment on alert in Malta for our crossing the pond.

We flew up the boot of Italy, let down over Rome, and landed for refueling. After refueling, we blasted off immediately for Chaumont. We flew by Corsica and arrived over Nice, France, before turning on course for Chaumont. We could see Lake Geneva from our altitude, but we had to be careful not to violate the Swiss border. We were pulling contrails, which could be seen by the Swiss who were fussy about their air space. Sometimes we did fly over the edge.

The beautiful green meadows surrounding those deep blue lakes were framed by the evergreen forests forever climbing up those towering snow-capped Alps. It was truly a picture to behold! Our white contrails in the light blue sky completed the movement of the scene. We departed the nostalgic moment and began our letdown to the Marne River, which parted the forest of the Ardennes.

We landed at Chaumont, taxied to the Marguerites (hangars), and shut down our engines. We got out of the aircraft and met the "mortal men" who manned the ground crew stations. By the time we had gotten over to the operations shack, we were among the mortals again, and had returned to the reality of the job at hand. We retired to the club for the evening fellowship with the awaiting support group types and dependents.

The next morning, we reported to the operations shack, and the operations officer notified us that we were replacing the 36th Fighter Bomber Wing on Iron Curtain patrol duty at Furstenfeldbruck and Bitburg while the 36th Wing went to Tripoli to receive its annual combat readiness training qualification. Our wing would cover the

Bavarian sector of the border and our other NATO countries like France, Belgium, Holland, Denmark, Norway, England, and Canada would be covering their sectors of the iron curtain. We saddled up the squadron and blasted off for "Fursty," a flight of only forty minutes. We arrived over the Bavarian wonderland and circled Munich before landing at "Fursty." We were giving the Germans a little informal notice that the green tails were back in town.

We landed at "Fursty," and went inside the hangar to set up our schedule. We would be on "ramp" or cockpit alert twenty-four hours on and twenty-four hours off, like a city fireman. When we were on scramble duty, we slept in the hangar. Our parachutes were already in the cockpit of the aircraft. The crew chief had the APU plugged into the electrical receptacle of the aircraft.

When the scramble horn bellowed, we would run to the aircraft, put on our parachutes while sitting in the cockpit, and then buckle in our seats. The crew chief would be starting our engine from the side of the plane while standing on the wing. Once the aircraft was started, the crew chief jumped off the wing and disconnected the APU after we switched the battery position on the bus bar circuit. We had the radio on and began to receive our takeoff instructions as we taxied out of the alert ramp. The tower had the runway cleared for us. Once we blasted off and got airborne, we went to the CGI command radio frequency for vector and altitude instructions. We climbed out to one thousand feet on top if there was weather. When it was clear, we climbed out to the highest vantage point like a couple of game roosters with our eyes scanning the horizon for any sign of Migs. The CGI controller advised us of the target location, altitude, direction, and speed. We raced up and down the border while the Migs shadowed our course on their side of the border. We had "hot" guns and were ready for any occasion.

We would stay airborne until our fuel reached the safe return level, and then we would be replaced by another element from our squadron. We would return to "Fursty," or our alternate airfield if "Fursty" was socked in by weather. Our alternate airfield was usually Bitburg, because Bitburg could launch us again with a full complement of fuel and ammo if necessary. Most of the time we landed back at "Fursty."

When we finished a twenty-four hour alert duty, we headed for Munich and the Hofbrau House, the social staging terminal. After my first tour of alert, I caught a train for Munich where I met some friends with a car. We drove to Garmisch-Partenkirchen in the Alps to scout the area and view the beauty. We were not disappointed in our expectations. We found the beer stops and the villages much to our liking. We also made some new friends.

We discovered that the armed services had developed a real presence at Garmisch. The Casa Carika was a nightclub with a sliding dance floor that would roll back when the ice capades were put on stage. This setup was developed for the American military officers and the noncommissioned officers in Europe and their dependents. The enlisted soldiers used the facilities in Berchtesgaden. Both developments were number one first-class entertainment and recreational facilities. We made future plans to limit the Hofbrau House activities and to engage in the more active and healthy Alpine festivities. I returned to "Fursty" with new ideas about my stay in Europe.

When our two weeks alert duty was over, we saddled up and blasted off for Chaumont. Another squadron of red tails had relieved us at "Fursty." On the flight back to Chaumont, I thought of the differences between the German economy and location versus the local Chaumont lifestyle. Chaumont was a provincial village where some of its citizens had never been to Paris. Although there were some big resort hotels around Chaumont where the Parisians made their annual pilgrimage to get away from the big city, there wasn't much cultural exchange between the Americans and the local Frenchmen.

Our lifestyles were miles apart. The middle-class French had little to do with us because we were temporary in our stay. The Upper Crust in France didn't need us. We had something to offer the peasants, but they were proud and didn't want anything that they didn't deserve. Therefore, we relished the journeys to Bavaria. The dependents and the support troops also relished an excursion to Switzerland or Paris on the weekends. They looked forward to these vacations, which they could afford about once a year.

The next day, I was designated to lead an element of thunder jets to Nuremberg along the Ludwig canal to make some simulated strafing passes on the camouflaged Army anti-aircraft guns emplacements there. Lieutenant Dick Linton was designated as my wingman. We saddled up our fighters and blasted off in the morning sunlight. I had already seen the folly of relying too heavily on the GCI controller and the forward air controllers. In short, I realized their limitations.

Dead reckoning with a high degree of pilotage[1] was the primary requirement for this type of operation. I did coordinate with the GCI and the stationary radio fixes, but I kept dead reckoning as my primary means of navigation to arrive within the radio range of my forward air controller. I further planned to locate the target without the help of the forward air controller, if necessary.

We had beautiful weather on the way to Nuremberg and we commenced our letdown to the target area. We found the canal and proceeded to make low passes up and down the canal. The forward air controller had radio failure and, thus, we were unable to make

---

1 "Pilotage" is the art of knowing where you are by reading a map and comparing it with the surrounding terrain and landmarks, while "dead reckoning" is the art of knowing where you currently are by using a compass, your ground speed, a clock, and an initial known position. *See,* Aircraft Owners and Pilots Association (AOPA), Marsh, Alton K., *Technique - Pilotage and Dead Reckoning,* March 5, 2016.

radio contact. We never located the gun emplacements either. When our fuel was exhausted for the sortie period, I pulled up and we flew back to Bitburg to refuel. The Army commander at Chaumont wanted us to return there to develop a procedure to initiate for those future times when we encountered a forward air controller who was having radio difficulty. We saddled up in Bitburg and blasted off on a low-level mission to Chaumont. As we crossed the Rhine River, I saw a long line of rain showers coming down like a curtain over the Rhineland. I looked for an opening where I could slip through without getting into the rain at that low level. My wingman was new, and I didn't want him to have any visual problems with the rain.

I heard the radio chatter of Captain Burke and his wingman Lieutenant Ulrich, discussing the situation on our tactical frequency. Ulrich wanted to skirt the weather, but Burke decided that the rain would just give the planes a good wash job. So, they plowed right through the thick of the weather band. I found a hole to the north and slipped through the curtain with no problem. I heard Burke and Ulrich talking about the hail in the thunder shower. They agreed that it got a little rough in there. We followed Captain Burke and Lieutenant Ulrich into the traffic pattern at Chaumont and landed. When we taxied to the ramp and shut down, we saw Captain Burke and Lieutenant Ulrich standing by their aircraft. The commander was with them. Those aircraft were beaten full of dents the size of baseballs. Hail can get big enough to ruin an aircraft, especially when striking a jet going four or five hundred mph. Those two aircraft had to be scrapped or "classed 26" because of the damage. Again, Colonel Peterson was able to explain away this unforecast hail as a hidden hazard for the aircraft on their routine mission.

I reported to the Army coordinating officer about the aircraft tracking exercise. He told us that the anti-aircraft batteries would shoot up two orange flares the next time we were in the area and could not locate them with the help of the forward air controller. Then, we could make several passes from lower levels and in many different directions. This would give the crew plenty of practice tracking incoming aircraft in the event of hostilities.

The next day the commander told me to report to Captain Fitzgerald in the wing instrument school. My annual instrument check was due. I was turned over to Captain Shadow who informed me that we were going to be flying together for the next twenty flying hours. He said that I would be familiar with every instrument letdown and low approach in the ETO when he got through with me.

The next day we blasted off in a T-33 two seated Shooting Star instrument trainer aircraft. We made about five penetrations at five different metropolitan airports in France that day. The following day, we flew penetrations and low approaches at the Belgium and Netherlands airports. The next day, we made about the same number of approaches at several airports in Germany. The following day we made the same number of jet penetration low approaches in England. The next day we flew penetrations and low approaches in Denmark and Scotland, and then we returned to Chaumont.

The instructor told me that we would practice some unusual positions the next day on our way to Le Bourget airport in Paris. He said he had called the French and gotten permission to fly the penetration and low approach, and to land at Le Bourget for our RON (remain overnight) mission. Finally, he said that he had confirmed that jet fuel would be available. The French comptroller told him that he was clear to get jet fuel under the usual civilian arrangement at Le Bourget. The captain had everything but the name of the French comptroller who gave him this permission. The captain did not coordinate this fight with the USAF or NATO because he didn't think it was necessary.

The next day, we blasted off for Paris in beautiful weather. We flew the instrument letdown and low approach. We circled Paris before landing to get a look at the Eiffel tower and to get oriented from the air. The Le Bourget tower requested that we make a couple of high-speed passes down the runway before we landed. We thought this was a bit unusual, but we took advantage of the opportunity. We dusted off the place a couple of times before landing and taxiing over to the parking ramp. We were surprised to see a crowd of people who worked at the airport coming over to observe our aircraft up close. We shut down and buttoned up the aircraft while the people were looking it over. We wondered what could be so interesting to them since we were only flying a two seated Shooting Star that had been in service for some time. We grabbed a taxi and headed for the American Hotel in Paris. When the cabby stopped in front of the first-class hotel in the center of Paris, we gave him our fare and a little tip. He kept asking for more tips. We gave him more and then he asked for even more. We caught on. He was going to ask as long as we would give. We gave him the wave off and checked into the hotel.

We made the night spots that evening, but we were not comfortable in these places for a number of reasons. The air was stale, and the smoke was thick. The costumes were too gaudy, and the music was too French. We turned in for the night rather early for Americans. We wanted to tour the city the next day before we flew back to Chaumont.

The next morning, we got up early and ate breakfast in an American styled restaurant. We then grabbed a taxi for the Eiffel Tower. When we arrived at the Tower, we found a large group of Americans waiting to go up. They were Jehovah Witnesses who had a world conference going on in Paris. The place was full of Americans as we went up to the Tower and looked out over the city. We came down out of the Tower and proceeded to the famous art museum, the Louvre. We went in and spent the rest of the day looking at the paintings and the visitors.

We came out of the museum and wandered along the Champs Élysée and along the Seine River before we went back to the airport.

When we got out of the taxi at Le Bourget, we found that the aircraft was not refueled. We inquired why the aircraft was not refueled and the personnel told us that no jet had ever been allowed to land in Le Bourget, except on special occasions. There was no provision for jet aircraft maintenance or fuel at Le Bourget. We got the message in a hurry. We got on the phone to the military detachment at Orly Field across town and told them of our predicament. They had a fuel truck haul us a load of jet fuel over to Le Bourget. We saddled up and blasted off for Chaumont, wondering what would come out of this incident.

The weather was still clear with seventy miles visibility. We roared into Chaumont, landed, and went over to the club. We had the Group Commander down our necks right off. Our operations officer assured the commander that the pilots involved in his squadron would pay for half of the fuel out of their own pockets if higher headquarters demanded compensation. This took some of the excitement out of our tour of Paris. We hoped that our mission could be considered official and, therefore, allow us to escape restitution in cash for the expense of the fuel burned.

I graduated immediately from the wing instrument school and reported back to the 492nd Fighter Bomber squadron the next morning. The operations officer informed us that we were going to receive a new model of the F-84. He told us that the F-84G, with in-flight refueling capability, was waiting for us to pick up at the port of Copenhagen. These aircraft had been shipped to Denmark, where the Danes had taken off the cocoons surrounding the aircraft and reassembled the wings back onto the aircraft. We had an engineering officer from USAFE (U.S. Air Forces in Europe), who had gone to Copenhagen and test flown the first shipment.

The commander told us that we would be given diplomatic clearances and train travel to Paris, where we would board SAS (Scandinavian) Airline for the flight to Copenhagen. We were all anxious to make this journey. I was with the first eight pilots selected to go to Copenhagen. We caught the fast freight out of Chaumont and rode through the beautiful green pastures of France to Paris on the Rapide train. We got off the train in Paris and caught a cab for Orly Field. When the cabbie let us off at Orly this time, we knew how to tip. We gave him what he wanted and then gave him the high sign.

We found our airline and went to their gate. When the time came to board the aircraft, we walked out the gangway and climbed up the steps to the airliner. The minute we spotted those lovely flight attendants, we realized that we were traveling first class again. The aircraft was beautifully painted white with light blue markings and stripes. The flight attendants had light blue uniforms and little blue caps with red, white, and blue patches showing on the front. The officer in front of me told the flight attendants that it was his birthday, and they both kissed him on the cheek. The flight attendants were used to the reserved English and European travelers, and they enjoyed the excitement of finding such active customers. We made the most of the opportunity. When the aircraft had taken off and levelled off on course, the flight attendants came by to serve us refreshments, which included free cocktails. We were in heaven at last! That was the only way to travel. We enjoyed the drinks, the passengers, and the lowland views below. By the time we got to Copenhagen we were reluctant to get off.

We grabbed a taxi after we cleared customs and rode to the best hotel in Copenhagen where the Americans were quartered. We got out of the cab and gave a nice tip. We went inside the hotel and registered. We went up to our rooms to clean up, then came back downstairs and retired to the bar. To our surprise, we found our commanders at the bar. Colonel Peterson bought us a round of drinks and gave us a little advice on how to stay out of trouble. We drank to the commander's health and to the success of this mission.

I offered to buy the Colonel a drink and learned right quickly that a Colonel buys the drinks at his party. The Wing Commander stayed with us for a couple more drinks, then he had to leave to visit with some local dignitaries. We ate dinner and sang a few songs before we decided to make the rounds around the heart of town. We visited a few market cantinas and returned to our hotel. We closed the bar that night before turning in.

The next morning, we caught the blue bus in front of the hotel and rode over to the big hangar at the airport where we were picking up our new fighters. Our fighters were ready to go and sat outside the hangar. The other aircraft were in various stages of assembly inside the hangars. We saddled up a flight of four thunder jets and taxied down to the run up pad on the takeoff end of the runway. The runway was just a few feet above sea level and the Baltic Sea was churning up waves only about 100 feet from the end of the runway. I made a mental note to land in the same direction from which I was taking off if I ever came into this place again and the runway was wet or slippery. An aircraft could slide into the ocean there without being noticed by the tower. We blasted off on a low level spread formation flying across the lowlands of Denmark, Germany, and France. The weather was good, but it was cold. We could see that the countryside was sparsely settled, and the population was in the cities. We flew over the lowlands of northern Germany and into the Rhineland of France. We were changing countries quickly in our jets.

We joined up in close formation before entering the Chaumont traffic pattern for landing. We landed and taxied to the parking apron where the operations officer was waiting for us. We handed him the paperwork as we climbed down the ladder and went over to the operation shack for the debriefing. After the critique, we were told that we would be taking the old F-84E's back to Copenhagen to be shipped out to other NATO nations.

We flew back to Copenhagen the next morning and discovered that we had the opportunity to test fly our new aircraft ourselves that day. We would get all the aircraft tested that day and leave the following day. I blasted off for a local test hop in my newly assigned F-84G Thunderjet late in the afternoon. I buzzed around Copenhagen a while, checked out all the systems, and then returned to enter the traffic pattern. I entered the pattern and pitched out on the initial for a landing. On the final approach, I noticed that one of my main gear lights had not turned green to indicate that the gear was down and locked in position. I put on full power and waited until I started to accelerate before I retracted the landing gear handle. Then I pulled up my flaps. I notified the tower that I had an unsafe landing gear light and that I was going around to try the gear again. I stayed in a closed pattern because of my low fuel and the weather. I dropped the gear again on the base leg. The three green lights came on indicating that my three landing gear were down and in the locked position. I didn't have to use the emergency crank down or manual gear lowering procedure. I touched down and applied the brakes. I was light on fuel and the runway was still a little icy. I began to think that I was going to have to try to turn the jet around by entering a turn off ramp and locking the main brakes. I finally gained traction on the last 1,500 feet of runway. I got a good look at those waves splashing up on the banks of the runway. I realized that under a little more adverse conditions, I could have slid into the sea. I taxied into the parking apron and was glad that I had no incident to report, other than the gear light problem.

The ground crew told me that they would put the aircraft on jacks and run a retraction check on the rear gears to find out if the gear was functioning normally or whether there was a true malfunction. They found that everything worked normally inside the warm hanger. Therefore, we concluded that the erroneous indication was due to the freezing weather. I thanked the ground crew and went off to join my fellow pilots at the hotel festivities. We closed the bar and turned in for the night.

The next morning, we blasted off for Chaumont. We climbed to one thousand feet on top of the weather and cruised at thirty-five thousand feet. We made our penetration and low approach at Chaumont. There had been heavy rain, and the runway was slick. We had a slight tail wind when the flight leader landed on the active runway. We were light on fuel, and I was the last to land. I had good spacing, and I was within the normal touchdown speed. However, after landing, I started having difficulty stopping. The other three pilots had been able to stop and turn off the runway onto the taxi strip. The runway had been undergoing repairs and water was standing on top of the fresh tar on the side of the runway. I saw that I was going to slide off the end of the runway if I didn't produce a quick solution. I decided to start my aircraft turning toward the last taxi strip. When I had slowed down as much as I could, I started turning the aircraft toward the last taxi strip. When I got a little arc going, I applied the brakes to the main gear. The nose gear did not have a brake. The nose gear held its traction, and the main gears began to slide. The aircraft slid around backwards and continued down the runway. I applied full power and utilized the thrust to stop the aircraft at the very end of the runway. The tail of the aircraft was hanging out over the end of the runway, but the wheels were on the runway. I chopped the power to a normal taxi and taxied into the ramp. No one knew how I had avoided the accident. I didn't bother to tell anyone either, because it would've been too hard to explain, not to mention believe. I was highly motivated to stay out of any more accidents or incidents. I parked the aircraft and headed for the club with the rest of the pilots. We closed the club again that night.

The next Monday the operations officer told us that we were going to Prestwick, Scotland to pick up the remainder of our F-84's. My flight was selected to go first, and we were given train tickets to Paris on the French Rapide passenger train out of Chaumont. I still remember the beautiful green pastures, the canals, the hedgerows, and the forests in France. Rural France was a livestock and vineyard country. While the cities were so big, the little villages were quaint and old. The cobblestones had held up for centuries and would continue to endure. We were in Paris before we knew it. We got off the train at the railway terminal and caught a French taxi to Orly Field.

Communicating with a French taxi driver was a challenge, and we were relieved when we saw the signs indicating that we were headed for Orly. We arrived at Orly and paid the cab fare plus a tip. We went inside and found our gate for the BOAC (British Overseas Airways Corporation) flight. Those British flight attendants in their gray suits were certainly a pretty sight. The flight took off on schedule. After we were airborne, the flight attendants began serving us drinks while they prepared to serve us our lunch. We were living in "high cotton" again. We looked out at the Seine River as we approached the coast. The weather was sunny and clear. We looked at the ships as we crossed the English Channel and ate our lunch as we approached the white cliffs of Dover. We marveled at the English countryside as we flew up the Thames River. We landed at Heathrow Airport in downtown London. We reluctantly got off the aircraft to go through English customs.

We were mildly disappointed when we learned that we would be boarding a local milk run airline to Glasgow. We missed the flight attendants already! The Fokker was loaded to the brim and had only one flight attendant. We decided to make the most of this low and slow flight across Britain by studying the English countryside and the industrial cities between London and Glasgow from the windows. We noted the rich limestone base of the English soil, which made the grass a lush blue green color. The countryside was beautiful with its hedgerows, castles, and country estates. The industrial cities were old and dirty with smog around the factories and row houses, but the suburbs were clean and attractive. The stucco homes of the middle-class people were small and close together by American standards. We stopped at Birmingham, Manchester, and Blackpool, to name a few cities. We saw a lot of golf courses near the cities and the villages where the aristocrats dwelled. The commoners must have had access to these public courses also because the courses were covered with golfers.

The Heathers (flowers) were in the flume (channel or ravine with a stream). We began to pass over the hills and dales as we approached Scotland. The sheep population grew in number as the cities and villages disappeared. We crossed Solway Firth and flew over the mountains to Edinburgh on the banks of Firth of Forth. That was a remarkable sight. The city was on the plains of the coast, and the Edinburgh castle overlooked the plains from the top of Castle Rock. We did not get to deplane at any of the stops.

We took off from Edinburgh and flew across the island to Prestwick Airport, just south of the city of Glasgow on the Bonnie River Clyde. We got off the aircraft and went into the terminal. I was immediately overwhelmed at the astonishing similarity of the Scottish people in their manner and their dress to our middle class in America. Their brogue was as prosaic as our southern accent. The lassies were dressed in the best woolen and tweeds. Their colorful scarves, tams, and floves certainly heightened our experience of the Argyle scene. We went into the terminal together, all four of us in uniform. While we were waiting for the limousine to come in from Glasgow, we had a little Irish coffee with a Scottish flavor. We were looking over the woolen in the terminal shops, and we decided to buy ourselves something. I purchased a tam and got several as souvenirs to send to the folks back home.

The next morning, we checked out our aircraft and blasted off for the continent. The weather was still sunny and clear with unlimited visibility. We flew at low level to catch the scenery. We flew over the channel and across the French countryside to Chaumont. The operations officer scheduled us to make a return trip to Scotland the next day, because we had been so efficient, and we already knew the ropes. The rest of the squadron had been called out on a maximum effort mission of some kind in Germany.

We got back to the Rapide train and repeated the journey to Paris. We caught another BOAC flight and had another ball while going to London and then on to Scotland. We landed in Prestwick and got off the aircraft. This time, I had another flight commander named Captain Okker. He had been stationed in Glasgow as an engineering officer in World War II and he really knew the ropes. We caught the Glasgow bus and checked into the hotel. Captain Okker took us to the Colosseum or Palladium ballroom. We went inside of this huge structure and found it jumping with music and young folks like us. Captain Okker had invited his old girlfriends to meet us there. The women so outnumbered the men that they were dancing with each other. We proceeded to have a ball.

The next morning, we went out to Prestwick to test fly our aircraft. We had already decided to practice some aerobatics with Captain Okker and put on a little airshow for Glasgow. We all blasted off at the same time and leveled off at ten thousand feet in formation. Captain Okker wanted to use this altitude as a safety measure in case any one of us had difficulty in the maneuvers. We started our first loop after a few barrel rolls. We soon realized that our aerobatic maneuvers were limited by the slow flow of fuel from our tip tanks. As we were coming over the top of our first loop, we all ran out of air speed and had to use our rudder pedals to fall away from each other. We burned off our tip tank fuel and joined up again to complete our maneuvers. We became quite proficient in a relatively short period of time. We then put on our little demonstration for Glasgow. We made a high-speed pass at Prestwick with their permission. Then we came in for a landing. This created some excitement for the local folks and gave us a little recognition.

One of the aircraft didn't check out, so we had to spend another night in Glasgow. We got the limo back to Glasgow and checked into our hotel. That night, I accompanied Captain Okker to a nearby pub. This tavern was filled with everyone from the local area. They were obviously well acquainted. I was introduced from room to room. The tables were in little rooms, which opened out to the ballroom and the bar. People would buy me a drink as I went around. They made me get up on a table and sing them a song. I wasn't feeling any pain by that time, and I sang "Way Back in the Hills" and a couple of other songs. The people wanted to hear my voice to get to know me. They would hit the floor themselves to spell us by singing a solo or two. The crowd chimed in on appropriate occasions. I bought the whole place a round of drinks and had to borrow a coin to get back to the hotel, where I was given a small advance from one of my buddies.

I returned the coin to my Scottish friend and turned in for the night. The next day, we blasted off for Chaumont. We were sent back to Scotland again the very next day. We made the trip that time without Captain Okker. What a party! It was a good thing we were drawing per diem for this duty, otherwise we would've all gone broke. When we saw Captain Okker's girlfriends, they asked us why he wasn't with us. One of the pilots took her aside and told her that Captain Okker "wasn't with us anymore." He spent the whole night consoling the damsel. What a line! I'm not sure the lady was all that disappointed.

We flew our aircraft back to France and the operations officer announced that we would be allowed to apply for cross-country flights if we traveled in pairs. Our fighter jets were equipped with only one radio, so another aircraft on the wing would ensure that we had an element up with at least one radio working in the soup. Also, in the event of a Mig intrusion into our air space, a two aircraft element would be essential to engage the enemy. The cross-country flights were part of an overall European familiarization program which USAFE had instituted. They wanted us to jointly participate in the NATO mock air battles, which were to be jointly executed that summer by all the participants in the NATO air umbrella. It was essential that we all became intimate with the letdown and low approach procedures at all the jet facilities in Europe and on the British Isles.

All I had to do was to talk a fellow fighter pilot into flying my wing every weekend. I applied for my first weekend cross-country flight to Menston Air Force Base, England near Dover. We blasted off to Menston and let down near Margate. We buttoned up the aircraft and headed for the dance hall in town where we found the action a little slower than that to which we had been accustomed. The Menston crowd was not as used to transients as were the bigger towns. We decided that we had better blast off for Germany. We roared across the channel and landed at the Bavarian base at Furstenfeldbruck. We checked into the officers club and had another party in the club and in Munich. Sunday night we flew back to Chaumont.

When I landed at Chaumont, I began to realize how small our jet world had become. We were just a couple of hours away from anywhere that we wanted to go. The next day, the operations officer told us about a new arresting barrier, which had been devised by the Air Force at Edwards Flight Center in California. This barrier was much like the Navy's arresting hooks on their carriers.

A Colonel Simler at the new base at Landstuhl, Germany, was going to demonstrate the operation of the device. The operations officer and the commander flew up to Ramstein to witness this demonstration. Colonel Simler taxied a fully loaded F-84 to the end of the runway and ran up the engine wide-open. He released the brakes and charged down the runway. The barrier, called the "rabbit catcher," was supposed to engage the landing gear, and bring the aircraft to an abrupt stop without any significant wear and tear to the aircraft or the pilot. When the Colonel hit the barrier, he went right through it. He stopcocked the aircraft, but not before he had overrun the runway, crossed a ditch, pulled 12 G forces on the aircraft, and sheared off the gear. In short, the test personnel witnessed an accident.

When the investigation was over, it was learned that there are only certain speeds at which a pilot can engage the barrier successfully. That speed happened to be about 110 knots. That would be the highest speed at which anyone would ever slide off the end of the runway while trying to stop. Colonel Simler was traveling at about 150 knots. We all got the word, simultaneously, on how to engage the rabbit catcher, and how not to engage the barrier.

The operations officer informed us that we would be flying a mission to practice in-flight refueling procedures soon. The F-84 G's were equipped for in-flight refueling, but no one had said much about it until then. We all gathered in the operation shack and went over the inflight refueling procedure. The procedure required the pilot to simply join up in close formation with the KC-97 aerial tanker and then maneuver the fighter below and slightly behind the tanker aircraft. Next, the pilot would pull forward to within three or four feet of the probe or gas hose extension. The crew member in the tanker aircraft would guide the hose into the leading edge of the fighter's main wing.

I got the first scramble to try out the refueling technique. We blasted off from Chaumont on course to rendezvous with the tanker aircraft, which was orbiting left over Toul Air Force Base, France at ten thousand feet. I took a flight of four aircraft up to the rendezvous point. We joined up in turn and took all the fuel the tanker had to spare. In fact, I made a dry hookup just for practice after that. The fighter pilot had to slow down to the transport speed of 200 knots to refuel. We returned to the base and landed. The operations officer had us brief the rest of the pilots on how simple the operation was.

The next day, we were scheduled to practice a group gaggle over Chaumont. We lined up for takeoff by squadrons. Colonel Norris led off our squadron with the first element. His second element got about halfway down the runway when the number four man elected to abort for some mechanical reason. The number four man slid off the end of the runway, hit a ditch and exploded. Colonel Norris told us to take off through the smoke. He said, "Nothing can be done for that pilot now." We blasted off through the black kerosene smoke because "the show had to go on." It was too bad that we didn't have that rabbit catcher installed at that time. The pilot who aborted just didn't know that you could not stop an aircraft fully loaded with fuel that far down the runway without running off the end of the runway. The ditch just happened to be there because of a perimeter road used by the Air Police to patrol the airbase.

The operation officer next notified us that we were scheduled to participate in a USAF flyby at Wiesbaden. A General was retiring after about 30 years of service. This would not only be a tribute to the man, but a real training exercise for the Air Force in Europe. The frag orders had been written and we had our assigned takeoff times, altitude, and airspeed. Our rendezvous points and time frames meshed to fit in a mosaic umbrella. The weather forecast indicated that we would have about twelve thousand feet broken and seven miles visibility with occasional scattered clouds at eight thousand feet.

We amassed on the runway for our Wing takeoff. There were about seventy-five aircraft on the runway. The runway was packed with jet fighters down to the one-third marker. The Wing commander was in the lead aircraft. We had to turn on 100% oxygen to avoid all the jet fumes. We blasted off at the appointed time. We climbed to about six thousand feet and throttled back to conserve our fuel and arrive at our rendezvous point at the appointed time, altitude, and airspeed. Neither I, nor most of the other pilots, knew the full details of the flyby.

As the plan unfolded, the slow aircraft like the C-119's and the transport aircraft were scheduled to fly over the base in between the jet wings. There was also an airborne exercise which would involve a company of paratroopers jumping out of their transport planes as they crossed the base. The timing of the various components was critical.

We approached our rendezvous point at the proper altitude and speed, but we found the scattered clouds had become broken. There was an unreported scattered deck of clouds at five thousand feet. This sequence of events led the Wing Commander to request a lower altitude to stay on VFR. The Wiesbaden control tower took on the enormous responsibility of coordinating this request for a change in altitude. The density of jet and conventional aircraft was now highly compressed.

We were approaching our rendezvous point from the west. I was flying in the number four position in my squadron on the last flight. I noticed a scud or scattered layer of clouds at three thousand feet. I noticed some C-119's flying from south to north over a rendezvous point. They were flying at approximately our flight level, maybe a little lower. As the C-119's passed from our right to our left, I noticed the C-119's suddenly separated their altitude like a covey of birds. Next, I saw a big red ball of fire. I saw a second ball of fire plummeting toward the ground, and I saw some parachutes blossom. My first impression was that the paratroopers had some kind of fireworks associated with their descent. My next impression was that something had gone terribly wrong. I thought that a couple of those C-119's had collided. Then I heard the chatter over the emergency frequency. A flight of F-84s in front of us had flown broadside through a flight of C-119's. One of the F-84's had collided with one of the C-119's. The big ball of fire was the C-119, and the small ball of fire was the F-84. The parachutes were the survivors of the collisions. It looked like the fighter pilot and some of the crew of the C-119 had parachuted. We got word from the tower that the mission was scrubbed.

We returned to Chaumont and landed. After we parked the aircraft, we headed for the operation shack to see what had happened. The operations officer said that an investigation was underway. It appeared that both transports and fighters had been cleared to proceed to their rendezvous point with the assumption that both transports and fighters were VFR. The weather was marginal and both groups were trying to put on a good show despite the adverse weather conditions. The scud prevented both groups from seeing each other until it was too late, because they were traveling at 90° from each other. The C-119's were climbing to their new altitude and the fighters were descending to their new altitude. Unfortunately, a layer of scud passed between the two flights of aircraft just prior to their collision.

We headed for the club for supper. The next morning, the operations officer informed us that we were scheduled to participate in a joint NATO exercise that would involve us making pre-dawn raids at low altitude on our NATO Allies' air bases to see how responsive they were to attack. We would also make airstrikes on designated harbors and industrial complexes. We would simulate the strafing of vessels in the Straits of Dover. We were all ready for a little excitement. We got our briefing, which included the weather, our routes, and our refueling locations. Unknown to us, a photo reconnaissance aircraft would follow or shadow us and take pictures of our runs and our strikes for camera assessment later.

We blasted off the next morning in time to strike the Belgium base at dawn. We gave the Belgians a good dusting off or buzz job, which was sanctioned by USAF. We returned to our base and refueled. We had another target assignment for the next morning – to dive bomb a couple of ports on the French coast at first light. We got up early the next morning, but by the time we got to the flight line, the Belgium pilots had already dusted us off in the dusk of pre-dawn light of Chaumont. One of the aircraft came so low that his tail cut our utility lights, which were strung about twenty feet above the ramp on light poles. How the aircraft lucked out and flew between the two poles is a miracle. He couldn't have seen the poles or the cables. I am sure that that pilot took some electrical wires home with him. I'm also sure that that pilot had some tall explaining to do. He was probably as shocked as the operations officer when the wires were discovered.

We took off and headed for our targets at dawn this time. We flew to Calais and made our simulated dive bomb run on the ships in the docks. I remember aiming at one ship, then doing a roll and picking up another ship in my bombsight before I pulled out of the dive. We flew up the coast simulating strafing the ships at sea. I was taking gun camera films of my runs. We climbed back to altitude and proceeded to Amsterdam to make another strike before we returned to our refueling base of Bitburg. We blasted off from the recovery base of Bitburg and struck Rotterdam. We then proceeded to Oostende and simulated strafing the harbor before climbing back to altitude and returning to Chaumont. We landed at Chaumont and parked the aircraft. We had our usual gathering at the club to discuss the fun and the problems, as well as the solutions that we found during the aerial blitzkrieg.

The next day, the operations officer asked for three volunteers to fly to Tripoli with him in a flight of four on official business. I always need a little extra flying time, so I volunteered. We blasted off for Furstenfeldbruck to RON (remain overnight). We landed at "Fursty," parked the aircraft, and headed for the club to eat. Afterwards, we turned in for the night.

The next morning, I rose early and ate at the officers club. After breakfast, we headed for the flight line where we checked out the aircraft and saddled up. We blasted off for Rome, Italy. The weather was clear as a bell as we flew across the Alps and down the "boot" to Rome. We let down and landed at Rome for refueling. The Italians were slow, but they got the job done. We blasted off from Rome and headed for North Africa. This was like a dream come true for me. I enjoyed every minute of every flight. We flew across the blue Mediterranean and spotted the green spot called Malta on our way. I could see the dust rising off the desert before I could make out the palm trees and the city of Tripoli. We called Wheelus Field and got permission to descend and land. We came screaming down like eagles. We landed and headed for the post exchange. The operations officer went over to the base headquarters to transact his official business. We left the post exchange and headed for the snack bar where I noticed a jukebox in the corner. I had a milkshake made from powdered milk while selecting a record to play. I chose a record by Charlene Arthur[2] and I dropped a coin in the jukebox as I sat down to enjoy the rest of my powdered milkshake. About that time, one of the other pilots in the flight came in and introduced me to an airman who had been on guard duty at the aircraft. He was a sergeant from Grundy with the last name of Breeding – I knew his parents. We exchanged some pleasantries and Sergeant Breeding gave

---

2 Charlene Arthur was an American singer of boogie-woogie, blues, and early rockabilly in the 1950's. She was one of twelve children born to a poor, but musically inclined family from Henrietta, Texas. She was discovered by Colonel Tom Parker and even toured with Elvis Pressley. She was inducted into the Rockabilly Hall of Fame and praised for her influence on artists such as Elvis Pressley and Patsy Cline.

a little insight into the philosophy of the Italians in Tripoli. He had been dating one of the Italian girls and said that the whole family went out with him and the girl on a date. I finished my milkshake while pondering the fact that I had changed continents, but was still drinking a powdered milkshake, playing a jukebox, and talking to someone from home. We left the snack bar and went to the flight line. The operations officer had completed his business and asked us if we wanted to stay overnight in Africa or fly back to Chaumont. We elected to fly back to Chaumont.

We blasted off from Wheelus Field and set course for Chaumont. We flew over Sardinia and Corsica, before refueling in Marseille, France. The weather was still beautiful. We blasted off from Marseille and flew at low level up the Rhône valley.[3] We noticed the shot up German convoys still cluttered up the sides of the highways. The World War II flyers had had a field day in the Rhône valley. We flew over Lyon and Dijon before we spotted Chaumont. We landed at Chaumont and hit the club again to see what the other pilots had been doing in our absence.

The weekend had arrived, and I applied for a couple of F-84 Thunder jets to go to Furstenfeldbruck. The operations officer approved my request. I talked one of my friends into going along with me to fly on my wing. We saddled up and blasted off for "Fursty," only thirty minutes away. We flew at low level to see the sites, as usual. We crossed the Rhine River and skirted the base of the Alps by the Ammer Sea to "Fursty." We landed and stayed overnight in "Fursty."

---

3 The Rhone Valley differed from the Rhine Valley in that it was located mainly in France, whereas the Rhine Valley began in Switzerland and passed through Liechtenstein, Austria, Germany, and France before it ended in the Netherlands. *See,* Cruise Critic, A Tripadvisory Company, *Rhine vs. Rhone River Cruises,* August 21, 2018.

The next day, we wanted to take an aerial tour of Bavaria. We saddled up our iron horses and blasted off to Salzburg. We remained at low altitude and circled this town nestled in the Alps. We then headed up to Berchtesgaden and on to Garmisch-Partenkirchen. After we toured the Alps, we headed for the Danube River at Ulm and then to Stuttgart. I was looking at the autobahn, where I had seen those German Messerschmitt ME-262 jets some years back. I thought of how one could still use the autobahn in the event of an emergency. We flew on up to Heidelberg and looked over the Neckar River basin. We finally returned to "Fursty" to spend another night there.

We flew back to Chaumont the next morning, by way of Strasbourg. We were flying at low altitude to see the scenery and look for the next place to spend our vacation. We made a low pass over Longchamp before landing at Chaumont, so that my wife knew that I was back at Chaumont. We parked the aircraft and headed for the club. We found the pilots engaged in another sport. Poker had set in on the Wing like the measles. Fads came and went in an active setting organization, and I knew that this poker thing would run its course. I just had to stay out of it until it did. I never did like cards because there was too much time lost. I preferred dice, but my experience in Tripoli had weaned me off that activity. I closed the bar with the help of a couple of camp companions who didn't like poker either.

The next morning, I reported to the flight line to the operation shack, as usual. The operations officer informed us that, since a couple of Migs had shot down an F-84 near Furstenfeldbruck in 1951, we were due to receive some faster aircraft. He told us that we had a representative from North America aviation in Los Angeles scheduled to fly into Chaumont on Tuesday to put on a demonstration in an F-86F Sabre jet air superiority fighter for our benefit.

We flew our regular training flights that day and went by the Officers club tent that evening to discuss the coming event. We wondered how this demonstration would affect us. While we were talking, some Officers from USAF came into the tent and introduced themselves as part of the advance support party for the Bob Hoover[4] demonstration. These pilots had flown a C-130 into Chaumont with all the support equipment for the Sabre jet operation. We did not have the power units and special equipment needed to support the local operation of this new supersonic jet fighter. Our F- 84G's were subsonic fighter bombers.

The next morning, we went down to the flight line to the operation shack where the operations officer told us to standby for the big F-86 Bob Hoover demonstration. The base was closed to transient air traffic. Local traffic was suspended between the hours of ten and twelve o'clock. At ten o'clock, the airshow began. We were standing outside the operation shack looking for the approaching Sabre jet. We expected the aircraft to enter the pattern and land in the normal sequence of events, then taxi over to the ramp and shut down for our inspection. We were scanning the sky when we picked up some contrails just beginning at about thirty-five thousand feet above the air drome. It looked like an aircraft had started to descend from above the contrail level to begin a penetration in VFR weather. We didn't connect this activity to Hoover. However, just a moment later, we got the shockwave from the sonic boom that a supersonic aircraft

---

4 Robert Anderson Hoover was an American fighter pilot, test pilot, flight instructor, and record-setting air show aviator. He was born in Nashville, Tennessee and was a POW during World War II when he was shot down in 1944 off the coast of France. He later escaped in a stolen enemy aircraft. He was inducted into the National Aviation Hall of Fame and was listed by Flying magazine as 10th on its list of the 51 Heroes of Aviation. *See, Hoover, Robert A. Forever Flying: Fifty Years of High-Flying Adventures, From Barnstorming in Prop Planes to Dogfighting Germans to Testing Supersonic Jets: An Autobiography. New York: Pocket Books, 1997. ISBN 978-0-67153-761-6.*

causes when it passes through the speed of sound. The base quivered a little like someone had dropped a 250-pound bomb on a range nearby. That was the announcement that Bob Hoover was on stage. Just a couple of minutes later, Bob passed over the flagpole at about 100 feet at supersonic speeds. He pulled the aircraft straight up into the sun and did aileron rolls until he ran out of air speed. He stalled the jet out and entered a spin for a couple of turns. He recovered from the spin and came across the runway at minimum airspeed. The support personnel had a microphone in the C-130 on which they were describing the next maneuver that Bob would perform. We began to listen to the announcer. He said that Bob was flying at an incredibly low flying speed about 200 feet above the runway. He stated that Bob would land the Sabre in the first one-third of the runway length and then turn the aircraft around and takeoff in the same one-third of the runway. Sure enough, Bob Hoover did just that.

When his demonstration ended, Bob entered the pattern in the normal sequence and pitched out on initial and landed. Bob taxied over to the C-130 and shut down the Sabre jet. The crew chief began to refuel the aircraft so Bob could take off shortly to make another demonstration flight for another fighter Wing in Germany that day. We gathered around Bob and took him to the officers club for a snack while his aircraft was being refueled. We had looked over the Sabre jet briefly before we went to the club. By the way Bob talked, I got the idea that we might be flying this aircraft in the near future. We asked Bob a few general questions about the Sabre and then we let him eat. After Bob had a snack, we all went back to the flight line to see him takeoff for Germany. The C-130 had taken off while we were eating lunch with Bob.

As Bob disappeared over the horizon, we began to speculate on how long it would be before we would get to fly the Sabre jets. We predicted that our new mission would include air superiority, in addition to air to ground support. We wondered how we would get the new fighters since we were not checked out in the F-86F's. We had been checked out in the F-84's before we got them.

Someone had heard of an outfit in the states, which flew new aircraft out of the factories in California and across the North Atlantic, island hopping to Greenland, Iceland, England, and then on to the continent. This outfit was said to be a "high flight" operation. It sounded logical, so we assumed that it might happen that way.

Some of the pilots thought that a select cadre of Wing pilots would be flown to the training base in the states for check out in the new fighter, then be scheduled to shuttle the aircraft over the ocean to Europe. The swept-wing supersonic Sabre jet with its swept-tail fins had stolen our imagination. The landing gear was close together and relatively short. When one looked at the Sabre straight on from the front, while it was taxiing, it looked as agile as a blue hornet. The blue canopy also gave it good visibility. The aircraft was more responsive to the controls even while taxiing on the taxiway. We couldn't wait to get into the supersonic age of flight!

The next day a C-130 landed early in the morning with a detachment of ground school instructors with a mobile training display unit that contained all the systems of the Sabre jet. The crew had a mobile training unit set up in each squadron operations building by the time we reported to the flight line. We were informed that we were back in ground school for the next two weeks. We were anxious students. I had not seen a mobile training unit since I left one of the training bases back in the states. For once, I was in the right place at the right time.

We had ground school in the morning and flew our training flights in the afternoon for the next two weeks. The Sabre jet ground school was most informative and well handled by the instructors. We completed our ground school on a Friday as usual. The following

Sunday, the first contingent of twelve Sabre jets arrived at Chaumont, delivered by the "high flight" pilots who were stationed at Long Beach, California. We will all remember those aircraft, because all the tails were painted red in the event anyone had to land in the snow of the North Atlantic High Flight route. We went out to welcome the delivery pilots. They were anxious to get back to civilization, and a C-130 was standing by to oblige. We were shortly left with the aircraft, which was what we were really interested in anyway. We poured over them that day.

The next day, we reported to the operation shack. The operation officer told us that we were detailed to get the red paint removed from the tails of those aircraft. The ground crew were swamped and needed our help. The Group Commander himself assisted in this endeavor. While we were removing paint, the operation officer and the flight leaders were in Bitburg being checked out in the F-86 Sabre jet by the Bitburg instructor pilots. Bitburg received their Sabres a couple of weeks before we received ours.

After we got the paint off the aircraft, we were scheduled to go to Wiesbaden to take our annual physical flight examination and to go through the high-altitude pressure chamber. This pressure chamber had been flown over to Europe by aircraft and had been set up in a medical clinic in Wiesbaden for the express purpose of indoctrinating the jet pilots. We all took the examination as a matter of course. However, the altitude chamber caused a little anxiety, not because anyone was frightened, but because any sinus congestion could result in pain, blockage, or damage. It was wintertime and everyone had a little congestion. A couple of the pilots had some membrane hemorrhage, which was more scary than painful, but there were no cases of sinus blockage, sinus damage, or ear problems.

We returned to Chaumont ready for the F-86 Sabre. While we were gone, the engineering officer had test flown our Sabres and checked them out in various configurations and maneuvers. We reported to the flight line the following Monday looking at our schedule. The operation officer had the schedule on the bulletin board. I was scheduled to get my first chase ride in the F-86 at one o'clock. I studied the operating manual, while I waited for my turn. We had been required to spend two hours in the cockpit to be ready for the blindfold cockpit check.

I went out to the F-86 aircraft at noon and looked over the cockpit one more time before the flight leader told me to get my personal flying gear and report out to my assigned Sabre jet. I went out eagerly to the aircraft, as every pilot would. We saddled up and taxied out to the run up pad where the aircraft checked out on the ground. The Flight Leader told me to take the runway and he lined up on my right wing. I gave him the run up signal and nodded my head as I pushed the throttle gradually and firmly to the full forward position. I eased the throttle back a couple of percent just before I released the brakes. The Sabre sailed down the runway light as feathers and the lift off was barely noticeable. We were airborne and accelerating quickly. I lifted the flaps, and we were clean and climbing fast. This was the aircraft that I had been looking for! I took the aircraft through the scheduled maneuvers, and she performed like a top.

I wanted to put the F-86 aircraft in a dive and go supersonic, but the flight leader told me that we might disturb the French cattle and sheep, not to mention the peasants. I joined up on the flight leader's right wing and we let down to traffic pattern altitude. The flight leader then gave the order for me to fly lead. The flight leader moved his aircraft down and back, then he crossed under my aircraft and came up on my right wing. He was no flying wingman. I entered the traffic pattern and pitched out for a landing. My flight leader flew my wing to observe my airspeed and gear and flap operation. I rolled out on final with my gear down and locked and with full flaps. I had my correct airspeed when I started my round out and I held the nose in the flare out until I was ready to set the bird down. I touched down like a bird and held the nose well off to help slow the aircraft down and save the break pucks some wear. When the nose fell, I utilized the expert on and off braking technique to keep the brakes from getting too hot. I turned the aircraft off at the last taxiway and waited for the flight leader to make his "go around" and land. He went around, landed, and taxied off the runway at the taxi finger where I was parked. Then we taxied to the takeoff end of the runway and repeated the takeoff and landing two more times before returning to the parking ramp and shutting down. I climbed out of the Sabre and went into the operation shack for the critique. The flight leader told me that I had done a good job.

The F-86 was a dream to fly! I was scheduled for a couple of solo missions that day as well. I blasted off and really wrung out the bird. I practiced dead stick landings where I would come over the airport at five-thousand feet above the runway, reduce the throttle to idle, and commence my left hand descending circle. I dropped my gear, lowered my flats, and touched down in the safe one third of the runway. After touchdown, I applied full power to make another takeoff. One of the new dimensions of the F-86 Sabre was the fact that you did not have control problems when exceeding the subsonic limitations like the F-84 hogs did. When my fuel was down to the prescribed amount, I returned to the air base and landed. I taxied into the parking ramp in a new "age" of flying. I wondered if I would ever get the chance to blast a Mig out of the sky. I parked the bird and turned in my personal equipment. I could have said that I had had a good day's work, but that really wasn't work for me.

I went over to the club to exchange my experiences with the other Sabre pilots. We were a new breed of tigers in our minds now that we had the number one equipment. Everyone was incredibly happy about the performance of the Sabre. We looked forward to getting on the air-to-ground gunnery range and the air-to-air range because the aircraft had excellent stability. It was sure to make a good gun platform. The F-84 was passé. The F-84G was no match for the supersonic bird and everyone knew it. I wondered why the Air Force had not sent us this aircraft earlier. I surmised that it had something to do with the appropriations from Congress. The Air Force had a ceiling just like every other corporation when it came to funding.

The next day, we were scheduled to fly the Sabre with 200 gallon drop tanks for familiarity and for additional range. The bird flew beautifully with the drop tanks. The following day, some pilots from USAF came to Chaumont in C-130's to shuttle our old F-84's to the rest of the NATO allies other than England. While we were getting the supersonic birds, our allies were getting our hand-me-down F-84's. This gave the Americans and the Canadians the air superiority mission and left the air to ground mission to the allies. The Canadians in Europe were receiving Sabres, too. However, the Canadiens had their F-86's modified. For example, the Canadiens kept the VHF radios in their new F-86's. We got the all-new ultra-high frequency radios in our F-86's. I imagine we gave our surplus VHF radios to the Canadians.

Only certain allies could afford to participate in the air armada due to funds, the technical requirements of support personnel, and the lack of trained pilots. To those countries where the economy would not support an air force of any size, we simply detached aircraft to those countries on temporary duty at their largest commercial airports. Countries like England, France, Belgium, Netherlands, Norway, Spain, Portugal, and Denmark could support their own Air Force. Countries like Greece, Turkey, and Libya could not support an Air Force, so the Americans had large air bases stationed in those countries for our protection, as well as their protection. I'm sure we gave some of those

F-84's to former Yugoslavia, but I don't know what the arrangement was. Tito had his own thing going "under the curtain."

We flew our regular mission schedule with the new Sabre jets, while the shuttle pilots moved out the F-84's. We became more conscious of "air supremacy" with the Sabre jets. Our commanders instructed us to "bounce" every other aircraft in the sky, especially other fighters. By bounce, I mean we were to try to engage the other fighters in a dogfight action. The idea was to get sharp in patrolling the skies on every sortie. We would strive to get the jump on the other aircraft by getting on its tail before the other pilot saw us. We would take the gun camera pictures of our dogfights to our commander. This kept all our commanders aware of the alertness of their pilots.

We had gotten comfortable in the Sabre jet when the operations officer notified us that the annual air-to-ground gunnery range at Siegenburg, just outside Furstenfeldbruck, was open for utilization by our wing. We flew to Fursty and proceeded to have fantastic rounds of air-to-ground gunnery. Several pilots recorded over fifty and sixty percent scores! The swept wing of the Sabre did not detract from the stability of the aircraft in the gunnery pattern. Next, we went through our high angle strafing sorties. Finally, we flew our skip bombing and low altitude dive bombing sorties after that. Before we knew it, we had completed our combat readiness training on the ground gunnery range in Siegenburg. We saddled up and blasted off for Chaumont. We had a little celebration when we landed at Chaumont.

The next day, the operations office informed us that we would be flying some interdiction missions for the Army in Germany while staging out of Chaumont. I drew the first sortie. I blasted off for Stuttgart, Germany with a flight of two Sabres to make a mock attack on a twenty vehicle Army truck convoy traveling at about forty mph on a small hard top road going North out of Stuttgart. I calculated that it would take our element about thirty minutes to arrive at Stuttgart and about five minutes to let down and find the convoy. If the convoy left Stuttgart while we took off, they couldn't be over twenty to twenty-five miles north of Stuttgart when we found them. I knew the shortcomings of GCI, so I elected to fly at altitude by dead reckoning with the Stuttgart beacon as an assistant locator. We climbed to thirty-five thousand feet to get on top of the weather. I arrived over Stuttgart and crossed over the beacon, making a level turn, so that I would come back over the beacon on the heading on which I intended to commence my penetration. The weather was solid up to thirty-four thousand feet. I popped my speed boards over the high cone and reduced my power for the descent. We penetrated the clouds and broke out in our penetration turn inbound to the low cone. It was raining and it did not look promising. I already knew what I was going to do in the event of weather conditions. I crossed the low cone and proceeded north at about one thousand feet above the terrain. I had flown about four minutes north when I flew out of the rain for just a moment. I saw the hard top road with its rain slick surface reflecting the light. I looked up at the road for just a second and then looked back to the south for a second. I was right on top of the convoy. I notified my wingman of the position of the convoy and how we would attack it. I signaled him to move out in wide formation. The weather would permit us to do some aerobatic maneuvers to get in as many passes as possible in the short period of time that we had allotted to do the job. I cautioned my wingman to always keep me in sight and to follow my lead. I told him to consider the extra fuel load that we had left in the tip tanks in his maneuvers.

I proceeded to beat up the convoy. To my surprise, the trucks did not pull off the road or disperse in any way. The men did not take cover either. Those were bad habits for the troops. I felt sure the convoy commander did not expect us to find them in that weather. He was probably trying to figure out how we were going to handle the mock attack in that low weather. We completed our simulated attack, joined up in close formation and put on full power as we headed back to the beacon to commence our ascent on course for Chaumont, to the west this time. We climbed back on top of the weather and roared back to Chaumont where we made a weather penetration and a low approach. We landed, taxied to the ramp, and shut down. The crew chief buttoned up the aircraft and we went into the operation shack and gave the operation officer and the Army coordinator our report of a highly successful mission, as far as the Air Force was concerned. The wingman thought that I was either a wizard or the luckiest element leader in the ETO (European Theater of Operations). I never let him in on the secret of planning your flight and flying your plan, which was really no secret.

The next day, I drew up a mission to find a tracking sortie on that Nuremberg canal gun emplacement again. I had the same plan for Nuremberg that I had had for the Stuttgart sortie. I made Nuremberg my letdown point. I utilized GCI but relied on dead reckoning and pilotage. When I made my letdown at Nuremberg, I was unable to contact the forward air controller. However, I did observe the two orange flares that the gun emplacement personnel shot into the air, and we made several passes on the anti-aircraft batteries before landing at Bitburg to refuel and then returning to Chaumont as scheduled. Again, I gave the operations officer a successful report.

The next day, the operations officer informed us that we were going to Tripoli to qualify in high altitude bombing and air-to-air gunnery. We had not bombed from high altitude with the F-84 because of the Mach limitations in a high-speed dive. We looked forward to this next dimension as we saddled up the squadron and blasted off on course for Tripoli. We found that the F-86 Sabre jets were also real gun platforms at altitude. We blasted our targets with higher scores than we had attained with the F-84 Thunder jets.

While we were in Tripoli, one of the F-86's came out of inspection and was ready for a test hop. I had just been appointed an element leader, so I was eligible to test hop the aircraft. The engineering officer told me to test hop the aircraft. I was eager to fly the F-86 without drop tanks on a sortie that did not involve other aircraft or another mission. I wanted to break the sound barrier! This was my chance. I blasted off and climbed east along the coast until I had accomplished about half of my climb out altitude. I reversed my course and climbed back toward Tripoli along the beach, so I could attain my maximum altitude over the city of Tripoli. I was nearing fifty thousand feet when I was directly over Tripoli. I flipped on the gun sight and rolled over upside down and pulled the nose of the Sabre straight through the horizon until I was heading straight down wide-open on the city of Tripoli with my gun sight on. I put the gunsight piper on the beach of Tripoli because that is where I wanted the boom to rumble. My airspeed accelerated quickly. The earth was coming up at me like a brick wall. I had full forward trim rolled in the elevator in preparation for the stick pressures which would be generated as my speed increased. I felt the aircraft buffet slightly when I was approaching the sound barrier and I noticed that the flight instruments temporarily reversed their direction for a fleeting moment. I suddenly became aware of the thundering silence of the engine. I thought that I had gone so fast that I had blown out the fire in the engine. I noticed that the airspeed indicator registered that I was going faster than the speed of sound, so I decided that I would roll the aircraft while I was supersonic to see how she performed on the controls. The aircraft responded like a dream. I had plenty of altitude to pull out in case I needed to make an air start or dead stick landing approach for Wheelus Field. As I began my pull out, I noticed that the engine was still running. When my airspeed decreased back below the speed of sound, I could hear the noise of my engine again.

I must have run ahead of the speed of sound for a time. I never fully understood the phenomenon.

To maximize my fun on that test hop flight, all I had to do was line up with the runway, call for a magnetic speed run check at Wheelus Field, and make a high-speed pass at the gunnery camp. I called Wheelus Tower and asked for a mag check pass at the runway. The tower operators knew that those mag checks usually resulted in a high-speed pass, which they enjoyed as long as nobody complained. I gave the call sign of "Tiger One" so no one could identify my aircraft. I figured that I would have the element of surprise in my favor, and I would be going so fast that no one could read my tail numbers.

I lined up to come out of the desert, cross the base on the short runway, and disappear out to sea before anyone could grasp the situation. I was "Whistling Dixie" when I crossed over the gunnery camp just above the tents at the bottom of my arc. As I crossed the beach and came over the sea, I pulled the aircraft straight up and did aileron rolls straight up until I had about ten thousand feet of altitude again. I then reduced power and scooted east along the coast for a few minutes, waiting for several planes to land before I returned to the field and entered the traffic pattern for a landing.

I came in on initial and pitched for my landing. When I landed and taxied over to the gunnery camp, I noticed a big group of dignitaries along with the base commander standing at my parking space. I thought they'd come over for a routine inspection tour. I carefully taxied my aircraft into the parking space and shut down the engine. The crew chief put the ladder up on the side of my aircraft and the operations officer was up on that ladder before I could open my canopy. I opened the canopy, unhooked my oxygen mask from one side of my helmet, and leaned over to see what the operation officer wanted. He asked me if I had sonic boomed the base. I said, "Yes, did you hear me?" He never answered me, but climbed down to the ground and took the visiting brass over to his tent. I got out of the aircraft and climbed down the ladder. I asked the crew chief what the operation officer meant. He told me that the Arabs had gathered in the local mosque for their annual religious service and had requested that the base not fly any aircraft between 12 and 2 o'clock at mid-day during the two-week religious services.

Breaking the sound barrier was not a common experience for pilots at that time. Chuck Yeager had been the first pilot to do so in 1947 with the experimental plane, the Bell X-1 Glamorous Glennis. In 1953, most military pilots still did not have an appreciation for how much disturbance the sonic booms could cause. I thought it would be a noise like a cannon firing off in the distance. However, since I had continued my supersonic dive for some time, the sonic boom had multiplied to the point of causing physical movement of objects on the ground. Fortunately, there had been no actual physical damage. The mosque was located near the beach where I had put my gun sight piper to guide my sonic boom. The Arabs had gathered in and around the mosque, filling it to its capacity. They were just getting ready to begin their service when the sonic boom hit the mosque. The enormous noise shook the building and blew a fine dust out from and around the old clay brick walls of the Mosque. The flying dust made the Arabs think that they were being bombed again. They all fled for their lives, running out of the mosque to get away from the bombardment. The Arabs panicked and headed for the safety of the desert. When the Arabs found out that they were not under bombardment, they headed for the mayor's office to see what the American military had done to them. They thought that a Navy aircraft had dropped a stray bomb or that a submarine had accidentally fired a torpedo.

I was in trouble! When I got over to the tent, the commander told the base commander that he could set any punishment that he deemed appropriate for me for this incident. My commander told me to report to the base commander the next morning for the final disposition of this incident. I went over to the club where all the pilots were waiting on me to find out what had happened. I also wanted to find out how the commander knew that I had buzzed the base. The other pilots told me that, by coincidence, I was the only pilot flying that period of the day without wingtip tanks. The F-86 could only break the sound barrier without wingtip tanks.

I didn't know what the charges would be, but they could include disturbing the peace, buzzing an airport, performing aerobatics in a controlled zone, and unauthorized maneuvers while on an official test flight. We had a big party scheduled for that night. After the Commander and the Flight Leaders gave me the official scolding, they soon forgot about any future charges and asked me to tell them what had happened. They were curious about the handling characteristics of the F-86 at supersonic speed since none of them had broken the sound barrier yet.

By the next day, everyone had had time to reflect on the incident and were having some second thoughts. The Arabs had settled down to religious meditation again and were in a forgiving mood when they discovered that they were not in jeopardy of physical harm. At 10 o'clock, I reported to the office of the base commander, who had gone over the entire incident. It was the first sonic boom that he had heard, and he didn't want to do the dirty work for the Fighter Wing. He wanted to keep the goodwill of the visiting Fighter Wings. He told me that, since I had told the truth about the entire event and saved the base the task of an investigation, he would turn the disposition of the case back to the Fighter Wing. I reported to the Wing Commander next. He referred me back to the Group Commander, who discovered that a quota for a forward air controller had arrived from USAFE. This would require a fighter pilot to go to Germany and spend six weeks with the infantry directing air strikes. The Group Commander told me that the Squadron Commander had nominated me for this position. The rest of the pilots considered that assignment a punishment, but I recognized it as an opportunity to visit Germany for six weeks with food, rations, and transportation being furnished by the Government. My commander ordered me to take this assignment once we had completed our gunnery camp and returned to Chaumont.

The next day, we commenced our high-altitude dive-bombing training. I saddled up the Sabre with a flight of four and we blasted off for the bombing area in the desert about fifty miles south of Tripoli. I had the flight fall into trail formation with enough space in between each aircraft so that one aircraft could complete his dive and pull out before the next aircraft started his dive. We flew a rectangular pattern and leveled off at twenty thousand feet. I flew my approach to the target in a manner where I could see the target until it passed under my left wing. Then I rolled over upside down and pulled the nose of the aircraft through the horizon until I was coming straight down on the target with my piper on the bull's-eye. It was important to be coming straight down rather than slanting in any manner, so that the bomb would fall true.

I had my trim full, so that I could release back pressure with ease as the aircraft accelerated. I got my piper on target and kept it there before releasing the practice bomb on a flight path that would carry it to the target after I pulled out of the dive. We had a minimum altitude and a release altitude. It so happened that one could not read the altimeter, because it was unwinding so fast at the release point. However, you could estimate your altitude with the shorthand, which read the altitude in thousands of feet. I released my bomb when I was ready and pulled out in plenty of time to get out from under the other aircraft in the pattern. I turned out to be the most accurate dive bomber in the wing, which had about seventy-five pilots doing dive bombing. Some of the pilots never did get used to simultaneously going straight down at an ever-increasing speed, trying to coordinate the piper with the target, and monitoring the altimeter. One day I got five bull's-eyes out of eight drops. The squadron commander who was in that flight with me made a statement that he had never seen such consistent accuracy since he had been flying.

The supersonic capability of the F-86 aircraft also made it an excellent high-altitude bomber. We had a nuclear capability, as well as a conventional mission. We continued our bombing exercises until everyone had qualified. Those low altitude pull ups that ran into the overcast required proficiency and active knowledge of instrument interpretation. It was the surest way to take the edge off the younger pilots who tended to get cocky before their experience warranted it.

The next day, the operations officer notified us that we would be undergoing a physical training program which would consist of calisthenics followed by some sprints and some extended jogging around the parade ground. We donned our PT (physical training) gear and fell into formation. After fifteen minutes of warmups, we did a few short sprints. Before we turned in for the day, we jogged around the training field. That African sun sure could sap your energy fast.

After about three days of physical training, our commander notified us that we were going out to sea, at the courtesy of the Air-Sea Rescue detachment stationed at the port of Tripoli. We donned our flying suits and flotation gear and climbed aboard the two torpedo boats docked at the harbor. These orange speedboats motored us off the beach and out to sea in short order. After a display of seamanship by the able crew on the gunboats, the operations officer told us to jump off the boat and try swimming in our flying suits and flotation gear. We leaped into the water from the ship's deck. We splashed around a bit and became familiar with the flotation gear and the problems associated with moving around in the water under these conditions. Then the ship's crew threw the rope ladder over the rail, so we could climb back on the boat deck. This required physical exertion beyond what one might expect.

After we got back on board, the ship's captain told us that in our next exercise, a rescue helicopter would "rescue" us out of the sea using a pulley and yoke set up. When the rescue helicopter came out, I was the first to go overboard. The chopper hovered over me at an altitude of about twenty feet. The prop wash from the rotors gave me some concern at first, but I soon realized that the wind was more a sensation than a handicap. The helicopter crew lowered the hook or yoke on a cable, which had a heavy twenty-pound steel ball attached about three feet above the yoke. This steel ball stabilized the yoke in the wake of the chopper propwash and the prevailing surface winds on the sea. I was noticeably careful about watching out for that steel ball. If that ball hit me in the head, a frog man would have to jump into the sea and hook me up. When the yoke touched the water, I grabbed it, pulled myself inside the circle, and held the cable with my arms over the side of the yoke. The crew chief signaled me to give him an OK to start the pulley motor and hoist me up to the door of the chopper. I gave him the OK sign and away I went. Once I was up to the door of the chopper, the crew chief pulled me inside the door and helped me out of the harness. As soon as I was loose from the yoke, I jumped back into the water, so that the next man could be rescued.

Once in the water, we could swim back to the beach. I learned very quickly how that physical training program fit into the water survival program. Even though the beach was nearby, it looked a lot closer to us from the ship's deck than it did in the water. The operations officer asked me if I wanted to ride the one-man rubber boat to shore to practice paddling a small boat on the swells. I told the him that I would just swim to the beach. I was struggling by the time I made it to the life buoy at the edge of the beach area, and I had to hang onto that buoy to get my strength up enough to swim the rest of the way to the beach. I made a promise to myself as I swam to the shore, never to underestimate the sea. We all completed the water survival program that day and wrapped up our training program at Tripoli.

After we returned to Chaumont, I took a local flight as an element leader. I had just taken off and was still at traffic pattern altitude when I saw a B-57 bomber flying across Chaumont making contrails and heading towards Paris. I needed to know how long it would take and how much fuel would be used to reach altitude and get a "Bogey" (unidentified aircraft). I told my wingman that we were going to make a simulated attack on the B-57ft5, which was passing overhead at about thirty-five thousand feet. I knew that the B-57 would be traveling at about .7 Mach or 70% the speed of sound. Therefore, I had to climb out in excess of .7 Mach to close on my target while climbing to overtake him. We climbed out at .75 Mach and caught the B-57 over the city of Paris, which was about one hundred miles from Chaumont. We made one pass on the bomber and broke off. We noticed that a French Mystère jet had come up and begun to chase the bomber as we headed back to Chaumont.

When we got back to Chaumont, a high cirrus cloud layer had floated over the field. I had noticed this layer on my way up. Strangely enough, the cloud formation had not changed its structure. It was just floating above Chaumont like an island in the sky. I noted my radio beacon and the cloud formation and told my wingman that we were penetrating over Chaumont. He told me that he didn't believe that we were over Chaumont. We penetrated the clouds where I estimated Chaumont was located and, sure enough, I was right on the button. Some of the pilots were not so observant of cloud formation. We landed with ample fuel remaining.

The next day, my assignment required me to take a flight of two aircraft to southern France and make a simulated attack on the little coastal town of Biarritz, and then return to Chaumont. We blasted off with two aircraft. I had used a WAC (world aeronautical chart), but accidentally measured the distance with a "sectional" plotter. This made the distance appear to be only half of the actual distance. We climbed to altitude and leveled off on course. When I finally noticed the error, we were way up the coast from our destination. I elected to fly to the port at altitude anyway. We flew on down near the Spanish border, but cloud coverage prevented us from making a mock attack on the port. We turned around and started back to Chaumont but hit a jet stream headwind. I went to forty-nine thousand feet, but my wingman could only get to forty-seven thousand feet and stay in formation. We would be pushed for fuel, so I selected Dijon as an alternative landing site if the fuel situation warranted it.

We were quiet and calculating on our way back. We were mentally calculating the amount of fuel needed to make it back to Chaumont. We overheard some other squadron pilots in a dogfight near Toul. They had temporarily lost their orientation and were contemplating landing at Toul for fuel before returning to Chaumont. Although this was a proper thing for these pilots to do under the circumstances, I knew that they were making an unscheduled landing and would be "on the carpet" from the operations officer when they returned to Chaumont. When my wingman suggested that we go into Dijon, I told him that Dijon was a French base and that we would be "on the carpet" just like those pilots who were landing at Toul, France. I told him that we could make it to Chaumont.

We had a little cloud coverage when we got near Chaumont. I could see the St. Dizier airstrip, which was located north of Chaumont. I told my wingman that I would penetrate the thin layer of clouds covering Chaumont, and he should remain at altitude until I made my report from below the clouds. If Chaumont was not where I thought it would be, then he would go on to St. Dizier and land from altitude. I penetrated the clouds and there was Chaumont just as I had estimated. I radioed my wingman to come on down and join up and we could land at Chaumont. We landed and taxied into the Marguerite parking apron. We were exceptionally low on fuel, so I told my wingman to run the engine until the engine flamed out to check the fuel gauges while we had a good opportunity. We both flamed out our engines in just a couple of minutes. This prevented the ground crew from knowing how low on fuel we had been when we landed and, consequently, cut down on unwanted gossip which inevitably occurred in situations such as ours.

We went into the operation shack. The pilots who landed at Toul came into the operation shack a little later. The operations officer flew all over them for making the decision to land at Toul. These pilots looked to me for sympathy. My sympathy was with them, but I could not tell them that they had made the correct decision. I had had to push the regulations to keep from being "on the carpet" with them.

One day I received notification that it was time for my six week "punishment" tour as an air controller for Army maneuvers. An Air Force pilot flew me and my two duffel bags full of field gear to Furstenfeldbruck in an L-20.[5] An Army pilot met me in "Fursty" in an L-19[6] and flew me up to Grafenwoehr range, where their maneuvers

---

5 The de Havilland Canada DHC-2 (L-20) "Beaver" was a single-engine high-wing propeller-driven short takeoff and landing (STOL) aircraft that was a favorite of civilian Canadian Bush pilots. It was adopted by the U.S. Army as a utility aircraft for transportation of people, freight, or other supplies. *See,* Heritage Flight Museum, DHS-2 (L-20) Beaver.

6 The Cessna L-19 "Bird Dog" was a relatively simple strut-based, high-wing, single-engine aircraft used by American forces in observation and forward air control missions. *See,* Planes of Fame Air Museum, Cessna L-19 "Bird Dog."

were about to commence. I reported to the Army commander in the field and told him that I was his designated forward air controller for this maneuver. This Colonel impressed me as being "on the ball." He assigned me my vehicle and ground crew and gave me my instructions.

For the next six weeks, I reconnoitered the advance positions, much like the artillery observers do. I set up my equipment on vantage points where I could direct airstrikes for my assigned Army team. Our airstrikes came in the daytime for training and safety purposes, so I had the evenings free to visit the local rathskeller (basement tavern or restaurant) for a little rest and recuperation. On one occasion, I attended a German cinema and saw "Gone with the Wind," which was in English with German subtitles.

I completed an enjoyable six weeks of forward air control duty and got an L-19 Army pilot to fly me back to "Fursty." When we arrived over "Fursty," we found the airport closed for repairs to the taxiway – the tar or asphalt was being replaced between the concrete blocks. I asked the Army pilot to land in the grass and let me off so that I could live in the officers' club until the base opened in a couple of days. The Army pilot elected to land on the taxi strip. Although no one was working on the taxi strip because it was Sunday, the Air Police called the officer of the day to the base to investigate the landing of the Army plane on the taxi strip. There was no damage to the asphalt or the aircraft because the big tires of the L-19 just rode right across the ruts between the concrete slabs. We bounced a little and that was the extent of the incident. However, the officer of the day was furious that he had been called into the base from some social function on Sunday. He was going to cite me until I pointed out that there was no control stick in the backseat of the L-19, where I was a passenger. Then he berated me for letting an Army pilot land on a closed field. He could "let loose" on me because he knew me, but he couldn't "let loose" on the Army pilot who was only doing the Air Force a favor.

I checked into the club and cleaned up. I was going to enjoy myself until the L-20 arrived from Chaumont. The Air Force used the L-20 to haul support personnel around to the little airports where the larger and faster aircraft could not land. In fact, the L-20 hauled most of the beer from Germany to our various parties at Chaumont. So, I was waiting for the "beer run," not the "milk run," to arrive.

I lived it up for a couple of days, and then the blue L-20 showed up at base operations. I loaded up my two duffel bags and the L-20 lumbered off towards France. We enjoyed the scenery on the way back to Chaumont. I described the good time I had had with the Army on maneuvers to the base pilot flying the L-20. He enjoyed the company as we flew over the Rhineland. We saw several great vineyards on our way to Chaumont. We arrived in Chaumont, landed, and retired to the club to continue our conversation and have a beer.

We found most of the squadron pilots at the bar. The pilots were talking about a big NATO mock air battle in the making. It was to be a maximum effort. I found myself a little bored with this session, in as much as I had been given a hard time over the past couple of months. I decided that I needed to take a leave to the United States to visit my wife and family for thirty days. I figured that they could do without me for that long and maybe appreciate me a little more when I came back.

The next day, I made my leave request. The operations officer had a conniption fit. One would have thought that I was deserting. I held fast to my request, and he finally had to agree to let me go. I caught the L-20 to Frankfurt the next day.

In Frankfurt at the Rhein-Main airport, I waited for a space available flight on MATS back to the states. I caught a C-54 the next morning for the states by way of Prestwick, Scotland; Keflavik, Iceland; Bluie West One, Greenland; Goose Bay, Labrador; Gander, Newfoundland;

Halifax, Nova Scotia; Boston; and New York, before landing at Andrews AFB in Washington, D.C. The weather was beautiful.

I checked into the BOQ in Washington, D.C. for the night. The next day, I got on a C-47 enroute to Knoxville, Tennessee on a National Guard mission. We took off just a few minutes after I checked in. I sat in my seat until we leveled off, then I went up between the pilots and studied the terrain as we flew down the Shenandoah Valley and into the Holston and Tennessee River valleys.

The grass was lush and green, and the rivers were clear and flowing. The scenery always reminded me of a little Switzerland. We finally arrived at the beautiful McGhee Tyson Airport in Knoxville, Tennessee. I had called my wife in Knoxville just before I took off from Andrews AFB and told her when to expect me. She said that she would be waiting for me at the airport with our daughter Rebecca.

We landed at McGhee Tyson Airport and taxied over to the military side of the military base operation. I got out of the aircraft and saw my wife and baby in my ivory Ford convertible parked beside base operations. I carried my bags over and threw them into the backseat of the convertible. I gave my wife and baby a big hug and kiss, and then got into the driver's seat. My wife was trying to catch me up on the things that had happened while I'd been in Europe and the baby was busy trying to read my face with her hands. All I could think about was how beautiful these folks were. They looked like they had just stepped off the script in Hollywood. They were so calm and secure and with such a peace of mind.

I drew a breath of satisfaction that I was plowing a path for them to follow soon. I was going to see how they felt about leaving the United States and joining me in Europe. I wanted to get my family's reaction as well. We drove through the green pastures of Blount County and across the Alcoa bridge over the deep blue Tennessee River and Fort Loudon Lake. The elegant riverfront homes in Sequoia Hills along the opposite shore of the Tennessee River reminded me of English castles and their grounds. We crossed the bridge, and I looked over towards the campus of the University of Tennessee. Although no game was in progress, I could imagine the shouts and cheers coming from the big horseshoe stadium surrounding the football field. Three of my children would eventually matriculate from the University of Tennessee. I drove over to West Haven to 4303 Ball Camp Pike and turned into the Davis place where my wife and baby lived with my aunt and uncle.

I went inside and several of my relatives were already there waiting for me to catch up on the situation overseas. We had a big meal, and everyone got into his or her story. I tried to bring them up to date on my situation and they in turn apprised me of the local situation. We talked into the night and finally turned in late.

The next day, I left Knoxville and went to Kentucky and Virginia to visit my relatives like a traveling troubadour. I stopped in Grundy with my parents and checked in for the night. We talked until late. The next day, I went downtown to visit my friends.

I returned to Knoxville that weekend. My wife got off her job at GMAC insurance company, and we drove over into North Carolina to visit the Smoky Mountains Park and the Cherokee Indians. We lost ourselves together in the wonders of the Smoky Mountains for the weekend.

We returned to Knoxville and discussed our plans for my wife and baby to join me in France once I got back there and found a place for them to live. My family was against the idea. They wanted to keep the baby in Knoxville and let my wife go. I finally convinced the family that my wife and baby would be safe at the American base near Chaumont.

My brother was attending the Medical College of Virginia Dental School in Richmond, Virginia at the time. I decided to take my Ford convertible to him and let him keep it until I could get the paperwork arranged to ship it to Europe. My father went to Richmond with me to see my brother. My brother and his wife agreed to keep the car until I called them to take it to the port of New York. They wanted to drive me back to Andrews Air Force Base to catch a flight back to Europe.

We drove up to Washington. I checked into Andrews Air Force Base, and they told me about a General who was leaving Westover Field on a C-97 for an inspection tour of North Africa and the Middle East. My father, brother, and sister-in-law drove me to Westover Field so that I could catch the General on that inspection flight. They enjoyed the drive, and I enjoyed talking to them on the way to the airport.

I checked into the BOQ at Westover and turned in for the night. The next morning, I boarded the C-97, which was destined for Saudi Arabia via the Azores, Sidi Slimane, Tripoli, and Cairo. The aircraft was plush. There was a crew of three and the General's party was five in number. I found out right away that a General was always on an inspection trip. There were several passengers on board who were on duty throughout the middle east and a couple of secretaries headed for Tripoli and the oil fields. We took off over the Atlantic and climbed to an altitude of about ten thousand feet. We headed for the Azores off the coast of Spain. The Atlantic was blue, and the white caps were heavy.

I watched the waves until I went to sleep. When I woke up, I was in a mood to meet the passengers and find out where they were headed, where they were from, and what they were doing. This occupied my time until we reached the Azores. We became a family again, as was the case on these flights across the ocean. We arrived at the Azores just before dark and I got off the airplane heading for the hotel. We checked in for the night and then went down to eat, listen to the music, and have a few drinks before turning in for the night.

The next morning, we loaded up the aircraft and took off for Sidi Slimane, Morocco. We passed over the Canary Islands and over the coast of forbidden Morocco before landing at Sidi Slimane. When the aircraft door opened and the ladder went down to the ground, the sunlight was blinding, and I felt the heat from the hot sands of the desert rise up into the aircraft. I had lost my hat and I elected to stay on board the aircraft until we took off again. We didn't stay long on the ground.

We took off for Tripoli and I ate my food packet and went back to sleep. I was still asleep when we arrived at Tripoli. We landed and I caught the blue bus to the PX, where I immediately bought a hat. I went back to the base operation and checked on a flight to Europe. The base operations officer told me to check into the BOQ and he would notify me when I had a flight to Frankfurt. I checked into my room, cleaned up, and went over to the officers club to see if the place had settled down since I had left some time ago. Things were back to normal. The operations officer called me at the club and told me that he had a flight for me on a C-54 to Napoli (Naples) and Frankfurt the next morning. I had a little party that night with the passengers who had gotten off the C-97 at Tripoli and I turned in late as usual.

The next day, I boarded the C-54 bound for Naples and Frankfurt. The MATS pilot took off on schedule, as usual, and we leveled off at an altitude of about ten thousand feet. We had a box lunch and I visited with my new traveling companions. Most of these passengers were going to Germany on a little vacation. The rest of the passengers were going to Germany or other locations in Europe on regular military business. A couple of passengers were on emergency leave to visit their parents or some close relative who were sick or dead in the states. We flew by the green spot of Malta again. Four engine aircraft like the C-54 did not stop in Malta – the twin engine aircraft made that milk run. We flew up the boot and landed at Naples where a couple of passengers got off and we took on a couple of new passengers. We roared off the runway in Naples and flew up the boot across the Brenner pass and down the Rhine to Frankfurt on the Main. We landed at Rhein-Main airbase, and I got off the aircraft and went into base operations to check for a military flight going to or near Chaumont. There were no aircraft going to France in the Chaumont area, so I decided to catch a train. I caught a ride to the railroad station and bought a ticket for Chaumont. I got on board the "forty and eight" (by our standards), and the smoker chugged out of the station. We rolled through the Saarland and went through customs near Saarbrucken. The train was not fast like the Rapide. It was like the old "Katy Line" in Texas. It moved slowly and lost a lot of time at the station. I leaned over my barracks bag and went to sleep. The conductor woke me up when we arrived at Chaumont. I got off the train and caught a ride to the base with a couple of pilots who were going through town.

I went by the club and found all the pilots talking about the big air armada mission which had just been completed with NATO. They were reliving the air battles and the parties which were held on the staging bases during the operation. I realized that I had missed a big maneuver. I also noted that my flight had replaced me with a new element leader. He was a nice lad from Texas. That was the cost of being absent. I turned in for the night.

The next morning, I reported to the operation shack for duty. The Commanders wanted their pilots to stay in good physical condition, so a big new physical education program was in progress. We donned our sweatsuits and went for calisthenics. After about thirty minutes of warm-up, we jogged around the hangar five times. We all complained a little, but we really enjoyed the activity because we needed the exercise.

We flew our sorties after we got our physical conditioning out-of-the-way. The next day, I learned that our squadron commander was rotating to the states. He had been renting a French summer home with a maid in the little village of Longchamp located about thirteen miles from the base. I saw my chance to get a place for my wife and daughter. The Squadron Commander connected me with the French officer who owned the cottage but was currently living in Nice. He only came up to this village in the summer before the Americans came. Now he was making the place pay for itself by renting it to the Americans. I rented the cottage and even bought the refrigerator and a few hard to get items from the squadron commander. All I needed then was a big water jug to carry water from the base to the village for drinking purposes. The squadron commander gave me the five-gallon glass jar which he had used.

The squadron commander explained how I could get my dependents over to France. He said that I could have them go to the courthouse, apply for a passport, and then get their immunization shots. They could either come overseas by military flight as dependents or they could come over by commercial flight as tourists and apply for dependent status at the base after they arrived in France. The military shipments always had a backlog because dependents traveled at the government's convenience and priority. Dependents had the lowest priority in the mission and there were all kinds of delays. Everyone thought of dependents as unavoidable along the pipeline.

I elected to have my family sent over commercially, even though it cost a little more than $300. I wrote to my wife and gave her the pertinent information. She got busy and, in her own efficient way, got everything ready without any trouble. She gave the dates that she would be boarding an American Airlines flight to LaGuardia Airport in New York. She told me that she would catch a cab from LaGuardia over to Kennedy International Airport where she would catch a Pan-American flight across the Atlantic to Shannon Airport in Ireland, and then to Paris where the flight would land at Orly Field.

I left Chaumont on the day that my wife left Knoxville, Tennessee. I drove to Paris and waited at the Orly Field air terminal. It was December 11, 1953. As I waited in the terminal, I thought about the little cottage in Longchamp. I had told the maid that she should have the fire going and the house warm when I arrived back in Longchamp. We had a coal stove, which was about the size of a cracker box standing on its end. There was another wood burning stove in the kitchen. Coal was $60 a ton for the egg shaped pressed coal. The maid kept the wood burning kitchen stove constantly fired up in the winter months. The kitchen, living room, and dining room were downstairs. Our bedrooms and bathroom were upstairs.

A little brook ran through the middle of town dividing the commercial side of town from our residential side. The stone bridge was right in front of our cottage. I could see the entire village from our upstairs windows. I figured we could easily supervise our daughter in this village. The other French families and the one other American family let their children loose in the town streets, which had very little traffic. There was a railroad in the field by our cottage, but it was fenced off. There was an open well behind the neighbor's house, but it was surrounded with a wire fence.

While I was thinking about the new abode for my family, I saw a group of passengers coming through customs. I looked for my wife and daughter. I saw my daughter first. She had on a white knit hat and a blue overcoat. Her galoshes came up to her knees. She was holding her doll and attending to its bottle. I saw her mother showing the customer officials their papers. When she was clear, she came through the gate leading Rebecca by the hand. She was so sure that I would be there, and she didn't even look for me at that moment. I went over to her and asked her how the trip was. She told me that she and Rebecca had enjoyed the excitement on the aircraft while crossing the ocean. We left the terminal and loaded up in the gray Renault. We headed for Chaumont, which was about 150 miles east. I wanted to get to Chaumont before the snow caught us.

We didn't eat in Paris, but we did stop and get some French bread to tide us over. French bread tasted like cake because of the yeast the French used. We motored along the deserted roads admiring the beautiful countryside. The French stayed off those country roads in the wintertime. I made it to Chaumont in good time and we stopped at the base, where we got some groceries at the Post exchange before driving out to Longchamp. We stopped in front of the cottage and my wife loved it because it had a flower garden in the front yard, and it was very private. We went inside and the maid had not started the fire. The French were very frugal, and the maid just couldn't see starting a fire until someone physically occupied the house. My wife started the fire in the little coal stove, and we gathered around it. When the fire got going, we warmed our pajamas and jumped into the feather bed. Those heavy quilts and down mattress kept us warm throughout the night.

The next morning, I took my family to the base so they could fill out the papers necessary to have them receive dependent privileges at the base. I reported to the operations shack while my wife checked in at family services. The operations officer and some of the other pilots thought that I had been extravagant in flying my wife over commercially with a tourist status. I explained that I wanted my wife to get first class treatment on her first voyage to Europe.

We began to get involved in a lot of interdiction strikes by the Air Force in the Army maneuvers. My operations officer sent me to Germany to direct these air strikes, not only for our wing, but other wings as well. I saw an opportunity to show my family all the terrain that I had covered on ground and by air during both my Army tour and my Air Force tour in Europe. I knew that those permanent maneuver ranges were located all over Germany and the rest of Europe. The ranges were usually located on a hunting preserve and had permanent Army barracks, an officers' club, and guest quarters. The local villagers were generally large landholders who took advantage of the range during hunting season. The permanent party personnel who ran these country clubs saw to it that visitors had their every need met, so that the personnel could keep their positions there as long as possible.

I knew that the Army would only need me during the day for airstrikes, so I could spend the evenings and nights in the guest house with my family. I packed my duffel bag in the backseat of the Renault for my daughter to play on, and my wife occupied the passenger seat in front beside me. We headed for the Grafenwoehr range in Germany. I drove on those blacktop roads in France to Neufchâteau, where I got on the main drag for Metz and the Rhineland. I scheduled my refueling stops for Toul-Rosiere and the other American bases along the way. This allowed us to eat at the officers club and to shop at the post exchange during our motor trip.

My mission with the air strike maneuvers became like a vacation to my family. I toured all of Bavaria while going to and from those air strike ranges. We liked Munich and Garmisch better than the rest of Germany. Heidelberg was satisfactory for visiting, but Bavaria had the big recreational opportunities for the entire family. The Casa Carico nightclub and ice-skating arena took the cake. The skiing at the Zugspitze was very handy also. After a time, I forgot about my situation at Chaumont and the squadron. I was afraid the operations officer would find out how much I was enjoying the forward air controller duty. He thought that I was being punished.

One day the operations officer notified us that we were scheduled to fly the Iron Curtain patrol again. I saddled up with my flight to blast off to our staging base at Furstenfeldbruck, Germany. We landed at "Fursty" and set up in the alert shack. Someone found a pool table in the basement of the officers' club, and we would head over there for a big pool game after our tour of duty. After the pool game, the pilots started gambling on dominoes. I stayed out of these gambling sessions and was razzed about it. However, I still remembered how broke I was when I came to France from North Africa.

We returned to Chaumont and commenced routine training flights. We still took weekend flights to keep the Wing in high flying time hours. This was a measure of how much training in combat readiness the unit was performing. The Wings in Europe competed in flying hours like the Wings all over the world. Therefore, I was able to get a couple of birds every weekend.

One day about a year later, I got a notice that my Ford convertible had arrived in the port of Bordeaux, France. My wife was expecting our second child in the middle of February 1955. I hesitated to leave her to get my Ford, but the Renault was beginning to be mechanically unreliable. I notified the American family in Longchamp that I was leaving, and I would appreciate any assistance that they might give my wife if something developed unexpectedly while I was gone to Bordeaux. I caught a train to Paris and then to Bordeaux. I arrived in Bordeaux after traveling on the train all night and found my Ford in good shape. I drove it off the pier and headed towards Paris. I wanted to go by way of Paris in case my car had trouble. There were some car repair facilities in Paris. I made it to Paris and stopped at the embassy to eat at the cafeteria and shop at the PX. I left Paris and rolled down the country road for Chaumont. That Ford seemed like a big automobile after driving the Renault for a year. I was living in high cotton.

The brook in Longchamp flooded and brought six inches of water into the lower floor of our rented house. The floor had floated up, making the house uninhabitable. So, I went to Chaumont and rented a furnished two bedroom apartment, which had been vacated just that day by one of our older pilots and his wife, who were going back to the states. I moved my family into the new quarters, and we were much better off than when we had been at Longchamp. We had hot water for bathing, washing dishes, and washing clothes for a change, and we didn't need a maid. I reported to the operations officer the next morning.

My second daughter arrived a couple of weeks ahead of schedule on January 6, 1955. She weighed seven pounds and ten ounces, and we named her Patricia Lee. I sent a telegram to the grandparents and told them that all was well with my wife and child. I gave out a box of cigars to the squadron pilots.

The weather turned sour for about two months, so we sat around the squadron operations shack studying our operations manuals and regulations until we were bored stiff. The operations officer got a call from Wing headquarters. They wanted a ski team from the Americans in France to train for ten days at Garmisch and then participate in a ski slalom and downhill race with the American ski teams in Germany and England. When they asked for volunteers, I was the first to volunteer.

I loaded up my family in the Ford convertible and we left Chaumont on course for Garmisch. We elected to drive through Switzerland and a portion of Austria before going to Garmisch via Salzburg and Munich. We drove to Geneva and spent the night.

The next day, we toured Lake Geneva. The people appeared to be on an eternal holiday with no hurry or tension. I just wished that I had had more time to spend in that never ending wonderland. We drove to Zürich and on to Austria through the little country of Liechtenstein. We crossed the Augsburg Pass, then drove to Innsbruck and on to Salzburg. We left Salzberg and crossed over into Germany.

It was cold and the relatively straight road was covered with a sheet of ice. The snow was drifting across the road onto the ice. I was going a little too fast and the wind caught the car and almost blew us off the side of the road before I could slow the car down. This incident taught me a lesson about the wind on icy roads. I had never encountered this type of experience. We drove on to Furstenfeldbruck and spent the night.

The next day, we drove to Garmisch and checked into the Recreation Hotel. I checked in to the ski headquarters for training. My wife signed up for beginner ski lessons. The German nurses had a baby-sitting service in the nursery for ten cents an hour. We attended the nightly dances at the Casa Carioca. When I was not skiing with the ski instructor during practice sessions, I went ice-skating with the family on the open ice arena at Garmisch. I skated with relative ease because I had roller skated, but my wife had never skated, so she just walked around the edge of the arena holding on to the side boards. Rebecca skated on a pair of double-bladed ice skates for children and had a lot of fun.

I had positioned myself to lead the second squad of skiers for the American team in France. We skied for about nine days. We were going to compete for the record. I made my last run down the slalom and had just begun the downhill run on the Condara trail. It was snowing, and some of the other members of the squad elected to skip the run under those conditions. The first quad had gone down the run ahead of my squad, which was now reduced to four members. I made the first turn, but I hit some moguls on the second straight run and lost my balance. I didn't want to get off that little chute and hit a tree, so I tried to make a controlled fall. I was going too fast to salvage the fall. When I hit that 44 inches of snow, my body stuck momentarily, but the right ski did not release. Consequently, as I tumbled, I received a bad sprain of my right ankle, knee, and hip.

This happened in a flash. I was down and I did not have any feeling in my right leg for a short while. I thought my leg was broken. I just laid there until the rescue team arrived. The rescue team took off my ski, put me on the sled stretcher, and took me down the trail in short order. When I got to the doctor, he told me that I was incredibly lucky not to have a broken bone, but I did have three serious sprains in the ankle, knee, and hip. He kept me in the hospital overnight.

The next day, they put me on crutches and let me go. I picked up my family and drove back to Chaumont. I had enjoyed the vacation, but now I was back at Chaumont to recover from my sprains. I hobbled around for about a week before the flight surgeon would let me get back into an aircraft. I needed four hours of flying time to get my flying pay. I contacted the visiting operations officer and asked him to let me test hop a couple of his aircraft to get my flying time in for the month. He went along with the request. I blasted off on the first test hop and logged two hours. On my next test hop, I blasted off on the half taxi strip and logged another two hours of flying time. However, a little shower came over the airbase before I returned to land. There were a few little puddles of water on the taxiway that I was going to use for landing. I made a normal approach and touchdown. When I hit those puddles of water, the deeper side of the puddle grabbed at the aircraft wheel and pulled the aircraft in that direction. The next puddle pulled the aircraft the other way. I had my hands and feet full of rudder pedals and stick trying to keep that Sabre on the narrow taxi strip. I finally made it OK. I told the visiting operations officer what I had run into, and he canceled further flights off the taxi strip when there was any water on the taxiway. That was my last fight at Chaumont as a pilot. I had finished my overseas tour.

We sent our luggage home by ship, and we were scheduled to travel by train to Orly Field and board an Air Force C-54 at Orly for the flight back to the states. I got my new assignment – I would be reporting to the 1738th Jet delivery group at Kelly Air Force Base in San Antonio, Texas after a thirty day leave in the states called a "delay in route."

We caught the Rapide train out of Chaumont in August 1955 and rode it to Paris where we caught a cab to Orly where we boarded a C-54 chartered flight with Global Airways. The flight attendants had attractive green uniforms and the plane was loaded with dependents and their service husbands. We roared off the runway at Orly and climbed to ten thousand feet, where the pilot leveled off on course for Shannon, Ireland. We flew across the English Channel and over the British Isles. We crossed the Irish Sea at St. George's channel, flew over bonnie Ireland, and landed at Shannon Airport. The aircraft had something wrong with the generator, and we were asked to wait in the terminal building until it was repaired. We did not have time to clear customs, because we were in a little waiting room roped off for transient personnel. We all had something to eat and several of us tried some Irish coffee. We must've been waiting for bad weather to clear because it couldn't have taken that long to change the generator. I surmised that the pilot felt that the generator repair story would be more acceptable than a delay for bad weather.

We slept in the waiting room chairs for two or three hours. Finally, we were called to board the aircraft. We got on board and strapped into our seats. The pilot took off in the middle of the night and we climbed to ten thousand feet before leveling off at cruising speed on course for Kennedy International Airport in New York City. The pilot's flight plan was in the shape of a dog leg. We flew towards Newfoundland until we reached land, then we flew down the coast to New York. The flight took about eighteen hours and we arrived at New York International Airport early in the morning. We went through customs and caught a cab for the servicemen's hotel.

We arrived at the Hudson Hotel and checked in for the night. We went upstairs to the room and ordered six fried ham sandwiches with lettuce and tomatoes on toast. Room service brought the order up to our room on a pushcart. The bill was twenty-three dollars! I was shocked! I had been told that this was the servicemen's hotel. I had forgotten how inexpensively we had lived on the European economy by staying at the officers clubs, using the military camp commissary, and shopping at the nonprofit post exchanges. I told Ruby that if this was the servicemen's hotel, we had better head inland to our home area quickly. We ate the sandwiches even though they were expensive, cold, and clammy.

The next day, I got a cab and went over to the New York port and found my Ford convertible. I drove back to the hotel and picked up my family. I had called an old friend of mine by the name of Francis C. Mears, who lived up the Hudson River near Poughkeepsie and Schenectady. I told him that we would pay him a short visit and he told me how to get to his place.

It was raining "cats and dogs" when we arrived at his apartment. We went upstairs to his apartment, and he met us at the door. He was very pleasantly surprised and happy that we took the time to drive up to see him. He had married a beautiful girl, and they had a priest from Rome, Italy, fly over to New York to marry them. My daughter Patricia was only about six months old, so we only visited for a couple of hours. We had to cover a couple hundred miles before we could stop at a motel enroute to Grundy, Virginia.

We left but we didn't drive far. The rain made driving a real hazard, so I stopped at the first number one lucky motel that I saw, and we spent the night. The flight across the Atlantic had given Patti a little sore throat. Ruby gave her a baby aspirin and rocked her to sleep on the side of the bed. Rebecca was asleep when she lay down on the bed. Ruby and I turned in plenty tired.

The next day we had an early breakfast of ham and eggs and then hit the road. I found the Lee highway, and, except for gas and food stops, we didn't stop driving until we rolled into Grundy, Virginia. We drove into the driveway at the Liza Lee place at about eleven o'clock that night and mom and dad were waiting for us. They had heard the car turn into the driveway, and they had the coffee pot hot. They turned on the porch light and helped us get the babies out of the chill of the night.

We did a lot of talking to bring everyone up to date on our recent endeavors. Mother and Ruby talked about the new baby. Dad told me about business and what my siblings were doing. My brother, Keith, was getting ready to graduate from dental school in Richmond and he was coming back to Grundy to help my father, who had practiced dentistry for forty years on three generations of patients. My father welcomed the assistance that my brother would bring to his patients. My sister, Lois, and her husband, Andrew Calvin Baird, were living in Rossville, Georgia. Calvin had just graduated from the University of Tennessee with a master's degree in marketing and was employed as a salesman for the Cumberland Case company in Chattanooga. Lois had quit teaching school when Calvin graduated, and she was raising two children of her own. We turned in about one o'clock that morning.

The next morning, the visit started all over again at the breakfast table. We finished breakfast and I wanted to see about getting my car's leaking radiator fixed. The leak in the radiator had started when we were in Europe on the vacation where we crossed the Augsburg pass from Switzerland to Austria. The temperature gauge had gone full hot, and I had gotten some honey or "stop leak" to remedy the situation at the time. I now wanted to have the puzzling leak fixed while I was at home.

My wife visited with her father and mother over at Rose Ann, Virginia about ten miles south of Grundy. I went up to Riverside

Pontiac and had the Arringtons investigate my radiator problem. They showed me a cracked block. I told them to replace the motor with a short block. It only cost $254 to handle the short block and repair the radiator. When my car was ready, my mother and mother-in-law took Ruby over to Bristol, Virginia to do some shopping. They helped her spend $400 on much-needed clothes for her and the children.

**CHAPTER 26**

# 1738<sup>th</sup> Jet Delivery Group (Kelly AFB, Texas)

When my leave was over and it was time to head to my next assignment at the 1738th Jet Delivery Group, I picked up my wife and children in Grundy and we headed west for Texas. I stopped in Knoxville and visited my Aunt Lottie and Uncle Frank Davis with whom we spent the night. We drove on to Chattanooga and spent the night with my sister Lois and her husband Calvin. We drove on to Memphis and spent the next night there. Our next stop was in Dallas, where we spent the night with my cousin, Taylor Dixon, his wife Dorothy, and their three little boys. The following day, we drove to Kelly Field in San Antonio, Texas.

We drove to the officers club and found everything to our liking. The personnel and the golf course were very inviting. Billy Mitchell Village was an ideal apartment complex located right across from the officers club. The complex had just been completed and offered furnished or unfurnished apartments. We rented a furnished apartment.

*Harold beside his Uncle Frank Davis's*
*Fire Engine – Knoxville, TN – 1955*

I signed in at the big hangar which housed the famous 1738 Jet Delivery Group, which was attached to military air transport service for worldwide logistical purposes and chain of command. The group had been formed at Long Beach Airport in Los Angeles, California for the purpose of flying new jet fighters to the Fighter commands in the field directly from the manufacturers, which were located primarily in California. However, as the group grew to some one hundred pilots, the command relocated the group to the beautiful facilities at Kelly Air Force Base. Some especially important personalities were assigned to this group because of its diverse mission, which provided a wonderful opportunity to travel worldwide to the far-flung air bases around the globe. General Vandenberg's son had pulled a tour with this organization. The group not only took new aircraft to the far-flung bases, but they brought the older aircraft back to California for overhaul to be dispensed to our national air guard units scattered throughout the states. Some of these older aircraft were delivered to our allies around the world. Although the group was primarily concerned with jet fighters, the group delivered many conventional and multi engine aircraft as well.

Colonel Archibald Chatterley introduced himself to me as I signed in. He then introduced me to the rest of the cadre. I found the operations officer, as well as the rest of the staff to be highly professional. Colonel Chatterley explained to me that I would get all the travel that I wanted on the 'high flight' routes to Europe and South America. He said there would be plenty of group deliveries as well as individual deliveries. I couldn't wait to get started!

Colonel Chatterley introduced me to an instructor pilot who would check me out in the F-86 that day. The instructor was formally with the 36th Fighter Bomber Wing in Germany. We reviewed the normal and emergency procedures and got the tail numbers of two Sabres. We walked out to the aircraft with our personal flight gear as the instructor explained the ground procedures to be followed in the transition area. We blasted off and went through the paces. We engaged in a little private dogfight just to keep us sharp in actual combat situations and I got on his tail quickly by a gambling maneuver. We came in, landed, and went into the operation hangar to fill out the rest of the training papers and to critique the fight. My instructor complimented me on my proficiency in the Sabre.

Colonel Chatterley and I had a cup of coffee and discussed the mission of the group and how it worked harmoniously with manufacturers, as well as with strange units all over the world. He told me that this organization would stay intact until the new fighters, such as the new Super Sabre Jets, were in the field. They were due to get several new supersonic aircraft soon. The conversation segued into a cook's tour of the attractions and the social opportunities in the historic San Antonio area. Colonel Chatterley also covered the nice eating, shopping, and recreational facilities in the area. Finally, we got into where we were born and where we went to school. We dovetailed our careers right down to match each other's statistics. The instructor noted his watch and told me that we had a big flying safety meeting coming up that afternoon. He said that I was in luck because the subject was "The new Super Sabre and You." The Super Sabre F-100 aircraft was very new in concept, and there were very few experienced pilots in the new aircraft. The instructor excused himself and told me to report to the flying safety meeting after lunch.

*F-100 Super Sabre Jet – 1956*

We were going to receive the new F-100 Super Sabre aircraft to train the local pilots. The local pilots could then deliver the new aircraft to the units in the field. Some of the instructor pilots had already checked out in the F-100 C aircraft at Edwards Air Force Base in the high desert near Palmdale, California. In fact, some of the pilots were in transition at Nellis Air Force Base in Nevada at that time getting a formal two-week course in the F-100 D. Nellis was the advanced fighter training base, so it was natural that they would receive the new advanced fighter first. The course included the mobile training unit, as well as the flight training.

Command had decided that not all of us were going to be able to go to Nellis for two weeks to get the formal course. The pilots who got the formal course would check us out after we went through the mobile training course. Training Command would send the mobile training course to Kelly Air Force Base.

The lecture and the safety meeting centered around the F-100 D, which we would be flying soon. The aircraft was the first aircraft in the inventory that would exceed the speed of sound in straight and level flight. One of the F-100 D's had been flown in for us to see that day. The F-100 aircraft had a long snout of a nose, and the intake was small for that size aircraft. The pitot tube was at least ten feet long, and looked like it was made from one inch pipe. The wings were swept and low mounted. The tail was also swept, and the elevator was a flying elevator. That meant that stick pressures would be sensitive to small movement, because so much surface moved as one piece. The aircraft was a tall aircraft with five feet long landing gear. You needed a real ladder to climb up to the cockpit. The aircraft had a twin spool engine with an afterburner. The F-100 aircraft had some characteristics that had to be reckoned with if one wanted to survive. The aircraft did the job, but it had a few hitches that you had to learn before you blasted off. These subjects were covered at length at the course at Nellis, but at Kelly AFB, the pilots got a quick review in the flying safety meeting. If the pilot missed the flying safety meeting, then he would learn what the term "intrepid airmen" meant in flight.

The F-100 aircraft performed well at high speeds. However, at low speeds, the aircraft was cumbersome because of its weight and the slow acceleration of the twin spool engine. The flying tail gave the aircraft quick response at high speeds but could result in over control at takeoff and landing speeds. The flaps were described as "drag flaps." That is, they were to be used to regulate the descent and slow the landing speed. The flaps were so large that they could not be used for takeoff or go around procedures. The greater sensitivity of the flying tail could result in either a smooth takeoff with gentle back pressure on the stick or, if the pilot used too much back pressure, he could begin to porpoise on takeoff with all tires blown and a dangerous subsequent landing on three stubs with directional control problems and a possible fire or collapsed gear.

There were additional dangerous characteristics of the F-100. If the pilot did not know about the slow acceleration rate of the twin spool engine and tried to go around with full flaps, he could end up losing his life as well as the aircraft. Also, the F-100 had a four second delay in feeding fuel to the afterburner. This time delay could cause the loss of several miles of air speed, which could drop the aircraft behind the flying power curve and cause the plane to stall, which would be fatal anywhere in the traffic pattern with the F-100.

Because of the thin wings on the F-100, the plane had to be flown at such a high angle of pitch at low speeds, that the pilots had to always use 100% oxygen to keep from being poisoned by the carbon monoxide fuel which was pulled into the cockpit by the engine. There was also a critical touchdown speed for the F-100. If the pilot did not touch down between 150 and 165 knots, he ran into one of two problems. If he touched down at lower speeds, he would cause the tail skid to be knocked up through the afterburner, causing major damage to the aircraft. If the pilot touched down at faster speeds, he would cause the brakes to heat excessively if the drag shoot did not deploy. The magnesium brakes could ignite, and the fire could run up the brake fluid hose on the landing gear and cause the pilot to lose all brakes. Or even worse, the fire could cause the fuel drop tanks to explode. In short, the aircraft was nice, but only if you handled it correctly. You could enjoy the advantages of the aircraft, if you kept abreast of the few characteristics that could cause some quick headaches. The flying safety officer covered these points extremely well.

Next, the flying safety officer began to describe incidents which involved the neglect of these critical points. The first point was made by recounting the experience of the British Viceroy of the Air Ministry, who came to Dallas to check out in the F-100. He took a few hours of instruction and then summarily dismissed his instructor pilot as of no further use to him in his training program. The Viceroy had many hours of fighter bomber flying time. However, he let his airspeed get too low on final approach in the F-100 and subsequently crashed with the loss of the aircraft and a valuable pilot.

Next, we viewed a film depicting another unfortunate incident. One of the group pilots was scheduled to pick up an F-100 at the Palmdale plant and deliver it to Nellis Air Force Base in Las Vegas, Nevada. The pilot was a second lieutenant who had completed a successful check out program in the F-100 at Nellis Air Force Base only a short time before the flight. The pilot made his pre-flight inspection of the F-100 and climbed into the cockpit. He fired up, taxied to the runway, and blasted off. However, when the pilot attempted to pull the gear up, the nose wheel would not retract into the nose wheel well. The pilot notified the Palmdale Tower that he was going to return to the field and make a fly by to allow the tower operator to observe the gear with field glasses to see if the gear was down and, whether it was safe for the pilot to land and have the gear inspected by the crew chief. The tower operator observed the three landing gear and noted that the nose wheel scissor joint had not been connected before takeoff. This joint allowed the nose wheel to rotate 90° to either side when the aircraft was being towed by a tug by the ground personnel. The pilot was supposed to have caught the unconnected scissor joint during his walk around inspection, but he didn't. The tow personnel should have connected it up when they finished towing the aircraft out of the hangar, but they didn't. Therefore, a pilot was currently airborne with a problem. A B-47 was coming into Palmdale in an emergency, so the ground crew had a camera set up to monitor the B-47 landing. Since the F-100 had less fuel supply, it was given number one priority to land before the B-47. The F-100 approach was on camera. The pilot made an approach but found that he was landing too far down the runway, so he elected to take the aircraft around. He was too low on airspeed, so he elected to utilize the afterburner. The four second delay of the opening eyelids put the aircraft behind the power curve. The pilot had to touchdown or stall. He lost directional control of the aircraft at the high angle of attack that he was maintaining. The aircraft veered to the left of the runway as it was trying to fly. The pilot couldn't touchdown in the desert or couldn't see what was going on at this point. The airspeed dropped below flying speed and the aircraft stalled or dropped to the ground in a right wing low position. The wing struck the sand first and the aircraft disintegrated. The tumble resulted in an explosion. The pilot was thrown clear of the aircraft, but the force of the crash caused his body to be pulled under his seatbelt, which caught his neck. He died of suffocation.

The next day was Saturday and the commander had scheduled a golf tournament at the club for us to get to know each other better. We were paired off in groups of four, consisting of two new pilots and two pilots who had been at Kelly for some time. It had rained that morning and there were puddles of water on the course. Most of us were duffers, but the puddles caused some consternation in the better players. I didn't know the difference between a water trap and a sand trap. I shot my balls out of the water just like I would shoot one out of a sand trap. Unbelievably, I hit a ball in about two inches of water and the ball popped on the green near the hole. My flight had the lowest score and we won. We didn't even think we were in contention. The commander had the chef broil steaks after the golf match and our wives and children got to know one another.

The next Monday, I received my first delivery order. I was told to take an F-86F from Kelly Field to Tucson, Arizona. Tucson had a stockpile of surplus aircraft, which were destined for future use, future sale in whole or in part, or future placement in a scrapyard.

My designated aircraft was clean with no drop tanks. The sky was big and blue with no clouds anywhere. I called the weather station, which reported that El Paso was clear and had seventy miles visibility. Based upon my experience with the F-86, I knew that I could make El Paso my first stop. My knowledge of the aircraft enabled me to figure range and fuel on my rules of thumb. I would be making a maximum range fight, but this was certainly doable with the weather clear and seventy with no forecast of change for one hour after my expected arrival time. I had a crew chief top off the fuel tanks and then check the oil and oxygen. I filled out my flight progress card and filed my flight plan with base operations. I picked up my personal equipment and took a change of clothes along with my shaving kit. I had been designated a transportation officer, so I could return to Kelly AFB from any point along the route if I needed. I could use this "go home free card" in the event the aircraft was not ready to go, or it went out of commission, or there were no military aircraft readily available to catch at my destination.

I saddled up the blue iron horse and blasted off into the wild blue yonder. The wind was moving west to east, and a pilot could count on losing one mile per minute in ground speed when headed west. On the other hand, a pilot picked up one mile per minute when he traveled east.

I was sailing over west Texas looking down where the hill country gives way to the desert oilfields. I flew at the maximum altitude, which gave me maximum range, maximum speed, and maximum visibility. A jet uses less than one-third the fuel at altitude than it uses on the deck. As I continued my westerly course, I could see 200 miles, but I could not make out small objects on the ground. I was intensely studying the geography of the ground, looking for signs of the river, the highways, and the different colors of the terrain as the moisture table fell. I had a good Del Rio, Texas radio program playing on the low frequency radio. As I got about three-quarters of the way to El Paso, I thought about a safety bulletin that I had read about a Navy pilot letting down through a hole while enroute to El Paso, but finding out that he was further from El Paso than he thought. He had to eject due to lack of fuel. I told myself that I had eliminated that possibility when I devised a system whereby I didn't let down until I had station passage on my low frequency radio.

As I approached El Paso, I noticed a brown dust band in the atmosphere at altitudes of twenty to thirty thousand feet. I instantly thought of a sandstorm like I had seen in Tripoli. I just hoped that it had already passed El Paso. I radioed El Paso and they had closed the airport due to a wide sandstorm on the field. The tower operator had the airlines holding on different radio fixes in the area. I was committed and had to land in El Paso. I had the required twenty minutes of fuel remaining over my destination when flying in VFR conditions. However, the sandstorm not only changed the El Paso situation, but it messed up any alternate airport within 200 miles of El Paso, which was twenty minutes by jet.

I devised a plan to get into the field even with little or no visibility. I would corkscrew down over the airbase from altitude. Sometimes, a pilot can see down through restrictions of visibility, but cannot see forward once he gets into it. I ascertained that I could get into the field before I left altitude. I had two alternate plans if I could not get into the field. I could fly towards an alternate airport until I ran out of fuel, then glide the rest of the way. The second alternative would have been to circle the field at altitude at a low fuel setting and hope that the storm subsided by the time I got down to the landing strip.

I could have flown an instrument approach, but sometimes the ground controller takes twenty minutes to get permission for a pilot to make a landing approach below weather "minimums." Sometimes, the restricted visibility affects the accuracy of the controller's equipment, and the wind can also knock out their instruments, which are designed for multi engine aircraft with a lot of fuel. Of course, a pilot can always declare an emergency, but that frequently causes panic and mistakes. I just chose the surest and fastest way. I would use the other alternatives if I got lost in the soup at low altitudes. I made my initial high key on schedule just like any other flameout pattern approach. I touched down like a painting and taxied to the refueling area. I got out and told the ground crew to refuel me, while I ran over to the snack bar and grabbed a sandwich. I had a glass of milk and a fried ham sandwich with lettuce and tomatoes on toast, and then I returned to the flight line. The sandstorm had passed to the east and my aircraft was ready to go.

I saddled up the Iron Horse and blasted off towards Tucson. The weather was clear all the way to Tucson. I let down in Tucson and landed at Davis Monthan airport without further incident. I taxied over to the depository and pulled the bird into the parking spot in the desert, where it would remain until needed or sold. I caught a ride back to base ops with the ground crew. A staff cab took me to the airport.

I grabbed a Continental Airlines flight to El Paso and then on to San Antonio that night. The flight attendants were friendly and efficient. The food was good, and the trip was generally pleasant. However, I told myself that I would catch American Airlines to Dallas and on to San Antonio the next trip. Strangely enough, it did not cost any more to fly to San Antonio via Dallas than it did to fly to Dallas via El Paso. The government was paying, but I had to answer for everything and fall within the guidelines.

I called my wife from the airport, and she came and picked me up. I realized that I would be doing a lot of traveling and, thus, we might need two cars. Sometimes the pilots in the 1738th Jet Delivery

Group would be sent away for six or eight weeks at a time to Palmdale, California to shuttle aircraft to and from Warner Robins Air Force Base, Georgia.

The next day we went into our mobile training unit for the F-100. We studied the systems for about three days and filled out the questionnaires. We were then ready for the aircraft, and I was scheduled for a chase ride the following day. The next day, I had started my taxi to the runway when I discovered that my oxygen regulator was not operating properly. I signaled the instructor pilot that I was returning to the parking ramp to get another aircraft or get the regulator repaired or replaced. We returned to the starting line and shut down. The F-100 was easy to taxi with that nose wheel steering. The crew chief replaced the oxygen regulator, and we taxied out again. The tower cleared me into position, and I rolled onto the runway on the left side. My instructor rolled up in formation beside me on my right wing. I gave him the run up signal and the nod of execution. After I had rolled about fifty feet, we kicked in the afterburner, and I was welded to the back of the seat as that "Going Jesse" accelerated down the runway. I had the trim tabs in the neutral position. The aircraft took off itself and all I had to do was maintain a little directional control and keep the wings level. We had to get the gear up quickly before we exceeded the gear down speed. We got to altitude in a couple of minutes, came out of the afterburner, and went out to the transition area where we put the aircraft through her paces. She was good at speeds, but she was a "one pass" aircraft and didn't respond well during high altitude aerobatics. When I pulled too many G forces, the wind to the intake choked off.

The aircraft had the engine located in the central part of the aircraft frame. This caused the aircraft to have a tendency for a flat spin, so I didn't practice any spins in this "horse." The instructor pilot asked me if I wanted to go out over the gulf and break the sound barrier and I told him that I had already experienced the "other side of the wall." I came on in and shot a couple of "touch and goes" (landings without stopping but taking off again while rolling down the runway). That aircraft was a real "dog" in the traffic pattern. With all I had been told, I still couldn't believe how sluggish that aircraft was in the traffic pattern. I could see how critical it was not to let the engine go below 85% of full power. It was a "killer" if you did. The bird landed well, but it required a flat approach. Once the pilot got the wheels on the ground and popped the drag chute, he was "in business."

However, there was a caveat to popping the chute. It should never be deployed in a cross wind because the plane could be pulled off the runway. If the pilot could not deploy the drag chute, he had to rely strictly on the brakes to stop. That meant that the pilot would have to land at speeds which were recommended to stop without overheating the brakes. In fact, the originally designed full power brake had to be discarded early, because the pilots were balding the tires without realizing it. When the chute deployed, the pilot's feet and body weight shifted to the front. The weight of the pilot's shoes was enough to lock the brakes. We had a few minor incidents before the investigators revealed the cause. As a result, the engineering officer redesigned the brakes and put pulsating brakes on the drums. When the pilot landed with these brakes, the brakes would hold and release intermittently no matter how hard the pilot pressed on the foot pedals. That was the solution. My instructor and I landed, taxied into the ramp, and shut down. The instructor pilot gave me my critique and we discussed the emergency procedures. He checked me out on the training forms.

The next day, I reported to the operations hangar. I was scheduled to fly to Palmdale, California to shuttle some new F-100 D's to Warner Robins Air Force Base, Georgia. Palmdale was 37 miles from Los

Angeles. I would be spending the entire week out there. Four of us pilots grabbed American Airlines for Los Angeles. We were met at the Palmdale terminal by North American representatives in their company cars. They took us into the customer relations receiving quarters. I had never seen quarters more plush at a business establishment. The quarters must have been designed for the multi-million dollar buyers. We were introduced to our department heads, and our schedule was worked out while we had refreshments. We would spend the weekend in California and start our deliveries on Monday. The company issued us a green company car and we had rooms reserved in the Holiday Inn at Azusa near Pasadena.

We left those big green soft lounge chairs, loaded up in the green company car, drove to Azusa, and checked into our rooms. We cleaned up and decided to take in the "big city." The weather was sunny, warm, and beautiful. We motored over to the freeway and joined the "mad dash" for LA. We were clipping along on the freeway at 85 mph when a police officer pulled us over. I thought he was going to cite us for speeding. However, it was almost dark, and the police officer only gave the driver a warning for having an inoperative taillight. We rejoined the dragsters in the "California 500" on the freeway. We took in a few places in Los Angeles and then found a nice place to eat in Fontana. We turned in after eating.

The next morning, we ate and went over to the golf course for eighteen holes. After we finished golfing, we returned to our rooms and cleaned up. We ate at the motel this time. After eating, we drove over to Apple Valley to visit the Apple Valley Inn. We looked over the high desert for a while, then we drove down to Palm Springs to tour the place before returning to the motel for the night.

The next morning, we ate breakfast and drove into Big Bear Lake in the San Bernardino mountains. We toured the mountains before driving back down into the valley to visit the officers club at

Riverside Air Force Base, California. We left the club when it closed and drove back to the motel for the night.

The next morning, we ate early, drove back to Palmdale, and reported into the North American reception center. Our committee took us out to the big hangar where our new aircraft were parked. I was surprised to see a big black experimental X-15 sitting outside. The X-15 would fly twice the speed of sound and I thought that it would be hidden in a closed hangar. The monster X-15 looked like a rocket with wheels. The B-52 which hauled the X-15 aloft for release was sitting beside the X-15. I was fascinated by the presence of these history-making machines. Suddenly, I felt close to the project.

Our liaison officer gave us the paperwork and the tail numbers for our new aircraft. We had our parachutes and our jet helmets with us in our parachute bag. We walked over to our aircraft and stowed our luggage and strapped into the cockpit. We fired up and blasted off for Oklahoma City.

The F-100's were real "hustlers." We climbed to altitude in the afterburner. We were flying on another beautiful day and the visibility was clear and 200 miles. We roared across the countryside looking down on the globe like we were in a balloon studying the earth's surface. We arrived over Oklahoma City, where we landed and deployed our drag chutes once we were rolling down the runway. We jettisoned our drag chutes as we turned off the active runway onto the taxi finger. We shut down and climbed out of the cockpit to the concrete ramp. I told the ground crew to fill the aircraft up with high test jet fuel, refill the liquid oxygen bottles, and bring the oil up to full. We also asked the ground crew to re-pack the chute or to issue us a couple of chutes which were already packed. We took a staff car over to the officers club to eat. We went down to the post exchange after dinner, then called the flight line to see if our aircraft were ready to go. We caught a ride to the flight line with another pilot whom we had met.

We checked over our aircraft and blasted off to Warner Robins Air Force Base, Georgia. We didn't want to spend the night at Warner Robins, because the base was isolated from the big city. I noted how green the vegetation was across the southern United States as we blazed across the sky. We made it to Warner Robins without any delay and gave the paperwork to the engineering officer. We talked him into providing us with transportation to the commercial airport in Macon in time to catch the evening flight to Atlanta. We caught the feeder Southern Airlines to Atlanta, where we changed over to an American Airlines flight back to California. On the flight to California, I retired to the rear lounge to write postcards to my family and friends. The postcards were free, courtesy of the airlines. After I wrote to everyone that I could think of, I went back to my seat and took a little nap. The flight attendants woke us up when we were starting our descent to the Los Angeles International Airport. We looked outside and saw the lights of the metropolis of Los Angeles, covering around 100 square miles. I could just make out the coastline and the beach from the light pattern. The pilots on the airline were truly professionals and we landed with a nice, soft touchdown. We picked up our bags at the baggage counter and caught a cab to the Plaza Hotel in Hollywood, since we had missed the last Bonanza feeder airlines to Palmdale that night. The hotel had a swimming pool and the rooms cost seven dollars.

The next morning after breakfast, I bought shark skin swimming trunks and went swimming in the pool. I figured that if I was paying for a pool, then I was obligated to use it. I was the only one who used the pool that morning, but I was fresh and ready for the Bonanza flight when we caught the cab to the airport.

We made the Bonanza flight to Palmdale where the North American liaison officer was right there on the spot to take care of us again. We picked up our two F-100's and blasted off for

Warner Robins with a refueling stop at Kirtland Air Force Base, in Albuquerque, New Mexico. We couldn't land just anywhere with these F-100's, because only certain bases had the capacity to service the aircraft with liquid oxygen and drag chute packing. We were late getting off at Palmdale due to an assembly line stoppage. When we got to altitude it was dusk. I was leading the element as we were chasing the sun. The sky looked dark ahead, but we could still see the ground by looking back over the wing. My wingman reported that his airspeed indicator had dropped to zero. He first thought that he was losing air speed and was going to stall out. My airspeed indicator and Mach needle indicated that we were proceeding normally, but I realized that we would have a problem if the atmospheric conditions caused a similar malfunction on my aircraft. We were not too far from Kirtland Air Force Base, but after a few minutes, my airspeed indicator started fluctuating from 350 knots to 250 knots. I told my wingman that I now had his problem, but he told me that his indicator had started working normally again. I ordered him to take over as lead aircraft. I was going to try to fly his wing and get down on the ground without an airspeed indicator.

In a few minutes, his airspeed indicator went on the blink again. Strangely enough, my airspeed indicator started working normally again. I again took over the lead position and radioed Kirtland Field asking them to have base operations have a T-33 standing by ready to take off and let us fly its wing in to land if our air speed indicators continued to malfunction. We started our letdown for Kirtland. When we came down on final approach, I saw that my wingman could make it without my continued assistance, so I told him to land. I went around and landed on my next pass without further incident. We taxied into the transient parking apron and had the ground crew check out our pitot systems, but they could find nothing wrong. That phenomenon was common with ground checks. We surmised that some sand had gotten into the pitot tube and the moisture at altitude had momentarily blocked passage of the air until the pitot heat system dried out the moisture. Kirtland did not have extra drag chutes, so we had to wait on the night shift to pack the drag chutes. We caught a ride back to the flight line when the club closed at one o'clock in the morning. We drilled through the night until we reached Warner Robins. I began my letdown so that we could land in VFR conditions before the fog set in. I could see the sky turning to buttermilk as we let down. The temperature dew point spread was approaching two degrees.[1] That clear sky could disappear in a hurry when a warm sea breeze came through and met the cooler air. We got down not a minute too soon. That base was socked in by the time we taxied to the parking apron and shut down. We crawled out of the cockpit and took the paperwork into the engineering officer's office. We were stuck for the night, so we walked over to the officers' BOQ and checked in for the rest of the night.

The next day, we caught the commercial flight back to California. Our American Airlines flight landed at Dallas enroute to California. We ran into one of the jet pilots from Tinker Air Force Base in Oklahoma City, who was going to Palmdale to pick up an F-100 F. I had flown with him in France. He told me that his base had strict regulations which required a long check out procedure for the two

---

1 Fog forms when the difference between air temperature and dew point is less than 2.5°C (4.5°F). The dewpoint of a parcel of air is the temperature at which an air parcel would need to be cooled to become completely saturated with moisture (a cloud would form, or in more proper terms, the air can no longer hold the moisture). If the temperature and dewpoint are close together, then the air has lots of moisture in it. If the temperature and dewpoint are the same, then you likely have fog, low visibility, lots of clouds, etc. since the air is saturated and now the moisture that was a gas is becoming a liquid (and visible). *See,* FLY8MA Online Flight Training, *WeatherXplore Temperature-Dewpoint Spread.*

seater F-100 F. We talked over old times as we traveled to Los Angeles, California. Then we caught Bonanza Airline over to Palmdale. By the time we got off the airline in Palmdale, we had filled each other in on our activities between Chaumont and Palmdale.

When I went out to get my next aircraft, I saw that it was the two seater F-100 F. I climbed up the ladder and reviewed the two cockpits. I stowed the second cockpit and had the tech representative explain any significant differences of the aircraft in the normal and emergency procedures. The only difference was the method of closing the canopy. I fired up and we taxied out for takeoff. My friend saw us about to leave, so he radioed me requesting permission to tack on to our flight, making it a flight of three. In this manner, he would not have to file a flight plan. I answered in the affirmative since we were scheduled to land at Tinker Air Force Base anyway.

We blasted off and went into spread formation as we sailed across the continent to Tinker and entered the traffic pattern in the normal fashion. We landed and climbed out of the cockpit. I went over to my friend and kidded him a little about the "long" checkout procedure in the F-100 F. I told him that I had never seen one of those two seaters before that flight. I asked him to sign me off in the F-100 F in a check out form. He said he would, but he would have to use the name of one of our "mutual friends." We laughed about the incident, and it was quickly forgotten. He took us over to visit with a couple of the other pilots that I knew in France. They looked well enough, but I had the exciting assignment, and I knew it. I thanked him for his assistance, and we went back to our aircraft, which had been refueled and had the drag chutes re-packed. We saddled up and blasted off to Warner Robins on a direct flight plan.

We arrived at Robins on schedule and landed. We caught another ride back to the commercial airport with one of the pilots. We boarded Southern Airways, and the airlines whisked us to Atlanta.

We landed in Atlanta and caught the American Airline flight back to California. We got off the plane in Los Angeles and checked into the Plaza Hotel for the night.

The next morning, we caught the Bonanza flight over to Palmdale. We picked up two more F-100 D's. We were told to deliver these aircraft to Kelly Air Force Base, Texas. We blasted off on a direct flight to Kelly. On the climb out, my oxygen system began to malfunction. I leveled off at ten thousand feet and we flew at low altitude to Kirtland Air Force Base, New Mexico. We landed at Kirtland and had the ground crew check out my oxygen system. They did not have the required parts, so I elected to fly on to Kelly at low altitude. We flew to Kelly without incident, and I delivered the paperwork to the operations officer. I told him about the oxygen system, and he told me that the fumes could have slipped up on me in that situation in the F-100. I went home that day with the biggest headache that I had ever had. My headache must have been a delayed reaction to those fumes.

The next morning, the operations officer gave me instructions to proceed to Port Columbus, Ohio to pick up an F-100 KD. I called "Uncle" Bill Sexton's son, Leon, who was a technical representative for North American on F-100's at Columbus, and told him to meet me at the airport, so we could have a little chat while I was in town. He said that he would be waiting for my commercial flight to arrive. I called "Uncle" Bill Sexton's other son, Bert, and told him that I would be in Columbus overnight and I wanted to have dinner with him, his wife, and his family. I had not seen Bert since I left Garrett, Kentucky over twenty years earlier. Bert told me that he would meet me at the hotel and would reserve a room for me that night.

I boarded American Airlines for the flight to Nashville, where I caught a feeder airline to Columbus. Leon was waiting for me at the airport. We drove over to the hotel and caught up on the news. He left me at the hotel and told me that he would pick me up the next morning and take me to Port Columbus. He wanted to give me a tour of the plant. He said that Charlie McClanahan from Grundy was working on the F-100 assembly line at the plant. We planned to surprise him on the job.

Bert Sexton and his wife, Mae, came over to the hotel with her son. We had dinner and caught up on twenty years of news about each other and our families. Bert and his family had to work the next day, so I told them to turn in early.

The next day, Leon came over to the hotel and picked me up. We drove out to Port Columbus and went through the plant until we found Charles working on the wing section of an F-100. We chatted with him briefly and then I went to the flight line.

There was a message for me on the bulletin board telling me to fly the F-100 back to Kelly Field immediately, instead of taking her to Warner Robins. I saddled up with a full load of fuel even though the liaison officer did not want me to get a full load of fuel because someone had recently hit a crane while taking off from Port Columbus with a full load of fuel. I needed a full load to get me to San Antonio nonstop and, besides, the crane had been moved. I saddled up and blasted off for San Antonio on a direct flight plan. I zipped down to Kelly Field in short order and landed.

After landing at Kelly, I went into the operations hangar where the operations officer told me that we were going to fly commercially to England and pick up eleven or twelve Sabre jets and fly them back across the Atlantic to storage facilities in Tucson, Arizona. He told me to go over to the personnel equipment training pool and get checked out in the moon space suits. I drove over to the indoor pool and reported to the training officer. He helped me and some other pilots into the fire fighter-like suits. They were made from light rubber and were a hassle to get into. The neck was the only place that air could get air into the suit. They were hot and dehydrating. We leapt into the swimming pool and splashed around a bit to get the feel of the suit in the water. Then we had to practice riding a twenty-man rubber life raft, turning it over, and then righting the boat. Everyone took turns turning the boat over. When my turn came, the instructor left the room for a telephone call. I flipped the boat over towards me and it came down over my head. I had to fight the tendency to panic. There was an air pocket under the boat, but the rubber suit made it a challenge to get my head underwater enough to swim out from under the capsized raft. I finally started going up and down to get my head underwater far enough to swim out from under the raft. I climbed out of the pool and took off my moon suit. I was oriented.

The next morning, I reported to the operations hangar. Our commanding officer, Colonel Archibald Chatterley, and the operations officer, Major "Cactus" Jack Wiley, were also going on the reverse high flight. Eleven of us boarded an American Airlines plane at San Antonio and flew to New York LaGuardia Airport. We deplaned and caught a limousine over to New York's International Airport. We went through customs and boarded Pan-American Airways on the double Decker C-97 aircraft. The aircraft took off on a direct course for Shannon, Ireland. We went downstairs to the bar after dinner with the three flight attendants and had a few more refreshments. We came back upstairs and went to sleep in our laid-back seats. We were letting down at Shannon when the flight attendants woke us up. We landed briefly at Shannon and refueled before taking off for London. When we landed in London, we went through customs and boarded a British feeder airline to Prestwick, Scotland, where the bus took us to Glasgow. We checked into the hotel, cleaned up, and went out for a visit to the Colosseum.

The next morning, we test hopped several of the aircraft. The liaison officer only wanted to put fifty gallons in the tips, but I eventually persuaded him to allow me to fill my tips completely.

I blasted off on a local flight and went through the usual checks. Everything checked out except for the fact that the drop tanks would not start to feed until the internal tanks were about halfway down. I noted this discrepancy in the Form One after I landed.

We had to stay overnight in Glasgow again to get the remaining aircraft test flown the next day. The next day we got all the aircraft tested. My aircraft was signed off as corrected on the drop tank discrepancy. We all saddled up and blasted off in flights of four, except for the last flight of three. By the time we climbed out on course and leveled off at Stornoway beacon enroute for Iceland, I saw that my drop tanks were not feeding as they should have been. I figured out how long I could continue with the group before I had to decide to return to Scotland if my drop tanks did not begin to feed. I was about to turn around when the drop tanks finally began to feed.

We continued onward towards Keflavík, Iceland and made our radio check at Point Charlie to the circling SA 16 air rescue aircraft. We saw a lot of fishing boats just before we spotted land. We were glad to see Iceland because our fuel supply was limited at that point. The westerly winds cut our ground speed by about sixty miles an hour. We had an alternate landing base of Reykjavik, but it was so close to Keflavík, that it would have been socked in as well, if weather had moved into the area. The weather was beautifully clear and sunny just like the weatherman said it would be. We landed at Keflavík, taxied to the ramp, and shut down for the night. We caught the blue bus to the BOQ and checked into our room.

We cleaned up and headed for the post exchange. That post exchange had everything! The Americans were trying to impress the Icelandic visitors with the PX. Everyone was buying gifts for their friends back in the states, because the prices were so low and there were no taxes. I realized that I had so many friends that I would have to think of a gift that would serve an entire family. I spotted some

Schatz eight-day clocks, and I had several sent to my family and relatives on that flight. Eventually, I would purchase 119 of these clocks for my friends during subsequent flights.

When the weather was clear at our next stop, Bluie West One or Narsarsuaq, Greenland, we blasted off for that stop, and then continued on to Goose Bay, Labrador, and then Presque Isle, Maine, where we went through customs.

One of the other pilots wanted to exchange aircraft with me. I shouldn't have gone for the change, but trying to get along, I agreed. His aircraft had an inoperative navigational radio. I wrote the discrepancy up in the Form One at Presque Isle. While the ground crew was checking the circuits in the nose bay, they broke a latch. They wanted me to go back to Kelly AFB on a commercial airline. I protested vigorously and they used sheet-metal to replace the latch while we waited. We refueled and blasted off for Andrews Air Force Base, Washington DC. We flew over the "Big Apple" in spread formation and made it to Andrews around dusk.

We landed at Andrews for refueling. I noted that my navigational radio had not been repaired, even though the Form One indicated that it had ground checked OK. I began to see that the ground crews were "passing the buck" on the write ups. They would ground check OK and hope that they never saw the pilot again. This way they would make the pilot get the item fixed at the next destination. I insisted that a new radio be put in the aircraft, and I had to call the Major, who was at his home off base, to get it done.

Now that we were safe from the overwater perils, the commander decided to allow us to modify our flight plan to our final destination of Arizona. For a job well done, he allowed us to fly to our respective home airports along the way and spend the night with our folks. I was the only one who wanted to go by Knoxville. The rest went the northern route to Arizona.

I had to wait until after dark to get the radio changed. I checked the radio on the ground, and it operated properly. The bird-dog needle and the ural null navigational aids worked. However, I had some concern about the static and humming noise that I heard on the radio. I still believed the ground crew had put the same radio back into the aircraft. I saddled up and taxied out for takeoff. The bird dog needle on the navigational radio was doing some "tall" searching. I figured that it must be static in the area. I would give it an airborne check shortly. I knew we had some weather moving into Andrews, and I had to get out of there before I was socked in for a day or two. I knew the weather was VFR at Knoxville and clear over the Mississippi River. So, I blasted off the runway at Andrews at about eight o'clock that evening. When I left the runway, I ran into some scud and was immediately on instruments on the climb out. Radar had me on the scope and gave me steers to one thousand feet on top. I didn't break out until I reached forty-three thousand feet where I leveled off and set up my cruise.

I tuned the navigational radio or bird-dog to the next station in route and noted my time and altitude. When my dead reckoning indicated that I was at my next checkpoint, the bird-dog needle did not pick up the signal. I tried the ural null navigational function, but it was also inoperative. I would have to depend on ground control intercept (GCI) to steer me to Knoxville.

I was too far out of Washington for their radar to pick me up. I was also too far out of Knoxville for the Knoxville CGI to pick me up. I continued on course until my dead reckoning indicated that I was over Bristol, Virginia, and I elected to let down through several layers of clouds. The thunderstorms were producing lightning strikes, which occasionally let me see through the thin layers of stratus clouds in between the heavy cells. I knew that I would be shy of Knoxville, but this would give me time to pinpoint myself and correct my course for Knoxville. The lightning led me on a northerly course during the letdown. When I broke out, I saw the lights from a town up ahead with a radio tower in the middle of it. Suddenly, the lights from the ground went out at once. I knew that a mountain had come between me and that town. I pulled up in the soup and put on full power at the same time. I had to climb back up on top and fly further towards Knoxville before trying another letdown.

I thought maybe the Knoxville radar could pick me up when I got closer. As I was climbing through the eighteen thousand feet marker, lightning suddenly struck the little radar nose cup on my Sabre jet. Everything looked all white at first. I had a hole in the glove on my left hand and I got a brief electrical shock from the lightning. When I was able to see again, everything looked red shaded. It took a while before I could interpret my flight instruments again. Fortunately for me, I was so proficient in the aircraft that I could hold the attitude by the seat of my pants until my sight recovered from the bolt of lightning flash. I continued my climb, but I noted that my inverter was inoperative. I also noted that my standby compass or Boy Scout compass was magnetized and would not move when I changed the headings. Now I was flying without any means of direction other than keeping the aircraft upright. I radioed Knoxville and reported my approximate position, my altitude, and my circumstances. They responded, but still could not pick my aircraft up on their radar scope. They dispatched two all-weather fighters from McGhee Tyson Airport to scramble aloft to see if they could intercept me in the event the GCI unit ever picked up my blip on the radar scope. I broke out at forty-four thousand feet this time and leveled off. I had to read the stars for directions. I looked for the Big Dipper, which would point me to the North Star. I found it and corrected my heading to the west.

I was hoping that radar would pick me up, or that I would fly into some open sky. Knoxville radar got a report from William,

West Virginia that a jet aircraft had just missed their commercial radio tower. This was our first clue as to my position. The Knoxville approach tower turned me over to Fort Campbell radar since I was in that vicinity. Fort Campbell picked up a blip, but it was too weak and too far out to positively identify me. I asked Fort Campbell tower to give me a steer to the airstrip based on the blip on their scope, after I made some identifying turns for them. They were still not positive, and they wanted me to contact Greenville Air Force Base, Mississippi, which had a more powerful radar search locator. I gave Fort Campbell a negative on this suggestion because my fuel was down to about ten minutes at this time. The weather began to look like the thunder bumps were disappearing and leaving only high stratus clouds below me. I was hopeful of flying into clear skies shortly.

I had two plans of action. If I didn't find Fort Campbell when I flew out of the weather, I would fly to the town with the most lights and circle it until I located an airstrip, towards which I could fly or glide depending on my fuel supply. If I didn't break out of the weather, I would have to eject. Air Rescue from Nashville called me on the command radio and asked me to build three fires close together if I ejected that night, so that their helicopters could locate me.

The Nashville weather was high overcast, and this gave me some more hope. Suddenly, I flew out of the weather into the clear. I looked down from that high altitude and it took me just a moment to discern the light patterns below. I thought I spotted Fort Campbell about thirty-five miles to the southwest of my position. I radioed the tower operator and asked him to flash the runway lights on and off at my command, so I could positively identify the airstrip. He complied and I identified the airstrip. I lowered the nose, chopped the power, and popped my speed boards. I had to leave the engine running to keep the canopy from fogging up when I hit that warm air at lower altitudes. I made a dead stick approach to the field. The runway was eleven thousand feet long so I couldn't miss from my altitude, even if my engine flamed out from lack of fuel. I hit my high key point on the nose. I slowed the aircraft, dropped the gear, and lowered the flaps while the engine was still running. I only had a couple of minutes of fuel remaining. I noticed the first third of the runway lights were out. I asked the tower if some kind of construction was in progress on the approach end of the runway. They told me that they had turned up the lights so bright that the bulbs in the first third had burned out earlier. I touched down like a painter stroking the canvas with a brush. I was able to taxi into the ramp and shut down before the fuel gauge hit zero.

The officer of the day met me at the aircraft as I climbed down the ladder and thanked him for his assistance. I asked him to close my flight plan and pass my thanks along to McGhee Tyson and Lieutenant Lindy Gill and his wingman, who had gone up on the scramble mission to try to find me earlier. I went to the club and had a "dust cutter" to get the dryness out of my throat. It was the Fourth of July weekend in 1955.

The next morning, I found that Fort Campbell did not have radio parts for Air Force jet aircraft. The maintenance crews with radio specialties were off on a Sunday picnic. I had the aircraft refueled, and I checked the standby compass. The magnetism had bled off the Boy Scout compass and the weather had moved out to the East Coast during the night. I elected to fly VFR to Knoxville on the clear and sunny day. I called my wife the night before and told her that I would call her from McGhee Tyson when I arrived there. She had driven home to visit the folks while I was on this "high flight." I blasted off and flew low level by dead reckoning and pilotage to Knoxville. I landed at McGhee Tyson and wrote the radio up again. McGhee Tyson was an Air National Guard base and didn't have a spare radio either.

I called my wife at my Aunt Lottie Davis's home, and she came over to the airbase and picked me up in her new Ford. We drove through the quiet green countryside, and I thought how peaceful this place was for my wife and children. I didn't know how long I could enjoy that peaceful atmosphere because I had learned to live on action. We had an enjoyable reunion by going up to the Smokey Mountains for another picnic.

The next morning, my wife drove me out to the airbase, and I thanked the fighter pilots again. I saddled up my iron horse and blasted off on a VFR clearance for Dallas Naval Air Station at Hensley Field between Dallas and Fort Worth. After refueling in Dallas, I continued to my final destination of Tucson, Arizona. I landed and the officer of the day took me over to base operation in his staff car. He then provided me with transportation to the commercial airport downtown where I grabbed an American Airlines flight to Dallas. There were only about five or six passengers on the flight, and I went to sleep. The flight attendants woke me when we were coming into Dallas Love Field to land, and I caught a Braniff Airlines flight at one a.m. in the morning to San Antonio. While I was waiting on the flight in the lounge, the famous boxer Joe Louis and his manager came in and sat down to wait on their flight. I should've struck up a conversation, but for some reason I let the opportunity slip by. I was waiting to hear him talk, but he never said anything. I went to sleep in the lounge. The next thing I knew, the flight attendant for the Braniff flight to San Antonio woke me up to tell me that the flight was waiting on me. I ran down the corridor with her and we climbed on board. She was from Mexico City. We arrived in San Antonio about two in the morning. I got off the plane, picked up my baggage, and found my Ford convertible in the parking lot. I drove to Billy Mitchell Village to our apartment and went to bed very tired.

The next morning, I reported to the flight line. The senior officer in charge, in the absence of the commander and the operation officer, asked me where the other pilots were. I had arrived home before any of them. I told them that they probably got weathered in on the northern route or had hit a wishy front somewhere. He just laughed and asked me where I wanted to go next. I asked him what trips were available. He said there were twelve new Sabre jets scheduled to be picked up at Los Angeles and flown to Madrid, Spain. I told him that I wanted to be on that "high flight." He told me to rest until the remaining pilots returned, and I would be dispatched with the group to Torrejon Airport just outside Madrid.

I went over to the apartments and called home. My wife was enroute to San Antonio and my mother was flying down for a little vacation. This news gave me a real thrill! I grabbed my golf clubs and headed for the Kelly Air Force Base golf course. I shot eighteen holes that day. The next day, I reported for work, but the pilot still had not shown up. I went over to Lackland AFB and tried their thirty-six hole golf course. I found out about that hot Texas sun. I could hardly make it around nine holes.

I went back to the base and decided to cool off in the base swimming pool. I took a shower and dived into the cold water at the pool. I swam around a little and then I crawled out of the pool and went to sleep under one of the beach umbrellas on the sundeck. When I woke up, I took another cold shower and dressed for the evening.

I drove over to the apartment at Billy Mitchell Village and saw my wife's blue Ford parked in front of our apartment. I went inside and found my wife and children there with my mother. Mother had flown down to Texas to visit some historic spots with my wife, while I was away on jet delivery missions. I was incredibly happy about this development because I could show my family around on the weekends when I was in town.

We went over to the officers club for dinner. While we ate, we planned all kinds of side trips for my mother, my wife, and my family. They were excited about the possibilities. Ruby would go places with my mother that she would not go with me. We went back to the apartment that night loaded with an itinerary for the entire summer.

The next morning, I reported to the operations officer at the hangar on base. The rest of the pilots had arrived from England. The operation officer briefed us on our next "high flight." Twelve of us were selected to proceed to Los Angeles, California to the North American Aviation plant located on the Los Angeles International Airport to pick up twelve brand new Sabre jet fighters to be delivered in mass to General Franco at Torrejon Airport just outside of Madrid, Spain. We were to travel to Los Angeles by commercial carrier and then proceed to Spain via the North Atlantic "high flight" route to England and then to Spain. The operation officer instructed us to travel in civilian clothes, except when we were in our flying suits. This not only kept our business confidential, but it was requested by General Franco. We were scheduled to depart for Los Angeles the next day.

The operations officer dismissed us for the rest of the day, so we could go home and pack for the trip. I drove to the apartment and told my wife and mother about our next assignment. They took me down to Joske's Department store to buy some appropriate attire for the trip. I needed a summer civilian suit anyway. I found a light brown summer suit which had just a touch of dark brown stripes in it, which made it look like an expensive Texas oiler suit. It cost $38 and I selected it immediately. I then decided to travel in Texas style. I bought a pair of dark tan kangaroo cowboy boots to match my suit and a beige summer cowboy hat to set off my ensemble. I selected a light green shirt and a Bram rock string tie. I took an extra light brown shirt along also. I was ready to travel incognito. I doubted that my compatriots would recognize me if they hadn't already known me. I loved this assignment!

The next day, my wife and mother took me down to San Antonio International Airport to meet the other pilots and catch our flight to Los Angeles. The other pilots were already there. I introduced my wife and mother to the commander, the operations officer, and a couple of other pilots who were making the trip with me. We picked up our tickets and sent our parachutes and flight bags to the baggage counter. We carried our white jet helmets on our arms by running our hand through the chin strap and carrying it like a bucket. We did not want to get separated from our helmets or let them get crushed. We could replace everything else, but the helmet was a "hard to get item" even at a supply depot at the home base.

Mom and Ruby walked to the fly gate with us. We said, "so long" and then walked down to the American airliner. We climbed aboard the aircraft and waved again as we looked back just before entering the passenger door of the aircraft. The flight attendants instructed us to sit together, so she could collect the tickets from one representative. We took our seats on the left side of the aircraft so we could look out the windows and see our families again as we taxied out for takeoff.

Our first stop was in El Paso, Texas. We were allowed a little time in the terminal to shop as we changed planes for Phoenix and Los Angeles. I went to the terminal and found some beautiful fern green shawls for only a couple of dollars. I bought four of them, one each for my wife, mother, my sister Lois, and my brother's wife Mary. We reboarded the American Airlines flight and roared off on a westerly heading. Upon entering the letdown for Los Angeles, I looked out the window and saw Burbank and the Hollywood studio lots. After we landed, we grabbed a cab in front of the terminal and rode to the Plaza Hotel. We cleaned up, donned our civvies, and went out on the town. We toured the place by briefly visiting several nightclubs.

The next morning, we grabbed a cab over to the Los Angeles International Airport. We went inside the terminal, gathered up our flying gear, and came out on the street side to wait for the green North American company car to pick us up with our baggage and haul us to the other side of the field where the North American plant was located. I was standing just outside the terminal door by my parachute bag with my jet helmet laying on top. I was dressed up in my western gear. I thought I looked like a rancher. However, since I didn't see anyone else looking like a rancher, I became a little self-conscious. I was studying the crowd when one of my fellow pilots called out from the terminal door and said, "Here comes Clark Gable and Burt Lancaster." I never fell for that gag, so I didn't even turn around and look in the direction of the door. Just a minute later, I heard cowboy boots walking towards me. I looked around towards the terminal door and there came two cowboys dressed like ranch hands. When they got right beside me, I noticed that their faces looked familiar. Sure enough, it was Clark Gable and Burt Lancaster. They were looking at me and my cowboy clothes when I exchanged glances with them. They must've thought that I was coming in for some two-bit part somewhere. I didn't speak to them, and they didn't speak to me. I guess they had just finished a western scene from the way they were dressed. I was a little surprised to find that these "big names" were not as large in real life as I had imagined. The other pilots started laughing at me for not believing their announcement. I realized that I had had an opportunity to at least speak to them and I let it pass.

I wondered if they would be interested in making a movie based upon the book that I intended to write one day about my flying career. I jotted down a message on a postcard and dropped it in the mailbox, addressed to Burt Lancaster in Hollywood, California. I figured that Burt would be more interested because he was a director, as well as an actor.

The green North American car arrived shortly thereafter. We put our bags in the trunk, hopped inside and rode around the perimeter of the field to the gate leading to the aircraft plant. I noticed the noise-reducing iron fence at the boundary of the field off the end of the runway. The fence had slots that opened to prevent hot jet wash from surging into the surrounding suburbs every time a jet blasted off down the runway. The company car stopped at the hangar, and we followed our leader up the stairs to the green waiting room with those green plush couches and easy chairs. The liaison officer told us that our new Sabre jets would be pulled out of the hangar shortly, and we would receive the accompanying paperwork.

I looked out the big plate window at a grassy area near the end of the field where I saw a 4 engine Douglas DC-4 moored in the center of an asphalt circular parking apron with its nose heading into the prevailing wind. The aircraft had the bronze markings of Western Airlines on it, and I noticed that the four bladed propellers were not centered, indicating that they had not been shut down for long. The aircraft just sat there with the tail drag support pole dangling from the tail, and the plane gently swaying to periodic gusts of wind. I asked one of the officials what the aircraft was doing there. He told me that the aircraft belonged to Howard Hughes, who owned Western Airlines. He said that Howard Hughes had the plane sitting there 24 x 7, so that he could take off himself when he wanted to go somewhere.

The liaison officer told us that our aircraft were ready, and we took off in flights of four. I was the element leader for the second flight. We stopped in Tucson for refueling, then continued on to Kelly AFB, where we spent the night. My wife and mother picked me up at the base that evening, and we drove back to the apartment. I cleaned up and we drove out to dinner at the officers club again. I told my wife and mother about running into Clark Gable and Burt Lancaster. Mom suggested that I call my brother and tell him about the incident. We got on the phone and gave him the news. It made for good conversation. News was a premium in Grundy, and it traveled fast. This information fell into the "sensational" class of news in Grundy.

The next morning, we blasted off for our next refueling stop in Memphis, Tennessee. We then continued to Dover, Delaware, where we spent the night. The following morning, we flew to Presque Isle, Maine and landed for refueling. The weather remained clear, so we continued to Goose Bay, Labrador. The weather kept us at Goose Bay for several days. When the weather cleared, we took off for Greenland. We let down for Greenland in an overcast sky and broke out at 1,800 feet. We landed and checked into the BOQ and remained "weathered in" at Greenland for a week. Finally, the weatherman gave us the "high ball," and we blasted off for Keflavik, Iceland. We landed in Keflavik and again experienced a "weathered in" period of a week. Strangely, all the waiting was more tiring than the flying. We were getting impatient to reach our final destination. Finally, we got a break in the weather, and we blasted off for Prestwick, Scotland. We landed and spent the night in a hotel in Glasgow.

The next morning, we saddled up our jets and blasted off for Bordeaux, France. We climbed out and went into a loose formation. We flew down the British Isle without too much curiosity. We had partied until we were just interested in getting the aircraft to Madrid. We crossed the English Channel without paying much attention to the vessels in the Straits of Dover or anywhere else. We were set on one thing and that was getting the Sabres to Madrid. We flew down the southwest coast of France and noticed little other than some fishing boats and some vineyards. We arrived at Bordeaux and let down in clear weather conditions. We entered the traffic pattern and landed.

The Colonel climbed out of the aircraft and asked the airman on duty where the engineering officer was. The engineering officer was responsible for seeing that the refueling operation was carried out immediately. The sergeant told the Colonel that this was Sunday, and he was the only man on duty. The Colonel called the Air Police and sent them out to the maintenance officer's house to bring him into the base to recall the men necessary to get our aircraft refueled. The Air Police brought the indignant maintenance officer to the Colonel. The Colonel informed him that this was a military operation and that he wasn't sent to France on a vacation. The maintenance officer caught the spirit of the Colonel and started calling the regular crew back to the base. We were refueled in the shortest possible time under the circumstances.

We blasted off on course for Madrid, Spain, climbing out over the Pyrenees mountains and flying over the northern middle portion of Spain. The countryside was about half-green and there seemed to be a lot of vineyards. The country was rural all the way to the outskirts of Madrid. We commenced our letdown when we had the city of Madrid in sight. The Colonel decided to make a close formation "fly-by" over Madrid at about 450 mph. The Colonel led us across the rooftops of downtown Madrid on several passes in show formation before we headed for the base at Torrejon, just northeast of Madrid. We entered the traffic pattern and landed.

As I was getting my clothes out of the radio compartment, two Air Police came over to the wing of my aircraft with a civilian and started asking me about the flight over the ocean. I couldn't hear very well because one of my eustachian tubes had plugged up in the high speed letdown. I told him that we had no problems coming over. After he left with the Air Police, one of the other pilots told me later that the civilian was "three finger" General Brown.

We delivered the aircraft to the engineering officer and checked into the Madrid Hilton for the night. The base furnished us with a staff car to travel to Madrid. They must have appreciated the new Sabres to give us those quarters for the night. That hotel had bellhops, bar maids, and room service who all spoke about three or four languages.

We checked into our rooms and cleaned up for a night on the town. We found two or three different types of musical concerts going on in different parts of the hotel at the same time. The rest of the pilots took a cab and went to some night spot in Madrid. I moseyed around in the hotel and then ventured down the street a short way. I returned to the hotel when I realized that all the action was in the hotel. I visited all the bars in the hotel and turned in when the bars closed about three o'clock in the morning.

The next morning, we met at the breakfast bar. We were told that we would get to stay in Madrid for three days while waiting for a military plane out of Madrid. We decided to grab a commercial TWA flight back to the states when we didn't see any military aircraft scheduled to leave Spain during the next week. Our return flight had refueling stops in Shannon, Ireland, and New York, before we landed in San Antonio. I caught a cab to my apartment where my wife met me at the door. The children were asleep.

The next morning, I reported to the operations officer on duty at the base. He told all of us to take our prescribed three days of rest and return ready to make the same flight from Hollywood to Madrid again. We left to go spend some time with our families. I drove to Billy Mitchell village and told my wife and mother to get ready to make a quick trip to Corpus Christi and the lazy Rio Grande Valley while I was free.

We packed our duds into Ruby's four-door sedan and headed south. During the next three days we visited the nice beach at Corpus Christi, the famous Kings Ranch that spread out over 50 miles, the Mexican border town of Brownsville, Texas, and the University of Texas at Austin. By the time we returned to San Antonio, my wife and mother had been indoctrinated in the cultural and geographical aspects of Southwest Texas.

When it was time to begin another mission, my wife and mother told me that they would take me to the airport and bring the kids along. I packed light, and we loaded up the Ford. We drove out to the International Airport and saw that the other pilots were already there. The commander and the operations officer had our orders. We bade farewell to our families and boarded Continental Airlines again. We flew to Palmdale where we picked up twelve new F-86 Sabre jets to be delivered to General Francisco Franco at Torrejon Airport in Madrid, Spain. We flew a similar transatlantic route and General Franco met us at the airport again. We were very welcome visitors. The Spaniards loved those Sabres. They had joined the 20th century Air Forces. We were taken to the Hilton again. We checked in and asked about the bullfights. We were told that we would have our trip to the bull arena all arranged on our next flight. We settled for this arrangement and turned in for the night.

The next morning, I had time to take a taxi out to the apartment where my cousin was staying with her husband. I had been told by my folks to visit them on my next trip to Spain. Elma and her husband were stationed at Torrejon in the Air Force. I found Elma at home, and she was surprised by an unexpected visit from someone from home. Her husband was a master sergeant in the Air Force. We had a nice chat and he asked me to bring him some touch up paint for his yellow Buick on my next trip to Spain. They drove me back to the Castellana Hilton.

We caught a Pan-American C-97 type airliner out of Madrid this time. We stopped for fuel at Shannon, Ireland, then continued directly across the ocean at night to New York International Airport. When the flight attendants woke me the next morning, I spotted the Statue of Liberty out my window. We cleared customs and grabbed an American Airlines flight headed West. We had three days leave cut into our orders, so that we could visit our folks on the way back to Texas. I boarded an American Airliner for Knoxville, Tennessee. The "Double A" took off from New York and had stops in Washington, D.C., and Roanoke before reaching McGhee Tyson Airport in Knoxville Tennessee. I went into the terminal and picked up my parachute bag from the baggage counter. I stowed the parachute and my jet helmet in the padlock area in the terminal and caught the next limo into Knoxville. I got a cab out to my folks' place on Western Avenue at 4303 Ball Camp Pike. My uncle and aunt were glad to see me. I spent the night with them and gave them all the details of my jet deliveries for the Air Force. I borrowed their automobile and drove up to Grundy the next day to visit my mother, father, and brother. When I got to town, my folks had already identified those contrails which had been passing over Grundy at high altitude on the flights to Spain.

I spent the night with my folks and drove back to Knoxville the next day. I gave the automobile back to my aunt and uncle and my uncle took me out to the airport to catch the American Airlines to Dallas. I got on board, and the airliner took off for Dallas. I landed in Dallas and had to spend the night because the plane had engine trouble.

The next morning, I caught the Braniff connection to San Antonio. We landed in San Antonio, where I got off the plane and caught a taxi to Billy Mitchell Village. My wife let me in the front door, and I tiptoed into the bedroom so I would not wake my children and my mother.

The next morning, I reported to the operations officer at the base. He informed us that we were going to LA the next day to take another twelve aircraft to Madrid. He gave us a day off to get our duds together and arrange for the trip. I drove home, washed my clothes, and took my suit to the one-hour cleaners.

The following morning, my wife and mother took me to the airport again. We waved goodbye from the aircraft window and the airliner taxied out to the runway. We took off for El Paso, where we would change planes for Los Angeles. We arrived in Los Angeles just before dark. We reported to the North American plant and picked up our papers. We checked into the Plaza that night.

The following morning, we got a taxi to the airport, where we were taken by the green car to the North American plant reception center. We saddled up our Sabres and blasted off for El Paso, Texas. We refueled in El Paso and flew on to Memphis, Tennessee for another refueling stop. We flew next to Dover, Delaware, where we landed shut down for the night.

The next day, we started up the Eastern coast for Presque Isle, Maine where we landed and refueled before blasting off for Goose Bay. Fortunately, the weather was beautiful and clear as a bell. We spent the night at Goose Bay, then blasted off for Greenland the next morning. We spent the night in Greenland, then took off for Iceland the following morning. We landed in Keflavík, where a low front finally caught us. We had to spend several days waiting for the weather to break on the continent and on the British Isles.

The weather finally broke, and we blasted off for Prestwick, Scotland. By the time we landed in Scotland, we were weathered in again. The weather in England could deteriorate very quickly. We spent the next few days spending our money in Glasgow. Finally, the weatherman gave us the "go" sign. We blasted off for Bordeaux, France, where we landed, quickly refueled, and promptly blasted off for Madrid. We cleared the Pyrenees and blazed on into Madrid. We gave the Spanish another free airshow and made a couple of high-speed passes over the city at low altitude. We landed at Torrejon Air Base and the liaison officer took us to the hotel. We checked in and hurried out to the waiting cab that was taking us to the bull arena to see the bullfights. It looked like the whole town went to the bullfights. Every taxi in the city was enroute to the bull arena. It reminded me of an evacuation or a crowd going to a Tennessee-Alabama football game.

We got out of the cab and went inside to our seats. All kinds of ceremonies, pageantry, and dedications preceded the bull being ushered into the ring. The bull charged around the ring making passes at the matadors who stepped out from behind their stall to taunt the bull with a red cape. Once the bull made a pass with his horns, the Matador stepped back behind his fence. In time, the main matador stepped out and walked into the middle of the ring. The bull threw dirt over his back with his front feet. The bull started making passes at the matador. The other matadors distracted the bull from time to time, causing him to further tire himself for the eventual last round. It became apparent that the bull really didn't have a chance in the ceremony. Finally, the picador came out on horseback and gouged the bull with a long pole that had a sharp blade on the end to puncture the bull's aorta before the matador made the final plunge of the sword between the bull's shoulder blades. The bull died from exhaustion and loss of blood. I sat through the slaughtering of six bulls with the results always the same – one dead bull.

I was ready to go back to the hotel when the last bull was killed. Everyone rushed for the gate. We had made the mistake of not employing the taxi for the return trip. Our cabbie had left with another fare. We were lucky to get picked up by a cab that wasn't too overloaded. We paid double the price for our lack of foresight. We were glad to get back to the hotel. We went inside to discuss our very vivid recent experience.

Our liaison officer told us that he had made us reservations on Pan Am Airlines again for the next morning. However, the weather delayed our flight the next morning and we had to wait until the next day. The liaison officer had a little tour planned for us in appreciation for our delivery of the Sabres. We were taken by a limousine out to see General Franco's country villa, an impressive villa with soldiers stationed every 100 yards around the villa. Anyone trying to get in there would have been mowed down by rifle and grenade before they even reached the wall. The villa was a pink stucco surrounded by slim cedar trees.

We drove back to the hotel that night. The next day, we boarded the Pan Am flight back to the states via Shannon and New York. A weather delay on the direct flight to Dallas caused me to redirect through Chicago. I finally arrived home and received another warm welcome from my wife and daughters.

After another reverse "high-flight" of F-86's from Prestwick, Scotland to San Antonio, the operations officer told us to take a rest and report back for some shuttle flights. We left and went home to our families. Mother and my wife had decided to move into a home in the northwest subdivision of San Antonio near the airport. They took me out to Ava Maria Drive and showed me the little flagstone house which was for rent. The beauty of it was that the landlady wanted to stay in the three rooms at one end of the house and let us have the other five rooms. This was the ideal set up because my wife liked for someone to be near when I was gone. The landlady was a widow and she wanted someone there also.

We spent the rest of my leave moving into the Ave Maria Avenue address. The subdivision was a clean and quiet neighborhood with tidy homes and nice lawns. We moved into our new quarters, and everyone was happy. My wife got a little toy rubber swimming pool about one foot deep for the children to play in under the carport. I parked my convertible in the carport at night after the children finished with the rubber duck pool.

I reported back to the operations officer on the appointed workday. He informed me that I would be joining a F-100 "high flight" scheduled to leave Warner Robins AFB the next day. I rushed home, got my clothes, and had my wife drive me to the airport. I caught American Airlines to Dallas and then to Knoxville where I caught a Delta flight to Atlanta and then a Southern flight to Macon. I grabbed a taxi in Macon and rode to Warner Robins. I reported to the operations officer, and he told me the flight was leaving in the morning. So, I checked into the BOQ, and went to the club to "jaw" with the other "high flight" pilots after dinner.

The next morning, we blasted off with twelve F-100s for Dover, Delaware. We landed in Dover and shut down for the night. We drew our overwater survival gear and stowed it in the aircraft before we turned in for the night. The next morning, we blasted off for Goose Bay. The F-100's had a longer fuel range than the F-86s and, consequently, we didn't have to make as many refueling stops as we did in the F-86. We had to penetrate the weather at the "Goose" where the GCI let us down in the soup and then lost us on radar. I anticipated this situation, so I notified the controller that I was climbing up to twenty thousand feet and making a standard jet penetration and low approach to the "Goose." The other two flights floundered around in the soup until radar finally picked them up again. Everyone landed without incident. We taxied over to the transit ramp and shut down for the night.

The next morning, we ate breakfast and went out to check on the aircraft. I found that my aircraft had been signed off as "ground checked OK" by the crew chief, but when I got in the cockpit, I found the radio missing from the aircraft. I called the engineering officer from base operations in a hurry. He couldn't find the crew chief that checked my aircraft. I began checking the aircraft very carefully at that point, because I was going to fly it over the "pond." I got a radio installed, but when we were ready to start our engines, my engine would not start. The crew chief commented that I may have flooded the aircraft. It was this comment that made me realize that these crew chiefs were used to working on conventional reciprocating aircraft and were not current in pre-flighting jet aircraft. We were taking the jet to "jet units," and we assumed that we would have jet maintenance men all along the route. However, we were being refueled by ordinary support troops who were overseas and not necessarily qualified in jet maintenance.

The operations officer told me to stay with the aircraft until it started, and then fly back to Dover to get it checked out before the next attempt to fly it across the pond. I stayed the prescribed time with the aircraft, about seven days. They never did get it started. I had to get back to our unit in Texas, so I decided to catch a military aircraft when I discovered that there were no civilian airliners coming into the "Goose" on a regular schedule. I finally caught a C-54 going to Gander, Labrador. I loaded my parachute, helmet, and clothing bag on the bird, and we roared off to Gander. We landed at Gander, and I went into base operations. While I was talking to the base operations officer about my predicament, he heard the tower talking to a C-124, which was in the pattern practicing instrument approaches to the airstrip. I asked the operations officer to request their destination. The operations officer asked their destination, and they said that they were a National Guard unit out of Harrisburg, Pennsylvania. I requested that they make a full stop landing on one of their practice runs and take me aboard so that I could get back to the states where I could board a commercial aircraft for San Antonio. The operations officer made the request, and the aircraft commander honored the request. He landed and I climbed aboard and thanked him before we roared off to Harrisburg, Pennsylvania where we landed late that evening.

I caught a feeder airline to Washington, DC where I caught American Airlines to San Antonio via Roanoke, Knoxville, Memphis,

Little Rock, and Dallas. I began to know the flight attendants on the entire route, as well as some of the pilots. The airlines were like a railroad in the sky.

I delivered another F-100 to Wethersfield, England and then the Kelly base operations officer told me to take a vacation. We decided to visit our family in Virginia. My mother flew back to Virginia because the drive was too demanding on her. My wife and I drove both cars back to Virginia for a short leave. We drove from San Antonio to Chattanooga, where we spent the night with my sister Lois Baird on Signal Mountain, Tennessee. The next morning, we drove to Knoxville and visited with my Aunt Lottie and Uncle Frank Davis, with whom we spent the night.

The next day, we drove to Grundy where we met my mother who had already arrived in Grundy and told my folks what a good time she had had visiting Texas. After hearing of my mother's exploits, my brother and his wife decided to visit us in Texas as well. I told my brother and his wife that I would leave my convertible in Grundy, and when I got back to San Antonio, I would take an F-100 on a shuttle run to Macon, Georgia, and meet them in Chattanooga at my sister's house. All they had to do was drive my convertible to Chattanooga, and then we could drive my convertible back to Texas.

My wife drove me to Tri-Cities Airport so that I could catch a flight back to San Antonio. I caught a Piedmont flight out of Tri-Cities to Knoxville where I caught an American Airlines flight to Dallas and San Antonio. I spent the night by myself at Ave Maria Drive.

The next day, I made a request to the operations officer to let me shuttle an F-100 to Macon, Georgia. He granted my request and told me that I could come back in my car, rather than return by commercial flight. I blasted off from Kelly Field with an F-100 and blazed across the south in clear weather. I landed at Warner Robins Air Force Base, Georgia and turned in the aircraft and the paperwork to the engineering officer. I caught a cab to the local commercial airport and grabbed a Southern Airlines flight to Atlanta where I caught a Piedmont flight to Chattanooga. I got off the aircraft in Chattanooga and met my brother and his wife. They had my convertible and a little six-week-old black and white beagle pup, which they gave to me as a present. We drove back to my sister's house on Signal Mountain and spent the night.

The next day, we drove to Dallas, Texas. We stayed in the Dallas Hilton and paid the usher a little tip, so that we could take our pup into the room with us. Jane Mansfield had just been refused to allow her wolfhound to accompany her in the hotel. We left Dallas the next morning and drove to San Antonio where we visited the historic sites. My brother took many pictures and movie camera footage along the route.

The next morning, I reported to the operations officer and signed out on a three day leave so that I could accompany my brother and his wife to Monterrey, Mexico. We left the pup with neighbors and drove to Laredo, Texas. The border guards were looking for a robber who was in uniform, and they had the border sealed off. I had to convince the guards that I wasn't a suspect before I was allowed to cross the border. We drove to Monterey along the secondary asphalt road. This part of Mexico was poverty stricken and the natives were not necessarily friendly. We stopped to film a Gaucho's home and he came out ordering us to move along. We realized that the great difference in living standards made the natives a little resentful of Americans. We arrived in Monterey and put up in the best hotel there. We were serenaded and romanced with food in the dining room that evening.

The next morning, we drove around a little and decided to drive back to Texas for the rest of the visit. We came back over the only asphalt road to Laredo. The dead mesquite, rocks and cacti gave the goat farmers the range. We arrived in San Antonio and took in more of the local sites.

After my leave was up, my brother and his wife flew back to Virginia, and I reported back to the operations officer. He told me to pack my duds and report the next day to take a "high flight" to the Panama Canal zone to deliver a flight of shooting star F-80's. I reported to the San Antonio Airport the next day and boarded an Eastern Airlines flight to Mobile, Alabama. We were met at the airport by the liaison officer who took us to the airbase where we checked into the BOQ.

The next day, we test flew the aircraft before we flew to Miami International Airport. My F-80 had a malfunctioning oxygen regulator, and I told my fight leader about it. He told me that I could fly the aircraft that way, since I had had no trouble flying to Miami. I told him that we would be flying over 700 miles of water and that I would prefer that he flew my aircraft if he had no objections. He decided to get the oxygen regulator replaced.

We rented a car and checked into the Bluebird Hotel on Miami Beach for the night. We enjoyed the entertainment at the hotel, which had a dance every night. The next day, we went back to the airport and cleared customs. We blasted off for Guantánamo Bay, Cuba. The weather was sky blue all the way. We had to sit on a collapsed rubber life raft, which made me lean over to see out the window screen all the way. Unbelievably, some of the pilots had stowed their deflated rubber life rafts in the gun bays to keep from being uncomfortable. In the event of an emergency, we had agreed to circle them and throw them one of our life rafts.

We arrived at Guantánamo Bay without incident and checked into the BOQ. We had to take a launch over to the club. Guantanamo was a remote station with poor relations between the US and Cuba. We rode the launch over to the main side where we visited the post exchange and the officers club. We saw several sailboats in the water at this Navy base. We stayed a few hours at the club and returned to our quarters by the launch. I was surprised to see the morale low at a base location in the Caribbean Sea. We turned in for the night.

The next morning, we blasted off south over the Gulf of Mexico and climbed on course enroute to Albrook Air Force Station on the Atlantic side of the Panama Canal. We flew over the blue shark-infested Gulf and arrived over the canal on top of some weather. We penetrated, landed, and shut down. Just as we got out of the aircraft, one of those tropical rain showers hit. I had never seen so much water pour down in such a short time! A night landing in that torrential rainfall would be a real challenge.

The staff car took us over to the living quarters. The base was well manicured, and the houses were all on stilts. Their sides were white stucco, and the buildings were covered with tile roofs. We checked into the BOQ for the night and went over to the club. The place looked pretty enough, but there was nothing going on. It reminded me of Guantánamo Bay back in Cuba. We went to the post exchange before going back to the club to eat and have a few drinks. We met an officer in the PX who volunteered to take us into the city.

We drove along the canal and noticed that an American setting had been carved out of the jungle along the canal. However, there were two different worlds here. There was a nice American section, which included a cafeteria and a golf course. Then, there was a rougher native section of town, which included a "house of love" or a government brothel. The Americans stayed near their section of town for obvious reasons. We ate at the cafeteria and looked over the golf course before returning to the base. The only other place to go was the very conspicuous, white high-rise Hilton hotel, which was like a city unto itself and quite expensive. We had supper at the club and retired to the bingo game and a few drinks at the bar. The only company we had were the officers who were curious about our mission to the canal zone. We had a long talk with the base flight surgeon who explained that the Panama Canal was a remote station that could be a happy experience if one used their imagination and had some creative hobbies.

The next day, we tried to get a military flight back to San Antonio. During our three enjoyable days in the Panama Canal Zone, we had sensed the resigned commitment to the tour of duty that was etched into the gaze of the soldiers stationed there. Nothing was going to change. The canal would be left like it was found and everyone would have done their duty. It became obvious that we would have to fly commercially back to the states because there was not as much military air traffic as we had expected.

I requested that we take the milk run back to the states through the central American countries. However, the flight leader did not want to fly on those second-class flights, so we caught a first-class flight back to Miami and then on to San Antonio. We enjoyed the flight back to Texas, but I would have much rather made the tour of Central America. We landed in San Antonio, and I caught a cab to Ave Maria where my wife welcomed me home.

The next day, I reported to the operations officer at Kelly. He informed us that we had another mission. We were going to shuttle all the big F-86H's from the overhauling factory in Ontario, California to National Guard bases in the eastern part of the United States. The F-86H was larger than the F-86F, and it would fly faster, higher, and further. We studied the different operating procedures and systems in ground school for a couple of days. After taking and passing a written test, we were ready to proceed to California and start flying these "Going Jessies" to Memphis Municipal Airport, Andrews Air Force Base, Washington DC, Wilmington, Delaware, Martinsburg, West Virginia, and Logan Field in Boston. Massachusetts.

I was anxious to saddle up in the F-86H and was in the first group that was sent to Ontario, California to pick up the first couple of aircraft. I caught an American Airlines flight to LA via Dallas. I arrived in LA and caught a Bonanza Airlines flight to the city of Ontario, which was situated about 100 miles east of Los Angeles in the grape vineyards of the San Bernardino Valley near Chino.

When the friendship Bonanza touched down in Ontario, I noticed that it was a quiet little commercial airport. We taxied over to the small terminal building beside the one runway and shut down. The contractor met us and took us to breakfast while we were waiting for the assembly line to finish a plane. This contractor was most appreciative of his big contract for overhauling the engines of these F-86H's. It was the biggest contract that he had ever received. He wanted to be sure that everyone who visited his plant to pick up an aircraft was impressed with the personal attention. He took us to the best restaurant in Fontana. When we returned to the field, one of the big birds was sitting outside the plant ready to go. A reporter was on location to make a little "news" for the new factory. He asked me where I was going as I was putting my cowboy boots into the gun bays. I told him that I was going to the East Coast. He asked me where I was stopping. I told him that I would make one refueling stop in Hensley Naval air station in Dallas and then proceed to Andrews Air Force Base in Washington DC. When I climbed up the ladder to get into the cockpit, the time was ten o'clock. He asked me when I would be in Dallas. I told him that I would be in Dallas in two hours and three minutes or around twelve o'clock noon. I told him that I would depart Dallas and arrive at Andrews Air Force Base two hours and six minutes after that. The reporter made a quick calculation on his pad and remarked that I was going coast to coast in four hours and nine minutes as casually as the conductor on a train. This was "news" in 1956 since civilians were still restricted to conventional propeller-driven aircraft for their commercial flights.[2] He took a picture of me climbing up the ladder and asked if it would be all right to run it in the local paper. I said, "Sure, go ahead."

---

2 Like perhaps no other single technology, the *jet engine* revolutionized air travel around the world. Unlike the old propeller-driven planes that were powered by *piston engines*, jet planes could fly at tremendous speeds, thus cutting down travel time. Jet-equipped airplanes also could climb faster and fly higher. Both the U.S. Air Force and civil aircraft builders found these capabilities attractive in the years after World War II when international contacts stretched across the globe. There were, however, major concerns about transferring jet engine technology to the commercial aviation sector. Airline executives in the postwar era were aware that, although jet engines were simpler than the old piston engines, they also had high operating temperatures that required very expensive metal alloy components that ultimately would affect an aircraft's longevity and reliability. Moreover, jet engines used far greater amounts of fuel. The initially low takeoff speed would also require longer runways. All of this added up to increased costs. As a result, U.S. passenger air carriers did not support the building of jet airliners in the immediate postwar years and adopted a "wait-and-see" approach before embarking on this risky path.

Of all the airlines in the United States, Pan American, which the U.S. government considered its "chosen instrument" to represent the American commercial air fleet abroad, was undoubtedly a pioneer in embracing jet aviation. *Juan Trippe*, the airlines' legendary chief executive officer, had early on expressed a keen interest in operating a passenger jet service capable of flying nonstop across the North Atlantic. Having seen the bright promise of the British Comet fade, Trippe played off two of the biggest domestic airplane builders, *Boeing* and *Douglas*. Both companies vied to appeal to Pan American's needs and offered the Boeing 707 and DC-8, respectively. In October 1955, Trippe signed contracts with both companies to buy 45 of these jets (20 707s and 25 DC-8s). Exactly two years later, Boeing rolled out the first operational 707, a Boeing 707-120, and on October 26, 1958, amid much fanfare, Pan American inaugurated its New York-London route, ushering in a new era in the history of passenger aviation. On the very first flight, which made a stopover in Newfoundland, there were 111 passengers, the largest number ever to board a single regularly scheduled flight. Coach fares were $272, about the same as one would expect to pay for a piston-engine flight across the Atlantic. *See, U.S. Centennial of Flight Commission.*

I hit the air bottle button, which discharged and cranked the engine without the aid of an APU unit, and the engine fired up. The other pilot had to wait until two o'clock to get the next plane off the assembly line. I blasted off and climbed on course to Dallas. That F-86H walked right up to forty-five thousand feet and cooked along at around ten miles per minute. The weather was clear and sunny all the way. I flew along "Green Five" air-route all the way to Dallas. I popped the boards, chopped the power, and descended on Hensley Naval Air Station like a big eagle coming down on its prey. I landed at Hensley and told the ground crew to refuel the Sabre with jet fuel and liquid oxygen. I went over to the operation shack, had a ham and cheese sandwich with a coke, and called one of my friends who flew for American Airlines. I was lucky to find him at home. We chatted for a few minutes, and I told him that I would stop again when I had more time. I went out to the aircraft, saddled up, and blasted off on course for Andrews Air Force Base in Washington DC. I smoked over Little Rock, Memphis, Nashville, and Grundy before I arrived at Andrews Air Force Base. I came screeching down on Andrews and the controller advised me that there was a 160-knot speed limit in the traffic pattern due to the high density of aircraft in the area. I acknowledged the advisory and requested a straight in approach where I could come down on final at the 160-knot speed limit. I was cleared to enter the pattern and land. As I was making the dog leg onto final, I looked over on my left wing and a B-25 was about to run through me. I put on full power, pulled up, and notified the tower of my intentions. The tower advised me that the bomber was on a simulated instrument approach and was under the GCA controller. The lack of coordination between the air traffic controller and the GCA controller increased the likelihood of accidents happening in the airport control zone. The tower operator handled the VFR traffic, and the radar control alert handled the instrument aircraft. The controllers left the responsibility for aircraft separation to both the VFR pilot and the safety pilot in the instrument aircraft. Consequently, I always cleared myself, even if the tower operator gave me clearance to land. Those tower operators were limited when sitting in the greenhouse with field glasses among all the communication distractions. They tried to do more than they were capable of doing.

I came back around and landed when the bomber cleared. I taxied over to the terminal and shut down. The Air National Guard Colonel and his operations officer were there to greet me. They thought that I had flown out of Hanscom Air Force Base in Massachusetts. They did not think an F-86 of any kind could fly nonstop from Dallas. They took me inside and questioned me at length while I gave them the paperwork. They still did not believe that I had flown nonstop from Dallas. I told him to furnish me with transportation to Washington International Airport, and then they could check my flight plan to verify my point of departure.

They furnished me with a staff car, and I went to the commercial airport. I caught Piedmont Airlines to Tri-Cities airport, because it was Friday, and the factory would not get another aircraft off the assembly line until Monday. I wanted my brother to pick me up in Bristol and take me to Grundy to spend the weekend at home. He was waiting at Tri-Cities Airport. We drove back to Grundy, and I brought him up on the events which had taken place since I had last seen him.

We arrived in Grundy in time to catch the drugstore cowboys with whom we had grown up. We had a nice chat before I walked up Slate Creek to the Liza Lee homeplace. My brother had left me because he knew I would talk until everyone left. I liked to walk the 2,000 feet up Slate Creek that I used to run daily as a boy.

Mom had supper ready, and we ate while I brought them up to date on my travels. We listened to the radio after supper, and I read the paper after dad finished with it. I spent Saturday and most of Sunday with my brother and our friends who were aviation enthusiasts. We drove over to Richlands and took a couple of flights in the Cessna 180 that one of the boys owned. They wanted to see how well I could land a small plane. My tendency to float in the round out gave them something to talk about.

Joe Breeding, my brother, and a couple of other boys flew me to Tri-Cities airport on Sunday so that I could catch a Piedmont flight to Knoxville. In Knoxville, I caught the American Airlines flight back to California. I enjoyed the company all along the route because I had begun to know some of the people who regularly traveled by air and were connected in one way or another to the coal and oil fields. When I arrived in Los Angeles, I got off the plane and spent the night in the Plaza again.

The next morning, I caught the Bonanza flight over to Ontario. The factory owner met me at the aircraft. He had a copy of the paper with the front-page article about the overhaul program and the pilots who deliver the aircraft to the National Guard units. There was my picture and a little spread about jet travel. I had breakfast and went over to the factory with the owner. They had another F-86H on the ramp. I saddled up the bird and blasted off to Dallas. I was over El Paso when the generator overheat light came on and I landed immediately in El Paso. I taxied into the maintenance hangar and shut down. The ground crew went to work looking for the trouble. It was not long before the mechanic found that a generator had been installed without the packing being removed from the cooling openings. Fortunately for me, the high-altitude subzero weather had made the generator last long enough to get me to El Paso before it overheated in the warmer Texas air.

After the replacement of the generator, I blasted off for Knoxville. If I had to make an additional refueling stop, it might as well have been where I had relatives and could spend the night. I had missed my commercial aircraft schedule anyway. I landed in Knoxville and my uncle picked me up at the airport. I brought him up to date on my travels as we drove over to his house to spend the night.

The next day, I blasted off for Andrews Air Force Base. I smoked up the coast in short order and delivered the aircraft. The Colonel of the Guard had figured out the route of my previous flight and was very appreciative of my remarkable efficiency in fuel management. I caught Piedmont Airlines back to Knoxville and picked up an American Airlines flight for the remainder of the flight back to Los Angeles. I spent the night at the Plaza again.

After another delivery of a F-86H to Wilmington, Delaware and return by commercial airline, I spent the night at home. My pregnant wife told me that she wasn't going to have the baby for two more weeks. I drove to the base and checked out an F-86F and blasted off for Knoxville where my uncle met me at the airport again. We drove over to his home, and I visited with my folks. I wanted to know if one of them could go to Texas to be with my wife when the baby arrived. While we were talking, I got a phone call from San Antonio telling me that my wife had gone to the hospital. I got my uncle to drive me back to the base and I blasted off for San Antonio.

I had to refuel at Dallas because the F-86F didn't have the range that the F-86H had. When I landed in San Antonio, I drove out to the Baptist Hospital. I found my wife in the waiting room for expectant mothers. She told me that she had a practical nurse watching the other children. I told her that I would go out to the house and see how the children were doing and then come back to the hospital and spend the night with her. I left the hospital and started to drive out to Ave Maria, but I thought that I should get her some roses before I left the hospital. I purchased a dozen roses and went back upstairs to take the flowers to my wife. When I got to the room, my wife had already gone into the delivery room, and I heard a baby crying. The nurse came out and asked, "Are you father?' I quickly replied, "Yes." She said, "Congratulations on being the proud father of a son." She brought out that big scrapper and showed me that he was a boy.

I told my wife that I would go out to the house and take care of the other children myself. I drove to the house and dismissed the practical nurse. I had my hands full with the children, who were like a bunch of possums. I took about a week of leave to help my wife with the children. My boy was born December 24, 1956, on Christmas Eve day and we named him Harold Glenn Junior. He woke everyone up when he cried at night. The girls didn't have such raspy voices.

When my wife was on her feet again, I reported back to duty. The operations officer dispatched me back to Ontario, California on the shuttle run. I knew the drill and I caught American Airlines back to Los Angeles and spent the night at the Plaza again.

The next morning, I caught Bonanza back out to Ontario, had breakfast with the contractor, and picked up another F-86H destined for Dallas. I roared across the desert at 45,000 feet and came screaming eagle down at Hensley Naval Air Station where I refueled and blasted off for Martinsburg, West Virginia. I had picked up my F-86 at Ontario on their late schedule – consequently, I was going to arrive at Martinsburg at about eight o'clock that night. The weather was clear with some scattered cirrus at 20,000 feet. As I neared Martinsburg, I received a weather advisory that some scattered fog might develop around Hagerstown, Pennsylvania, which was close to Martinsburg. I calculated that I could make Andrews Air Force Base if the weather soured at Martinsburg.

I arrived over the Martinsburg beacon and commenced my jet penetration. When I notified the tower that I was in the penetration, the tower advised me that the base had landing lights on the old runway, but not on the new longer runway. I could see the new concrete runway even though it was night, so I notified the tower that I would land on the long runway. The tower advised me that the fire department was not on duty at this hour, and I quickly replied, "It's OK, I'm not going to crash anyway."

I continued my approach because I had left my altitude and had committed myself to land at Martinsburg as far as my fuel supply was concerned. I knew that I could go around and land on the old runway if I had any problems keeping the unlit runway in sight. I came over the low approach and was coming in on final with my gear and flaps down. At about 700 feet, I went through a patch of fog. It was just a puff that blew across the approach end of the runway. I continued my approach, passed through the patch, rounded out, and landed. The fog sure did fool me! The instant that I was engulfed in the fog seemed like an eternity. I was so low that I would have had to initiate a go around on the gauges in the round out. However, I broke out and landed without incident. This experience really made me alert for any future sudden developments in the traffic pattern where isolated weather conditions prevailed. I had no difficulty seeing the runway with my landing lights on this moonlit night. I slowed down, taxied to the terminal, and shut down.

The National Guard base had the usual skeleton crew on duty at that late hour. I turned the paperwork into the airdrome officer. I collected my duds and requested that the airdrome officer give me transportation to Washington National Airport. He was most appreciative of me bringing their unit the F-86H, so he drove me to the Washington National Airport. I discovered that I had left my cowboy boots in the gun bays of the aircraft that I had just delivered, when I collected my bags out of the staff car at Washington National Airport. I told the airdrome officer to keep them for me, and I would retrieve them when I brought him another F-86H back from California. He assured me that my boots would be at Martinsburg base operations when I returned. I caught American Airlines back to

California with the usual stops enroute on the milk run to Dallas. I flew nonstop to Los Angeles on the early morning flight and caught Bonanza to Ontario.

After breakfast, I picked up an early assembly line completed F-86H and blasted off for Dallas. I refueled in Dallas and blasted off for Martinsburg. I arrived at Martinsburg in the middle of the afternoon on a weekday. I picked up my boots in base operations and caught another staff car over to Washington International Airport. I grabbed the first American flight back to California. I slept most of the time on the way back and woke up when the flight attendant served the meal. We landed without incident in Ontario.

The next morning, I picked up another F-86H and blasted off for Dallas. I refueled in Dallas and roared off for Knoxville, where I refueled and continued on to my final destination of Schenectady, New York. I arrived over Schenectady on a beautiful, cold clear January day. There was some water left on the runway from rain the night before. As I pitched out in the landing pattern, I knew that I might encounter slick spots in the runway and possibly some ice patches. I touched down and held the nose off the runway as long as I could. When the nose dropped onto the runway, it began to hit the slick spots. I opened the canopy to further disrupt the air-flow to help slow the aircraft. The aircraft yawed and swerved, but I kept it going down the centerline. I hit a few icy spots, but got it stopped at the last taxi finger. I taxied to the terminal where the ground crew met me at the aircraft with a ladder. I collected my belongings and rode over to base operations in the staff car. I was well greeted again because these National Guard commanders really looked forward to receiving those new birds.

After I turned in the paperwork, the commander had a staff car run me over to Albany to catch a Mohawk feeder airline into New York. Once in New York, I caught American Airlines back to California.

We made only one stop enroute and that was in the windy city of Chicago. I flew all night again.

The next day, I arrived in Ontario for breakfast. After breakfast, I saddled up another F-86H and blasted off for Dallas. I refueled in Dallas and continued on to my final destination of Hanscom Field just outside Boston, Massachusetts. I smoked up the coast and arrived over Hanscom on a beautiful, clear day. I found another fighter, arriving in the area at altitude about the same time. I noticed that he wanted to engage me in a little aerial dogfight. I had enough fuel, so I went at it for about ten minutes. I got on his tail and then broke off the engagement. I landed and taxied into the terminal parking apron. As I was about to get out of my aircraft, a fellow pilot brought the ladder out and put it on the side of my aircraft. He climbed up the ladder and began to ask about the new aircraft and I recognized him as one of my cadet class members. We had a little reunion while I was getting unstrapped and collecting my gear.

Suddenly, I saw the aircraft with which I had been dogfighting entering the traffic pattern. I knew the F-86H was a heavier bird than the F-86F. We paused to watch our colleague fly his pattern, but I noticed that he was making too long of a downwind leg with power off. I told my classmate that the pilot could get in trouble if he didn't add some power on the turn to the base leg. My classmate didn't think that I knew what I was talking about. Of course, I knew that he had not flown this F-86H yet.

When the pilot turned base, I said, "If he adds power now, he might make it to the runway." Sure enough, he didn't add power and he stalled and went in. He landed in the mud off the end of the runway still in the same direction as the base leg. He was an extremely lucky pilot for several reasons. One, he made a partial recovery, which broke his descent just before striking the ground. Second, the gear folded and absorbed some more of the shock. Third, the aircraft didn't catch on fire. He waved a handkerchief from the cockpit for someone to get him out. I suspected that he had a broken back. I got out of my aircraft to catch a ride over to the accident, but the firetruck and rescue units went right by us.

I went into the terminal and discussed the accident with my classmate. I told him what I thought he did that contributed to the situation. I asked my classmate to keep me out of the investigation because he witnessed the accident also. I caught a staff car to Albany, caught the feeder airlines to New York, and caught an American Airlines flight back to California.

Next morning, I was back in Ontario to eat breakfast again. After breakfast, I saddled up another F-86H and blasted off for Dallas, this time headed for Logan Field in Boston, Massachusetts. I arrived over the Boston beacon on another beautiful day and entered the traffic pattern. I ran into a flock of pigeons on my final approach, but fortunately, I didn't inhale any of them because they broke down away from my flight line.

I went into the Boston Statler Hilton to spend the night because I couldn't make connections that night back to California. I had duckling that night in the dining room because it was the least expensive meal, but I would've had pheasant under a glass if I had known how sweet duckling was. I couldn't eat it.

The next morning, I went downstairs to pay my room bill and they only charged me nine dollars. When I checked in, they told me my room would be twelve dollars. I appreciated the consideration they had for servicemen. I figured that must've been a routine discount for service personnel. I got a cab to the airport and boarded American Airlines back to California.

I arrived back in Ontario the next morning. They didn't have an aircraft ready for me, so they took me to the Holiday Inn where I checked into a room. I rested several hours before they had an aircraft ready for me to deliver to Memphis. I blasted off that evening for my first stop in Austin, Texas. I had not seen my wife and children for a couple of weeks, so I was going to have her meet me at Bergstrom Air Force Base in Austin. I landed at Bergstrom and shut down for the night. My wife came up and we visited until about 10 o'clock, when she had to drive back to San Antonio. I discovered that the weather was socked in at my destination in Memphis, so I had to spend the night at Bergstrom.

The next day, I had to get the ground crew to refuel me. Those SAC folks were not concerned too much with fighter pilots. They would rather we stayed out of their locations. I blasted off for Memphis and landed there without any problems. I turned in the aircraft and caught an American Airlines flight back to San Antonio where I caught a taxi home that evening.

The next morning, the operations officer told me to take a rest and report back to be a part of a mass delivery of F-86 H's out of Memphis to Logan field. I drove home and rested for a couple of days around the house, on the golf course, and in the base swimming pool.

I reported back to the base operations on the scheduled day. We all left for the airport as a group in a couple of staff cars. There were only about six or seven of us. We boarded American Airlines and roared off to Dallas and then on to Memphis. We enjoyed the refreshments and dinner on the flight, and we joshed around with the flight attendants. We got off the aircraft in Memphis and rode over to the Air National Guard hangar in the staff cars.

We had to test fly the birds before we blasted off for Boston. We took off on a local test flight. It wasn't long before we had a big, mock air battle in progress. I had observed the aircraft which had taken off before me, so I had their flight path zeroed in. The aircraft were turning in a big circle around 50,000 feet as I climbed towards them. I was able to slip up on the tail of all six aircraft in the mock battle which was in progress. The lead aircraft realized that he had all six aircraft on his tail and immediately broke straight up, banked 90°, and pulled the nose of his aircraft through the horizon until he was traveling straight down at full throttle. I managed to hang onto my whip crack position as we yo-yoed up and down. We all came screaming eagle straight down in the Memphis area. I realized that we might break the sound barrier and the seven aircraft booming at one time might have a devastating effect on the windows and other fragile structures on the surface far below. Therefore, I had the presence of mind to glance at my airspeed indicator to see when I would have to pull out of the dive to avoid being in the sonic boom barrage. Unfortunately, I was already exceeding 1000 mph, so I knew then that I had to break away from this group and not land with them. I was sure that the community would be waiting for them on the ground as a reception committee.

The other six aircraft went on with their mock air battles, unaware of the possible consequences of supersonic activities when pointing their noses toward the ground. After about twenty minutes, the other aircraft went into the base and landed. I was circling overhead at altitude so I wouldn't be associated with the other six aircraft. I heard the tower operator request that the leader of the flight report to the base operations officer after shutting down.

I let down and landed after a few minutes and taxied over to the Air Guard ramp and shut down. I buttoned up my aircraft and walked into the base operation to see what kind of violations were in store for all of us. Our sonic booms must've struck outside the city in unpopulated areas, because all the airdrome officer wanted was our departure time so that he could have the aircraft refueled in time to meet our takeoff schedule.

The high altitude had helped diminish the effect of the sonic booms, because we remained above 30,000 feet in the mock air battle.

I drew a big sigh of relief, but I don't think the other pilots knew what we could've been in for. After the ground crew refueled the aircraft, we saddled up and blasted off on course for Logan Field in Boston, Massachusetts. We soared up the East Coast in the contrails like a flight of wild geese. The weather was sky blue and clear as far as the eye could see.

We arrived over Boston and let down in show formation. We shifted into echelon on the turn on initial approach. We broke at four second intervals and came around the pattern and landed. We kept our eyes peeled for those flocks of birds that had a habit of gathering on the end of the runway and suddenly flushing up in front of the plane just before the round out. We were fortunate that day that the birds had already been flushed. We landed without incident, taxied over to the Air Guard ramp, and shut down. The Air Guard staff met us at the aircraft and relieved us of the paperwork. We caught a staff car to the civilian side of the airport where we boarded American Airlines and roared off in a westerly direction.

The next morning, the operation officer informed us that we would be leaving for California to pick up twelve more F-100s to take to Bitburg, Germany, over the "high flight" route. We flew to Los Angeles, and the North American liaison officer drove us to Palmdale to pick up our F-100's on the ramp. We had an uneventful transatlantic flight and landed in Bitburg, Germany, where we spent the night. Before I caught a commercial flight back to the states, I made a visit to my Grundy friend Nick Street and his wife, who were stationed in Furstenfeldbruck. Nick was a legal officer at Furstenfeldbruck. I grabbed a train to "Fursty" and called Nick who came out to the base and took me home with him for supper. We caught up with each other on what had happened since we had last met. His wife June was a fabulous cook. I borrowed Nick's car that night to visit some friends in Munich.

The next morning, I brought his car back to him and he took me to the airport to catch the Pan Am flight back to the states. He asked me to tell his folks that he and his family were doing well. I cleared customs at Munich and boarded a big two-story C-97. I met some of the same flight attendants with whom I had previously flown over the Atlantic. We had some more Irish coffee at Shannon, Ireland while the aircraft was being refueled. We flew across the Atlantic again at night and arrived at New York International Airport the next morning. I cleared customs and caught the limousine over to LaGuardia Airport, where I boarded American Airlines for San Antonio. I turned in for the night at Ave Maria Drive.

The next morning, the operations officer notified us that the mission of the 1738th Jet delivery Group had been accomplished for the most part and that there was a cut back in appropriations. The group was disbanding, and we were advised to request an assignment. The Colonel told us that we would be lucky to find positions to our liking.

# CHAPTER 27

# TAC George AFB, California (Victorville, California)

**I** requested an assignment to George Air Force Base in Victorville, California. I was warned that the base was already full of pilots who wanted to fly the new F-104, which was scheduled to arrive at George soon. I decided to take my chances. A couple of pilots were "riffed" or cut out of the group as "surplus" before we left the base.

We shipped our belongings to George by North American Van lines. My son, Harold, Junior had something close to pneumonia. That damp, cold Texas weather could be hazardous. The doctor told us that my son was ok to travel with us and I knew the weather would get warmer as we traveled westward.

We loaded up the two Fords and drove to El Paso the first day where the weather was indeed warmer. On our second day, we drove into Phoenix, Arizona, but found that every motel was full of people who had come to Arizona for the winter. One Best Western Hotel got us a room in a private dwelling where we slept on a screen porch for $20 that night.

The next day, I drove to Apple Valley, California and found a suite available in the Apple Valley Inn. The suite cost $25 per night. We ate in the expensive dining room while the combo played soft music and the Chinese waiters served the meal. We would have preferred another setting for the family, but the motels were full in the high desert with tourists visiting for the winter. I kept the family in the Apple Valley Inn until I could find another place to stay. The Apple Valley Inn was a Fieldstone structure, and the most beautiful motel in the area. I thought that we might as well go first class since we were in a bind for quarters.

Apple Valley was a resort community just east of Victorville, where base housing was not available. The local real estate agency could build you a house under a contract agreement. There were a couple of furnished homes available, but a movie star could not afford the rates. I finally found a little seven-unit motel on Bear Valley Road between Apple Valley and Victorville, which had just opened. The lady rented me a kitchenette set up for $25 per week. The motel was in Hesperia, California, which included only a couple of old homes and a post office. My wife and children loved the place at first sight, and I didn't think it was wise to buy a home under the present economic squeeze, in as much as I was considered surplus for the moment. Congress had limited the Air Force to 100,000 pilots. The reduction in force was not over.

I reported for duty at George AFB. Colonel Lavin gathered us in the auditorium and informed us that he would be lucky to find positions for some of us. He told us that we would be there only temporarily until the Air Force could find positions for us or discharge us. I had to find a position in one of the tactical squadrons.

Otherwise, I might not be interested in remaining in the Air Force. I was offered the non-flying position of Hedren squadron commander for one year, after which I might be assigned to fly in the squadron full-time. I wanted an immediate flying position, so I turned this proposition down.

I was next offered a position as a simulator officer, which trained pilots in the F-104 simulator training. This made flying a secondary duty. I had had enough of "secondary duty flying," so I refused this duty as well. Finally, I was assigned as a passive defense officer with flying as a secondary duty. It looked like my flying days were numbered. I began to concentrate on enjoying California with my family and taking cross-country trips in the base operations T-33.

I went over to Apple Valley flying club and joined because the club had a T-34 Mentor, a small two seater low wing single engine trainer. I wanted to fly my wife and family around the area for their pleasure when I had time. I was checked out by a pilot who had only ninety total hours. When I started to do some aerobatics, he informed me that a parachute was required to fly aerobatics in a T-34. I hardly realized that I was flying without a parachute. The T-34 flew like the T-28.

The first weekend I took my family to Disneyland. We drove across the Cajon Pass and down the canyon to the San Bernardino valley below. I drove through the side roads to Anaheim so that my wife could appreciate the countryside in the valley floor. My wife and I enjoyed Disney world as much as the children did. I drove my family out to Hollywood and Beverly Hills after we left Disneyland. We looked at the movie stars' homes then drove down to Santa Monica Beach to see the beach and the old millionaires' homes along the beach. We returned to Hesperia satisfied with the trip.

The next weekend, I drove my family up to the top of the San Bernardino mountains. The top of the mountain was flat and covered with evergreen pine trees. The headwaters of the streams were dammed up into beautiful, crystal-clear lakes. The motels and village shopping centers were constructed of expensive Redwood timbers. This area was truly a resort at the top of the mountains. The lakes were covered with boat docks and there were a bunch of sailboats on Big Bear Lake. We drove out to the location of the movie "Trail of the Lonesome Pine." We especially enjoyed this tour because our "roots" were back in Virginia and Kentucky in the actual "Trail of the Lonesome Pine" area. The rolling and gentle hills on the mountain tops in Bear Creek were covered with white pines. Whereas the mountains in eastern Kentucky, southwestern Virginia, and East Tennessee were covered with knotty pines mixed with scrub oaks, white pines, and yellow pines.

Big Bear Lake looked like the place for movie stars to retire. We drove through the tops of the mountains and visited the other little villages. One village had a candy shop with a Santa Claus motif for a draw. They had some reindeer in a fenced area nearby. The smell of the candy drew us off the road and into the parking lot. The place, called Santa's Village, became a regular pitstop for the children.

We drove back to Big Bear and ate. We went out on the sundeck to the shopping center cafeteria and relaxed, while looking over the boating and sailing activities on the lake. I wanted to do some water skiing and sail one of those sailboats. I would put that off until I had time one day.

The next week, I flew the T-33 to Hill Air Force Base and to Eglin Air Force Base, Florida, gathering up parts to support the flying operation at George AFB. The operational squadrons were flying F-100's, and the attached air defense squadrons were flying F-102's. The T-33's were loaded down with more instrumentation than had originally been planned for the aircraft. Inverters were always in demand because of the heavy workload on these aircraft. I was flying everywhere looking for inverters and getting inverters repaired.

These flights enabled me to visit Knoxville and Grundy, and to stay overnight on the weekend and visit my family and friends. In fact, my friends could not understand how I could come home so often to Virginia, Kentucky, and Tennessee. They thought that I was in the Air Force.

My brother called me one day and told me that he was going to Darlington, South Carolina to see the stock car races. I told him that I would fly a T-33 into Douglas field in Charlotte, North Carolina and meet him at the airport terminal. I flew into Charlotte, met my brother, and drove on down to Darlington. Everyone was in town for the races and all the hotels were filled up. We either had to drive to Myrtle Beach or sleep in the car. We drove to Myrtle Beach and every motel was filled there as well. We were about to consider sleeping on the beach when we found a motel with a vacancy sign. We approached the motel owner, who told us we would have to take the room for two nights for fifty-one dollars. We thought it was "highway robbery," but we didn't have a choice.

The next day we took in the races. Everybody and his brother was there. We thoroughly enjoyed the noise and the race. We drove back to Charlotte that night where I saddled up the T-33 and blasted off for California and my brother drove back to Grundy. I landed in Dallas, refueled, and blasted off for Victorville. I almost went to sleep in the aircraft over Blythe, California, because everything was so silent on the radio. I landed at George in the wee hours of the morning.

The next weekend, I drove my family up to Las Vegas, Nevada. We drove to Barstow and turned west for about fifteen miles to visit the movie location for several western movies. Calico was an old mining town that had long since been abandoned. The main street was separated by the old railroad track which had been used to pull the oar out of the mountains. The place was hot as blazes! It was in the scorched part of the desert on the edge of the high mountain cliffs. The terrain looked like the ashes of an old coal stove and the cliffs looked like the sides of the grate in a potbelly stove.

We sweltered around the old plant buildings until I wanted to get back on the road to Las Vegas. We drove back to the main highway, and I drew a sigh of relief. I wouldn't want to have car trouble on that side road. We had a couple of water bags hanging on our bumpers to use in case of an emergency. The water bags seeped through the burlap-looking containers just slow enough to keep the container moist and cool. We had some rations in the truck and some goodies in the car for the children. We drove through the desert until we arrived at the green grasslands around the Luxor Motel on the western end of the famous strip of Las Vegas. The motels had irrigated the land around the buildings. There was a golf course and swimming pool behind every motel. We studied the resort motels just like we looked at those Beverly Hills homes.

We drove up to a couple of resort motels and went inside just far enough to see what they looked like inside. We drove on into town and passed McCarran Field and the big airport tower there. We parked the car and walked the streets for a while. It was too hot and there were too many "saddle tramps"[1] on the sidewalk to suit us. We drove back to the strip to eat at one of the motel buffets.

After dinner, we drove out to Boulder city and were awed to see that Lake Mead "ocean" in the middle of the desert. Hoover Dam was so strategically located in the narrow canyon that it was not large in comparison to the water that it held back in Lake Mead. I wanted to take the family out to Death Valley just to see the edge of it, but we ran out of daylight and had to return to Hesperia.

---

1 A saddle tramp in the Old West was a person who wandered from place to place on a horse. *See,* Texas Tech University, History and Traditions, "Saddle Tramps."

The next flight took me to the Naval Air Station at Naval Oceana in Virginia Beach. I landed there on another beautiful day. I had a friend in the Navy, who flew conventional aircraft. His name was Lawrence Combs, and he was from Grundy. I called him out to base operations. I had an extra jet helmet and parachute in the backseat. I told him that I was going to give him an orientation ride in a jet, and he was delighted. I put him in the front seat, and we blasted off and flew around the area, as I gave him a little instruction on the differences between jet aircraft and conventional aircraft. Lawrence Lee would never forget that flight! He was in training and didn't know whether he would get his wings or not. I reassured him and told him how to conquer those self-doubts.

That night, my brother took me to Richmond to a big national dental meeting where he was campaigning for president of the Virginia Dental Society. We sat at a table in the bar room with my brother and a few of his friends from Roanoke, Richlands, and Johnson City. Dr. Frank Anderson was there from Johnson City, Tennessee. After the meeting, Dr. Frank Anderson asked me to fly one of his Air Force friends back to Sheppard Air Force Base, Texas for him. I told him I would be glad to accommodate him, and I told him to have his friend meet me at the Navy Oceana base operation building the next morning.

My brother drove me back to Virginia Beach where we had a little party at the Naval officers club. The next morning, I met the Major who was going to fly to Sheppard Air Force Base, Texas with me. We suited up and blasted off for Shepard, which I made in one nonstop flight on that clear and sunny day. I landed at Shepherd, let the Major off, refueled, and blasted off for Victorville. I flew over Las Vegas and checked my fuel before deciding to continue to George nonstop. I had to check the desert weather because I would have minimal fuel when I arrived over George, and I didn't want to run into any sandstorm. I made it to George and landed without incident.

The next day, I flew to Tampa, Florida looking for parts. I refueled in Dallas enroute. I visited with my mother who was living in Tampa for her health. The Gasparilla Pirate Festival was in progress, and I took in that entertaining activity that night.

The following day, I blasted off for Colorado Springs. I had a friend, Dr. John Harmon, stationed there as an Air Force dentist. As I let down in the traffic pattern to land, I was informed by the tower that a directive had just been published, prohibiting jets from landing at joint military and civilian fields, unless directed there by specific orders. I explained that I had not received those orders, so they cleared me to land. With one stroke of the pen, the government had cut out 1,800 air bases at which I could have landed prior to this order. Later, the Air Force restricted reserve pilots to a 200 mile radius of operation from their home field. The crunch was in full bloom. Major John Harmon met me at the base operation and he and his wife took me to their home. We attended a dance at the officers club that night.

The next day, I blasted off for California. The weather was still good when I flew into George and landed without incident. I had a leave coming up, so I decided to take my family on a round robin tour of California while I had the chance. My wife would not fly, so we left Hesperia in my wife's four-door Ford. We drove to Burbank, and then drove up the San Fernando valley for a short stretch before we headed for the California coastline at Ventura. We arrived at Ventura and found the weather beautiful. The temperature was 72°F. The beautiful blue Pacific was our backdrop off the coast. The coastal mountains rose off the coastal plains majestically. The climate was arid, although there was enough rainfall to handle the garden crops.

We drove on up the coast to Santa Barbara. The entire coastline was one big resort. We visited Vandenberg Air Force Base where we ate lunch and visited the post exchange. We drove on up to San Luis

Obispo and picked up Highway # 1, a secondary road to Morro Bay. We were traveling along the rural coast of California. We came to San Simeon and could see the stately Hearst castle, high up on the mountain overlooking the ocean. We didn't have time to drive halfway up the mountain to visit the castle, so we continued along the coastal Highway to Big Sur. The road ran along the cliffs with the ocean slapping up against the rocks some 100 feet straight down below us. We did not want to be inattentive along that road – we had heard that the Pacific water was cold! We discovered that California did in fact have a rural area along this coastal drive. Big Sur was a place to get away from it all. Those white Spanish missions were scattered throughout the coastal towns and villages along the road. The sun made the white stucco structures look even whiter. We drove into Carmel, the most lavish resort area we had seen on the trip. We visited Del Monte and drove out to Pebble Beach, the golf course on the edge of the Pacific Ocean. It was something to behold. The greens were lush, and the golf course was about thirty feet above the waves of the ocean. The twisting wind had curved the green cypress trees surrounding the perimeter of the golf course.

We toured the shopping center and then drove on to the Monterey Bay area. I stopped the car, and we gazed across the blue waters of the bay. We could see the mountains in the distance rising above the dusty mist hanging over the bay. The white stucco Catholic missions stood out in the distance with the sun reflecting off their surfaces.

We drove around the bay to Santa Cruz and stopped in the middle of town to have dinner at one of the Spanish restaurants. It felt like we were in an actual Spanish village. We drove on up to the Big Basin redwoods. There was some road construction in progress, so we had to detour through the sugar beet farms along the coast. The sugar beet farmers must have come from the Azores, Portugal, or Spain. We had to stop at one point on the side of the road until a farmer finished milking a cow right in the middle of the road. The children enjoyed this interruption.

We drove on to Half Moon Bay and then to San Francisco where we drove across the Golden Gate Bridge. We spent the night in San Rafael. The next day, we drove across the bay from San Francisco to Oakland. The bay looked much like Monterey Bay, only it was inland and a little dryer. There was a lot of farming along the bay. Fishing and shipbuilding were big occupations in the built-up area. We drove down the San Joaquin valley to Merced, where we had dinner. This was cotton country where the farms were irrigated, and the soil was rich.

After dinner at Merced, we drove into the Sierra Madre mountains to visit Yosemite National Park. As the terrain rose, the water supply increased, and the cattle ranches sprang up everywhere. We drove up to the big Redwood Forest. The cool breeze was a refreshing experience. We visited the big waterfall and then drove down to the valley below.

We drove into Fresno where there was an airport that had a vintage P-51 mounted on the gate signifying that it had once been a P-51 fighter training base. We drove up into the Sierra Madre again to Sequoia National Forest and toured the giant Redwood Forest where we drove through a tunnel in one of the huge trees. We left Sequoia and drove to Bakersfield, where we spent the night.

The next day, we drove to Mojave and passed through the mountain pass into the high desert. We then drove down to Lancaster and Palmdale, before returning to Victorville along the canal of California.

The next day, we drove down to the San Bernardino Valley and eastward out to Palm Springs. I saw many nice homes scattered around the motels and golf courses. We drove around the Salton Sea and studied the date farms with all the palm trees before driving back to Indio to spend the night.

The next day, I drove back to George AFB and reported to work. I could take the rest of my leave at another time. I blasted off for McClellan Air Force Base in Sacramento to get some parts at the depot. I landed at McClellan and had to spend the night to pick up the parts, so I caught a bus into Sacramento, which was green and clean much like Denver, Colorado. The trees and buildings were well planned. I walked over to the capitol building and the impressive arbor. The blue spruce trees were most decorative. As I walked back to the bus stop, I saw a beautiful woman walking down the street towards the capital. I asked her if she was a movie star. She said, "No, but thank-you for the compliment." I hoped to spend more time in Sacramento in the future.

I went back to the base, took in the club, and spent the night. The next day, I blasted off back to George AFB with my parts. As quickly as I delivered the parts to base operations, I was dispatched to Stead AFB in Reno. I had just changed clothes when I got the word to proceed to Reno. I changed back into my flying suit and blasted off for Reno. I climbed out to China Lake and looked over Death Valley on my right. I cruised by Mono Lake and came over Lake Tahoe, which was situated at the top of the mountain above Reno in the Sierra Madre mountains. Lake Tahoe was another resort like Big Bear, but the lake was miles across. The resort villages had A-framed homes lining the edges of the lake. I let down over the lake to view the area from a good vantage point. I landed in Reno, where the base was at a high elevation. I caught a bus across town to the base commissary and post exchange area. I went to the post exchange to get a check cashed, so I could walk downtown and visit some of the gambling casinos while I waited for the parts to arrive from the storage depot. I had left my pocketbook back at George when I changed clothes. The lady at the post exchange told me that I had an "honest face" and cashed my $10 check anyway.

I caught a ride downtown and went into Harold's place in Reno. The tourists were hanging onto the slot machines like they were being pulled by magnets, just like they do in Las Vegas. I enjoyed the floor show but didn't stay long. I blasted off for George. When I landed at George, I found my pocketbook just where I left it on top of the locker.

The next day, I was the Airdrome Officer for the day. There was an air strip out in the desert near Adelanto, called Shadow Mountain. It was a little dirt strip, where glider pilots always played around with the air currents off the Sierra Madre mountains. We could see the dust devils coming off the desert out that way from the base operations building. The dust devils helped the glider pilots climb up out of the desert to the winds aloft.

We went into base operations that morning, drinking coffee, and getting ready for the heavy traffic to commence. About that time, a big one wheel metal glider swished down on the parking apron, coasted over into the F-102 compound, and fell over on one wing tip. We called the Air Police because the military base was a restricted area. We commanded a staff car and raced over to the compound. We met the pilot and detained him until the Air Police arrived. He spoke with a foreign accent, and we thought he might be there to spy on our facility. He claimed that his glider ran out of air current, preventing him from making it back to Shadow Mountain. He had to land where a light plane could pull him off the runway again, so he picked George AFB.

After we took him through our investigation and interrogation procedures, we charged him for landing on the military compound, as prescribed in the regulations. We then let his light aircraft fly in from Shadow Mountain and pull him off again. Never a dull moment around an airport!

The next day, I was dispatched to Castle Air Force Base in California, near Merced to take an airman on an emergency leave.

The airman showed up at base operations with his duffel bag and his guitar. He had to leave his duffel bag and take a handbag instead. I had him get into the T-33, and we tried closing the canopy without damaging the guitar. We barely made it. I blasted off and climbed on course for Castle Air Force Base. We buzzed over to Castle, let down, and landed. I taxied over to the ramp and the airman climbed out of the aircraft, thanking me for the flight.

I went into base operation and called a friend of mine from Hurley, Virginia, who was stationed at Castle, flying B-52's. I asked him to come out to base operation and visit me for a while. Lieutenant Jimmy Davis came out to base operations, and he was glad to see someone from home. He couldn't move around the country like I could because he was flying B-52's and they could not land anywhere. After a nice chat, I walked out to my aircraft and blasted off on my return trip to George.

When I landed at George, I was dispatched to Kansas City, carrying a nurse who was taking an emergency leave. She climbed aboard and I blasted off for Kansas City. The weather was clear and sunny. I streaked across the sky and landed at Kansas City where the nurse climbed out and thanked me for the flight. I took off for MacDill AFB in Tampa, Florida. I arrived at MacDill and remained overnight, so I could visit with my mother again. I flew back to George the next day.

It had snowed that weekend in Big Bear Lake. We had spotted a little ski resort named Rebel's Retreat on a previous trip to the mountains. We decided to take the children up to Rebel's Retreat to let them learn about the snow. When we drove up to the resort, we could not park within a mile of the club, because there were so many people with the same idea. California had a population that could move fast. No wonder they had to go to Aspen or Sun Valley.

We settled for a stop at Santa's Village and dinner at the Big Bear Lake lodge. The next day, I reported to base operations and was issued an aircraft to make parts run to Reno Air Force Base and Hill Air Force Base in Utah. I climbed into a T-33 and blasted off on course for Reno. I was cruising on a clear day just below Mono Lake near Bishop, California. I looked over to my right in the direction of the Tonopah, Nevada test range and saw an explosion start on the ground and kick the dust straight up to 30,000 feet before the mushroom developed. I was cruising at 35,000 feet when I slowly realized that this was an atomic bomb detonation. I wondered if I was out of the reach of the radiation, and I wondered why no NOTAMS (Notice to Air Missions issued by the Federal Aviation Administration) had indicated that an explosion was planned in that area. It may have been an underground test that got away from the test personnel. I landed in Reno and picked up the part at base operations. I blasted off and climbed on course for Hill Air Force Base. I landed at Hill, picked up some more parts, and blasted off back to George.

That night, I was scheduled to take an airman to Knoxville, Tennessee. The airman was on an emergency leave. I saddled up the T-33 and blasted off for Dallas. The airman did fine on that first leg on the flight. We refueled in Dallas and blasted off for Knoxville. We were flying over an overcast which reached up to 37,000 feet. The stars were bright and made the overcast look like murky water on a river. I was about ready to descend over the Knoxville beacon, when the airman told me that he was air sick and might vomit in the oxygen mask. I put the aircraft in a circle and began reassuring him that everything was fine, and that this was just a routine penetration. When his voice sounded more confident, I commenced the penetration. I talked to him on the way down, telling him how to clear his ears and assuring him that I would level off anytime he felt uncomfortable. We got down without further incident. We landed in Knoxville, and he caught a bus over to the North Carolina border where he lived. I told him that I would meet him at base operations at McGhee Tyson Airport on Monday to take him back to California. I visited with my aunt and uncle in Knoxville.

On Monday, I picked the airman up at base operation and flew back to California in the daylight. I began to think that passengers should go through the high-altitude pressure training to familiarize them with high-altitude flying if they were going to make regular flights as passengers. I was fast becoming a mercy pilot at George for emergency leave personnel.

The next day, I was dispatched to Langley Field near Virginia Beach, Virginia. I blasted off and sailed to Hensley Naval Air Station in Dallas to refuel. I blasted off from Hensley and roared into Langley Air Force Base where I picked up my parts at base operations. I checked the weather, and it wasn't good enough for me to land at my first stop on the return flight, so I visited the post exchange and lounged around base operations until the weather improved.

When the weather had improved, I took off on course for Salina, Kansas. It was getting late when I arrived at my destination. I refueled and filed my flight plan for George, but the airdrome officer thought that I was stretching my fuel. I told him to calculate the distance from Langley to Salinas, from which I had just come. He did and decided that I knew what I was doing. I blasted off and climbed on course for Las Vegas. I had a habit of "cruise climbing" enroute after I got on top of the weather. As I burned down my fuel, the aircraft became lighter and I could climb higher, thereby increasing my range of flying time. I was cruise climbing at about 40,000 feet just outside Pueblo, Colorado and the overcast was climbing up with me. I figured the weather was higher over the Rockies. I noticed that the overcast had some whitecaps like the air was being disturbed just ahead. I got ready to go through the weather until I could climb back on top. When I entered the clouds, I got some turbulence that caused my wings to roll through 90° of travel before my full control action righted the aircraft. Then the aircraft rotated the opposite direction through 90°. I used full controls to right the aircraft. The move was sudden and violent. The thin air at altitude usually buffered the turbulence.

I tuned in Pueblo radio and listened to the weather report. There had been a tornado, which suddenly developed fifty miles southeast of Colorado Springs. The top of that tornado must've stretched over to Pueblo. I realized that I was in the eye of that tornado. Fortunately, I was at high altitude. I braced to go through the other side of the cup. Sure enough, I got the same movement when I penetrated the rim again. I flew on to Las Vegas and noticed that I had plenty of fuel to get to George, where the weather was good. I let down and landed without further incident. I had gone from the east coast to the west coast against the westerly winds with only one refueling stop. A pilot had to know his or her aircraft, the weather, and the winds to do that within the regulations.

The next day, I applied for the test pilot school at Edwards Air Force Base. The age limit was thirty-two. I was thirty-two, but I could make it if my application came through before my 33rd birthday. Some of the other pilots told me that they would not want to fly those canned missions, but I saw more in the research and development aspects of the school.

The people around the high desert had been good to the Air Force and the test pilot school was well received. In fact, George was well received in the Victorville area. The Air Force brought a large payroll into the high desert. When Captain Joe McConnell returned from Korea as a triple jet fighter ace, the local real estate people at Apple Valley had a home built for him at no cost to show their appreciation for his efforts in Korea. Captain John McConnell was subsequently killed in August 1954 while test flying an F-86H aircraft out of Edwards Air Force Base. I heard that the flying tail control came disconnected and Joe was trying to land the aircraft with only the trim tabs when the desert turbulence upset the flight path near the round out. The crash was fatal to Joe. His wife still traded at George Air Force Base and utilized their services.

One day, an order came down from the Air Force to dispatch ten pilots to Mobile, Alabama to pick up ten surplus F-80 shooting stars and deliver the aircraft to some South American countries. I was one of those selected to make the flight. We grabbed our bags and boarded Bonanza at Apple Valley and flew to Phoenix, where we boarded Eastern Airlines to Houston and on to Mobile.

Eastern Airlines did not appear to be as passenger-friendly and image-conscious as American Airlines. We got off the aircraft in Mobile and caught a staff car over to the BOQ. We cleaned up and went down to the officers club, which overlooked the bay. The view was beautiful in the candlelight dining room, but the action was too mundane for fighter jockeys. The permanent party didn't have much more going on than bingo. You could hear a pin drop in that bar room. We didn't patronize the bar for long. We turned in for the night so we could get up early in the morning and test fly those old warbirds.

The next morning, we went to the Flight line after breakfast. Our liaison officer gathered us in base operations and gave us a little briefing. He told us that two of the aircraft were going to Ecuador, two more were going to Chile, and the remaining seven aircraft were going to Uruguay. We drew straws to see who took the short flight and who took the long flights. I drew one of the short straws. My aircraft was going to Peru.

I saddled up the F-80 and blasted off on my test hop. The aircraft went through her paces, but the engine lacked one percent power to make the flight. Everyone else's aircraft checked out. Eight of the aircraft blasted off for Miami that afternoon. I had to select another aircraft and test it the next day. One other pilot stayed with me so we would have two radios when we flew into Miami to join the other eight pilots. We spent another night at the slow club, relaxing.

The next day, I was given another aircraft to test fly and that aircraft flew to specifications. When I landed, I was given orders to take the aircraft to Uruguay also. We blasted off for Miami in clear and sunny weather. We landed at Miami International, taxied over to the ramp, and shut down. We had to spend the night in Miami before we could clear customs. I imagined the Duck Butts had to have twenty-four hours' notice before they could get ready to monitor our progress across the Gulf of Mexico.

We grabbed a taxi to the Fontainebleau for dinner. We soon realized that we were out of our element at the Fontainebleau. We just walked around the inside of the place before we got a cab over to the Blue Waters Hotel on Miami Beach. We checked in for the night and attended the local dance in the hotel ballroom that night.

The next day we got a cab out to Miami International. We cleared customs and went out to check out our aircraft. The flight commander had a friend who wanted to go to Uruguay, so he asked me to take his friend's aircraft to Ecuador and let his friend take my aircraft to Uruguay. I told him that I was sticking to the written orders, but I would switch with his friend if Mobile changed the orders. They dropped the subject.

The weather was clear and sunny. We blasted out of Miami and climbed on course for "Gitmo Bay." We sailed across the water and crossed Cuba. We let down over the Gulf and came inbound to the city of Santiago de Cuba. The maps indicated that there were gun emplacements around the city, and it was a prohibited zone. I thought the flight commander was lost or had orders to harass the city when he buzzed over it. The thought occurred to me that we might get shot! Our relations with Cuba were not the best at that time. They had been wanting the Naval base back in their hands for some time. We flew over to Gitmo and landed. We were taken by launch over to the main side, where the BOQ, officers club, and post exchange were located. We checked into the BOQ and visited the post exchange before settling down in the officers' club for the evening. The club was located on a hill overlooking the bay and we could look out the window and watch the sailboats coming into port for the evening with their multicolored sails.

I saw a sailboat with a red sail. I felt that the person who wrote the lyrics for the song "Red Sails in the Sunset" must have been here. Gitmo was an isolated station, like an aircraft carrier. The base personnel were confined to the base and its activities. I noticed a little strain showing on the veterans who had been there for a while. We didn't cause much fuss there.

The next morning, the launch motored us back across the bay to the airstrip. We saddled up and blasted off across the Gulf of Mexico. The 700 miles passed rather quickly. The weather was clear with seventy miles visibility. We arrived over the Panama Canal and commenced our letdown. The flight commander again ignored a prohibited zone on the map and flew right through it.

We landed at the Pacific end of the canal at Howard Field because it was concrete and five thousand feet long. The concrete sections of the runway had settled in the marsh and our shock absorbers bottomed on the nose and main gear every time we crossed a section. It sounded like a train on the rails. My right brake had some air in the system, which made the brakes soft and mushy. I landed in such a way that I could do a little more breaking with my left brake. I was able to stop by landing from left to right after the other aircraft got off the runway. We taxied up to the ramp and shut down for the day. We buttoned up the aircraft and rode the blue bus about twenty-five miles back to Albrook Air Force Base. We checked into the quarters and came down to the club for dinner. Again, we found a general lack of enthusiasm around the dining room and lounge. That was normal for this type of location. We ordered dinner, and for dessert, I requested some ice cream with chocolate syrup on it. The syrup was crystalline and old. I shouldn't have eaten it. We had a few drinks and turned in for the night. I had just laid down on the bed when I experienced searing gas pains. That chocolate had given me food poisoning. I stayed in the bathroom all night trying to vomit that stuff off my stomach.

The next morning, the flight leader wanted me to give up my aircraft again. I told him that I didn't get an opportunity like this very often and that I would take the aircraft to Uruguay. We went to base operation for our weather briefing where we saw some cloud coverage on the radar scope. The weatherman told us that this coverage was in the northern section of the area and that we would not run into this weather going south. He then brought in a weather map which was eight years old! Some South American had authored a dissertation on the weather trends at altitude in the southern hemisphere. We reviewed these maps for what they were worth. There had not been any need for high altitude maps in South America before this time, because jets were just coming to South America.

We saddled up, blasted off, and climbed on course for Lima, Perú. We hit dark and turbulent clouds at 14,000 feet and began climbing through them. We had been in the clouds for about one minute when we encountered the worst turbulence that I had ever experienced in or out of clouds. The rain was so heavy that I could not see out of my canopy half the time. The updrafts and downdrafts were pitching us up and down by each other, twenty and thirty feet. I was just getting ready to break down and get away from the formation when the rain and the turbulence let up. We were incredibly lucky that we did not collide in that long forty or fifty seconds when we were in the heart of that turmoil.

We flew over the gulf of Panama. The Colombians had stoned Vice President Nixon's automobile just before this trip and we didn't want to get in their air space. We finally broke out on top of the weather at 35,000 feet some 80 miles later. When we leveled off and throttled back to cruise, my canopy seal suddenly pulled away from the canopy rails to the inside, inflated like a big king cobra, and wrapped around my headrest. I experienced decompression and my command radio went dead. I was going to have to communicate by hand signals.

When we got abreast of radio Quito in Ecuador, the pilot flying the jet destined to land at Guayaquil, peeled off our left wing and headed toward the radio station to make his penetration. We continued to radio Lima, Peru. We closed our formation over the beacon and let down to the west out over the sea so we would not run into those cloud covered Andes mountains, which rose to 23,000 feet along the western coast of South America.

We finally broke out under the clouds at 1,200 feet inbound to the coast. We had to dodge some islands which stuck up out of the water about 1,000 feet on the way into the coastline. When we arrived over the base, we broke on the initial and commenced our four second interval spacing. The lead aircraft landed, and immediately stirred up so much dust on the runway that the rest of us pilots had to take our aircraft around the pattern and re-enter after the dust settled on the runway.

We spaced our aircraft long enough apart to avoid landing in the dust stirred up by the previous aircraft. We taxied to the ramp and shut down for the night. After we cleared customs, we were taken into Lima and quartered in the Hilton hotel. We cleaned up and dressed in civilian clothes to avoid speculation by the natives and possible controversy. We had a little reception at dinner, and a tour of the Inca Indian ruins was scheduled for us the next day. We went out on the streets that night for a short time. The natives were weary of strangers, so we returned to the bar and the hotel. We talked to some American diplomats in the bar. They didn't have much to say either. Lima wasn't the jovial place we had anticipated.

The next day, we took the bus out to the Inca Indian ruins. The natives lived in rural poverty outside of town and the road was strictly secondary at best. The natives used the llama as the beast of burden. The llama looked like an oversized goat but was as big as a buck deer. The natives carried their wares on this animal, some of which were big enough to ride.

The natives hung around the tourists at the ruins to sell llama skins and decorative rugs. I bought two llama rugs. We returned to the hotel and lounged another day until our diplomatic clearance had been processed. The next day, the weather was fair, and we blasted off on course for Antofagasta, Chili. We climbed out to sea until we penetrated the thin overcast. We then turned south, and continued our climb along the coast, noting the Andes mountains running along the coastline reaching up to 23,000 feet. Those snow-capped mountains were a real barrier for the natives, or anyone else who had to cross them on the ground or in the air. I noticed that the coastal areas were somewhat arid, even though they were so close to the sea. I surmised that the prevailing Westerly winds came ashore but did not drop the moisture on the beaches. The rain fell up in the mountains, after being carried aloft to the cold temperatures all over the mountain. Most of the rainfall fell on the eastern side of the Andes Mountain range. As we sailed down the coast toward Antofagasta, I noted the lack of roads or development along the coast. I began to realize why South Americans had to travel by air, boat, or horseback between the few metropolitan areas.

We were over a coastal desert when we commenced to let down to land at Antofagasta. We landed on the airstrip in the desert close to the coast. As we taxied to the parking ramp, I noticed four Navy corsairs on the ramp with Chilean markings on them. There was one British jet fighter parked on the ramp also. The British jet must've flown off a carrier. The British may have been trying to sell their jets to the Chileans.

We shut down and got out of our aircraft. I had a big jungle knife hanging off my pistol belt. I had bought the knife in Panama in case I had to jettison in the jungles. There weren't any jungles here, but I kept the knife on my belt anyway. The Chilean groundcrew met the aircraft with one of our liaison officers who was stationed there. The ground crew were all looking at my knife.

We were told to give the ground crew cigarettes to refuel our aircraft. I told my ground crew that they could have the cigarettes after they completed the refueling and after I checked the tanks. This turned out to be irritating to the ground crew who were refueling my jet. The other pilots gave their ground crews cigarettes before they refueled their aircraft. The ground crew reported my proposition to my flight commander. The liaison officer and my flight commander had a few words for me, and they weren't good. I gave the cigarettes to the ground crew immediately after this confrontation. We walked over to the snack bar where the Chilean officers had some salami, brown rice, bread, and some beer for us to eat and drink. I had to pass up the offer, since my stomach was still a little fuzzy from the Panama incident.

The ground crew reported to the liaison officer that my aircraft had blown the canopy seals. The liaison officer jumped on the opportunity to keep the aircraft at Antofagasta for repair so he could complete the delivery himself. My flight commander was ready to agree with the liaison officer. However, I exercised my prerogative as the pilot to continue the mission with the knowledge of the discrepancy and its ramifications.

We went back out to the aircraft and blasted off for Santiago, Chili. The weather was clear with seventy miles visibility. I climbed up along the side of the towering 23,000 foot Andes. The snow-capped mountains were a natural barrier of long-standing duration and continued to pose transportation problems.

I could see that the vegetation was a little green around the coast as we approached the airport at Valparaiso, Chili. We let down out to sea and came inbound to the coast. We entered the traffic pattern and landed on the one long east-west runway. As we slowed our aircraft while rolling down the runway, I spotted four more Navy corsairs parked neatly on the ramp. I suddenly realized why we had sold surplus Navy fighters to the South American countries along the Andes Mountains. Our Navy could support the aircraft from a carrier stationed offshore in the event of an emergency.

We turned off the runway and taxied up to the jet parking area by following the ground crew instructions. We parked the aircraft and shut them down. As we were climbing out of the aircraft, the entire Chilean Air Force marched out on the ramp and came to a halt. The band began to play the Chilean national anthem. We stood at attention by our aircraft. Then the band played the American national anthem. After the music stopped, our flight leader reported to the commander of the Chilean Air Force and saluted. We were escorted to the waiting bus and transported to Santiago.

We were quartered in the first-class Hilton Hotel in Santiago. Our flight commander told us to get ready to attend a dinner reception that evening in the hotel dining room. We hadn't realized how important our mission was to the South Americans. We had flown jets for so long that we had taken the jet age for granted. The South Americans were showing their appreciation to us for ushering in the jet age for them. We cleaned up and reported to the ballroom where we were given the reception of full-fledged diplomats. We responded by playing the role.

After the official function was over, we retired to the bar. It was winter in South America, and it was too cold to go outside of the hotel that night. Besides, there wasn't much going on around the city, except for the influx of ski tourists. I was window shopping in the hotel hallway when I recognized a former legal officer who had served with me in the 48th fighter bomber squadron in Chaumont, France back in 1953 to 1955. He recognized me immediately. We retired to the bar to catch up on what had happened to us since we were in Chaumont.

He was no longer in the service and was in South America on a ski vacation. He was practicing law in New York City. I told him that I suspected that he was in South America on a CIA mission. I could hardly believe that his practice had been that successful in five years. I began to suspect that he may have inherited his wealth. He denied being connected with any government agency and told me that he had been skiing with a bunch of Midshipmen and Navy carrier pilots who had come to Chile on the aircraft carrier Enterprise.

The Enterprise aircraft carrier had just pulled out of port the day before we arrived. It was making all the ports of call in Central and South America for the benefit of the cadets, and to reassure the South Americans that the Monroe Doctrine was a continuing reality. The Enterprise had come down the Atlantic side and was going back to America up the Pacific side of the southern continent.

While in the bar, I saw a polo saddle hanging over the bar mirror with the associated tack. I could have bought that rig for $110 and it would've been a good souvenir to hang over the mantle at home. However, I considered the difficulty of mailing them back to the states and decided against the purchase. The South American nobles took great pride in their ability to manage the horse. The polo games in South America were followed as closely as we followed our major sports. We closed the bar and turned in for the night.

The next day, we lounged around the hotel, waiting for our diplomatic clearance to come through. The weather finally broke and the Chilean commander placed an unprecedented phone call from Santiago to the commander of the Argentine Air Force, as well as, the commander-in-chief of the Uruguayan Air Force, requesting permission for us to depart Santiago, fly over Argentina, and land in Montevideo. We were cleared to blast off.

We left two jets for the Chilean Air Force and the pilots of those two jets caught commercial flights back to the states from Santiago. We saddled up the remaining seven Shooting Stars and blasted off for Buenos Aires and Montevideo. We circled the airport and climbed out to sea until we were sure that we could climb over the 23,000 foot mountains just east of Santiago.

We turned east at about 15,000 feet and climbed over the Andes Mountains at 30,000 feet. We passed over the tops of the mountains and we were in Argentina. The weather was clear and sunny. The mountains had been left behind when we passed the radio beacon at Mendoza. The terrain below was flat, and the vegetation was green. The land looked a little on the marshy side and I began to understand why Argentina had hundreds of cattle ranches on those plains. No wonder Argentina was big in exporting beef.

I spotted the city of Buenos Aires, a sprawling city of approximately six million people. I located the big 11,000 foot, just completed, asphalt airstrip just south of the city. The new 1,500 foot concrete overruns on the ends of the asphalt runway made the airport easy to locate from the air. General Lemay had just completed a 6,000 mile nonstop flight in one of his B-52 bombers from America to Argentina just a few days prior to our arrival to demonstrate to the South Americans how accessible South America was for our strategic Air Force.

We let down over the Rio de la Plata and the bay between Buenos Aires and Montevideo. We entered the traffic pattern and landed in one flight of four and another flight of three jets. We taxied to the ramp where we found another Air Force waiting to give us a military welcome. We climbed out of our aircraft and stood at attention again, while the two national anthems were played by the military soldiers. The entire Uruguayan Air Force officer corps had gathered on the ramp to meet us. This was a big day for the Uruguayan Air Force. Even the retired members of their Air Force were on hand for the occasion.

We cleared customs and were whisked off to the Hilton Hotel in Montevideo. After we cleaned up, we were taken out to the home of the Commanding General of the Uruguayan Air Force for dinner. We were famished by the time we arrived at the General's home. His wife was most gracious, and the spaghetti and ravioli were exotic. The General had many questions, and the flight commander had a lot of answers. The General told us that we could get some fur coats made from South American nutria skins at a very reasonable price in town. After dinner, we all went down to the little fur shop, where Mamie Eisenhower had bought a coat. I bought three coats for about $1,000 in 1957 dollars. I intended to give one to my wife, one to my mother, and one to my sister, when I got back to the states. I also bought myself a maroon kangaroo smoking jacket. We returned to the Hilton, and I placed the fur coats in the safety deposit box with a hotel security officer. We retired to the bar.

I wanted to catch a commercial flight back to the states, which would take me through as much of South and Central America as possible. We would not be able to catch a flight for a couple of days. The flight commander didn't care how I flew back to the states. We closed the bar and turned in for the night. The next day, I found out that I could catch a seaplane over to Buenos Aires. I went down to the seaplane mooring dock and found out that the aircraft made about three round trips per day to Buenos Aires. I bought a round-trip ticket and waited in the terminal for takeoff time. The seaplane had six engines. When the pilot showed up, it was "raining cats and dogs." The pilots made their 360 degree inspection of the aircraft while we waited in the passenger terminal. The pilots tried starting the engines, but they drowned out. Not one of the engines would start. I cashed in my ticket and returned to the Hilton Hotel.

Montevideo was a modern city on the bay. As I lounged around the bar waiting for a reservation, I pondered the economic and social conditions that I had found in South America. The difference in the standards between the top class of South Americans and the peasants was a wide gap to be sure. The wealthy individuals controlled politics and the economy, much like the royal families in Europe. The middle class was not large considering the population of the country. In comparison, America's economy and industrialization allowed for a large middle class of people. Economic opportunity abounded for our middle class. However, the limited opportunities in South America left five or six families in the driver's seat in 1957. I could not really appreciate our form of government until I had seen the economies in the South American countries.

My thoughts drifted to the fact that no matter how dire the economic circumstances, some individuals seem to rise above their surroundings. A perfect Argentinian example was Luis Angel Firpo aka "the Wild Bull of las Pampas," who came out of the bulrushes of Argentina to fight another outstanding personality of yesteryear, Jack Dempsey, for the heavyweight championship of the world in 1923.

I closed the bar and turned in for the night. The next morning, I checked out my rugs and furs, and caught a taxi over to the airport. I checked into the airport terminal building and waited for my commercial flight, which was delayed. I finally boarded the flight near dusk. The Airliner had three flight attendants who were most receptive to our friendliness. We enjoyed the food and refreshments, as well as the chatter until we went to sleep. The airliner lost an engine as we came in for a landing in São Paulo, Brazil, but managed to land successfully.

We rested in the terminal lounge while the engine was repaired. We loaded up the airliner when the engine was repaired and roared off to Rio de Janeiro. The coast of Brazil was green. We arrived in Rio early the next morning and approached the city from the sea. The city was as sprawling as Buenos Aires, but it lay at the foot of some substantial mountains. I could see the enormous statue of Christ on top of the mountain just west of town. This was the largest statue that I had seen besides the Statue of Liberty. The airport ran right out into the bay. We landed to the west on the east-west runway, taxied in, and shut down at the terminal. I elected to join the rest of the troops, who caught a cab to the Copacabana Hotel on the beach in the south part of Rio. The city was beautiful with wide and well laid out streets. The buildings were elegant and metropolitan. The city was clean and reminded me of a resort city in the south of France, like Nice or Monte Carlo.

As we drove through the center city, I had the driver stop by the American Embassy. I wanted to go into the cafeteria and the post exchange to see if there was anyone there that I might happen to know. The first thing I heard when I got out of the cab was a record playing an Elvis Presley song. The Embassy was not open for the day yet, so the cabbie gave me a tour of the beach. Afterwards, we headed back to the Copacabana. I had to get some sleep before I caught another flight up the coast. I had my furs and rugs with me, and the cabbie recommended that I leave the furs and the rugs in the locker boxes at the airport. We drove over there, and I checked my loot into the lockers. The cabbie took me back to the hotel, where I tried to sleep, but it was difficult because the weather was hot.

The next day, I checked out of the hotel and caught a cab to the airport. I had been scheduled on a milk run flight, which would land at every major hamlet along the eastern coast of South America. We roared off and climbed on course for Salvador. We landed at Brasília for a brief passenger stop and then took off for Salvador. After a refueling stop at Salvador, we roared off and landed at Recife, which had been a point of departure across the Atlantic during WWII for our B-24's when weather did not permit taking the northern "high flight" route. Everyone who had gone through Recife had purchased a pair of kangaroo boots for about five dollars. I didn't need any boots because I already had kangaroo boots.

We took off from Recife and flew up the coast to the mouth of the Amazon River at Belem. We were in the tropics. We refueled in Belem and roared off on course to Georgetown in Guyana. After a brief stop in Georgetown, we took off for Port of Spain on the island of Trinidad, just off the coast of Venezuela. We landed in Port of Spain for a passenger and mail exchange. We flew along the tropical coastline until we arrived at Maiquetia Airport, which served the capital city of Caracas. We walked off the aircraft to wait in the lounge for the next connecting flight. The terminal was flooded with construction workers who had come into the airport to be flown to the new oil fields. Venezuela was the richest country in South America in the development of natural resources.

I couldn't get a flight until the next morning, so I called the Caracas Hilton, which was located twenty-five miles inland in the mountains. Rooms were going for $50 per day, so I decided not to bother. I spent a hot and uncomfortable night in the terminal. Fortunately, my departure aircraft left in the early hours of the morning. We roared off the runway and headed west for Barquisimeto. We flew over the mountains and cattle country where the grass was green, and the undergrowth was heavy where it had not been cleared.

We adjusted our manifest at Barquisimeto and roared off on course for Maracaibo. As we let down over Lake Maracaibo, we could see many of the 2,000 oil well rigs pumping oil out of the lake. As we approached the runway, I saw hundreds of people running out on the taxiway toward a C-47 parked on the ramp. I thought that we were going to witness another banana revolution in progress. I asked the pilot what was going on and he told me that Ida Pieri, Miss Venezuela, and participant to the Miss Universe Beauty contest of 1958, was on board the aircraft that was parked on the taxi strip. The crowd mobbed the aircraft.

We landed, turned off the runway, and stopped until the dignitaries took Miss Pieri to the terminal, followed by the crowd. After we let off our passengers, we took off, climbed over the mountains, and landed at Barranquilla, Columbia briefly, and then took off and flew over the Gulf of Darien to Colon on the border of Panama.

We refueled and took off on our run through Central America. We landed at San Jose, Costa Rica for our first stop where I noticed four P-51's and two P-47 fighters sitting in the staging area on the ramp. Those planes constituted the Costa Rican Air Force.

We flew on up to Managua, Nicaragua, where I spotted four more P-51's and two P-47 fighters on the ramp. We discharged our passengers and the mail, and took off for Tegucigalpa, Honduras. When we landed at Tegucigalpa, I spotted four British Marine fighters on the ramp, which made sense because Honduras was a British protectorate.

We departed Honduras and landed at San Salvador, El Salvador, where I saw four more P-51 fighters. We flew out of San Salvador and landed in Guatemala City, Guatemala where I again saw four more P-51's and two P-47 fighters. We flew out of Guatemala, and landed in Belize, where I spotted two more British Marine fighters. We left Belize and flew up the Yucatán peninsula to Mexico City, Mexico.

Mexico City was located high in the mountains. After landing, we taxied to the ramp. My next flight did not leave until the next morning, so I checked into the Hilton Hotel, which was noisy because of repairs being done. However, after having seen the facilities of

Central America, I was ready to put up with a little noise. I had dinner with one of the passengers who had come through Central America with me. She had been to Venezuela to visit her husband, who worked in the old fields there. We discussed the pros and cons of South America as we ate.

The next day, I boarded an American Airlines flight for San Antonio. We roared off the runway and climbed out on course for San Antonio. After leveling off, I unfastened my safety belt and waited for the flight attendant to bring us some refreshments before dinner. When the flight attendant came back to check the passenger manifest, I thought she looked familiar. I was busy talking to the lady who sat next to me, who was the daughter of the Chrysler dealer in San Antonio. We were talking automobiles.

Finally, the flight attendant came by with refreshments and I then recognized her. She was the flight attendant that I had met in Dallas and promised to look up if I was ever in Mexico City. I told her that I had forgotten about her living in Mexico City. I said that I had been living too fast and I promised to slow down on the next trip. The airline pilot circled around the Temple of the Sun and Moon, which the Aztecs had built upon great pyramids centuries ago. We studied the project from our windows in the clear and sunny weather. We soon arrived in San Antonio and landed. I cleared customs and had to pay some duty on my loot. After clearing customs, we boarded the aircraft for the flight to Dallas to connect with the American Airlines flight going to Los Angeles.

We roared up to Dallas and landed at the Amon Carter field. There was a short wait before my next flight, so I called Bob Leonard and found him home for a change. He drove over to the terminal to see the fur coats and to hear about the flight to South America. We chatted until my flight was paged for Los Angeles. I boarded the LA flight and settled down for refreshments and a delicious meal. I thought about all that I had seen in South America. I fell asleep and the flight attendant woke me up in time to buckle my seatbelt for the landing in Los Angeles. I went into the Los Angeles terminal and waited on my bags. I noticed that the florist in the terminal was selling orchids for five dollars each. The orchid was encased in a lovely paper box with a clear top. I bought one for my wife. I picked up my bags and boarded the Bonanza flight over the mountains to Apple Valley.

When we landed in Apple Valley, I called my wife to come over to the airport to pick me up from Hesperia. I had spent $1,300 on my 26-day flight to South America. My wife came up in her Ford with the children. I gave her the orchid and she looked at me like I had been up to something. I carried my bags to the car, and we drove over to Hesperia to the Bear Valley Motel. I took the bags inside and showed my wife the fur coats. I told her to pick one out for herself. She picked one but thought that buying coats for other family members was somewhat extravagant. I told Ruby as much as she wanted to hear about South America, and we had dinner. The children had a hundred questions about the trip. We finally put the children to bed and turned in for the night.

The next day, I reported to George Air Force Base. It was Friday and I was able to check out a T-33 to take my furs to Grundy. I loaded up the aircraft and put the fur coats in the gun bays. I blasted off and refueled in Dallas before flying on to Knoxville. I landed at McGhee Tyson airport and my uncle drove me over to Knoxville. My mother just happened to be visiting my aunt and she really appreciated the fur coat. I called my sister in Chattanooga and offered her the other coat. She told me that her husband had just bought her a mink stole, so I told her that I would give the remaining fur coat to my brother, and he could give it to his wife.

I drove to Grundy with my mother and took the remaining fur coat over to my brother's house to give to his wife. I also showed him my smoking jacket to which he took a shine and told me that he wanted it too. I told him that he could wear it, but when he got a little miffed, I just told him to keep it. He was happy as a baby. I spent the night telling my folks about the trip to South America.

The next day, I went downtown on the streets of Grundy, meeting my friends and telling them a little something about the trip. On Saturday afternoon, my brother and I went golfing. The next morning, my brother contacted Joe Breeding, who flew me back to Knoxville in a Cessna 180. I thanked my brother and Joe, and then climbed into the Shooting Star. I blasted off for Hensley Naval Air Station and flew back to Victorville. I landed at George and drove back to Hesperia.

I reported to the base the next morning and we had a meeting of all pilots. Colonel Lavin explained that Congress had put the squeeze on the funds for flying personnel in the Air Force. He explained that some of the pilots occupying positions with flying as a secondary duty would most likely be administratively grounded. This meant a cut in pay and a real adjustment in the career field. I was counting on my application coming through for the test pilot school at Edwards, but it hadn't shown up. After the meeting, I ran into Colonel Chuck Yeager over at base operations and asked him what the situation was over at Edwards. He explained that he had just arrived at George himself because the test pilot program was currently full up.

I made a trip to Colonel Lavin's office and requested that he transfer me out of the command into multi engine rather than have me face administrative review. I told Colonel Lavin that I would like to go to the Commanding General of TAC and plead my case if he could do no more. Colonel Lavin sprang out of his chair, put his foot up on the chair seat, and informed me that he was my Lord and Master, and that he would decide my fate that day. I was immediately put on orders to report to Randolph Air Force Base, Texas for a three month commanders course for the KC- 97. Afterwards I was to report to Malmstrom, Air Force Base, Montana to fly the KC- 97 tankers aircraft for SAC (Strategic Air Command). I was "out of the skillet and into the frying pan."

**CHAPTER 28**

# SAC, Malmstrom, AFB, Montana

I took a thirty-day delay enroute to visit Grundy with my family. I had ten new Firestone 500 tires put on my two cars. We packed our bags and sent our belongings to Malmstrom Air Force Base to be stored until we arrived there. We departed Victorville by automobile and motored to the Grand Canyon on the first day. My wife and I enjoyed the scenery, but the children didn't notice it that much. The next day, we motored to Gallup, Albuquerque, Taos, and Amarillo. We paid Hulen Burke a short visit and then drove to Chillicothe, Texas, where we spent the night with my old friend, Dr. James Howard, and his wife.

The following day, we drove to Dallas and visited my cousin Taylor Dixon and his wife Dorothy. We drove on to Texarkana, Little Rock, and Memphis, where we spent the night. We then drove to Knoxville for a two-day visit before driving on to Grundy. We spent a couple of weeks in Grundy, driving around to all the relatives in

Virginia and Kentucky, and introducing my children. My mother had gone to Tampa, Florida, so we motored next to Chattanooga to visit my sister. We spent a short visit there on Signal Mountain and drove to Macon, Georgia to visit my cousin, Frieda Marion and her husband, Jack. Jack was working with the civil service at Warner Robins Air Force Base.

The next day, we drove to Tampa, Florida. My mother had not seen my son, Harold Junior. We spent a few days in Tampa before motoring on towards Tallahassee. I planned to travel the Jeff Davis coastal Highway to New Orleans to spend the night. The drive was beautiful. The evergreen pines lined the highway, and the ocean breeze kept the route cool in the evening.

We spent the night in New Orleans. The following day, we motored to Houston and crossed the plains to San Antonio. We drove out to the little town at the gates of Randolph, called Shirts. I found a little house within walking distance of the base. I rented the bottom furnished floor at a reasonable rate. The old man who owned the place lived upstairs.

I reported to Randolph for the aircraft commander course the next day. My wife put the children in the local schools. The ground school for the KC-97 covered the operation of that tanker and the mission from stem to stern. When ground school was completed, we flew every conceivable mission that the aircraft was capable of flying. I quickly got used to the nosewheel steering wheel and I passed the course "with flying colors."

By the time I completed the course, winter had set in. We packed our bags and motored out of Shirts, Texas enroute to Chillicothe, Texas to spend the night with Dr. and Mrs. James Howard. We made it to Chillicothe without any trouble and spent the night.

The next day we motored north to Amarillo, Walsenburg, and Colorado Springs, where we spent the night. The next day, we motored on to Denver, and ate at the Lowry Air Force Base officers club. We left Denver and drove toward Cheyenne, Wyoming. We ran into a little snow flurry just south of Cheyenne in the open range and sheepherding country. Snow covered the plains and blue ice covered the roads. My wife was a little leery of driving on the snow covered highway. The overcast sky gave the area a wilderness look. At one point, I spotted a sheep herder just off the road with his herd. He must've been driving them back to the barn in the cold temperature.

My wife and I were in separate cars. I instructed her on how to drive in the snow. I told her to let up on the gas if she hit a slick place rather than putting on the brakes. I also told her to let up on the gas easily and to apply the accelerator smoothly in the ice and snow. I came over a little hill and hit a slick place. I let off the gas easily and looked through my rearview mirror to monitor my wife's handling of the situation. I saw her auto start to swerve from one side of the road to the other. The rear of her car finally passed the front of her car, and she disappeared over the snowbank in reverse. I stopped my car, got out, and ran back to the place where she went over the bank. I only saw tracks. I looked out in the field and saw the automobile sitting there. It had not turned over. I waded through the fourteen inches of snow out to the car. My wife was still clutching the steering wheel, wondering what had happened. I got into the driver's seat and started the car. I put the car in drive and, remarkably, it moved. The sage grass in the snow gave the tires the traction they required. I decided to drive along the road until I found a low place, and then take a run to climb out of the field and back onto the road. About that time, we spotted a snowplow coming over the hill. The snowplow driver was looking at us over in the field and almost ran into my convertible parked on the road.

I drove my wife's Ford south in the field along the highway until I came to a low section of the road where I gunned the Ford to climb the snowbank. Once I was on top of the bank, I entered the highway and turned around to drive north back towards where my Ford was parked. I told my wife that we would drive on to Cheyenne, where we would spend the night and rest up. My wife was still a little shaky, but she agreed to drive the remaining twenty miles to Cheyenne.

We drove into town, parked at the best hotel there, and checked in for the night. We had a good warm supper and turned in for the night. The next morning after breakfast, we loaded up the cars and drove over to the service station where we filled up with gas and oil and checked the antifreeze and the battery water. Towns and cities were far apart in Wyoming. We drove up to Casper and had lunch before driving on to Billings and Butte, Montana. We had supper in Butte, and then drove to Great Falls that evening. We arrived in Great Falls at dusk. The white blanket of snow was about twelve to fourteen inches deep. As we drove over a little crest, just on the edge of town, I spotted the airbase. The base was located on the eastern outskirts of the city. The lights of the city and the blanket of snow gave the appearance of a Christmas postcard. Great Falls was situated on the Prairie along the banks of the Missouri River. The Rocky Mountains formed a backdrop to the west. We drove to the base and checked in the BOQ for the night.

The next day, we had breakfast and drove into town where we bought a newspaper and started looking for furnished houses for rent. We found a little four room house on 17th St., just six or seven blocks from the front gate of Malmstrom Air Force base. We rented the house immediately. The shopping center and schools were nearby, and Columbus Hospital was just six blocks north. This was an important consideration because my wife was expecting our fourth child. We loaded the cupboard and settled down for our first meal in our new home. We planned to explore the Northwest United States on our weekends, just like we had explored every other place we had been stationed. We drove all over town that day.

The next day, I reported to the base commander, Colonel Tex Barnes. His deputy directed me to report to one of the Air Refueling squadrons. I reported to the squadron commander and was assigned to a KC– 97 as a copilot trainee. I would fly in this training status until I was fully checked out and given a copilot position on a combat crew. There was the possibility that I could become a permanent copilot on this training crew after we became combat ready.

I was scheduled to fly a training mission that night. We reported to the personal equipment room three and one-half hours before takeoff. We drew our equipment and commenced the pre-flight inspection. We did everything but grease the aircraft. That was the most detailed inspection that I had ever witnessed. No wonder Colonel Burns had such a crack outfit. We lumbered off the runway on schedule and climbed out on course to Missoula, Montana. We were scheduled to refuel a B-52 over Missoula. We crossed the Rockies at dusk and the mountain views were wonderful. The elk, moose, and bear were scattered throughout the Rocky Mountain range. The elk was protected and ran free in the game preserves along with the bear. The moose were mostly confined to Yellowstone and Glacier parks. We leveled off at our cruising altitude and placed the plane on autopilot. We got out our box lunches and began to eat supper. That was an experience that I had not been able to enjoy in a fighter aircraft. I walked back to the tail section to observe the boom operator getting ready to refuel the approaching B-52. The instructor pilot and copilot were manning the yoke or controls.

When the B-52 came up behind us, the wake of the B-52 nudged the KC-97 upward. The instructor pilot made the correction to hold his altitude. The B-52 pulled up to within range of the telescopic boom. The boom operator flew the boom nozzle down into the opening in the back of the cockpit and on the dorsal portion of the B-52. The boom operator then directed fuel from the tanker's belly down through the boom into the fuselage tanks of the B-52. It only took about fifteen minutes to refuel the bomber. The boom operator hit the disconnect switch and the boom came out of the bomber's dorsal tank. The boom operator then retracted the boom and flew it up to the stowed position. I complimented the boom operator for his professional skill.

I returned to the cockpit and took over the copilot position for the return leg of the flight. On the way home, we started talking about automobiles for relaxation. I indicated that I wanted to trade my two Fords for a Cadillac. The instructor pilot told me where the Cadillac agency was in Great Falls. The flight engineer told me that he knew a local dealer who could get me a Cadillac from Choteau, Montana, if the local dealer didn't trade with me. We let down and flew a low approach to Malmstrom where we landed without incident. We taxied to the parking spot and shut down for the night. I drove home and turned in for the night.

The next day, I told my wife that we really didn't need two cars in Montana. After some convincing, she reluctantly agreed. I had promised myself a new Cadillac if I worked extremely hard before I was thirty-five years old. It was 1958 and I was thirty-three years old at the time.

That afternoon, I had my wife drive her car and follow me in my car to the local Cadillac dealer. We stopped out front and went inside. The salesman wanted to know what I had in mind. I told him that I wanted to trade cars and he asked me to pick out one. I selected one in short order and told him that I had two automobiles to trade, both of which had less than fifty thousand miles. He told me that he would drive them around the block. I went with him, and he found a lot of little things wrong with each car. When we completed the test rides, he told me that he would only take one car in on a trade. I thanked him and walked out to our cars and told my wife to follow me back to the house.

After we drove home, my wife told me that she didn't like the color of the Cadillac anyway. I told her that I was going to contact the local used car dealer who had a connection with the Chevrolet Cadillac dealer in Choteau. I drove over to the used car lot and found my connection. He had a Cadillac just like I wanted sitting on the lot. I think the engineer had tipped him off to the fact that I was looking for a green four-door Cadillac with Texas windows. I told him what I wanted for my two Fords. He agreed to the price, and we traded. I drove the 1959 Cadillac with the classic tail fins to the house that evening.

I was set for the west. I had my cowboy get up and my 1959 Cadillac. The next morning, I didn't have to go to work. I had breakfast, put on my golfing togs, and strolled out to my Cadillac parked in front of our house. My wife came to the door and watched me carry my golf clubs out to the car. I opened the trunk and set my sticks gently inside. Then I sat down on the lip of the open trunk and proceeded to take off my boots to put on my golfing shoes. My wife asked me where I was going. I told her that I was thinking about going over to the municipal golf course and playing a round of golf. She told me that she didn't think that I was going today. She told me to look at the tailfins of my Cadillac. I looked around to my right. Those beautiful 75 mm twin cannon shell shaped taillights were missing. Only the pigtails hung out of the receptacle. I thought that I would drive with one set of taillights, but when I looked around to the left side I saw only pigtails hanging from the socket there. I was dumbfounded at first. Then I became a little upset.

I went into the house and called the police to come out and investigate the theft. I found some fingerprints on the fins and some footprints in the dust on the ground. The screws which held the taillights in place were also on the ground. The pieces of evidence indicated that the theft had taken place right in front of my house.

The police came out and dusted the fingerprints and told me that every 1959 Cadillac in town on the car lots had been raided and the taillights stolen.

The police had been informed that an interstate theft ring was going through cities and hiring juveniles to steal the taillights. The theft ring was sending the taillights to California, where some outfit customized Chevrolets by putting the cannon shell tail lights in the three taillight slots on each side of that model of Chevrolet. Unbelievably, the police caught the thieves that day. I had to go to my insurance company to get my tail lights replaced. The twin tail lights cost $17 each. I had the taillights replaced that day and was able to go out to the golf course and play nine holes anyway.

I continued my training missions. We refueled B-52s and B-47s all over the western states, but those long flights made me sleepy. I had never spent over four hours up in a fighter, but these KC-97s would fly all day. The reality began to sink in that this type of flying was not as exciting as my former jet flying days. I also realized that I had not taken a cross-country since I had been at Malmstrom, and we always landed back at our base. In short, I had been cut off from the world to which I had been accustomed — traveling about at my leisure. I mentioned the fact that we never went on any cross-country trips to the other pilots. They said that they had never asked for a cross country because of the mission. I told them that the mission could be performed on a round robin cross country – we could refuel on every leg and land at a different base at the end of each leg of the flight. This type of flying might keep our routine from getting dull.

The next thing I knew, we were scheduled for a big round robin flight. We took off from Malmstrom and refueled a bomber on our way to Denver. We landed in Denver and parked our aircraft on static display for the open house that the base was sponsoring. We met the throngs all day. This was as interesting to us as it was to the milling crowds. That night, we went over to the officers club and lived it up a little bit before turning in for the night.

The next day, we roared off for Tucson, Arizona. We were climbing out when one of the engines had to be shut down because of excessive smoking. We returned and landed at Lowry Air Force Base. The ground crew checked the engine out and replaced some items. We roared off again toward Tucson. We refueled another bomber over Santa Fe before we continued to Tucson. As we were letting down in the traffic pattern for Davis-Monthan Air Force Base at Tucson, the faulty engine went out for good. We landed at Tucson without incident on the three remaining engines.

We checked into the BOQ, put on our civvies, and walked over to the officers club. The bomber pilots were having a bingo game and a party. We joined the party and were just getting to know the folks, when the flight line notified us that the engine had been replaced, and the aircraft was ready to go. The ground crew had changed engines in only six hours.

We headed for the BOQ to pick up our duds and then headed for the flight line. We saddled up the aerial tanker and roared off for March Air Force Base, in Riverside, California. We refueled a bomber over Blythe, California before we landed at March Air Force Base. We were scheduled to remain overnight at March Field and participate in a command golf tournament at Riverside the next day. I was scheduled to play with the Commanding General because we had the same handicap.

The next morning, I went out to the golf driving range early to hit some practice balls to warm up. Well, I hit too many too hard. I pulled a muscle in my shoulder and ruined my long game. I wanted to beat the General, but I knew that I would have to have an exceptionally good short game and my putting would have to be out of this world. We paired off and played the course. The General beat me handily. I just didn't have my heart in the game with that aching muscle, which got more sore as I continued to play. I finished the round and complimented the General on his good game.

We returned to the flight line and loaded up the tanker. We roared off for Castle Air Force Base at Merced, California. We refueled a bomber over Paso Robles on the coast before we flew on to Castle and landed. I called Jimmy Davis, the B-52 pilot from Hurley, Virginia, who was stationed at Castle. He came down to base operation and we had a nice chat. I gave him some reassurance that his parents would appreciate.

We blasted off from Castle and climbed on course for Great Falls. We refueled a bomber over Salt Lake City before flying on to Malmstrom and landing. I drove home that night and slept like a baby. The round robin had been a real morale booster.

The next day, the base was snowed in again. On my way to the base, my new Cadillac slid right through an intersection. Luckily for me, no one was traveling through the intersection at the time. I resolved right then to buy an old Ford to drive to and from work. My wife didn't like the idea of being without a car while I was at the base anyway. I found a 1952 Ford advertisement in the daily bulletin and bought it for $250. I had to have the radiator hoses replaced, but outside of that, it ran like a top. My wife was overjoyed at having wheels again.

The next night, we were scheduled to fly some night formation. We roared off into the night and climbed out to our rendezvous point. We joined up with three other KC-97's. We flew about one mile apart and monitored our position on radar. We flew down to Pocatello and rendezvoused with four B-52's. We refueled the bombers as we flew in formation. After completing our hookups and offloading the fuel, we disconnected and stowed the boom. We then started for home. We were monitoring the radio at Great

Falls where the weather had turned for the worse and the snow was coming down at the home base in pelts.

The Great Falls Municipal Airport had a component of the Air National Guard and Reserve unit, who were flying the all-weather F-89 fighter. The F-89's were up in force that night to intercept our tanker in a mock exercise. The F-89's completed their intercept mission and were headed home to Great Falls. Those jets easily out-distanced our conventional tankers. The airbase had a NOTAM out to the fact that the approach end of the jet runway was under construction in the overrun. The construction crew had dug down three feet at the lip of the runway to pour more concrete and extend the asphalt runway for the KC-135 jet tanker, which was scheduled to replace the KC-97 tanker at a future date. A transient T-33 came into Malmstrom on a cross-country flight and touched down a little short of the runway in the construction area. When his aircraft struck the lip of the runway, the landing gear sheared off and the T-33 continued down the runway another 1,200 feet before it slid off the side of the runway into the snow. The base closed the runway until the ground crew could get out to the runway and clear the debris and the aircraft off the runway. The pilots in the T-33 were not hurt, however the F-89's couldn't land at the municipal airport because the snowstorm had closed that airport by that time. The F-89's circled patiently waiting for Mälmstrom or the Municipal Airport to open the runway to traffic. We were monitoring the situation as we approached Great Falls. We had plenty of fuel and we could go to an alternate airport in the event we were directed to do so. The Malmstrom ground crew took too much time clearing the runway and the Municipal airport continued to have below minimum weather.

Finally, the F-89's had to proceed to an alternate airport. Four of the F-89's did not make their alternates and had to abandon their aircraft by ejection -- all were rescued the next day. We continued to circle Malmstrom for a couple of hours until they reopened the runway. I drove home that night and slept well.

The next day, I was assigned to the accident investigation board by SAC. We began the preliminary questioning of the pilots involved and I got to know the base operation personnel. The base operation officer was an old fighter pilot, who had flown fighters at Malmstrom when the Russians had come down from Alaska and picked up the P-39's that we had sold them. He had remained in Malmstrom when SAC arrived to complete his tour of duty before retirement. During our discussions, I discovered that base operations had one T-33 and one C-47 assigned to carry their operational load and I decided to look into the opportunity of me getting some flying time in that T-33.

The aircraft Investigation was finally turned over to ADC (Alaska Defense Command) personnel, since so many of the Air Defense Command personnel and aircraft were involved. I began pulling that famous SAC alert. We would remain housed in a barracks on the flight line for two weeks at a time on standing war alert. We would only take off if war were declared, but we didn't leave that area for anything during the two-week shift. We had books to read and a couple of pool tables available.

After so many days and nights in this location, one had trouble telling days from night. We wound up sleeping in the day and staying up most of the night. I began thinking that I was wasting my time sitting there on alert. I knew it was necessary because we were the Minutemen of modern times. However, I wanted more action than that, so I applied for a transfer to a jetfighter organization. I knew the chances were slim to none, but I applied anyway. When I was off alert, I played golf over at the municipal golf course, which was located on the banks of the Missouri river.

One Sunday, my wife asked me to drive her over to the Columbus hospital. The day was July 19, 1959. She was ready to give birth to our fourth child. I drove her over to the hospital and checked her in with the reception clerk. I drove the children back to the house and told my wife to call me when she went into labor.

About two hours later, I got a call from my wife at the hospital. She had given birth to a 10 pound and 13 ounce boy. We named him Keith Dennis after my brother Keith and my uncle Denys Caudill. Keith was a bouncing baby boy with the energy of a bear cub. His appetite matched his general exuberance for life. He was happy to join the family and his disposition was uncanny. The other children couldn't get over the new addition. They were old enough to enjoy the occasion and appreciate a new playmate.

As soon as Ruby was able to get on her feet again, we went downtown and bought everyone western outfits for the winter season. I knew that we would be going back to Virginia to visit, so we had to deck out in full regalia to represent the best in western living.

*Becky and Patti in Western outfits – 1959*

My request for transfer to a jet unit was denied and the position of Headquarter Commander came open. Colonel Tex Burns assigned me to this position and attached me to base operations for my flying duty. I liked the new assignment and went about my business with great anticipation and enthusiasm. Colonel Burns liked what he saw. I got the squadron in top shape in no time and commanded the troops in an admirable fashion and with excellent results.

I reported the base operations and got a check out flight in the T-33. Everything began to look up. Shortly after I flew the T-33, the SAC Commanding General transferred the T-33 to March Field. This left the C-47 for all of us base operation pilots to get in our flying time. My check out in the C-47 proved to be a long drawn-out affair. That C-47 was flying everywhere getting parts to keep those KC-97s in the air. There was little time allotted for transition flying. The pilots already flying this C-47 were in no hurry to check anyone else out because they were getting most of the flying time under the circumstances. I knew that I would have to change the situation, but I wanted to secure my position in the headquarters squadron before I started influencing the policies at base operations. Colonel Tex Burns scheduled a base golf tournament, and I played in Colonel Burns' golf flight. I practiced golf every evening when the weather permitted and began to lower my handicap. My best score was 88 for 18 holes.

One weekend we drove down to Yellowstone National Park and entered from the north end. We really appreciated the beauty of the giant waterfalls on the Yellowstone River just inside the north gate of the park. We admired "Old Faithful" and looked around the hotel for a while. Then I noticed that my parking ticket stub indicated that I could fish in the park without charge. We drove out to the stream where the moose, the bear, and the elk were absent. I stopped by the stream and got my fishing gear out of the trunk of the car. I had just tossed my spinner into the water and was reeling it into the bank when a Forest Ranger tapped me on the shoulder. He asked me to show him my lure. I pulled the lure out of the water, and he told me that he would have to take my gear because I wasn't allowed to fish with a lure in this stream. He told me to follow him to the ranger station. I was dumbfounded. I wouldn't have fished at all if the park entry ticket had not given me the opportunity to fish. I should've read the detailed regulations on fishing in the park which explained that you could only fish in certain bends in the river and with certain bait. I was mad by the time we arrived at the ranger station. I guess I could have surrendered my fishing gear and left the station, but I wanted to keep my gear. I requested to talk to the head ranger. We waited about two hours. Finally, the Ranger took me into the summary court. I explained my position and they gave me back my fishing gear. I thanked them, drove out of the park, and returned to Great Falls.

The following weekend, we drove up to Browning to see the Blackfoot Indians in their Pow Wow. We watched the Indians dance around that big circle inside of the tents, which surrounded the festival grounds. We then drove out to East Glacier Park. The club was in the evergreen forest where a cold wind was blowing. The snow-capped mountains cooled the air currents, and it was chilly. The golf course was in the pine thickets and the clubhouse was sturdily built and had the best of everything in facilities and services. We had dinner in the club and drove out to Lake Mary Ronan before we returned to Great Falls.

The following weekend, we attended the chuckwagon races and the running horse races at the fairgrounds in Great Falls. The children liked all the action associated with the horses.

I took a leave to take my family back to Grundy to introduce my new boy to my relatives. We drove out of Great Falls and motored down to the Black Hills of South Dakota, where we visited Mount

Rushmore. We drove through the Badlands and across the Prairie to Sioux Falls, before we turned south to Kansas City.

That Cadillac was so much fun to drive that I wanted to drive straight through to Grundy without spending the night anywhere. The "caddy" had enough room for the children to sleep comfortably while I drove through the night. We motored to St. Louis and then to Louisville where we stopped to spend the night.

The next day, I drove my family through Bardstown where we visited "My Old Kentucky Home" Museum briefly. We next drove through Danville, the home of my alma mater, Centre College. We continued on through the mountains to Grundy and arrived at one o'clock in the morning. We drove into the Liza Lee yard, stepped into the house, and put the children to bed. Mom got up briefly and saw that we were squared away. She told us to get some rest and we would all visit with the baby in the morning.

The next morning, the whole family, including my brother and his wife, came over to see the new baby boy and get in on the news. My family really got a charge out of our western outfits. After breakfast, my brother and I went out to look over the new caddy. I told him how wonderful Great Falls was and that I would have an opportunity to take a big game hunt soon. He told me that he had a Springfield M1903 rifle (a five-round .30-06 caliber rifle) that I would need. I told him that I had a golf hand cart that I would trade him for the rifle. He was glad to make the trade. I took the handcart out of the trunk of my car and gave it to him, and he took me over to the basement of his office and gave me the rifle. I stowed the rifle in the trunk of my car.

We drove downtown to show off the caddy. I drove around the courthouse a couple of times, then I parked in my father's private parking lot. My brother and I got out of the car and walked down to the drugstore where my friends hung out on Saturday. They didn't ask me how I was doing because my new caddy answered that question. They did, however, ask me how I felt.

We caught the courthouse crowd next and visited every office. It took me about a week to get around to all the friends and neighbors. We drove over to Kentucky to visit relatives and friends from Inez to Hazard. After visiting Kentucky, we drove down to Knoxville to visit relatives and friends. We made a little tour of Gatlinburg before we decided to return to Great Falls.

I had not visited my old B-24 crewmate, Art Aro, in Iron Mountain, Minnesota. I planned to motor up to Iron Mountain by way of Louisville, Indianapolis, Chicago, and Duluth. We left Knoxville and drove straight through to Iron Mountain. Art lived just east of Iron Mountain in Hoyt Lakes. We drove over to Hoyt Lakes and inquired at a local service station where Art lived. Everyone knew that "Finn." We drove out to Art's home and stopped in front of the little white house. Our timing was good. That little mining town was just letting the iron ore open pit miners off from the evening shift. I went up to the front door and rang the doorbell. Art's wife came to the door. She was in the process of preparing supper for the family. I introduced myself, but she knew who I was even though we had never met. I imagine Art had told her stories about our activities over in Germany in World War II. We met Art's three children, two girls and a boy in the same age group as my children. Art and his wife had bought a little ice cream concession stand to operate in the summer with the help of their children. It wasn't long before the children were off to the stand to eat up the profits for the day.

Art arrived shortly thereafter and saw the caddy out front. He came in the door and greeted me like he had been expecting me any day. He asked me why I took so long to visit him. We both knew the answer to that. We were working people, and this was the first time the trip could be economically arranged.

We had supper together and Art had to take us out to the local pub to introduce us to his friends who frequented the establishment. We left Art's oldest girl to babysit, and the adults went over to the pub. The women had tea and Art started to suds it up a little. We met his friends. Every one of them insisted on buying us a round of drinks. We closed the bar while reliving those truck driving incidents back in old Germany. We returned home and turned in for the night.

The next morning, we departed for Great Falls. We rolled across the great Northern Prairie at a fast pace. The grass was green and knee-high across the plains. We were passing through cattle and horse country. The land between the few towns was sparsely settled and the towns were stretched wide apart. The sky was blue, but you could see the hot air raising those cumulus clouds fast in the heat of the day, which would later produce good thunderstorms in the evening and night. The water table was high in that region.

We drove through Grand Forks, Minot, Williston, and Malta on the Milk River, before we turned southwest to Great Falls. We arrived in Great Falls the next morning. I drove to the little green house on 17th St., and we went inside where everyone got into bed to rest up from the twenty-four hour drive we had just completed. We slept until noon.

We got up and had dinner. I even felt like playing a round of golf, so I donned my golf togs and went over to the municipal golf course where I played eighteen holes. I came home, had supper, and turned in for the night.

The next day, I reported to the base for duty. Colonel Tex Burns encouraged the officers in command positions to play golf regularly. After five o'clock, we would all hit the golf course. My wife became interested in learning to play golf. This was a sport that we could enjoy together. I got her a set of sticks and some plastic air balls to practice with in the backyard of our home until she felt confident enough to go to the golf course with me. She would get so flustered trying to play a good game that her heart would start to palpate, and she would have to go back to the car and wait for me to finish my game.

My base operations officer was an avid hunter. His friends over at the Municipal Airport and the National Guard and Reserves were also avid hunters. He organized a seven-day packhorse hunt, which would leave from Choteau, Montana by horse and cross the Continental Divide at 7,500 feet elevation and continue down the western slope of the tributaries of the White River to an old, abandoned logging campsite. I was fortunate enough to be invited along on this big elk hunt. I gathered up the gear that I would need and stored it in the back of my car. I took my rifle over to the firing range and put it in a vice to see that the sites were accurate.

When the big day came, we drove up to Choteau and drove into the hunting guides parking lot. We secured our automobiles and took our hunting gear over to the corral where fifteen horses were waiting for their riders. The five or six pack horses were loaded with the grub stake (supplies). We climbed into the saddles of the trail horses and rode out of the corral trailing a hunting guide, who was riding up front. The pack horses followed the saddle horses up the trail. We rode over to the foot of the mountain and stopped. The trail boss gave us our instructions.

He told us that we would stop at hourly intervals to check on the horses, saddles, and blanket fittings. We were to be on the lookout for anything that might spook the horses. The trail was quite steep, and a stray bear, or any wild animal or bird, could cause a horse to buck or stampede on the trail, and toss the rider over the high canyon walls. I doubted that many of us could stay on a horse in a full gallop down that trail. We were riding a potential powder keg. We were not to shoot anything out of the saddle, because it might spook the horse.

We would be in the White River game preserve until we reached the White River tributary on the western slope. We mounted up and started the climb in string formation. Sure enough, the trail quickly became a goat path, up one side of a canyon and around another. Switch back or hairpin turns became a challenge to negotiate.

On one steep climb, a pack horse reared up on his hind feet and broke the rope which was connected to the saddle of the next horse. The pack horse fell over backwards down into a 100 foot ravine to its death. The guide rappelled down to the horse to finish off the dying horse with a bullet, before he recovered most of the gear.

We passed through dense undergrowth and over bald points with only the big rock outcroppings for footage. The horses' hooves were not very secure on the rocks. The horses would step on loose gravel sometimes and have to fall on their knees to hold their footing to keep from going over the cliff. This hunt began to get serious. We were on a survival trail!

I was wearing the skin off my bottom side, as well as, on the insides of my legs around the knees from swinging back-and-forth in the saddle. The sweat was not adding to the comfort of these tender places. I got off the horse and walked a little, but the trail was too rough, so I got back on the horse. We finally mounted the top of the gap where we had a rest stop. The scenery was something to behold! The view was breathtaking, looking off the mountain in either direction.

We mounted back on the horses and started down the western slope. I thought riding up the hill was rough, but riding downhill was even tougher. We continued down the winding trail until we arrived in the western flats of the mountain. We rode north while still descending gradually to the stream bed. When we arrived at the stream side, we were out of the game preserve.

We rode on a couple of miles until we arrived at the old logging campsite. We rode up to the corral and stopped the horses. The guide climbed off his horse and began helping the less hardy get off their horses. I told the guide that I would get down in a minute after my horse rested for a little while. I wanted to wait for the feeling to come back into my legs below the knee so that I could get off my horse. I didn't want folks to think that I couldn't get off my horse. I finally managed to wiggle my toes and get the circulation going again. I also relaxed my leg muscles because I was experiencing leg cramps. It took a while, but I finally got my feet out of the stirrups. I swung my leg over the horse's back and slid down to the ground. I held on to the saddle horn until my walking legs came around. Then I took the saddle and blankets off the horse and laid them on the fence rail of the corral. I rubbed the horse down before I put him in the corral and took off his bridle. The corral had corn in the stall and the water trough was running over, where it had been piped in from the stream into the old hollowed out log. I took my sleeping bag and placed it on the pile of straw which had been laid on the ground under the tent where we were going to sleep.

I went over to the kitchen tent where the cook had coffee waiting for us. The cook was a retired Great Northern Railroad cook of thirty years. He was cooking some elk meat that had been left by the previous hunting party. The meat sure smelled sweet. When dinner was served, I do believe that the meat was the tenderest and juiciest meat that I had ever tasted. I could see why everyone wanted to hunt elk. After dinner, the old hunters broke out the refreshments and the cards. I slipped off to the creek, removed my clothes, and took a cold bath with some soap and a towel. It gave me shivers, but I felt clean enough to slip into the sleeping bag for a good night's rest. I was asleep in two shakes of a sheep's tail.

Early the next morning, I heard the kitchen utensils clamoring like someone was tearing down the kitchen. I looked out of my sleeping bag with blurry eyes. The morning fog was only about one foot above my bed. I looked over to the kitchen tent, which was about four feet lower than our sleeping tent, and saw a big, shiny black bear up on the table pulling a slab of our meat off the tree limb where the cooking utensils and elk meat were hanging.

I could've gotten a shot at the bear which was only about seventy-five feet from our tent. However, I was afraid that I would hit one of the hunters, who was getting up and yelling at the bear. The big slick, jet-black bear disappeared into the pine thicket with the meat in short order. The rest of the hunters were ready to go elk hunting, but it was bone chilling cold, and I had a little sore throat from taking a bath in that cold water. I decided to remain in bed until the sun came up, hoping to reverse my throat condition before it got worse. I went back to sleep.

I woke up about ten o'clock, got dressed, and went over to the kitchen to get breakfast. The cook fixed me eggs and bacon plus some flapjacks with syrup. After breakfast, I went over to the corral and saddled up on my horse. I rode out of the corral and up the trail along the creek looking for a place to stop and stalk big game. I had gone about two miles when I came upon a blueberry thicket covering both sides of the trail. The horse sniggered and stopped. The horse knew that bears liked blueberries, and it was trying to flush anything out of that thicket before we entered the undergrowth. We would be at a distinct disadvantage in the undergrowth, if a grizzly bear charged us in close quarters.

I studied the situation and saw some bear droppings on the side of the trail where we had stopped. I decided to tie up my horse and stalk from this location. I got off the horse and tied him to a tree. I climbed on a big log nearby and waited for whatever might come out of that thicket. If the bear had charged out of the thicket, that bridle would not have kept my horse waiting for me. It would've been me and the bear. The elk were not likely to be this far down in the valley. The elk were higher up in the dense forest grazing under the protection of the fog. I didn't see anything all morning, so I decided to ride back to camp.

I mounted up and started riding down the stream. I came upon a fellow hunter on horseback. He told me that he had a saddle bag full of mountain trout. I looked in his saddle bag and saw trout up to thirty-two inches in length and weighing up to six pounds. I asked him what gave him the idea to go fishing. He told me that he had seen a big trout in the water that morning, so he got his fishing gear and went to get that fish rather than go elk hunting. He said the trout would not bite or spook, so he made a loop out of his fishing line and slipped it over a big trout's head and jerked quickly, thereby lassoing the critter. After that, the other fish started biting. I never questioned his story because I saw the results. We rode back to camp together and saw that the other hunters were back. They had bagged an elk and were dressing and quartering the animal. My friend took his fish to the stream's edge, and after everyone got a look at his catch, he started dressing the fish. We had another party the rest of the day.

The next morning, I crawled out of the sack with my friends, and we had coffee and breakfast. We saddled up and rode up into the high country following the guide to the elk feeding ground. The going was rough up the trail, but those trail horses lived up to their name and managed it well. We arrived in the fog and waited above a clearing near a big clump of pine trees. The guide told us that the elk had bedded down in that clump of trees the previous night, but they were spooky that morning and didn't come out to feed at the expected time. They got wind of us and slipped out to the other side of the grove of trees into the dense forest. We caught a glimpse of them just before they disappeared into the big forest, but they were too far away to shoot. We returned to camp where we had another party. We had plenty of meat and fish and the refreshments were plentiful. I went to sleep while the other hunters continued their poker game.

The next morning, one of the hunters wanted someone to go with him to hunt mountain goats. He had a rifle with a powerful scope. I wanted to see where these white mountain goats ranged anyway, so I volunteered to go along with him. We saddled up and headed for the bottoms of some crafty peaks. We climbed through the underbrush until the horses could no longer scale the cliffs. We tied the horses up and proceeded on foot to the top of one of the lofty points.

We slipped out from under the cover of the evergreen pines, which were growing on the cracks in the rocks, and got behind an old log. The hunter began systematically scoping the opposite ridge with his binoculars, where he spotted three mountain goats. Two were grazing about twenty feet below the ridge in plain view with the glasses, but not noticeable to the naked eye. One big billy goat was lying down sunning near the other two goats. The hunter gave me the binoculars and told me to sight him in, and he commenced firing. I was to announce where his shots landed and give him a correction in feet. He only had about five shots to get off before the goats would disappear over the crest of that ridge.

I zeroed in on the goats. He fired and the shot fell twenty feet directly below the goat lying down. I gave him a correction and he fired again. He hit ten feet below and online this time. He fired again and hit only about four feet below the goat lying down, at which point the goat jumped up and all three disappeared over the ridge in the blink of an eye. We didn't get any goats, but we learned how to reach them and how to fire with scope and binoculars. We climbed back down to our horses and rode back down the mountain to our camp. We had another party that lasted into the night.

The next morning, we split up into two hunting parties to try to find the elk. We climbed up to another feeding ground and set up our stalking positions. The elk evaded us again. We must've made too much noise on the climb. We returned to camp and found that the other party had shot an elk, but the trail was too rough to recover the elk even after they had cleaned and quartered the animal.

We all rode back out to the location where the elk was felled. The hunter had shot the elk from a high cliff, which dropped one hundred feet down to a little wooded ledge around the cliff. There was another 100 foot cliff below that little belt line of loose ground. The gully down to the exact location of the elk was straight down and the ground was loose. If we lost our footing, we would tumble down the mountain like loose rock. We made the old college try until we scared ourselves. We got a couple of pack horses bogged down in the forest above both cliffs. We had brought them along to pack the meat out of the mountains. They were tied together by a rope. They slid down on opposite sides of a tree, and we almost never got the horses up on their feet and untangled from that rope. We were lucky to leave the meat for the bear or mountain lions. We spent all day getting down out of the mountain with our pack horses. We rode back to the base camp and had another party.

We hunted for a couple more days without any luck. We quit hunting and just relaxed at the camp the rest of the time, enjoying the food and drinks, and spinning yarns. The card game was left to the experts. The time came to make the trip back across the divide. We saddled up and rode up the trail. We were a little more experienced for the trip back. We climbed out to the top of the mountains and rested before coming down to the other side. We rode out of the mountains and onto the plains of Choteau.

We were rested up mentally but worn out physically. We had had a lesson in the problems of survival in the Rocky Mountains with the horse and hunting equipment. We rode into the corral and dismounted. We took the saddle and blankets off the horses and then took off their bridles. We gave the guide seventy dollars each and thanked him for the trip. We loaded up our hunting gear in our automobiles and drove back to Great Falls. We should've spent some time in the town of Choteau where a lot of big-name Hollywood sidewalk cowboys came up to Montana to hunt out of that town.

I drove back to the little green house on 17th St. that evening. I pulled up and stopped in my parking place out in front of the house. The children heard the car and came running out to see what I had brought back with me. I told them that we had eaten all the elk meat, but I promised them that I would take them elk hunting when they got big enough. We went inside, and my wife asked me how the trip went. I told her that we had become like brothers on that journey. I told her that I would have a better chance of survival if I ever had to bail out over that terrain, now that I had lived out there in the wild for a week. My wife followed this story with more curiosity than an active interest. The children wanted to know all the details of the hunt and I filled them in on the big things. I took a bath, shaved, and ate supper with the family. We turned in early that night and I went to sleep easily.

The next morning, I reported to work as Hedron Squadron Commander. I brought my squadron up to top notch and went down to base operations to catch up on my flying schedule. While I was down at base operations, we got word that our base operations officer dropped dead with a heart attack. We all went over to his widow's house for the wake that night. He had a lot of friends.

The next day, I drove up to Havre to pick up some of his kinfolk who had come out by train from back East. We all missed this fabulous officer with a brilliant career. He was a stable influence in the Air Force in times of uncertainty and always an inspiration.

My next flight was on a C-47 to Edmonton, Canada. We flew over the Alberta plains, landed at the Canadian air base, and shut down for the night. We caught a cab into the city to the first-class hotel. We cleaned up and went out to the Peacock club for the evening's entertainment. We heckled the performer until one of the Canadians wanted to start a fight. We backed off when we realized we were in poor taste as guests of the neighboring country. We returned to the hotel and spent the night.

We completed our business the next morning and went out to the airport. We had our aircraft pulled out of the hangar and when we cranked up the aircraft's left engine it died. We had to pull the aircraft back into the hangar and have the spark plugs pulled out and dried before we could start the engines again. The cold weather in Canada froze the spark plug points if an engine died after a start in winter. We finally got the engine started and flew back to Great Falls.

We got lots of flying time to various parts depots like Hill Air Force Base in Utah, Minot Air Force Base in North Dakota, Boise, Idaho, Rapid City, South Dakota, and Sioux City, Iowa. We were assigned a new base operations officer who was preoccupied with his upcoming retirement. Flying time became a scarce commodity. A couple of the instructor pilots began taking all the flights. We were left to be reviewed by the administration's annual flying review board. I complained to the Inspector General's office that this was unjust, and I got results. We began flying again, but the instructor pilots tried to get me grounded for my efforts. The Colonel put a stop to this endeavor.

The Colonel entered us commanders in a golf tournament at the Great Falls Country club, with the benefits going to some charitable organization. We had a great time until a thunderstorm moved in and stopped the tournament for the evening. Those high winds would stop a ball in flight.

The next day, the tournament continued and Colonel Burns finally won the tournament in a sudden death playoff on the third hole. The following day, I discovered that the USAF was screening pilots who were flying as a secondary duty with the intent to administratively ground as many as possible to meet a quota set by the USAF. In fact, I did not realize it at the time, but I was on a flight which took the review board findings back to Washington. We filed an IRR (restricted instrument rating) plan and flew into Andrews Air Force Base. We were not used to the inbound and outbound Corridors. We flew inbound on the outbound Corridor with the permission of the ATC (air traffic control). We spent the night at Andrews where it was nice to be back at the center of the action. Great Falls was remote in comparison, but it had the advantage of easy access to the great outdoors. We completed our business and flew back to Great Falls. The review board had determined that I was "essential" to remain on flying status.

We volunteered to fly over the western half of the United States chasing parts for the KC-97's. The C-47 was slow and low, but it was an enjoyable bird to fly. The climb out to altitude took its toll on the old engines. One night, one of the engines went out over Missoula, but two pilots managed to land at Missoula at night.

We had to be careful when we flew west to Spokane because we had a service ceiling limit in the C-47 of 14,000 feet, and that was only for two hours without oxygen. We had to fly through the mountain passes to accomplish our mission on these western flights. We became remarkably familiar with the Northwest passage for the C-47. We had to be especially careful around Sheridan, Wyoming near the Big Horn Mountains.

One weekend, I took my shotgun and drove up to Fairfield to hunt for Brant geese. I saw four geese circle a stream on a farm and I watched them land from the highway. I pulled onto the farm road and drove out to the farmhouse to get permission to hunt on the property. When I drove up into the front yard of the farmhouse, a bunch of children were running around having a birthday party. The old lady who lived there was a widow and she would not let anyone hunt on her property, because some years back a hunter shot one of her cows. She was in a good mood that day. I told her what I had seen, and who I was. She let me hunt the geese, provided that I checked in at her house before leaving and had some ice cream and cake with her and the children.

I proceeded to the tree covering the stream bed. I slipped up on the geese, flushed them, and blasted away as they came up out of the water. I bagged three out of the four. I went back to the farmhouse and had that ice cream and cake with the old lady and her grandchildren.

I returned home proud of my kill. I went into the house and laid the dead geese on the floor. I intended to give the geese to my neighbor who cut our grass and liked to eat wild fowl. My oldest boy, Harold Junior looked at the ducks for a long time before speaking. He was about four years old. Finally, he came over to me and asked, "Daddy, why did you murder those ducks?" I had a big time explaining why folks go hunting that night. I got those geese out of my house real quick. We couldn't have eaten them with that kind of attitude in the house anyway. My neighbor was very grateful.

I applied for a school. I wanted to get a degree in one of the natural sciences that was recognized by the services. I was going to convert my Bachelor of Arts degree into a Bachelor of Science degree. I also made an application for an overseas transfer if I did not get my school assignment.

I was practically cut off from flying time during this period. I went over to the Montana National Guard and flew to the Air Adjutant General's conference in Asheville, North Carolina to build up my flying time. I was able to arrange this TDY, because of the close ties that I had made with the Guard pilots who I had met on the elk hunt. My organization could not afford to complain. We spent three days in Asheville at the Oak Grove Hotel, where we played several rounds of golf. Asheville was green and beautiful in the foothills of the Smoky Mountains. It was no small wonder why so many VIPs in the military retired there after they got out of the service. We flew back to Montana in the C-47.

One of the Guard pilots asked me if I was still up to date in the T-33. I told him that I had not flown a jet since I had been at SAC. He scheduled me for a recheck in the T-33. We blasted off and flew locally for a couple of hours while I put the bird through its paces and shot several landings. By the time we made our final landing and taxied to the ramp, I was up to date in the T-33 again. I was ready for any kind of transfer.

My request for school was approved, and my request for overseas assignments came through the same day. I told the personnel officer to arrange for me to take both assignments. I could go to school TDY (on temporary duty) and report to an overseas station after school. The personnel officer never managed to see my point. I decided to resign my commission to go fly with the airlines while I was young enough to make the switch. I submitted my resignation.

# CHAPTER 29

# Alaskan Air Command (Patrolling the Frozen North)

I thought the situation over that night and withdrew my resignation the next morning. I received an immediate transfer to Elmendorf Air Force Base in Anchorage Alaska. I advertised my old Ford for sale and sold it for $400. I took a delay enroute and we drove back to Grundy. We traveled by way of Glendive and Fargo this time, just to see different scenery and get to know the location of available airfields and their relation to the cities that they served. This information could be used in case of future emergencies.

We arrived in Grundy in good shape after a straight through trip. That caddy could stand the pressure. The entire family studied the maps together to determine the route to take to Alaska. The research didn't take long. There was only one road to Alaska from Montana. You drove north to Edmonton and then fifty miles out of

Edmonton you picked up the gravel road called the Alcan Highway for 1,280 miles to the Alaskan border. We spent the entire leave talking about the trip. My wife finally told me that she would go under one condition. She would go, providing that she could leave if she didn't like the place. That was all right with me.

We made the usual contacts on this leave as we did on our other leaves. We engaged in much the same activities on this vacation as we did on other vacations. We discussed Alaska frequently with our friends and neighbors. We never ran into anyone who had been stationed there. When we were ready to shove off, we took the southern route out west. We drove down to Knoxville and Chattanooga to visit my aunt and my sister. We spent the night with my sister Lois on Signal Mountain.

We departed Chattanooga the next morning and rode to Dallas to visit my cousin Taylor, Dixon, and my friends Ran Holman and Bob Leonard. We spent the night at Taylor's house. He had been stationed in Alaska and he told us how he earned that assignment. He returned from WWII as a hero in the battle of Italy. He was sent to Fort Collins, Colorado to train troops to be combat ready. Taylor was a little over enthusiastic in his command and recommended more realistic training methods. The Commanding General took offense to these suggestions and had Taylor transferred over to the hospital to see if he was suffering from combat fatigue. This infuriated Taylor and he had a few choice remarks to make about that situation. Shortly thereafter, Taylor was transferred to a weather station floating on a large iceberg in the Beaufort Sea surrounding the North Pole. Taylor was put in command of the weather station. He told me his main mission was to survive and send in weather reports when he could get through. He elected to get out of the service after he returned to the "lower 48."

We drove up to Chillicothe, Texas the next day to spend the night with Dr. James Howard and his wife. Dr. Howard was glad we came as usual. I had one thousand dollars in a sock in the trunk of my caddy to be used as needed on our trip to Alaska. Dr. Howard recommended that I put the money in the local bank and take a certified check up on the Alcan Highway with me as a safety precaution to keep the money from being stolen. I followed his recommendation. This left me with about $90 in each of my pockets plus my credit cards with the major oil companies, and an American Express card, which I understood was acceptable everywhere.

We drove out of Chillicothe early the next morning. We ran into some snow flurries at Childress, Texas. I thought that we were in for a rough trip. We continued to Amarillo, where we looked up Hulen and Polly Burke and visited them for a few minutes. Then we "set sail" on the highway enroute to Colorado Springs. We drove straight through. We began to sweat the weather and decided not to visit Colonel John Harmon. We pushed on to Denver where we spent the night at the BOQ at Lowry Field. We checked out of Lowry the next morning and drove to Great Falls via Cheyenne, Casper, Billings, and Butte. As we passed through the remote sections of Wyoming, we saw antelopes traveling in wild herds along with the buffalo. The antelope had a rich brown color with white markings and were as agile as the gazelle in Africa.

I grazed one of three deer that night when I popped over a little hill. The three deer, who were on one side of the road, darted across the road at the last minute. I hit the last deer, but he kept going.

We drove into Great Falls and checked into the BOQ for the night. The next day, we pulled out of Great Falls and drove up to the Canadian border at Sunburst. We cleared customs along with Steve Chitwood and his daredevil driving group. Chitwood had a couple of cars on the ground and a carrier truck with five racing cars on it. He was going to Alaska to make the fairs and put on a show on the NASCAR circuit. We were glad to be traveling with someone from the U.S. who was going all the way up the Alcan Highway. I felt like we could depend on Steve to help us get to the nearest town along the remote Alcan Highway, if we had car trouble.

We drove up to Lethbridge and had lunch. We refueled and drove to Calgary. The horses and chuck wagons were everywhere. The Calgary stampede days must have been in full swing, and we saw a big rodeo in town. We stopped and watched three cowboys try to lasso a wild horse in the stadium. That horse was a furious animal. I am sure that these cowboys received some broken bones in the event.

We ate and drove up to Edmonton to spend the night. Edmonton was a sprawling city with 300,000 people. It was modern and the last metro stop on the way to Alaska. We found a nice motel and checked in for the night.

The next morning, we rose early and began the long haul to Alaska. The road was paved, but it was no superhighway. It was just a two-lane paved road. We rolled into Grand Prairie, refueled, and got a bite to eat. I went over to the bank and tried to cash the certified check. There wasn't a bank in Canada that would cash a certified check for an American passing through the country. I still was not worried because I had my credit cards and my American Express card.

My son, Keith, had a temperature, so we took him to a doctor in Dawson Creek, the last outpost of civilization on the way to Alaska. We refueled there and when I tried my American Express credit card, they told me that they only took Carte de Blanche. Apparently, someone had used a stolen credit card while passing through Canada and the service stations had been unable to collect the charges on the foreign credit card. Consequently, the service stations had limited the credit cards that they accepted to Carte de Blanche.

We encountered a gravel road right outside of Dawson Creek made from broken river rock. During hard rains, the big trucks had made the road full of potholes, so we could not travel at a speed of over thirty-five mph. I thought this was just a bad stretch of the road, but I learned shortly thereafter that this was the general condition of the Alcan Highway all the way to the Alaskan border near Tok. The only route through the territory was actually a wilderness road through the Lob Lolly pine groves. There were no facilities along the highway and no homes or businesses — just forest. We realized that we would have to fill up with gas every time we found a service station, which were about fifty miles apart. When we crossed the Peace River, we were in "another world" and many of the service stations were closed.

We stopped at Fort St. John and ordered six hamburgers. The hamburgers were thick, and the meat wasn't well cooked. The meat tasted like sawdust and the children would not eat the burgers. I lost my appetite too. We realized that we would have to drive straight through day and night, even though there was a sign along the road recommending not to travel the Alcan Highway at night.

We soon ran out of Esso, Shell, and Texaco gas stations. We had a Chevron credit card that was good at BP service stations, so we began to fill up gas at BP stations to save our pocket money. The gasoline was only 88 octane, making my engine run rough. The valves clanged, but that caddy 325 hp engine purred on like a diesel engine. Big trucks came by and the rocks following their big dual wheels flew up, broke two of our headlamps, and cracked my windshield. I had four headlights, so I was not without lights. We came around one curve, and the bridge across the shallow creek was missing. There were no signs or warnings. I stopped at the edge of the water and pondered how I was going to get across the creek. I looked up in the brush and spotted a road gang sitting on a caterpillar eating their lunch like they didn't expect anyone to come by today. I blew my horn and the caterpillar driver cranked up the diesel and drove the Cat down across the creek and turned around in front of my car. One of his helpers jumped off the Cat and hooked the cable to my front bumper. He told me that he would pull me across. That sounded good, but I wasn't sure that my muffler would be intact after I hit those ruts in the creek. The car's bottom drug but nothing came off. We came out on the other side in good shape. I wasn't happy about this predicament, but I had to compromise due to lack of other alternatives.

We drove on up the Alcan Highway, which was built by the Americans during World War II just in case we had to fight the Russians in Alaska. The United States had to protect important military and naval bases along the coast of Alaska. I had my old Springfield rifle on the floor of the backseat where I could reach it in a hurry if I needed it. We stopped once to check the tires. I was about to get out of the car when I saw a pack of yellow-eyed timber wolves running out of the trees towards the car. The children piled into the front seat with my wife and me. I pulled out and we drove on to the next service station before stopping.

We filled up with gas and used the restrooms when we found them. There were little airports cut out of the forest along the highway, usually near one of these service stations, outposts, or if you stretched your imagination, trading posts. I thought we could summon air support if a real emergency arose.

We crossed two huge rivers, the Peace, and the Laird. They looked bigger than they were because we did not expect to run into such streams. We crossed the Yukon River next, just before we arrived at Whitehorse in the early morning. I began to see pieces of rubber tires scattered all over the road on the outskirts of Whitehorse. I told my wife, "It's a good thing that I don't have recapped tires." About that time, my first tire separated. I stopped when I heard the flopping and knocking of the rubber flying off the tire. The road was so rough that tires would only hold up to Whitehorse before they started separating.

I changed tires and elected to drive on to Alaska with four tires. If I had seen the cracks on the rest of the tires, I would've returned to Whitehorse and attempted to purchase five new tires with my Chevron credit card. We drove on in ignorance, but we drove slower. We passed some resort lakes with some nice cottages on their shores. The cottages looked closed, so I surmised that the owners flew into these lakes with fly planes on floats during the hunting season.

We were anxious to reach the Alaskan border because we had heard that a paved road began there. We received an unpleasant shock when we reached the paved road. The sixteen feet of permafrost had melted under the road, and the big trucks had caused the blacktop to sink, tear apart, and separate. That road looked like saltwater taffy covering a banana split. There were so many sinkholes and crevices, that I had to travel slower than I did on the old gravel road! Our bumper dragged on the swags, and we were down to 15 to 20 mph.

We began to see moose standing along the road. A big black bear ran across the road in front of us once. I tried to wake the children, but they were hibernating in the front seat with us. They had all been in the front seat ever since we had left the pack of wolves back at Fort St. John. They were huddled around us like pups and kittens.

I finally drove into Tok where we refueled and turned southwest on the road to Anchorage. We drove through that marsh country and across the mountain called Goat Mountain in the middle of the night. As I was coming down one of those mountains, I could hear the seashore tide echoing off the mountains. I couldn't quite figure out the noise. I later discovered that the tide in Alaska could be 30 feet high.

The next morning, I drove down the Matanuska Valley where we could see land that had been cleared for pasture. The grass was green, and the cattle were grazing. The houses were built like cellars – underground to withstand the cold winters.

We finally came into the big seaport of Anchorage. We could see the Western Hotel high-rise from quite a way out. It was strange to find a metropolitan city after all the wilderness that we had come through. It was a lovely sight! The Cook Inlet separated the city from the big airbase at Elmendorf. We drove over to the base and checked into the BOQ. I drove over to town and bought a paper at the Western Hotel to start looking for an apartment or home to rent. I felt sure that all the houses would be occupied in this far north country.

I found a new apartment which had just opened near the shopping center. The apartment had three furnished rooms and rented for $165 per month. I took the place immediately. It was a high price, but it was all that was available. I moved my family into the apartment that day. My wife liked the location because the shopping center was within walking distance, and so were the schools for the children.

We had dinner and proceeded to drive around Anchorage before I thought of reporting into the base for duty. We found Anchorage a lovable city. We drove out to the civilian airport and found that the aircraft had priority over automobiles when crossing the road near the airport. Alaska is much like South America. There were only two major roads in Alaska. One road led from Tok to Anchorage, and another road led from Tok to Fairbanks. Therefore, the aircraft and ships were the primary means of transportation in Alaska. They were supplemented by the automobile and the dog sled.

The people were friendly in Alaska because they were more dependent on each other for survival. The challenge in Alaska was the winner and the weather. The light aircraft used pontoons in the summer to land on the lakes, and the same aircraft used skis to land on the same frozen lakes in the winter. The bush pilots in Alaska were looked at in the same manner as they were in Africa or South America. They were the lifeline between the natives and civilization.

Everything in Alaska was informal. We had lunch at the airport where I ran into Andy Step, from Inez, Kentucky. I spoke to him in the terminal, and he asked me where I was from. When I told him, he remembered who I was. We used to play together when we were children. He had come to Alaska in the Army and had gotten out of the Army and gone to work building houses. He later went to work for Ford Motor company for the dealer in Anchorage as a service writer. In time, he advanced to service manager and was transferred to Brooklyn, New York for a time as a troubleshooter. He came back to Anchorage and got on the sales force. He became the sales manager and eventually bought the Anchorage Ford dealership after about twenty years. He had just purchased the Chrysler dealership in Fairbanks also. Andy was delighted to run into someone from back home, so that he could relay his success story and be appreciated. He was an important member of the business community in Anchorage and Fairbanks. He had encouraged some of his friends from eastern Kentucky to come to Alaska and invest. The Jett family from Pikeville, Kentucky had purchased a motel in Anchorage. Andy and I caught each other up on the big interval between our last contact, while we enjoyed dinner at the Cloud Lounge. When we parted, I promised to stop by his Ford dealership when I had a chance.

The next day, I drove out to Elmendorf Air Force Base and signed in at the main gate for the security service headquarters. I was introduced to the commanding officer who welcomed me to the security community but was careful to emphasize that flying was not the primary mission of his command. He told me that I would be allowed one day a week to fly as an attached pilot with the Alaskan Air Command. I was assigned as an administrative assistant in the headquarters of the security command. This position didn't look promising, but I thanked the Colonel and left the compound to drive over to the Alaskan Air Command headquarters to report to the base operations support group. I gave my Form Five to the operations officer and he assigned me to the T-33 section. Our mission would be to support the Alaskan Air Command. The headquarters building itself was decorated with the symbol of a Polar bear and a giant twelve foot white polar bear was mounted in the upright position in a glass case in the lobby entrance. I was glad to be attached to this command.

I would be flying all kinds of target missions for the benefit of the Air Defense Command, which was charged with flying all the intercept missions to protect Alaska from enemy air penetration. I could see that I would be living for this one day per week. The Alaskan Air Command and the Air Defense Command had high morale because their mission was real. The extreme weather and terrain conditions made each flight a piece of history.

I saddled up in the T-33 with an instructor pilot to get an orientation check out ride. We blasted off on course for Fairbanks, climbing over the Matanuska Valley and Mount McKinley, which reached up to over 20,000 feet. I could see the winds tearing at the snow-capped tops. One would have to be careful at night around that natural and hazardous barrier.

The weather was clear and sunny. We let down in the Tanana River Valley and landed at Fairbanks. We went over to the officers club while the ground crew was refueling. The doors to the club bar were two-way swinging doors like the old Red Dog Saloon in Juneau and the club was full of cigarette smoke. We went inside the bar where some outfit was having a party. I had never seen so many people drinking with a drink in each hand. They hardly noticed us enter. They were too far absorbed in their mission for the evening. We fulfilled our curiosity and went over to the post exchange where I spotted some interesting postcards. One card had a picture of a beautiful Intuit maiden dressed in a decorative sealskin parka. I bought fifty of these cards to send to my mailing list.

We went back to the flight line and blasted off on course for Galena on the Yukon River near Norton Sound. Some air defense fighters intercepted us on the way in a planned practice intercept mission. We were flying over an immense wilderness and could see a mountain, some lakes, and stands of evergreen pines everywhere.

The Yukon River, which flows into the Bering Sea and is the third longest river in the U.S., looked bigger than the Mississippi River. The tops of the rugged mountains in the background were all snow-capped and the valley was wide and flat. The river meandered easily through the valley floor of evergreen pines. We let down at Galena Air Force base and landed on the 5,500 feet runway. We had to be careful to avoid the dike, which kept the river from over running the runway at high flood. The dike was just off the end of the runway and about four feet high. We taxied over to base operations and shut down. When we opened the canopy, the mosquitoes nearly annihilated us in the cockpit. Those were the biggest and most persistent insects that I had ever encountered! Our flying equipment helped protect us – our helmet and our gloves came in very handy.

We got out of the cockpit and went into base operations at Galena and ran into the ADC pilots who were on high alert. I imagined some of these pilots were the ones who had intercepted us on our way over to Galena. We were welcome visitors and we enjoyed dinner and small talk with these pilots. We went back to the aircraft, saddled up, and blasted off on course for King Salmon Airport at Bethel, near the mouth of the Kuskokwim River. We were intercepted again by the ADC interceptors.

We arrived over King Salmon Airport and let down, landed, and taxied over to base operations. We opened the canopy and got another swarm of mosquitoes, even more persistent than those at Galena. We fought our way over to the alert shack and base operations. We went inside and met another contingent of ADC fighter pilots on scramble alert. We talked to the pilots until our aircraft was refueled. We went back out to the aircraft and blasted off on course for Anchorage. We climbed over some of the active volcanoes on the eastward journey back to Anchorage. Those mountain tops were smoking and threatening, but not erupting.

We were intercepted again about halfway between King Salmon Airport and Anchorage by the ADC interceptors. They made several passes simulating combat and then returned to their base of operation. We let down over the Cook Inlet on our practice instrument penetration. I made a low approach and landed at Anchorage. We taxied over to base operations and shut down. I climbed out of the aircraft as a newly checked out pilot in the T-33 for the Alaskan air command. I turned in my equipment and drove back to the base officers club. I went downstairs to a bar where I could lounge in my flying suit after a mission. I ran into all kinds of pilots there. We had a few beers before I left for the apartment. I drove home, went into the house, and met my wife and children, who were happy to see me. In Alaska, one does not spend much time out in the open even in the summer, unless you are well dressed. The breeze was always cool. I turned in after supper tired but satisfied with the day's mission.

The next day, I reported to my desk job. Every evening, I would stop by the pilots' lounge to hear any exciting news for the day. I managed to get occasional flights on a C-123 during their round robin resupply missions to build up my flying time to get my senior pilot's star. Flying jets only one day a week required some supplementary flying. The C-123 flights were sandbag flights on which I just rode backseat for orientation purposes. I studied the operator's manual, but there was no formal course on the bird for attached pilots. I got to visit the remote radar landing strips that dotted the Alaskan wilderness. The C-123 planes could land on dirt strips and reverse their props to stop in short distances.

On the weekends, I began to take my family on motor trips to familiarize them with the Alaskan countryside. We drove up to Matanuska Valley near Palmer on the first weekend to the movie location where Clark Gable and Lana Turner starred in "The Call of the Wild." We were thrilled to drive around the location of a movie city. The roads around these lakes were made of river bottom rocks and sand, which had to weather sudden summer rains. The raindrops were big and cold. We drove back to Anchorage and turned in for the evening.

I hibernated in the security command all week until I could get another flight. I was able to get a flight on a C-54 out to the Aleutian Island chain one evening. We landed at Kodiak and went into the Navy officers club where we received a warm welcome. We ate and climbed back aboard the C-54 and flew out to the westernmost island of Kiska, where we landed at night. The wind was something fierce and the rain was horizontal. We taxied over to the terminal and parked. We had to hand walk a rope to pull ourselves along the icy ramp to get into base operation.

We refueled and roared off at night, climbing on course for Anchorage. We landed at Dutch Harbor or Kodiak on the way back. I was asleep most of the time and we landed at Anchorage in the wee hours of the morning. I drove back to the apartment and turned in for the night.

The next weekend, we motored down toward Homer on the Kenai peninsula. We found more wilderness, but the land looked like it could be cultivated. We drove back to Anchorage over the muddy road. I stopped at a Texaco station in Anchorage and had the car washed. The attendant washed the car in the wash bays. The wind was too cold to wash a car outside, even in the summer in Alaska. The attendant charged me four dollars for the job. Labor was high in the summer. A lot of the labor force were out of work in the winter.

We drove back to the apartment, and I let my wife and children out. I drove over to the officers club to the pilot transient center in the basement. There were all kinds of people passing through Anchorage, processing in and out of the remote radar cities. These people were allowed in the club at a certain GS (General Schedule) level. You could gather a lot of news from these travelers. The USO often had troupes passing through Alaska, making the circuit of the military outposts. We got to hear these troupes perform from time to time.

The Army base adjacent to Elmendorf had a big club also. We visited their club and they visited ours. The clubs were the center of social activity for the military. The Western Hotel was too expensive. I would spend a couple of hours at the club and come back to the apartment. My wife never cared much about going to the club. She was preoccupied with the children.

The base held a golf tournament on the day that the sun shined for twenty-four hours. I played in the tournament during which it rained, causing the greens to be wet. It was not uncommon to see moose hanging around the golf course. I saw a mother moose and its calf standing on the edge of the forest. I kept an eye on the mother Moose because she could have charged us at any time. I began to think that one should keep a rifle in one's golf bag in Alaska. I completed the thirty-six-hole tournament, but it was an ordeal in the rain.

We began to fly low level penetration missions for the benefit of the protective radar line. We would fly out to one of the satellite air strips, refuel, and fly a zigzag, low level course out over the coast before then turning to penetrate the ADIZ (Air Defense Identification Zone). These flights were exciting and necessary. We learned a lot more about Alaska on these low-level flights. We saw a lot of salmon canneries along the coastal area. The salmon industry was a major capital industry in Alaska. Seal hunting was also big. We buzzed the fishing fleets and flew over the mountain ranges and through the mountain passes. We located a herd of white mountain goats for future reference. We observed the grizzly bear in the tundra.

On one deployment, I was dispatched to Nome, Alaska. The weather was clear and sunny. I blasted off to Galena, where I refueled. I bored on and climbed westward on a course for the little fishing village of Nome on the coast of the Seward peninsula. I could see for miles over the green, flat tundra. Every now and then, I would spot a big dredge digging for gold. I surmised that the Intuits must have had reindeer or caribou running around the marsh in the summer.

I commenced my letdown on the coast. I had to look carefully to locate the fishing village of Nome. When I spotted the village, it was just some rough finished buildings lining the edge of the beach near the 5,500 feet asphalt airstrip. I made a low approach so I could study the terrain before landing. I landed and taxied over to the parking apron and shut down the aircraft. An Intuit man in an olive fatigue suit came out to the aircraft and placed a couple of rocks under the main gear. There were no wooden chocks for the aircraft in Nome – I was in the wilds of Alaska.

I saw a couple of Malamute husky dogs running around the airstrip. The animals belonged to the attendant, who looked like he was half Intuit and half Caucasian. I raised my canopy and unstrapped my shoulder harness and seatbelt. I unbuckled my parachute, climbed out of the cockpit, and hopped down on the wing of the T-33. I asked the attendant where the tie downs were. He told me that he didn't have any. I didn't believe that too many jets had ever been into Nome – I may have been one of the first. I had a takeoff time three hours after landing.

I decided to walk down to the main street along the beach, which was the only street in town. I waited for the attendant to refuel my aircraft and then we walked a quarter of a mile into town together. I asked him why he didn't go down to the lower 48 states and learn a trade or something. He told me that he had just finished eight years in the Air Force in California. I asked him why he got out and returned to this remote location. He told me a strange story. He said that he never understood the people in the Air Force, who were always in a rush. He said that everyone rushed through their job, rushed through their meals, rushed home after work, and drove as far as they could from the base on the weekend so they could just barely get back in time to go to work again. He said that he thought these people were in a racetrack pattern and were running themselves to death. He told me that he thought that he would be better off coming back to Nome and enjoying the simple things of life before time ran out.

He stopped at the first shack; it was obviously his alert quarters since it was nearest the airstrip. I walked down the street to visit the three or four shops and the two so-called hotels in town. I discovered a beautiful Intuit girl in the first shop selling ivory-carved animals depicting polar bear-hunting Intuits in confrontation with a standing bear. I was suddenly intrigued by the natural beauty of this maiden who had a gold crown on her tooth when she smiled. She spoke excellent English and was one of the daughters of a soldier who had retired out of the US Army in Nome and married an Intuit. For a long moment, I realized how someone could become attached to this paradise.

I looked over the hardware and thanked the lady for her attention. I walked down to the other shop, went inside, and found much the same set up. I left the second shop and walked over to the hotel, which was more like a boarding house. The dining room and the bar were all in one room. I obtained an excellent lunch while gazing out the front window at the Bering Strait. I pondered how close Russia really was to our continent. I talked to the hotel owner and the help. The owner told me that most of his business in the summer came from tourists. He told me that, in winter, he had several polar bear hunters scheduled in the hotel at different intervals during the hunting season.

When my take off time approached, I strolled back up the dirt straight to the airstrip. I saddled up my T-33 and signaled the attendant to pull the rocks out from under the main gear. I fired up and blasted off from the airstrip. I looked back as I climbed out on the first leg of my mission. I wanted a good mental picture of that airstrip and the contour of the surrounding beach. If it snowed suddenly, which could happen in the far north any time, I wanted to be able to find that airstrip by using the shoreline as a guide.

I climbed to my altitude on course for Point Barrow. I crossed over the Arctic Circle as I flew over Kotzebue and Kotzebue Sound. I noted the airstrip at Kotzebue for future reference and I continued north over the great white desert of snow. The winds over the snow-capped country carried the snow up into the air, much like the wind carried sand over the African desert. I could see some tiny movements in the snow. It must've been dogsleds because nothing else could cross that great barren wasteland.

I flew over the coast and out over the Arctic Ocean for a short time. I turned around and flew down to Point Hope on the Chukchi Sea before returning to Galena. I refueled at Galena and returned to Anchorage, where I landed. I stowed my personal equipment and drove by the officers club, where I entered the pilots' lounge. I ran into the other pilots who had been on various assignments that day. Somewhere in our conversation, I learned that a midwinter aircraft tour was offered for the military, which made the Dillingham, Nome, and Kotzebue circuit with a party at each location to relieve the military personnel of cabin fever during the long winter months. That sounded like a trip that I should put on my schedule, since the pilots could take their wives. I thought that would be an unforgettable journey for my wife. I drove back to the apartment and told my wife about the wonders of the far north. She was skeptical, to say the least.

The next day, I got a telegram that my grandfather, R. B. Caudill, was extremely ill. I took a leave, went over to the air terminal, and caught a ride as a courier on a C-124 to Norton Air Force Base in Marysville, California. We roared off and lumbered along over Canada before landing at Seattle to refuel. We then roared off on course for Marysville. We flew down to Norton and landed that night. I completed my courier mission and checked into the BOQ.

The next morning, I went over to the officers club for breakfast. The dining room overlooked a man-made lake. The big oak trees surrounding that western setting was a calming sight. After breakfast, I went over to base operations to see what was moving east or south. Late that evening, I found a Cessna 310 going to McClellan Air Force Base in Sacramento and I was given a seat on that aircraft. We roared off down the valley to McClellan. When we landed, I thanked the pilot in command for the ride.

I went into base operations and asked what aircraft was scheduled to go East. I was told that General Greer was about to take off for Tullahoma, Tennessee. The General had already started his aircraft, but I asked base operations to radio the General and ask if I could catch a ride. The pilot radioed that he would have a ladder down at the rear door of the C-54 when I got out to the aircraft, so I could climb aboard. I rushed out to the aircraft and climbed up the ladder. The flight engineer pulled up the ladder and closed the door. I went up to the cabin, thanked the General and then buckled into my seat. The General's C-54 roared down the runway and lifted off into the night. We climbed out and turned toward Tullahoma for a nonstop flight. I went to sleep.

When I was awakened, we were in the traffic pattern for the airstrip at Tullahoma. The lights were not on at the field because we were landing so late. The General's pilot was so used to the runway that he only needed his landing lights to land. We landed without incident and climbed down the ladder to the ground. I went into base operations and called my brother in Knoxville and asked him to meet me at the airbase. He reminded me that it was three o'clock in the morning. I told him that I would spend the rest of the night in a certain motel in Manchester. He told me that I could call my sister in Chattanooga, and she would pick me up the next morning on our way to Knoxville. I called her and she agreed to come by.

The next morning, I had breakfast while my sister was in route to Manchester. She soon picked me up and we drove up to Sparta, and then turned east to Knoxville, where we stopped for lunch. We continued the drive up to Blackey, Kentucky, but discovered that my grandfather had already expired in the hospital at Whitesburg. We went up to the funeral home in Whitesburg for the wake and stayed with friends that night.

The next day, the funeral was held at the Presbyterian Church in Blackey. Preachers of all denominations spoke a few words. Reverend I.D Black preached the sermon. We buried my grandfather in the Caudill cemetery just below Blackey above the barn.

I drove back to Knoxville with my sister, brother, mother, and father. We all gathered at my Aunt Lottie and Uncle Frank Davis's house. The family urged me to consider buying a home in a new subdivision in Knoxville called Cumberland Estates, just a couple of miles west of my Aunt Lottie's house. We all drove out to the new subdivision and drove through the development. I spotted a two-story colonial brick fronted home on an estate lot at 4505 Crestfield Drive. The house had four pillars on the front porch which reached from the second floor roof to the porch. I told my family that that was the home that I would buy.

A sign in the yard indicated that it was built by Cockrum Construction. My uncle called Bigelow Real Estate, and Newton Jones answered the phone. We made an appointment with Mr. Jones to inspect the house. Newton came out right away and we looked over the house inside and out. We negotiated a price with Newton, and I was able to get the house for $500 down on the G.I. Bill. I told Newton to get the papers in order and send them to my address in Alaska, so that I could have my attorney look over the contract and have my wife sign them with me. We returned to Aunt Lottie's for the night.

General Greer had told me that the Commanding General of the Alaskan Air Command was presently attending a conference at Wright Patterson Air Force Base in Ohio. I got on the phone and called Wright Patterson base operation officer to confirm this information. He arranged for me to occupy a seat back to Anchorage with the Commanding General's permission. I caught a commercial flight out of McGhee Tyson to Dayton, Ohio. My cousin Freida Marion met me at the airport with her husband Jack. They took me to their house for the night.

The next morning, Jack took me out to the base and let me off at base operations where I met the Alaskan Air Commanding General and his pilot. We boarded the C-54 and roared off the runway enroute to Anchorage. We flew to Spokane, landed, and had lunch while the ground crew refueled the big bird. We re-boarded and roared off up through Canada to Anchorage, where we landed that night. I thanked the General and drove over to my apartment. I slipped into bed after a hot shower.

The next morning, I told my wife about our new home. I told her that, if she didn't like it, we would not sign the papers. She told me that she was getting ready to leave the far north anyway, and Knoxville was her choice of a home city, because it was near the University of Tennessee where our children could further their education. My wife planned to fly back to Knoxville for Christmas with the children and the move was going to be permanent -- she was leaving Alaska for good! It was December 1961 and Christmas was only a week away.

I reported back to the base and was given my next flight on a round robin with a pre-dawn takeoff time. Our new base operation duty officer had figured out our flight plans for us. We would not know our destination or course until just before takeoff time. The reason the flight was planned this way was to ensure that the target pilots did not tell the interceptor pilots about their courses. We were together so much that this information was usually transmitted in pre-flight conversation.

I came to the base operations about four o'clock the next morning. I picked up my flight progress card along with the other pilots. We were told to check the routes for accuracy. Because I knew the duty officer, I made an almost fatal error. I decided that he knew what he was doing, so I didn't check his heading and distances. I had a new pilot assigned to fly with me on an orientation flight. We went out to the T-33 aircraft and made a 360 degree inspection. We were to maintain radio silence to further enhance the reality of the mission. We saddled up and blasted off into the frozen north. I was checking my heading to get an idea where we would be flying out over the coast and where we would be penetrating the air defense area as we climbed out to altitude. I failed to notice that the distance had been figured on a WAC (World Aeronautical Chart with a scale of 1:1,000,000) rather than a Sectional Chart (with a scale of 1:500,000).

The jet winds in the far north were extraordinarily strong at times, particularly at low altitudes and near the poles. In addition to this complication, we were flying over mountains with active or current volcanoes at their tops. The air currents around the mountains could cause some clear air turbulence at altitude. The heat coming off the volcanoes churned up the air currents, causing severe turbulence at low altitudes.

I proceeded on to my furthest checkpoint. I thought that it was taking an unnecessarily long time to reach each of my station passes. I figured that I must be fighting against a westerly jet stream wind. I knew that I could make up the time when I turned over my destination and got the jet stream wind on my tail. I got a radio call from one of the pilots who broke radio silence. I didn't answer because I thought that he had forgotten about the radio silence. He called three times, but I never answered. I still had not reached my turning point.

I began to get a little suspicious about the flight plan. I started checking the distances with my times and I caught the error. I was twice as far out over the Bering Sea as I should've been. I must've been halfway to the Kamchatka peninsula. The Russians had probably already scrambled MIG-21 all-weather fighters out of Petropavlovsk and Anadyr after me by then.

I turned the aircraft around and headed for the Alaskan coast. I must've been beyond the Pribilof Islands and St. Matthew Island near Russia. I refigured my distance and time. It was going to be close on fuel whether I could reach the Alaskan coast or not. I broke radio silence and requested a steer to the nearest airbase. I notified the pilot in the rear seat of our predicament, but he kept his cool. He had been just a passenger until this development. Now he quickly began making some calculations of his own. It was mighty cold to have to bail out over that white icy ocean. Maybe we could get close enough to the shoreline to land on the ice.

We needed to know exactly how far out we were to calculate our range properly. Radar could not pick us up. We just kept continuing through the early morning darkness. Near Nunivak Island, radar picked up our blip on the scope. The GCI controller gave me our approximate position and the nearest available airstrips.

There was a gravel strip with an 8% grade running up the point near the radar dome at Cape Newenham. The airstrip was only used by the C-123 cargo aircraft because the runway was only 3,000 feet long. The other possibility was the 4,000 foot civilian airstrip at Dillingham. However, Dillingham was about eighty miles further inland, so I had to plan to go to Cape Newenham.

I would fly a Navy traffic pattern with power, touch down on the very end of the runway, and open the canopy to create more drag to slow the aircraft down faster. I would also stop cock the engine to get rid of the 30% thrust created by an idling jet engine. Now all I had to do was hope that daylight would come in time for me to locate the radar dome near the airstrip. I requested that ADC scramble a couple of interceptors to locate us in the event we had to bail out on the ice. Major Lindy Gill and his wingman scrambled their F-102s from Bethel King Salmon air base.

The interceptors could circle in shifts until a chopper could fly out and rescue us. Maybe the ice would hold up the weight of the T-33, and we could land on the ice. I began to see daylight. A short time later, the two F-102 interceptors came alongside our aircraft. We got on the same channel. I thanked the fighter boys for their prompt interception and requested that they help me find Cape Newenham airstrip. I finally saw the snow-white mountains on the shoreline. The gravel strip blended into the white mountains like camouflage. I knew that the strip would be a leveled off point with a big lip dropping down into the sea.

I spotted the radar dome. I requested that the interceptors fly down and drag the strip, to make recommendations on how to approach the airstrip. The fighters bored down on the strip ahead of me. I had to remain at altitude due to my minimum fuel until I was within dead stick range of the strip.

The radar crew had gotten in on the action by now, and some of the troops had driven a vehicle down to the upper end of the strip to watch the attempted jet landing. They did not realize that if I slid off the runway, I would slide right into their vehicle. I radioed the GCI controller to notify the radar station to move the vehicle at once.

In the meantime, I got busy estimating when to make my letdown and how to dissipate my airspeed so that I could make the field even if I ran out of gas. The ADC fighters buzzed the vehicle on the end of the runway and popped their afterburners to attract the attention of the spectators, but to no avail.

I approached the high key point just like the book indicated for my air speed and configuration. I dropped my landing gear and commenced the final circle. I lowered my flaps on the low-key point. I had everything like I wanted it, but I had to adjust my eyes to the snow. Fortunately, some gravel lay on top of the snow in places on the incline. I touched down on the first one hundred feet of the runway. I opened the canopy, and the aircraft was slowing so well that I didn't have to stop cock the engine. In fact, I began to think that I would have to use the engine to keep from sliding back down the incline when I stopped the aircraft on the slippery ice. I had to use power to taxi up to the far end of the runway. I held power until the ground personnel found rocks to chalk my main gear. I turned the aircraft around, and the ground crew secured the chocks. I shut the engine down as I was 90° in the turn, otherwise the aircraft might have jumped the chocks.

I unbuckled my parachute and climbed out of the cockpit. My passenger met me on the wing. We hopped off the wing and rode the vehicle up to the radar living quarters. We took off our shoes to go into the building because the radar commander kept the floor extremely polished and shiny. We thanked everyone concerned and requested that my commander have some jet fuel sent out by C-123, so that I could fly back to the base. We settled down to a good breakfast.

The C-123 arrived in about four hours. My commanding officer and the safety officer were aboard. They had to see the aircraft to believe the report. They brought two jetto bottles to secure on the fuselage hooks on the underside of the aircraft. The jetto bottles would be fired as the aircraft began to takeoff, to give the aircraft added thrust on such a short runway. There would be no such thing as an aborted takeoff because the aircraft would slide over the end of the cliff at the bottom of the runway. They insisted on flying the aircraft out because they were currently trained in the use of jetto takeoffs.

I told him to be sure to travel down the side of the runway that did not have any gravel showing, otherwise they might inhale gravel and have engine failure during takeoff. They saddled up and blasted off. They had rolled about fifty feet when the jetto bottles were fired. Only one of the bottles gave off a big thrust. The other just fizzled. The aircraft pulled off the runway near the three quarters mark. The jet engine was a real performer in cold climates.

The pilots circled the strip, jettisoned the jetto bottles in the Bering Sea, and climbed out on course for Anchorage. I climbed aboard the C-123 and we lumbered off on course for Anchorage. I went to sleep in the rear of the plane. They woke me up as we were in the traffic pattern at Anchorage, and we landed without further incident. We taxied over to base operations and shut down. I climbed out of the aircraft and went into base operation where the duty officer apologized for his error. I told him that it was as much my error as his since I was the pilot in command. I drove back to the apartment and told my wife about my delay enroute to Cape Newenham. That weekend, I helped crate our belongings to ship back to Knoxville.

My next flight was a routine check ride. We flew up to Galena and my instructor gave me a passing grade. Upon landing at Galena, we went into the alert hut and had to wait for the weather to improve back at Anchorage before we could fly back to Anchorage. It began snowing like it snows in Alaska. It became a complete white out and it snowed in sheets like heavy rain. We stayed in the alert shack until about 9 o'clock at night before it quit snowing. The howling wind had blown the snow off the taxi strip and the ramp.

We saddled up and taxied out to the runway. We were running through some snow drifts on the taxiway. We thought the runway would be clearer because it was wider, and the snow tended to blow off the runway better than the taxiway. We lined up on the runway at night and received our instrument flight clearance. I was going to make an instrument take off so that I would have a better chance of staying on the partially covered runway. The centerline was not always visible.

I ran up the engine to full throttle and released the brakes. The instructor pilot was the observer in the front seat. We accelerated down the runway until we started running into mounds of drifting snow that had clung to the runway despite the cross wind. When I hit these mounds, the nose wheel split the snow, causing the intake to inhale the flying snow which resulted in the cockpit filling up with instant fog from the change in temperature. We could not see out of the canopy, and momentarily, we could not see the instruments either. The aircraft would not accelerate over ninety-five knots, and we were not able to lift the nose wheel off the runway due to the snow drifts. The instructor pilot stop cocked the engine and commenced braking. He used the heading indicator to keep going straight down the runway. We were able to stop in a short distance due to the snow drifts at the far end of the runway.

We opened the canopy and saw that we were in a snow drift. I asked the instructor if we were still on the runway. He said, "I don't know." We decided that the snow drifts must have kept us within the confines of the runway despite our heavy fuel load. We made a battery start and called the tower to notify them of the developments. We asked the tower to close the runway until the snow removal unit could clear it. We taxied back to the ramp through the snow drifts. This had been another close call, but all in a day's work. We spent the night at the alert hangar with the ADC pilots.

The next morning, we blasted off and flew back to Anchorage. We flew over the mountains where the volcanoes were cooking and smoldering. We let down over one of the volcanoes and picked up some sharp turbulence. We were going through a hole in the clouds and really didn't know that we were near the volcano. It was a good thing that we had our seatbelts and our chin straps buckled snuggly in that turbulence. We flew on into Anchorage in visual fly conditions and landed without further incident.

My wife was very much pregnant with our fifth child. That weekend, I took my wife and the children over to the international airport to catch the Northwest Orient Airlines jet to Chicago. They boarded the aircraft, and I watched the big bird taxi out and take off. My wife would change planes at Chicago O'Hare Airport and fly Southern Airlines to Knoxville.

I drove back to the airbase and checked into the BOQ. The next day, I was assigned to attend the Ellison Air Force Base arctic survival course to be held after the holidays. In the meantime, I attended every Christmas party held on the base. The officers club was my main social setting now. We ushered in the new year of 1962 at the club.

When the weather broke, I gathered my survival gear and boarded a C-54 at base operations along with several other pilots who were new to the North country. The C-54 flew up to Ellison AFB and landed. We got off the aircraft and took our gear over to the terminal. We were picked up by the arctic training instructors and taken to the school barracks, where we would receive our classroom instructions before being taken out into the wild to survive in the wilderness for three days and nights with only our flying equipment and parachute for shelter.

We received our instructions from every viewpoint, from the medical considerations to the hunting for food and water. We saw some colored films showing how the hazardous elements had taken the lives of crews of aircraft who had crashed in the wilds of Alaska. The films depicted actual incidents. It was not a pretty sight when we realized that we would be facing the same elements if we had to bail out the next day. We appreciated the insight.

When the classroom instruction was over for the day, we would retire to the Red Dog Saloon at the officers club. When the day came for us to graduate from the classroom, we gathered our gear and boarded a blue bus. The bus drove us out on the snow-covered tundra, some several miles from Fairbanks, and dropped us off in the snow in an area designated for survival training. We had assignments for each day.

The first day, we had to take our parachute and build a big tent, where six or eight of us could spend the night. We all cooperated as fast as we could to get the tent up before nightfall. We found dead trees small enough to use as tent poles and set up our teepees. We had to put our parachute around the poles in two layers with a space between the layers of about eight inches wide. We left a hole in the top of the tent. The inside layer of the parachute reached the ground and the outside layer of parachutes had to start about six or eight inches above the ground. The idea was to have a fire in the middle of the tent for the night. The fire would cause the hot air and smoke to rise up through the hole in the top of the tent. The cold air from the outside of the tent would come in between the two layers of parachutes and rise between the layers, drawing the smoke off the teepee at the top.

We laid our sleeping bags on top of the parachutes we had laid around the inside of the tent. We gathered firewood by breaking small trees down and hacking them into stove sized pieces. Then we built a fire in the center of the tent. Once we got our tent up and our fire going, we stacked wood around the inside of the tent.

Next, we went out and set up some snares to catch a rabbit. We found rabbit tracks in the snow leading into the brush. We set the snares at the edge of the brush where the rabbit would have to pass. We returned to the tent to get into our sleeping bags. We wore thermal underwear under our insulated flying suits. We took off our phosphorescent orange flying suits and boots or mukluk boots (canvas boots with three layered cotton soles and padding) and crawled into our sleeping bags.

Something went wrong with our ventilation system. We left the tent door open and killed our draft, or else the wind was too calm to pull the smoke out the top of the tent. It was 35° F below zero. A couple of hours after we had crawled into our sleeping bags, the smoke gathered in the tent down to about six inches above our faces before we realized the situation. We unzipped our sleeping bags and put on our mukluks and flying suits in short order. We got out of the tent in the middle of the night and decided to put out our fire for the moment. We jumped up and down, doing calisthenics while the smoke cleared.

We finally got back into the tent, took off our flying suits and Mukluk boots, and jumped into our sleeping bags. The moisture from our bodies had moistened the insides of the sleeping bags, which were ringed with a thin sheet of ice. The zipper was frozen and would not zip up. We had to get back into our boots and flying suits and get the fire going again to dry the sleeping bags.

We were up all night trying to get things ironed out. The next morning, we melted snow over the fire to get water to drain. Some of us scraped down in the snow, hoping to find ice to melt. About three feet deep we found ice. We chipped the ice and began to melt it. We noticed that the ice had mosquitoes frozen in it. We went back to melting snow.

We decided to check the snares. We found a rabbit in one of the snares, but it was frozen solid. We tried unsuccessfully to cook the rabbit while pondering how we could thaw out a frozen rabbit at 35°F below zero. We determined that we had to cook the rabbit before it froze in the Arctic.

The second night, we had to build individual tents out of our parachutes. I got some sticks and laid them over the snow and put some poles between three trees upon which to lay my parachute. I had a lean-to. I built a fire at the mouth of the tent and laid my wood where I could reach it without getting out of the tent. I fed the fire all night to stay warm, but I shivered continuously from the cold. I never got a bit of sleep. I should've made the tent reach down into the snow, so that the wind could not get under the edges.

The next day, we all got together and decided to set up one large teepee tent for the last night, since we had a choice on the third night. We were getting better at building the teepee and gathering wood. We built our teepee and gathered wood for the night.

The survival instructors told us to gather pine trees and put out a help sign in the snow. They had given us two red flares to fire in the event we heard aircraft in the area. We spelled out "help" with the pine trees and waited to hear a helicopter. We heard the chopper and waited until it was in sight before we set off the two flares. The chopper came over and threw out a sock full of corn bread for us to eat and then flew back to the base. The chopper was checking to see that we were all making the field trip in good condition.

On the last night, we got the teepee working pretty well. We had discovered the secret to keeping the wood fire going. We split the tree limbs and melted the ice off before we threw them on the fire, and this had the added benefit of cutting down on the smoke.

The next morning, we were ready for the blue bus to pick us up. The blue bus came by, and we folded our tent and gathered our gear. That bus sure seemed like a Waldorf Astoria. We fell asleep on the bus as it returned to the Ellison Air Force Base terminal building. We got off the bus at the terminal building, stowed our belongings, and went over to the BOQ to shower and get into some clean clothes before we went to the club to eat. We ate like a pack of wolves and walked over to the terminal, laid down on our sleeping bags, and went to sleep, waiting for the C-54 to come in from Anchorage. I don't know how long we slept, but the C-54 pilots came into the terminal and woke us up for the flight. We boarded with a great sense of appreciation for any place that was warm. We flew back to Anchorage and landed.

The C-54 pilot taxied the aircraft over to the parking apron at base operations and shut down. We filed out of the aircraft with our survival gear. I carried my gear over to personal equipment and turned it in along with my parachute and my field infantry pack. I jumped in my car and drove to the pilot's lounge where I found a lot of activity. Many civilians and military personnel were rotating to and from the states and were waiting in the lounge for flights out to the radar cities or back to the states.

I mingled with the local pilots and began to recount my experiences in arctic survival school. The other pilots who had been through the school recounted their experiences also. They finally told me that I was now eligible to apply for one of those polar bear hunts on the ice pack. They told me that I now had a better chance of survival on the ice. We laughed about this private joke. The polar bear hunt cost $1,200 per person. If you killed a polar bear, you were charged another $600 to have it stuffed and sent back home as a trophy.

A couple of the ADC pilots had just been rescued from a goat hunt. After spotting some goats, they had rented a light plane and flown out to the base of the mountain where the goats were feeding. They landed on a glacier floor, climbed the mountain, and shot a couple of goats. When they came back down the mountain to the aircraft, the sun had melted a portion of the ice and caused some mud to flow over the takeoff run. The two pilots saw no problems in taking off on this muddy ice. They cranked up the aircraft and began their takeoff run. The mud clung to the tires of the aircraft and slung over the propeller. The propeller, in turn, slung the mud over the windshield. The pilots lost the horizon and struck a snowbank with a wing tip. The aircraft cartwheeled and came to rest in the snowbank, with a broken propeller and a slightly bent landing gear. The pilots were not injured in this freak accident, but they had to remain overnight on the headwaters of the glacier. Fortunately, they had the presence of mind to notify the base of their predicament by communicating with a bush pilot in the area before their radio went dead. They wrapped themselves up in the two goats skins and remained overnight in the cockpit of their aircraft. The base rescue attachment picked the two goat hunters up the next morning with a helicopter. They planned to take another light plane out later, replace the propeller, straighten out the landing gear skis, and fly the aircraft back to Anchorage.

The local hunting guides had heard about the goat hunt and came over to the lounge. They were retired military pilots and they wanted to know about the accident. They also wanted to recruit the next hunting party, which would take a feeder airline to Kotzebue for the polar bear hunt. The guides had several single engine two-seater light aircraft in position at Kotzebue or Nome to be utilized on the actual hunt on the ice cap. The guides took two hunters on each trip. One of the hunters flew one aircraft and the guide and the other hunter flew another aircraft. The guide led the formation of two aircraft out to Point Hope and turned west to fly out over the ice cap and over the Chukchi Sea. When the guide spotted a polar bear, he landed upwind of the bear. The second aircraft remained airborne and circled the aircraft that had landed on the ice pack. The circling aircraft performed two missions – monitoring the hunter and monitoring the polar bear.

The guide and the hunter on the ice would deplane and proceed to the location of the polar bear. If the polar bear ever got wind of the hunters, then the hunters became the prey, and the bear became the hunter. The polar bear was king of the ice cap and was not afraid of anything on the ice or in the water. If the polar bear became the hunter, it would circle the hunters in an ever-decreasing circle until it charged them. Therefore, it was imperative that the airborne party kept in touch with the ground party by walkie-talkie.

After the stalking was over and the hunt was a success, the ground party cleaned and skinned the bear. The guide and the hunter with him loaded the bear hides up in the aircraft and flew back to Point Hope along with the circling aircraft.

Just in case the aircraft on the ice pack did not start, the circling aircraft would land and pick up the guide and hunter and fly them back to Point Hope. The guide would send an Intuit party to find their bear meat while the guide then flew back to Kotzebue with the hunters. Once back in Kotzebue, the guides got in the aircraft with the second hunter and the routine was repeated until all hunters had had a chance to get a bear.

Firing a rifle or pistol at 50°F below zero posed some problems. The mittens that had to be worn were cumbersome. Also, guns had been known to freeze up after the first shot. Therefore, the bear hunt taught the hunter some of the basics of arctic warfare in a sportsmanlike manner.

I communicated with my wife by letter and telephone. Telephone conversations were expensive in Alaska. Long distance calls to the states cost three dollars per minute. I had to list my planned topics of discussion on a pad before my telephone calls. I would have about ten items to discuss during each phone call. I went over to the Western Hotel on Sunday morning to have blueberry hotcakes and steak for breakfast before making my telephone call.

I ran into Governor Bill Egan and introduced myself. I told him about a friend of his in Montana who had asked me to pass along his best regards. His friend hadn't bothered to tell me that Bill was the Governor of Alaska. Bill got a big kick out of the way his friend managed to send him a good word from time to time. Bill asked me to be sure to attend one of his moose barbecues later in the spring. I told him that I would be there.

I made my telephone call and walked out of the hotel to get into my car. I saw a couple of dog teams with sleds behind them coming down the street. In stark contrast to this long standing way of life, I saw a large truck going up the other side of the street pulling an oil derrick on a flatbed. I wished that I had had a camera to capture the iconic moment.

I asked someone what the dog sleds were doing coming into the center city. They told me that the annual fur rendezvous was coming to town. I drove back to the base and went down to the pilots' lounge. I met some of the pilots who had been in Alaska a couple years and knew what happened at the rendezvous. They told me that the trappers and the natives came to town to sell their furs at auction. The furs were leftovers after the exporters had selected the best pelts.

The entire community took advantage of the occasion to come out of hibernation during the winter. I was also told to be careful about any real bargains in mink wraps, because some of them might turn out to be coyote hides. The natives took over the town until the furs were all sold, then they bought their grub stake for the next year in the bush. After the purchase of next year's stake, the natives participated in their own version of gambling by betting on the dog team pulling contests of weight and speed. I watched some of the sled races with great interest. The dogs crossed the tundra like nothing else could.

The natives could get drunk and wild during the rendezvous with tossing blanket dances in the street. It was not wise to ever get in one of the blanket tosses. One G.I. broke his leg after being tossed up and coming down off the blanket onto the hood of a car. A lot of fur brokers flew up to the rendezvous to make sure that they had gotten all the good fur.

One day I was returning to Elmendorf from King Salmon on a late mission in a T-33. I was coming down the chute when two F-102s were scrambled. I had to break off my penetration until the interceptors got airborne. The weather was just cold enough that the hot gases coming out of the tailpipe of the fighters caused the runway to turn to buttermilk and become socked in. I had to divert and fly over to the civilian airport at Spenard, which was almost socked in as well. I was told that the airport was testing a new light system, which would serve as a visually referenced glideslope. There were light systems on each side of the approach end of the runway. These lights beamed three different colors to the aircraft on final approach. The pilot was on the glideslope if he saw a green light. If the pilot dropped below the glideslope, he would see a red light. If a white light was seen, the pilot was above the glideslope.

I came down on final and found the light references highly effective. I landed without incident. I taxied over to the parking ramp and shut down. I climbed out of the aircraft and went into the terminal to wait until I could fly back to Elmendorf. I told the tower operator that the light system should be used at all airports for night approaches, as well as for restricted visibility. The lights were very inexpensive and would be great safety devices.

The weather never got better that night. I left the aircraft at the civilian airport and rode the limousine back to Elmendorf, where I spent the night. The next day, I rode the limo back to Spenard and flew the aircraft back to Elmendorf.

As summer approached, we began to get personnel from Juneau, an area little known by the people in Anchorage. I met some educated natives who were on high priority missions of some sort for the state government. They may have been civil service personnel. Anyway, I saw a beautiful native Indian, who was well educated and very cultured, come down to the lounge with an escort. I realized that the natives had all kinds of potential. I had wondered privately how the Intuits would fare if educated in the modern age. Well, my observations dispelled my doubts.

As the summer came, I took motor trips up the Matanuska Valley. I had never seen so many big, red salmon, which came up to the heads of all those little tributaries to spawn and die. There were enough fish in the streams to feed the starving world for a few days. The fisherman actually reported accidents where the salmon jumped into their boat in their frenzy to reach their spawning grounds before they died.

I began to concentrate on my career dream – to fly with the US Air Force Thunderbird Jet aerobatic team in Las Vegas. I applied for a transfer to Nellis Air Force Base, Las Vegas. I had over 3,000 single engine jet flying hours, I had the desire, and I was qualified. The security service reacted negatively to my application to leave their command. They requested that I voluntarily give up my wings to ensure completing my twenty years as a non-rated officer. I found this suggestion utterly ridiculous. Flying was my major interest! I decided that if I didn't get my transfer, I would resign.

I received a telegram from my wife. She had given birth on February 21, 1962, to our fifth and last child, a baby girl. We named our new daughter Charlotta Jane. When the weather broke, I took a leave. I left Anchorage, drove up the valley, and started across Goat Mountain. I hit slick snow about where you can hear the tide. There must've been a warm current brushing up the mountain that morning to make the snow so slick. I got out of the car and jacked up the rear wheel to put on snow chains. I got the chains on, but I almost got frostbitten fingers in the process. I put chains on the other wheel and drove on over the mountain. I found the going easier once I crossed the mountain, so I took the chains off.

I wanted to get through Canada to civilization before I got caught in a snowstorm. I drove day and night. I was fifteen miles out of Dawson Creek before the snow came. It was snowing in sheets, and I had to stop by the side of the road. I thought I was stopped, but I was moving slowly with the moving sheets of snow. I opened the door to get some fresh air and noted that I was going to be in the ditch in a few more minutes if I didn't move the car.

The snow finally let up. Someone came by the next morning in a station wagon with oversized snow tires. I followed him until the snow was about eighteen inches deep, and then I couldn't keep up with him. I slipped, slid, and spun until I reached the pavement about twenty-five miles north of Dawson Creek. The big trucks began coming by me and leaving ruts in the snow. I could drive in the ruts, but it was hard to get out of those ruts when I met another vehicle. I somehow managed not to slide off the road.

By the time I arrived in Edmonton, the snow was gone, and the weather was clear and sunny. I gassed up, ate breakfast, and took a cat nap in my car before going further. I decided to motor over to Jasper on the Yellowhead Highway and drive through Banff National Park. I had heard that the road was four lanes. I motored over to Lake Louise through those beautiful mountains. This was one of the best stretches of roads in Canada and the most scenic.

I arrived in Banff, a resort town located in a big green basin much like Cades Cove in the Smoky Mountains of East Tennessee. The resort was first class in every respect. and the hotels were superb. The Royal Hotel up on the mountain resembled a majestic castle. I spent the day driving around the city, looking at the tennis courts, golf courses, and the gardens. I walked down the main street and visited the stores and shops. I went into a drugstore and the ophthalmologists were having a convention in town. A lady sitting next to me overheard me order a chocolate milkshake. She asked me if I was a southerner from the states. I told her that I was. She asked me if the Southerners still had strong feelings about the Yankees. I decided to let her imagination work for her. I told her President Jefferson Davis was a personal friend of mine, but I added quickly that some of my friends felt more strongly about the South. She didn't know what to make of the situation. I kept a straight face so that she could have fun at the convention relaying the story as she interpreted it. I visited the riding stables and ski lifts. I generally surveyed the resort for further reference before I motored down the pike.

I drove into Calgary where I refueled and ate again. I took another cat nap. I departed Calgary and motored along the Trans-Canadian highway across to Medicine Hat, Moose Jaw, Regina, Brandon, and Winnipeg. The Trans-Canadian highway from Regina to Winnipeg began to take on an American look. The Kentucky Fried chicken shacks began to appear near the outskirts of the cities. I drove into Winnipeg and stopped at one of the new shopping centers. It was Saturday evening, and I left my Cadillac to be gassed up at the service station. I walked over to the nearby restaurant, went inside, and ordered myself a sandwich and a milkshake. The place was packed with a local Saturday night crowd. I went up to the counter, took a seat on one of the stools, and ordered a fried ham sandwich and a chocolate milkshake. The crowd immediately knew that I was an American and began to speak French in a derogatory manner. I hadn't expected this reaction and I sensed that all was not well in Winnipeg. I quickly ate, got in my car, and drove south toward the American border.

I drove down to Fargo, North Dakota, and turned east towards Chicago. I motored straight through Chicago and drove on to Louisville, Kentucky, where I stopped for a nap. After my nap, I drove out of Louisville towards Knoxville. I was four days into a five-day journey, traveling day and night. I was so tired that I couldn't sleep.

I finally arrived in Knoxville and spent my first night in the home that I had bought back in December. The children were a little leery of me -- they held onto my wife's dress and asked her if I was going to spend the night. My wife and I had our private laugh and I realized how much I had been gone from the children. I stayed around the house waiting until I could get a good night's sleep. Finally, I got the expected letdown and slept for twenty-four hours without waking up. I was fresh when I woke up, but after I visited for a few days, I decided that I would not use all my leave at that time.

I had my wife drive me over to McGhee Tyson airport so that I could catch a flight out on my return trip to Alaska. I caught a C-130 to Salina Air Force Base, Kansas on a beautiful day. However, when we landed, I quickly discovered that Selena was not a place to get a connecting flight. The traffic was on a local 200-mile radius restriction to conserve fuel and consolidate maintenance. A Cessna 310 on an emergency parts run out of Tinker Air Force Base in Oklahoma landed and taxied over to base operations. I managed to get aboard that evening on their return to Tinker. We took off and circumnavigated some rain showers. When we landed at Tinker, I went into base operations and found a good friend on duty as the dispatcher. I told him to get me a ride to Alaska. He made a few calls and lined me up with a B-47 crew that was flying to Fairbanks, Alaska that night.

I boarded the B-47 and we blasted off into the night. We landed at Eielson Air Force Base in Fairbanks in the middle of the night and checked into the BOQ for the night.

The next morning, I caught a T-33 heading to Anchorage. We flew by Mount McKinley at 30,000 feet on a clear and sunny day. The snow was twisting around the tops of the mountain with the shifting winds at 21,000 feet. When we let down into Anchorage, I noticed a gusher of water sprouting out of the Cook Inlet. I asked the pilot, "What is that?" He replied, "Some oil company drilled an offshore well and struck natural gas." That water spray must've been 500 feet high. We decided that the gusher would make a good landmark for a landing at that airport. We landed and caught a ride over to the pilots' lounge.

I needed wheels, and I knew that some of the pilots in the National Guard, Reserve, and SAC had old cars that were used for their short periods of active duty and summer camp TDY. These cars were sold to the next troops who came up to relieve the transients. I purchased a 1962 Ford for $60 before I left the lounge. The car didn't have a fan belt on it, but it didn't need one in Alaska. The Ford operated beautifully, and I drove it for 2,200 miles without any maintenance.

**CHAPTER 30**

# ATC Nellis AFB, Nevada (Air Training Command)

I finally got my transfer to Nellis AFB in Las Vegas, and a bad OER (officer's efficiency report) to go with it. I sold my '62 Ford for $5 and boarded a MATS C-54 bound for Warner Robins Air Force Base, Georgia. I slept most of the way. We landed a couple of times enroute at Hill Air Force Base, Utah, and Kelly Air Force Base, Texas, before reaching our destination of Warner Robins.

I got off the aircraft in Georgia and caught a C-130 flying out to Smyrna Air Force Base in Murfreesboro Tennessee. I asked the pilot to make a dog leg and let me off at Knoxville, and he obliged. I got off the aircraft at McGhee Tyson airport in Knoxville, where my wife met me and drove me back to Knoxville in the caddy.

I told my wife about the Nellis Air Force base assignment and about the possibility of flying with the Thunderbirds. She told me that she was finished traveling with the children. She wanted to stay in Knoxville at our new home while I gallivanted around the

452

country. She loved our new home, and my family was pleased with the arrangement. My mother gave my wife her 1958 Chevrolet as a grocery wagon, so that I could take the caddy to Las Vegas with me. In the next few days, I realized how tranquil my wife and children were in their new home. I agreed that they should stay in Knoxville. If I didn't get on the Thunderbird aerobatic team, my future in the Air Force would be over anyway.

We were so happy with our new two-story home that we named it Lee Lynn, after the middle names of our first two daughters. I made the rounds up in Kentucky and Virginia, visiting friends and relatives. I returned to Knoxville to bid my family farewell. I drove out to Dallas and spent the night with Taylor Dixon and his family. The next day, I drove up to Chillicothe and spent the night with Dr. James Howard and his wife. The following day, I drove to El Paso and kept going to Las Cruces, New Mexico, where I stopped for a cat nap.

The next day, I drove to Phoenix and checked into the BOQ at Williams Air Force Base at Chandler, Arizona. I went over to the officers club and met some of my friends who had been transferred to "Willy" to instruct the new cadets. We caught up on each other's careers.

The next day, I drove to Las Vegas, by way of Wickenburg and Kingman, Arizona. I wanted to see some of the desert over which I had flown so often. The Joshua trees added to the natural beauty of the desert. I felt like I was in another world in this backcountry. People in these remote locations were friendly, but wary of outsiders. I drove over to the Hoover Dam and on into Las Vegas, where I spent the night at the Desert Inn. The next morning, I was ready to check into Las Vegas at Nellis Air Force Base. I reported to the Base Support Group Commander and was told that I would be assigned to the Support Group as a passive defense officer and attached to base operations for flying until something else opened.

My first flight took me to Los Angeles on a Cessna 310. A couple of us went to the North American plant at Los Angeles International Airport to fly the first T-39 Sabre Liner twin jet back to Nellis. The T-39 would later become immensely popular among the business world executives. It flew like any Sabre jet, but it was of course, subsonic. The idea was to favor payload rather than speed. We landed in Nellis and shut down. The aircraft would be utilized to train fighter pilots to monitor radar over a closed course. I made a few flights in a T-33, chasing parts for the tactical squadron that was flying F-100s, like the Thunderbirds.

I finally got my chance to request an assignment to the Thunderbirds. I was told that there were 200 applicants ahead of me. I was also told that President Kennedy had a hand in the final selection of the candidates. In short, I was turned away. I was extremely disappointed. I felt like the Air Force had passed over a real asset. I went on with my duties, but without much enthusiasm.

I spent most nights on the strip, catching the free floor shows. I tried to get assigned to one of the tactical squadrons without success. There was a RIF (reduction in force) in progress. The war in Asia had not developed enough at that time to have an impact on the RIF. In time, the Air Force would need more pilots, but the wheels of bureaucracy turned slowly.

I remained on duty in Nellis for one year. I was assigned various clean up details during the interim. We painted and refurbished the officers club as one of the projects. I was passed over for Major during this period. One day, on November 22, 1963, we got word that President Kennedy had been assassinated. We were saddened that our top official had been picked off. The Thunderbirds stayed on the ground for one month in memoriam of President Kennedy.

Finally, I realized that the needs of the Air Force no longer coincided with my interest in flying jets. I couldn't foresee this situation changing anytime soon and I missed my family. I decided to resign my commission and pursue a career in the private sector in Knoxville. On September 1, 1964, I received my orders, terminating my active duty and my temporary commission. I turned in my flying gear and picked up my severance pay. I grabbed my bags, loaded up my caddy, and drove off the base. I never looked back as I drove out the gate. I really had no regrets. I would now have a future which I could control, and I would only look to the past to draw experience for the future. The Air Force had been good to me. I wouldn't take anything for the experiences that I had been able to enjoy.

**CHAPTER 31**

# Roundup

I returned to Knoxville and started my new career as a Ford car salesman. I loved the job because it allowed me to meet new people every day as I assisted them with their transportation needs. I became the number one salesman at Ted Russell Ford and, over the forty years that followed, I sold 5,000 cars and trucks to various friends, relatives, and acquaintances. I began to have more free time to spend with my family and to continue my flying activities with the Knoxville Downtown flying club.

One Sunday afternoon on December 9, 1973, my sixteen-year-old son, Harold Jr., whom I had enrolled in flying lessons, came over to the couch and asked me to come down to the airport with him. He told me that he was ready to fly solo, but his pocketbook, which contained his flight physical card, had recently been stolen along with the pocketbooks of all the other West High School football players. He told me that his instructor, a University of Tennessee professor, Hall Roland, Ph.D., wanted me to verify that my son had taken the

*Ruby and five children – Becky, Patti, Bud, Keith, and Jane – 1965*

physical and passed. I got up off the couch, got into the car with my wife, and drove to the airport. My wife wasn't quite ready for the experience, but I assured her that the instructor was well qualified and would not let our son solo if he were not ready.

We met the instructor at the airport. The instructor and my son, Harold Junior, climbed into the Cessna 150 and taxied out to the runway. They took off and flew in a closed pattern. I knew my son was flying the aircraft. The pattern and the approach were perfect. The landing was a beautiful sight. They taxied over to the taxiway and the instructor climbed out. My son taxied down to the approach end of the runway for the run up check. He took the runway, made a beautiful take off, climbed out, and turned on crosswind. I knew that he had this flight pattern down pat. We watched him on the downwind leg and on the base leg. He turned on the final leg and came down like a professional. He rounded out and held the aircraft off until it stalled on the runway from about six inches above the runway. He held the nose up until the flying ground speed was gone and it dropped gently on the runway. He turned off the runway onto the last taxi finger.

He taxied down the taxi strip to the takeoff end of the runway again. He made his run up check, took off, and flew around the pattern in closed traffic for another landing. He made one more takeoff and landing before he returned to the parking ramp and shut down the aircraft.

We met him at the aircraft as he was climbing out of the cockpit. I extended my hand to congratulate him on his solo. He was not moved enough over the occasion to shake my hand. He just asked me to help him tie down the aircraft so he could get back to his studies. I was glad to see him so confident. The instructor gave him a little debriefing and my son went on his way.

I told the instructor that I was immensely proud of the confidence that he had instilled in my son. The instructor told me that my son had that confidence when he came to the flying club. I thanked the instructor anyway.

My wife and I walked back to our car and drove back to the house. I pulled into our driveway and shut down the motor. We got out of the car, walked into the house, and sat down on the couch. I began to reminisce over the last ten years with my wife. We had gotten the children through the little leagues and other childhood activities. My mother and aunt had both passed away eight or ten years earlier. My oldest daughter, Rebecca Lynn, who had graduated from the University of Tennessee with a degree in physical education, had married John Makla from Camden, South Carolina. They would later have three daughters and reside in Marietta, Georgia and Pensacola, Florida. My second daughter, Patricia Lee, graduated from East Tennessee State University in Johnson City with a degree in dental hygiene. She would later return to dental school, become a Periodontist, marry a dentist, have two sons, and set up practice in Virginia Beach, Virginia. Harold Junior was a senior at the University of Tennessee studying pre-dentistry. He would later go to dental school, marry his dental school classmate Grace E. Hall, have one son and two daughters, and set up practices in the Memphis and Nashville areas. My son Keith was attending West high school and would later follow me into car sales. My youngest daughter Charlotta Jane was attending Northwest Junior High school, and would later graduate from MTSU, move to the Atlanta area, marry John Flaspohler, and have two sons and one daughter. **LIFE HAS BEEN GOOD TO ME!**

*Harold and Ruby in 1981*

# Timeline:
# A Memoir: My Father, the Pilot

- Harold Glenn Speer was born October 25, 1925, at Cumberland Kentucky son of Dr. Harold and Elizabeth Caudill Speer DDS.

- Enlisted in the Army Air Force from Grundy, Virginia after a semester at Eastern State University on December 23, 1943.

- Attended Aerial gunnery school at Tyndall Air Force Base Florida.

- Assigned to B-24 Air crew at Chatham Field, Savannah Georgia.

- Assigned to 453rd bomb group 735th squadron at old Buckenham airfield near Norwich England. Our crew flew our B-24 from Bangor Maine to Bangor England via the north Atlantic High Fly route of Goose Bay, Canada, Narsarsuaq, Greenland, Keflavík, Iceland and the British Isles.

- Flew four missions over Europe before being transferred to the 36th Texas Oklahoma infantry division in Ulm, Germany as a 2 ½ ton truck driver. Drove army trucks all over Europe delivering rations, troops, prisoners and logistics from Marseille, France to Berlin, Germany and from Antwerp, Netherlands to Frankfurt, Stuttgart, Munich and Oberdorf, Germany.

— Assigned a third marine infantry division at Bad Wildengun, Germany as truck driver. Attended seventh army ski school at Fulda for basic skiing and later to Obers Dorf, Germany for Advanced skiing instruction.

— Honorable discharge April 29, 1946, at Fort Dix, New Jersey.

— Entered Center College in Danville, Kentucky in 1946. Played football as tackle and guard with the Colonels. Graduated with a BA degree in 1949.

— Assigned as teacher of science and mathematics and coach for football, basketball, and baseball at Hurley high school in Hurley, Virginia 1949-1950.

— Married Ruby Catherine Cox of Deel, Virginia on October 1, 1949. Ruby attended Radford College as well as Knoxville Business College.

— Accepted as an aviation cadet in the USAF at James Connolly, Waco, Texas, October 27, 1950. Graduated as a pilot and Officer from the jet fighter pilot school at Williams Air Force Base, Chandler, Arizona, Class 51G.

— Assigned tour of duty with the 48th fighter bomber group, 492nd squadron at Chaumont Air Force Base, France 1952 to 1955. Broke the "Sound Barrier" in 1953.

— Flew F 84G and later F 86F on NATO maneuvers on training missions. Patrolled the Iron Curtain staging out of Furstenfeldbruck and Bitburg. We flew to Tripoli, Libya via Rome. Maintained combat ready status by bombing and strafing on the desert range and flying Aerial gunnery missions on the Gulf of Sidra range.

– Assigned to the 1738th jet delivery group at Kelly Air Force Base San Antonio, Texas 1955 to 1958. Our mission was to deliver new jet fighters from the aircraft plants in California and Ontario and fly the replaced jet fighters back to California and Arizona to be reconditioned and flown to the USAF reserves throughout the USA. We flew our surplus jet fighters (F-80) to our South American allies. We literally took the jet age to South America replacing old P-51 and P-47 propeller driven fighters.

– Assigned to SAC at Malmstrom Air Force Base Montana flying KC-97 tankers from 1958 to 1961.

– Assigned to Alaskan air command at Elmendorf flying target missions in the T-33 jet from 1960 to 1963.

– Assigned to Nellis Air Force Base Nevada flying the Sabre liner and the T-33.

– Honorable discharge at Nellis Air Force Base Nevada September 1964.

– Began selling Ford automobiles, trucks, and A1 used vehicles at Hull Dobbs Ford in Knoxville Tennessee from 1964 until 1978 when the dealership ownership transferred to Ted Russell Ford. Continued selling Fords until my retirement in 2008, at which time I had sold over 5000 vehicles.

– Harold passed away peacefully one month short of his 92nd birthday in September 2017.